HANABATA DAYS

HANABATA DAYS

MICHAEL HOYT

Hanabata Days

This project was written and drawn in unceded and occupied Dakota territory.

Written and illustrated by Michael Hoyt
michael-hoyt.com

Printed and bound in the United States of America
ISBN: 978-0-578-29098-0 (softcover)

HANABATA DAYS

HANA TRANSLATES TO NOSE FROM THE JAPANESE LOANWORD
"HANAKUSO." BATA REFERRING TO THE ENGLISH WORD "BUTTER."
HANABATA DAYS IS A HAWAI'IAN PHRASE REFERING TO ONE'S
CHILDHOOD OR THE AGE WHEN KIDS RAN AROUND WITH
RUNNY NOSES.

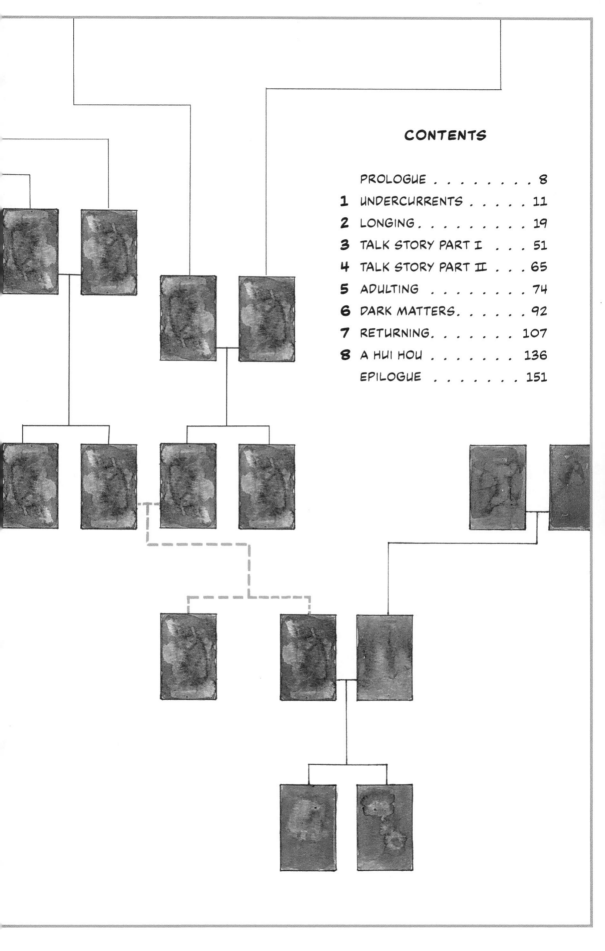

CONTENTS

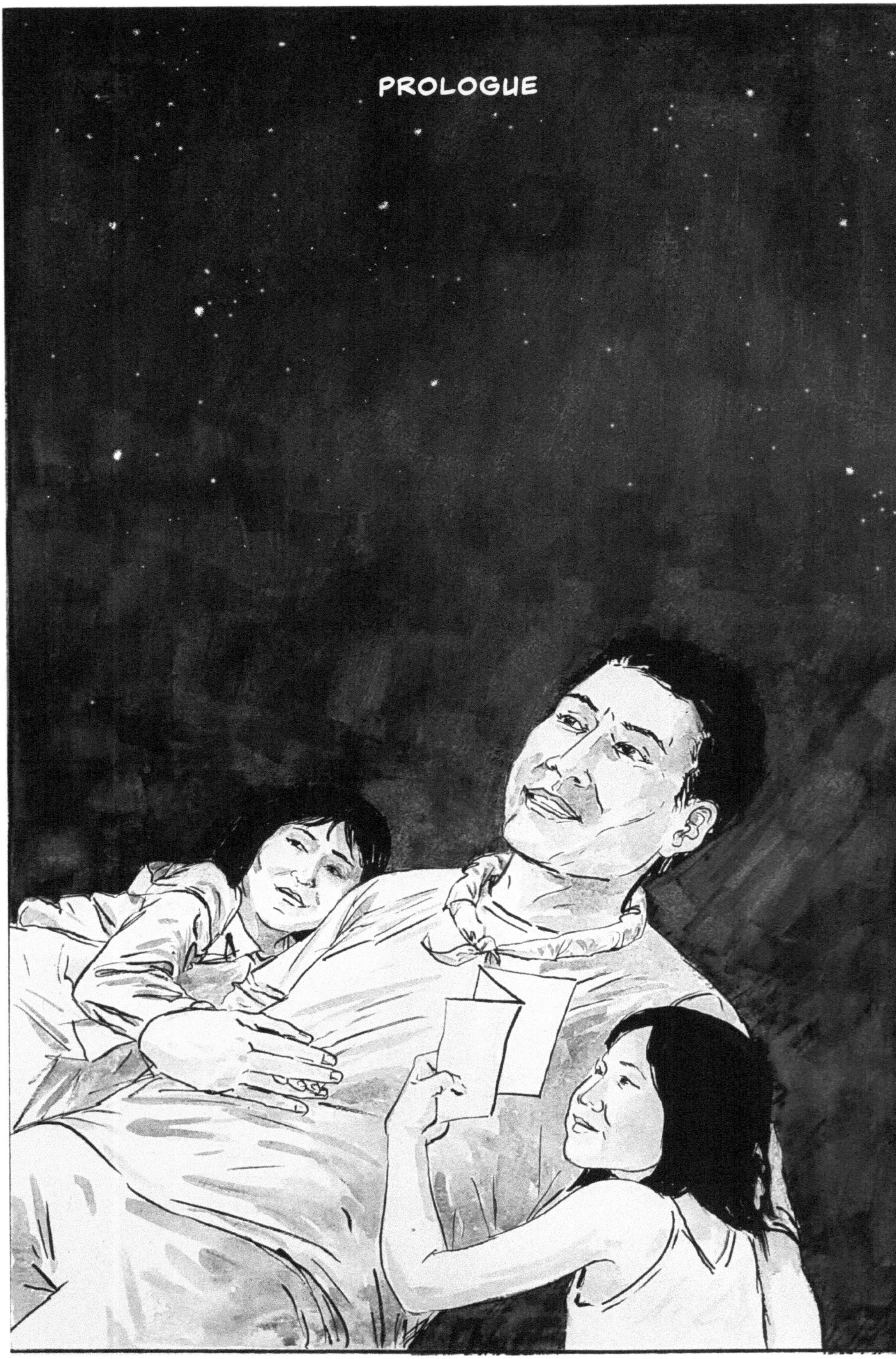
PROLOGUE

DEAR DAUGHTERS,

I OFTEN THINK BACK TO ONE OF OUR MANY MAGICAL MOMENTS
TOGETHER CAMPING NEAR THE NORTH SHORE OF SUPERIOR.
KA'ELANI, YOU WERE 6. TUULA, IT WAS TWO DAYS BEFORE YOUR
FOURTH BIRTHDAY. WE WERE LYING ON OUR BACKS, FANNED OUT IN A
CRESCENT, LOOKING UP AT THE INFINITE FIELD OF STARS. THE
KIND OF STARGAZING THAT WE RARELY EXPERIENCE FROM OUR
HOME IN THE CITY. IT WAS WELL PAST YOUR BEDTIME BUT ON
THIS NIGHT YOUR MOTHER AND I MADE AN EXCEPTION.

WE HAD JUST LEARNED ABOUT THE *MAKOCE WICANHPI WOWAPI**,
AND WE WERE TAKING TURNS TRACING STAR STORIES FROM THE
LAKOTA KNOWLEDGE PASSED DOWN TO US. I AM EMBARRASSED TO
ADMIT TO YOU THAT IT WAS ALL NEW TO ME, EVEN IN MY 40'S.
I HAD NEVER LEARNED ABOUT THE INDIGENOUS STAR MAP FROM
THIS REGION OR, FOR THAT MATTER, EVER CONSIDERED THERE
WERE OTHER WAYS OF LOOKING AT THE STARS THAN THE WESTERN
CELESTIAL ATLAS I LEARNED AS A CHILD.

I REMEMBER THINKING TO MYSELF HOW NAIVE I WAS IN THIS
REGARD. THAT THROUGHOUT HISTORY PEOPLE ACROSS THE ENTIRE
PLANET HAD THEIR OWN CULTURAL PRACTICES AND SYSTEMS OF
NAVIGATION AND WAYS OF MAKING MEANING OF THE COSMOS, AND
I HAD NEVER CONSIDERED IT BEFORE. I QUIETLY HOPED THIS DID
NOT MAKE ME A POOR FATHER. I WONDER TODAY IF THAT NAIVETE
HAD SOMETHING TO DO WITH MY STRUGGLE TO FEEL CENTERED,
TO LOCK IN MY INTERNAL COORDINATES.

THROUGHOUT YOUR SHORT LIVES, YOUR MOTHER AND I TRIED
VERY HARD TO BUILD WITHIN EACH OF YOU A SENSE OF
CONNECTION AND ATTACHMENT TO BOTH PEOPLE AND PLACE.
WE DIDN'T WANT EITHER OF YOU TO BEAR THE SENSE OF BEING
UNMOORED AND PERPETUALLY ADRIFT--SOMETHING THAT WE
BOTH EXPERIENCED FOR THE MAJORITY OF OUR LIVES.
THIS IS PROBABLY WHY THIS LITTLE MOMENT STICKS WITH
ME ALL THESE YEARS LATER: TRACING NEW ANCIENT KNOWLEDGE
TO EXPAND OUR UNDERSTANDING AND NAVIGATIONAL LANGUAGE.
I'M JUST SO THANKFUL TO HAVE LEARNED ALONGSIDE YOU BOTH
IN THAT MOMENT.

*LAKOTA STAR MAP

LOOKING BACK, I VIEW THIS AS ONE OF THE COUNTLESS GIFTS
YOU BOTH HAVE GIVEN ME, THE EXPERIENCE OF LEARNING
TOGETHER FROM THE SAME STARTING POINT. IT HAS, YOU HAVE,
MADE ME AWARE THAT THERE ARE MOMENTS WHEN THE MYSTERIES
OF THE WORLD EXPAND AND UNFOLD FOR US SIMULTANEOUSLY.
THROUGHOUT OUR LIVES, I HOPE THERE WILL BE MANY MORE
MOMENTS LIKE THIS WHEN YOU ARE THE TEACHER AND I AM
THE STUDENT. FOR NOW, I CLING TO THIS MEMORY.

LIE BACK WITH SOFT FOCUS.
HALF CIRCLED ATOP A BLANKET OF LUSH GRASS,
OUR SHOULDERS AND HEADS BRUSHING.
WE PASS EACH OTHER WARMTH.

TWILIGHT AND FAINT MOON AGLOW.
OH GREAT SUPERIOR, LAPPING ARCTIC RELICS
UNDULATE.

WHAT DO YOU SEE?
PLEASE, GIRLS. SHOW ME.
WHAT DO YOU FEEL?
PLEASE, GIRLS. PRESS CLOSER.
SMILE WITH YOUR EYES.

PLEASE, MEMORY. FLICKER ON YET NEVER DIMINISH.
RETURN LIKE THE MOON, EACH REMAINING NIGHT.

FOR I CLENCH IT TIGHT,
AS YOU BOTH ARE OUR ATLAS
TO OUR DESCENDANTS.

-M

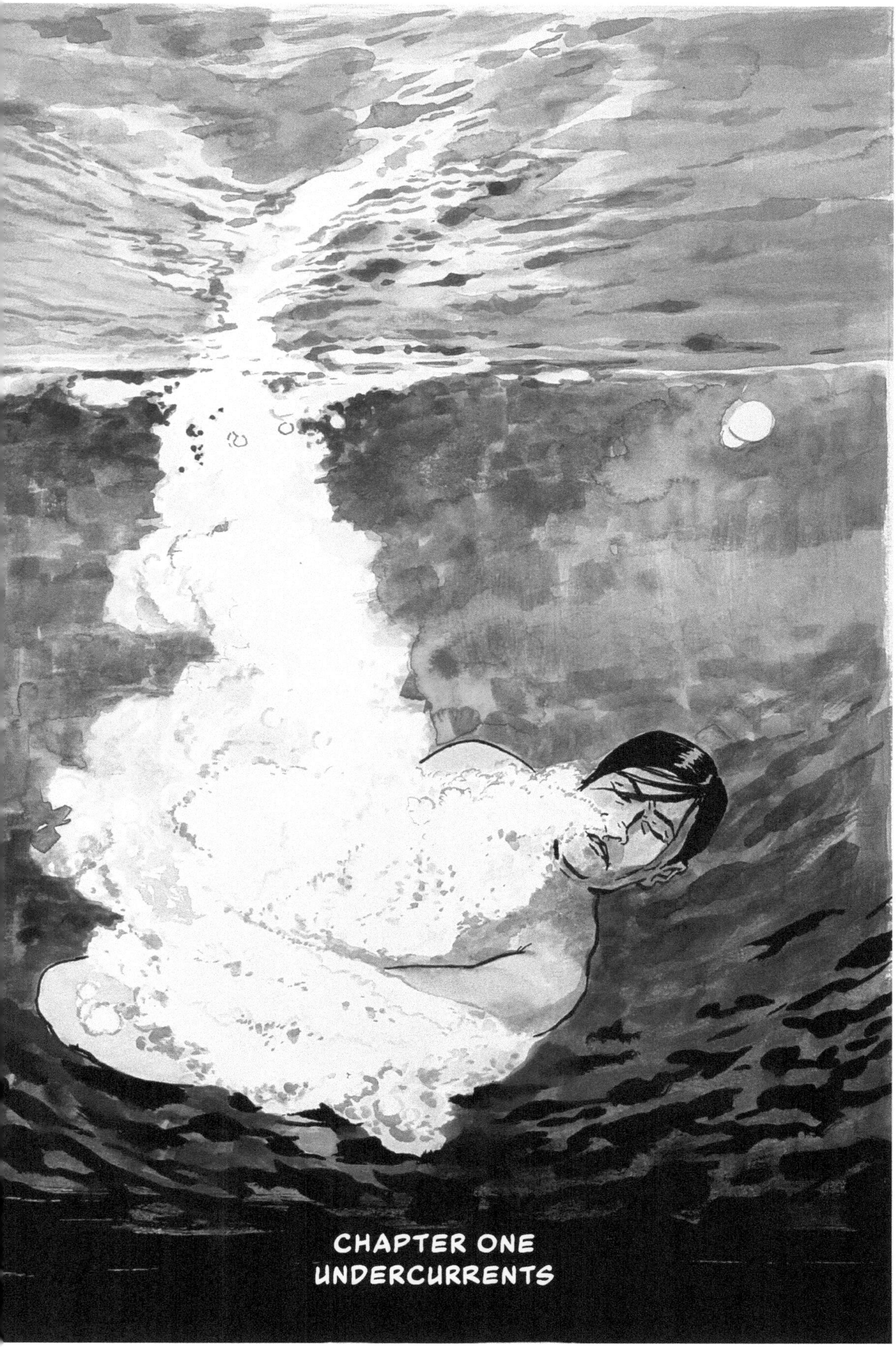
CHAPTER ONE
UNDERCURRENTS

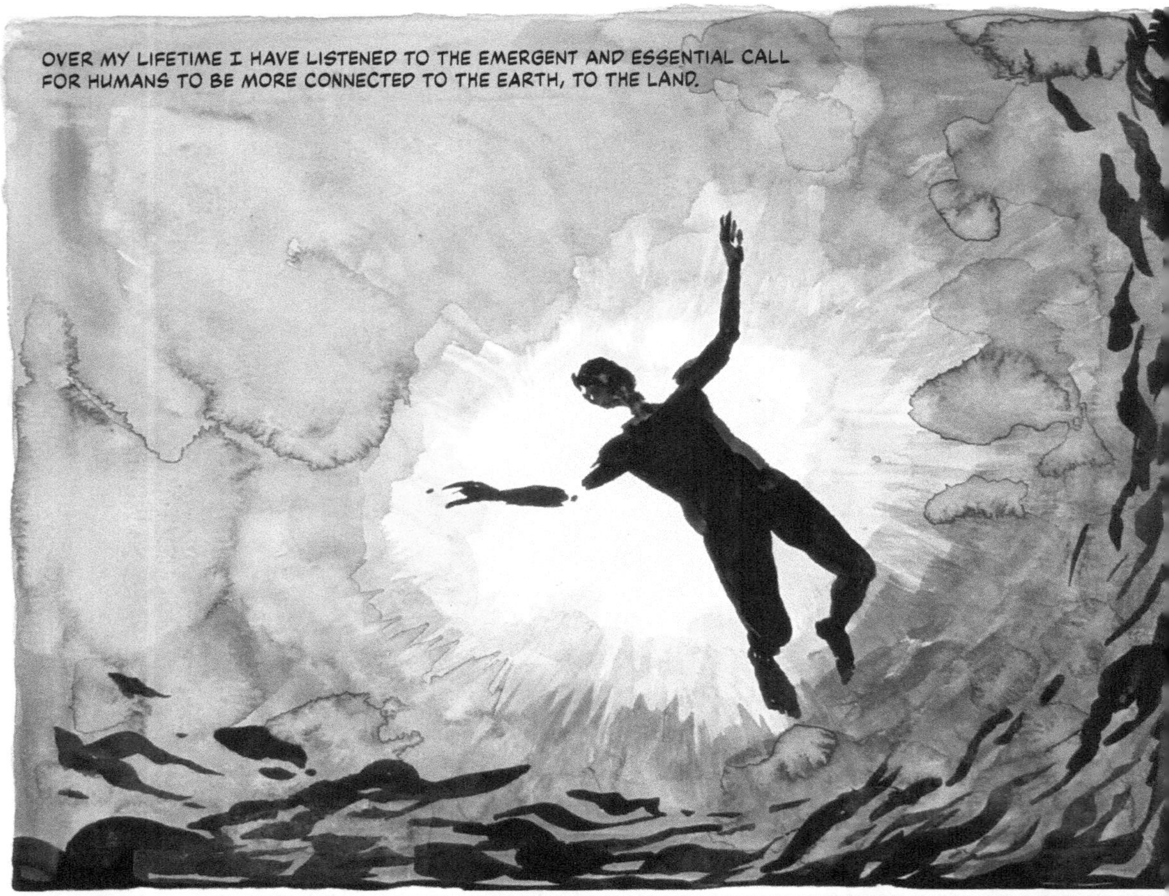
OVER MY LIFETIME I HAVE LISTENED TO THE EMERGENT AND ESSENTIAL CALL FOR HUMANS TO BE MORE CONNECTED TO THE EARTH, TO THE LAND.

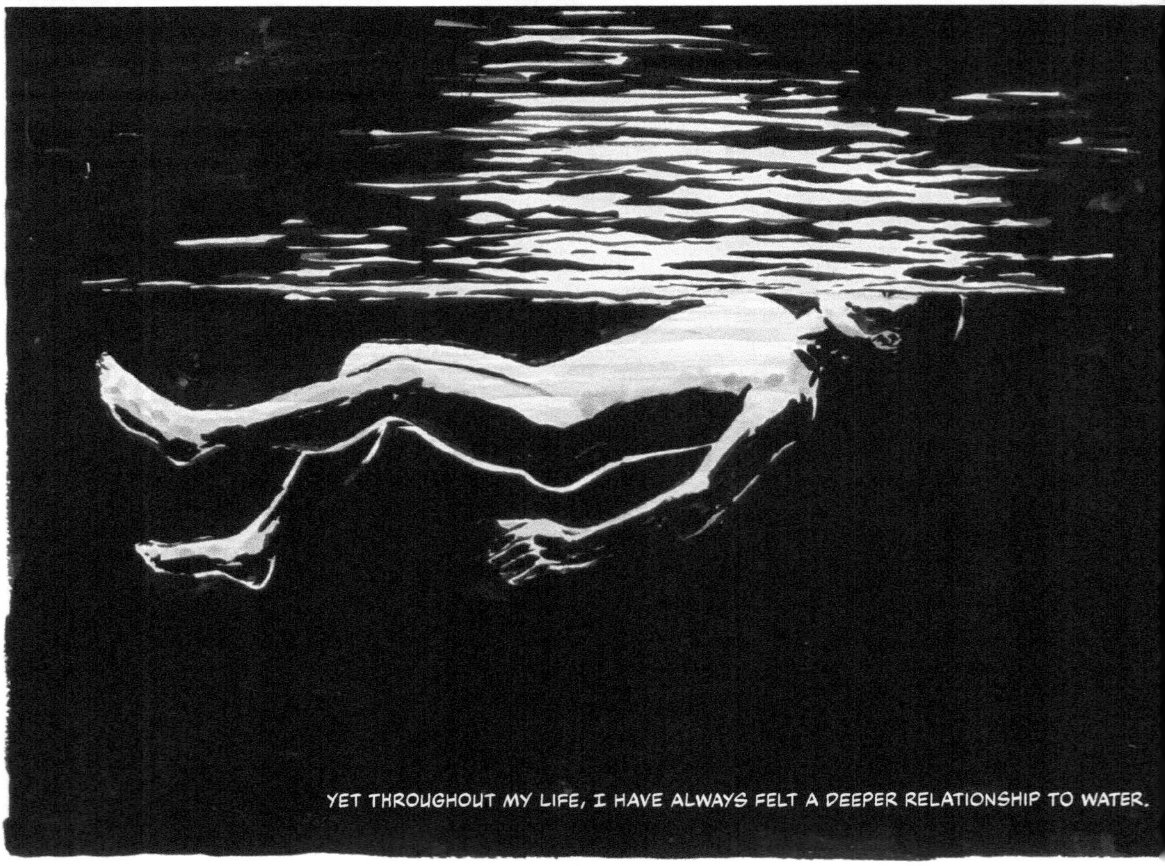
YET THROUGHOUT MY LIFE, I HAVE ALWAYS FELT A DEEPER RELATIONSHIP TO WATER.

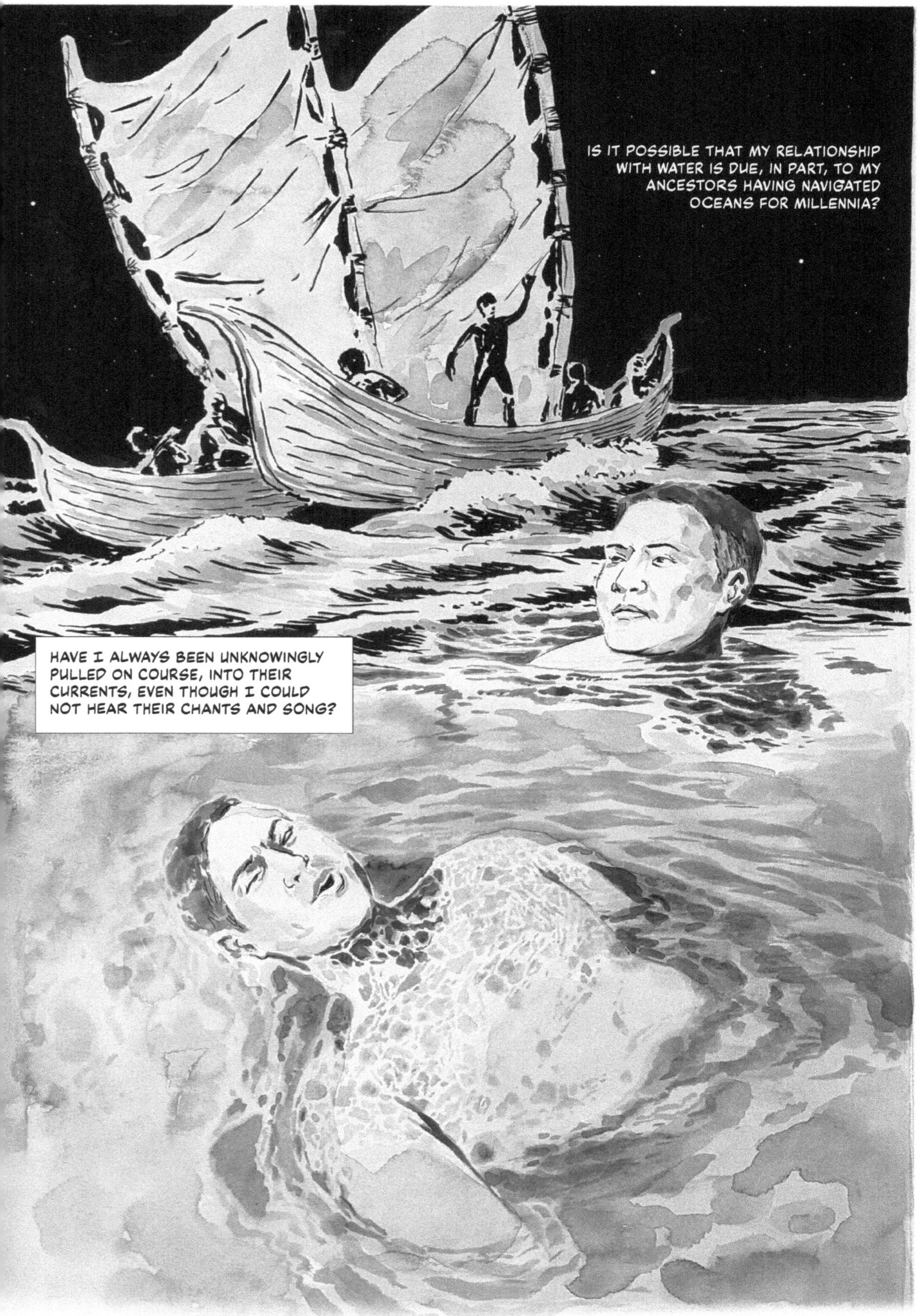
IS IT POSSIBLE THAT MY RELATIONSHIP WITH WATER IS DUE, IN PART, TO MY ANCESTORS HAVING NAVIGATED OCEANS FOR MILLENNIA?
HAVE I ALWAYS BEEN UNKNOWINGLY PULLED ON COURSE, INTO THEIR CURRENTS, EVEN THOUGH I COULD NOT HEAR THEIR CHANTS AND SONG?

OR WAS IT A DESIRE TO NOT FEEL LANDLOCKED IN THE MIDWEST? A QUIET LONGING TO SEEK THE WATER'S EDGE?

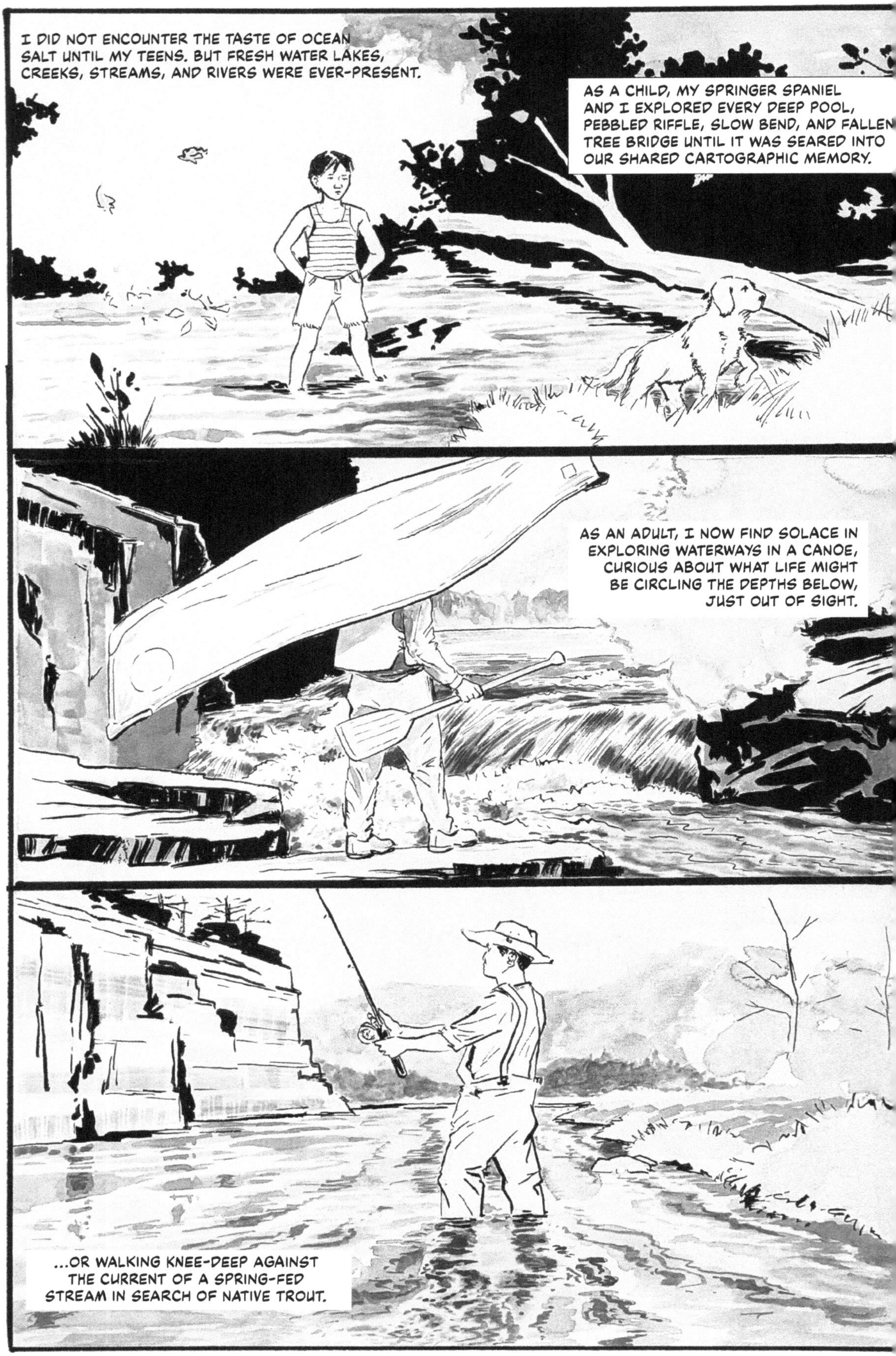
I DID NOT ENCOUNTER THE TASTE OF OCEAN SALT UNTIL MY TEENS. BUT FRESH WATER LAKES, CREEKS, STREAMS, AND RIVERS WERE EVER-PRESENT.
AS A CHILD, MY SPRINGER SPANIEL AND I EXPLORED EVERY DEEP POOL, PEBBLED RIFFLE, SLOW BEND, AND FALLEN TREE BRIDGE UNTIL IT WAS SEARED INTO OUR SHARED CARTOGRAPHIC MEMORY.
AS AN ADULT, I NOW FIND SOLACE IN EXPLORING WATERWAYS IN A CANOE, CURIOUS ABOUT WHAT LIFE MIGHT BE CIRCLING THE DEPTHS BELOW, JUST OUT OF SIGHT.
...OR WALKING KNEE-DEEP AGAINST THE CURRENT OF A SPRING-FED STREAM IN SEARCH OF NATIVE TROUT.

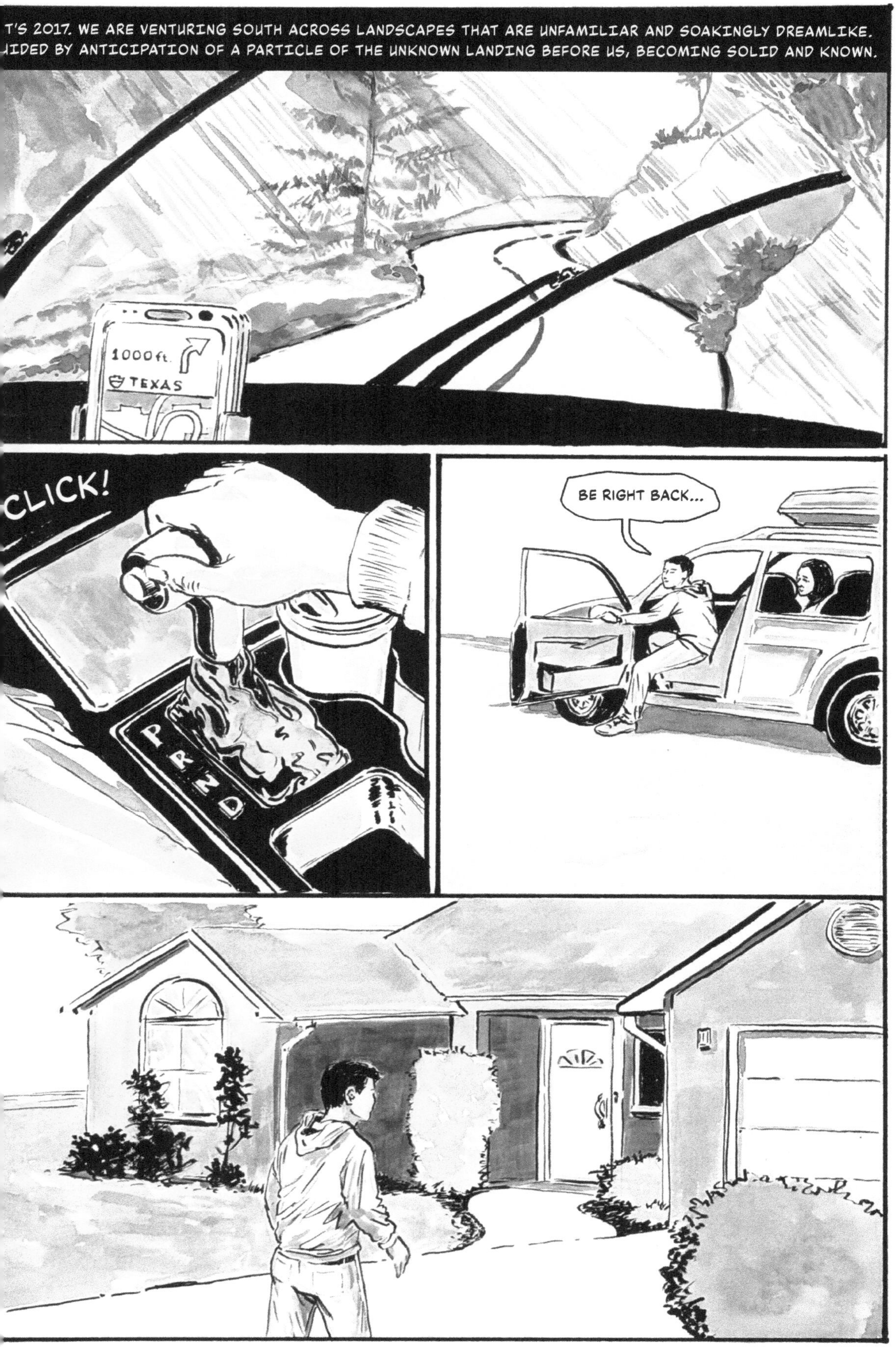

T'S 2017. WE ARE VENTURING SOUTH ACROSS LANDSCAPES THAT ARE UNFAMILIAR AND SOAKINGLY DREAMLIKE.
UIDED BY ANTICIPATION OF A PARTICLE OF THE UNKNOWN LANDING BEFORE US, BECOMING SOLID AND KNOWN.
1000ft.
TEXAS
CLICK!
P
R
N
D
BE RIGHT BACK...

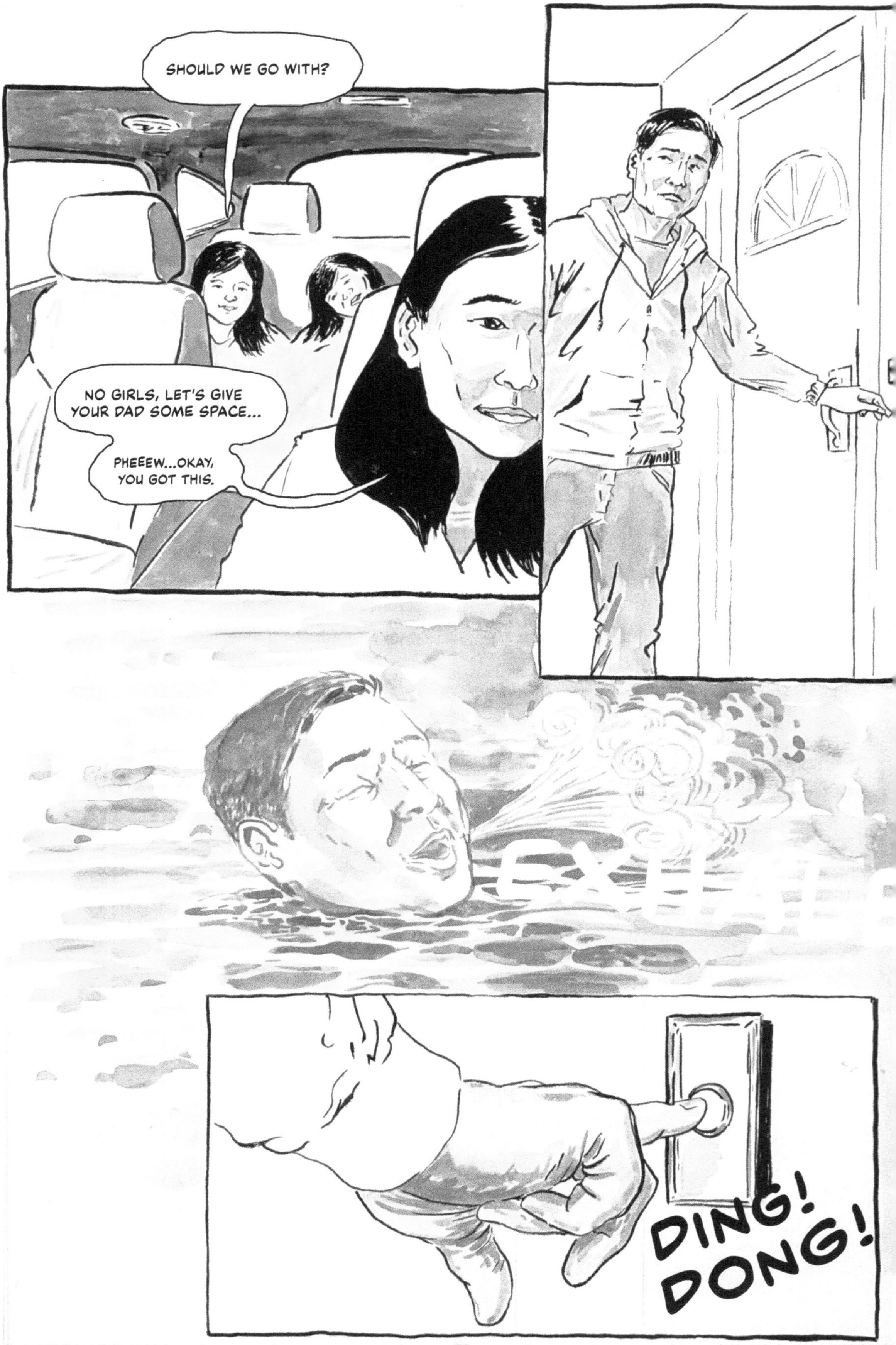
SHOULD WE GO WITH?
NO GIRLS, LET'S GIVE YOUR DAD SOME SPACE...
PHEEEW...OKAY, YOU GOT THIS.
DING! DONG!

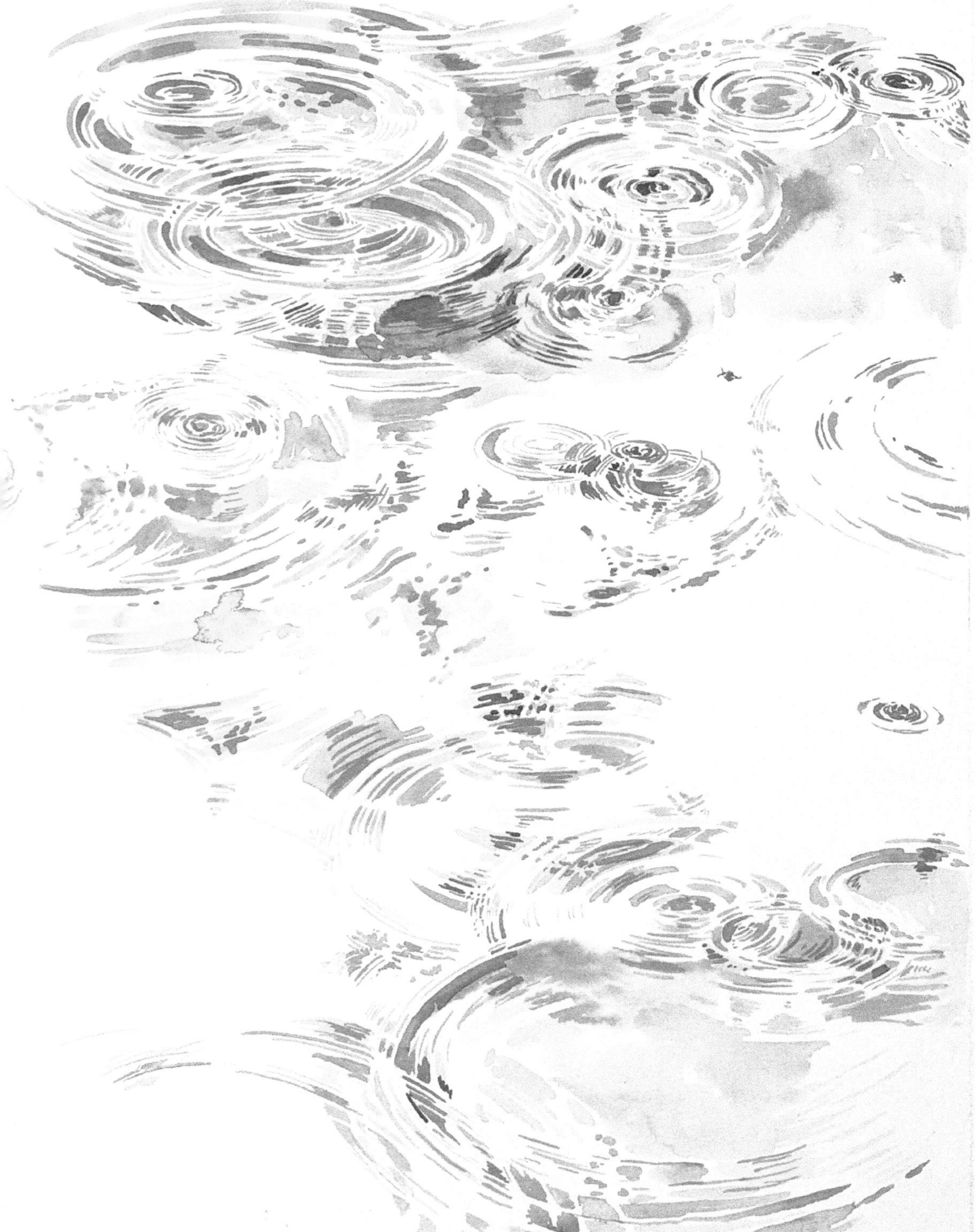

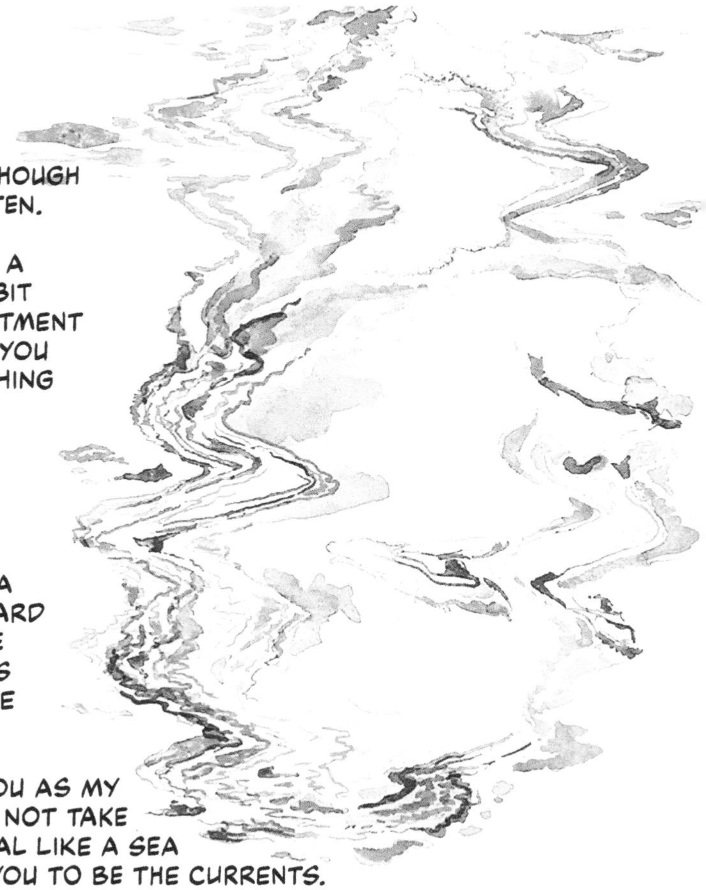

DEAR ANTICIPATION,

IT HAS BEEN A WHILE SINCE WE HAVE CONNECTED. I HAVE BEEN AWAY FOR SOME TIME, ALTHOUGH I HOPE YOU ARE WILLING TO LISTEN.

YOU ONCE TOLD ME, POSSIBLY IN A DREAM, MY RECOLLECTION IS A BIT FUZZY, THAT YOU WERE THE ENACTMENT OF KNOWING FORWARD. BUT HEY, YOU KNOW ME, UNKNOWING IS SOMETHING I AM QUITE ACCUSTOMED TO.

THIS IS PROBABLY WHERE THINGS BETWEEN US GOT OFF COURSE, OR STALLED OUT. I ADMIT I HAVE NEVER BEEN A PLANFUL PERSON. I'M MORE OF A MEANDERER. I'VE COME TO REGARD THIS AS A SKILL THAT MAKES ME RESILIENT, ALTHOUGH MAYBE IT IS SOMETHING I SHOULD FEEL MORE HUMBLE ABOUT.

AT TIMES I HAVE THOUGHT OF YOU AS MY *AUMAKUA**, BUT ONE THAT DOES NOT TAKE THE PHYSICAL FORM OF AN ANIMAL LIKE A SEA TURTLE OR OWL. NO, I IMAGINE YOU TO BE THE CURRENTS.

OPERATING ON THE BELIEF THAT ONE'S PAST CAN NEVER BE KNOWN, I SEE NOW, HAS LED ME TO DISAVOW YOU. MY HABITUAL INERTIA RESISTS YOU. AND WE BOTH KNOW I'M A STRONG SWIMMER. BUT I'M NOT TRYING TO MAKE EXCUSES.

I WANT TO MAKE AMENDS IF IT IS NOT TOO LATE. EVEN NOW AS I RELEASE ISOMETRIC MOMENTUM, I UNDERSTAND IT MIGHT FEEL AWKWARD. AND AS I ALLOW YOU TO FLUIDLY ENCAPSULATE ME, YOU ARE PROBABLY THINKING, "WHO DIS HITCHHIKER COME CALLING AFTER ALL THESE YEARS?" AND YOU WOULD BE RIGHT. YOU DON'T OWE ME ANYTHING, DO YOU?

BUT YOU KNEW I'D COME BACK AROUND ALL ALONG BECAUSE HEY, PREMONITION IS YOUR THING.

MIGHT I SUGGEST, IF YOU ARE WILLING, THAT WE TAKE IT SLOW? I'LL CONTINUE TO WADE IN IF YOU PLEASE KEEP REMINDING ME EVERY SO OFTEN THAT YOU ARE STILL THERE. I WILL MAKE A CONCERTED EFFORT TO BE MORE PHYSICALLY ATTUNED. I AM READY TO NOT ONLY REFLECT ON THE WEIGHT OF WHO I AM, BUT ALSO RECEIVE THE BUOYANCY OF WHO I AM BECOMING.

I BELIEVE WHAT YOU ONCE TOLD ME IS TRUE, THAT ALL STREAMS AND RIVERS EVENTUALLY FIND THEIR OCEAN.

-M

*A PERSONAL OR FAMILY GOD THAT ORIGINATED AS A DEIFIED ANCESTO

CHAPTER TWO
LONGING

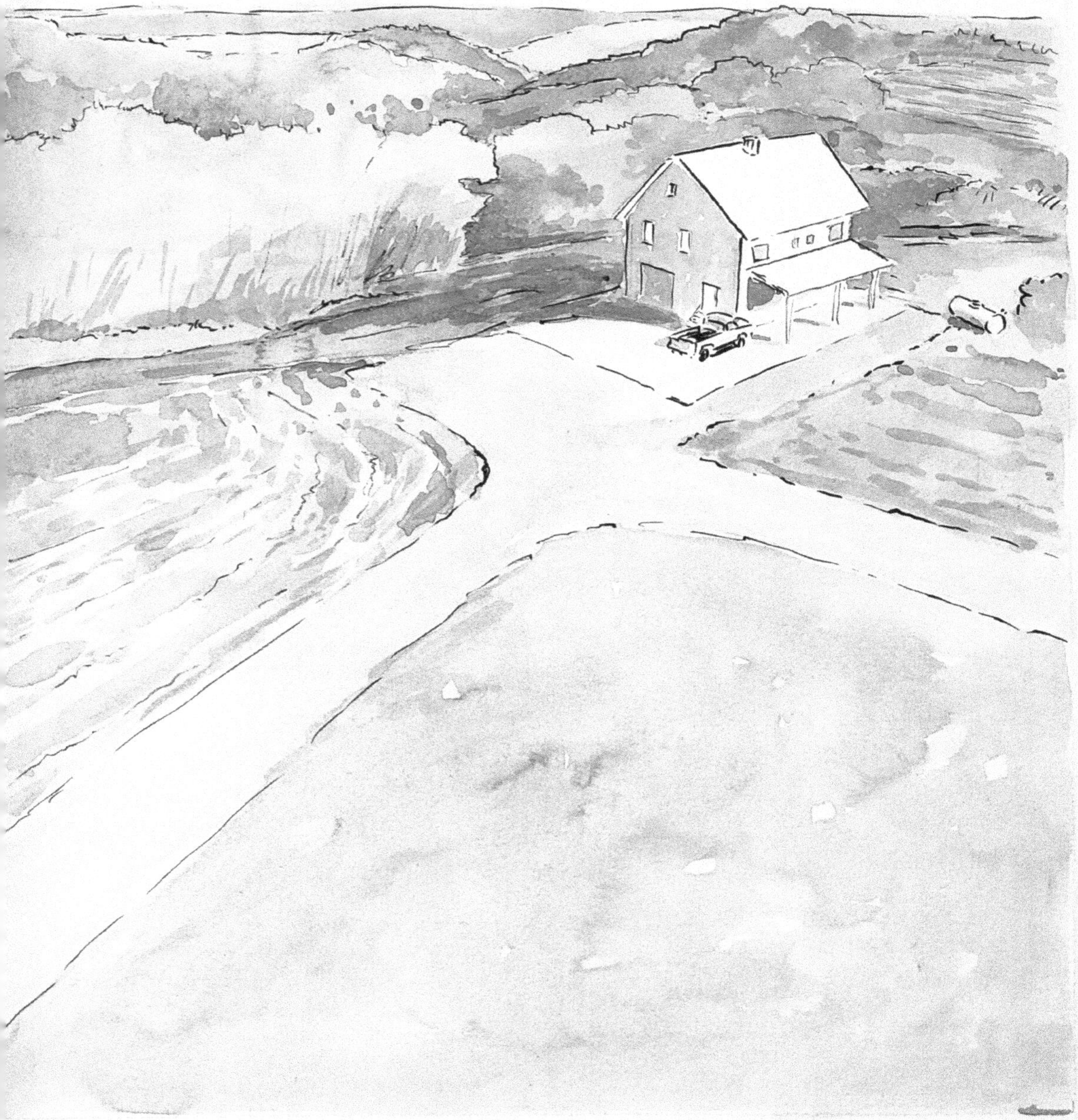

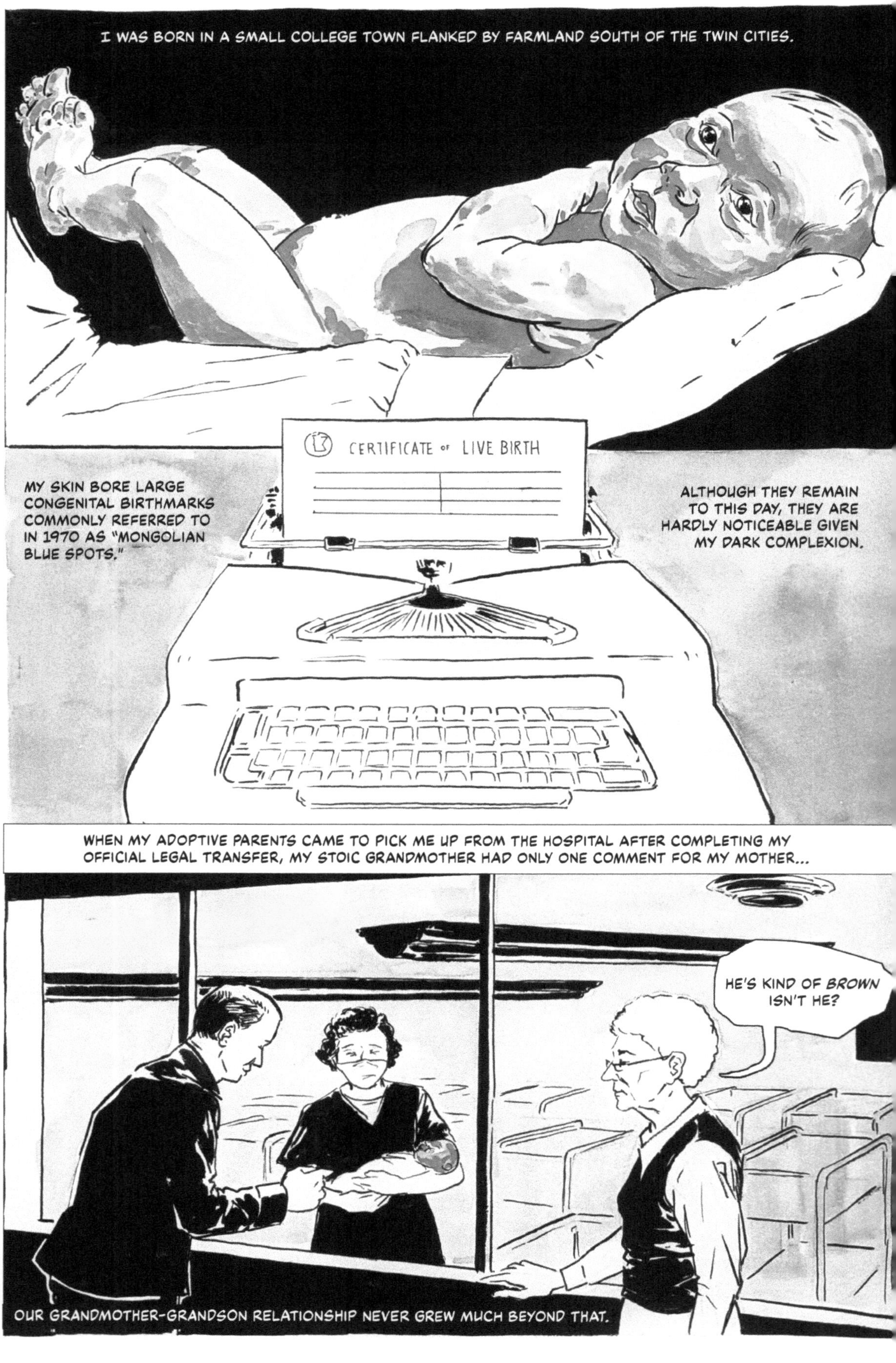
I WAS BORN IN A SMALL COLLEGE TOWN FLANKED BY FARMLAND SOUTH OF THE TWIN CITIES.
CERTIFICATE of LIVE BIRTH
MY SKIN BORE LARGE CONGENITAL BIRTHMARKS COMMONLY REFERRED TO IN 1970 AS "MONGOLIAN BLUE SPOTS."
ALTHOUGH THEY REMAIN TO THIS DAY, THEY ARE HARDLY NOTICEABLE GIVEN MY DARK COMPLEXION.
WHEN MY ADOPTIVE PARENTS CAME TO PICK ME UP FROM THE HOSPITAL AFTER COMPLETING MY OFFICIAL LEGAL TRANSFER, MY STOIC GRANDMOTHER HAD ONLY ONE COMMENT FOR MY MOTHER...
HE'S KIND OF *BROWN* ISN'T HE?
OUR GRANDMOTHER-GRANDSON RELATIONSHIP NEVER GREW MUCH BEYOND THAT.

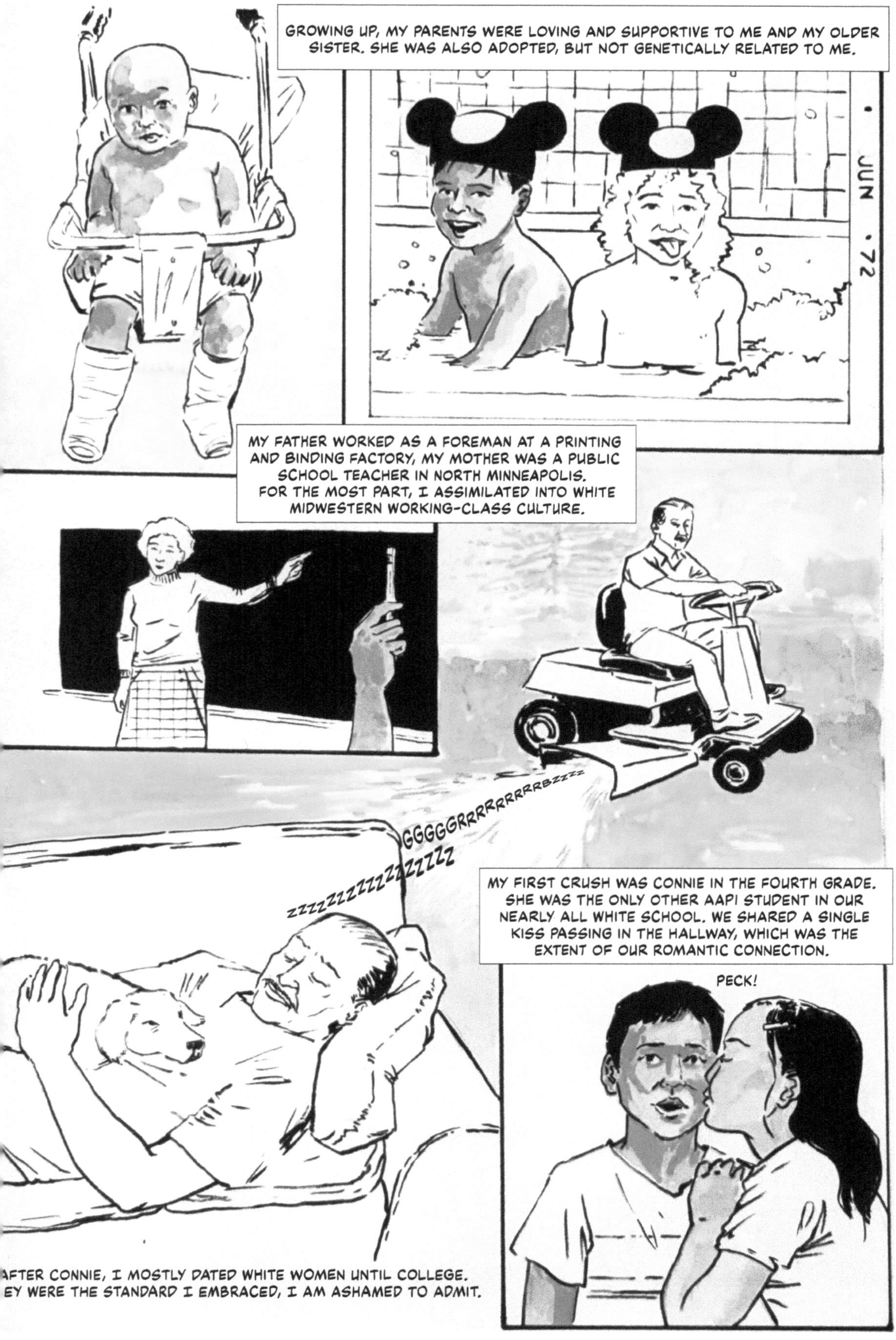

GROWING UP, MY PARENTS WERE LOVING AND SUPPORTIVE TO ME AND MY OLDER SISTER. SHE WAS ALSO ADOPTED, BUT NOT GENETICALLY RELATED TO ME.
JUN •72
MY FATHER WORKED AS A FOREMAN AT A PRINTING AND BINDING FACTORY, MY MOTHER WAS A PUBLIC SCHOOL TEACHER IN NORTH MINNEAPOLIS. FOR THE MOST PART, I ASSIMILATED INTO WHITE MIDWESTERN WORKING-CLASS CULTURE.
GGGGGRRRRRRRRRRBZZZZ
ZZZZZZZZZZZZZZZZZ
MY FIRST CRUSH WAS CONNIE IN THE FOURTH GRADE. SHE WAS THE ONLY OTHER AAPI STUDENT IN OUR NEARLY ALL WHITE SCHOOL. WE SHARED A SINGLE KISS PASSING IN THE HALLWAY, WHICH WAS THE EXTENT OF OUR ROMANTIC CONNECTION.
PECK!
AFTER CONNIE, I MOSTLY DATED WHITE WOMEN UNTIL COLLEGE.
EY WERE THE STANDARD I EMBRACED, I AM ASHAMED TO ADMIT.

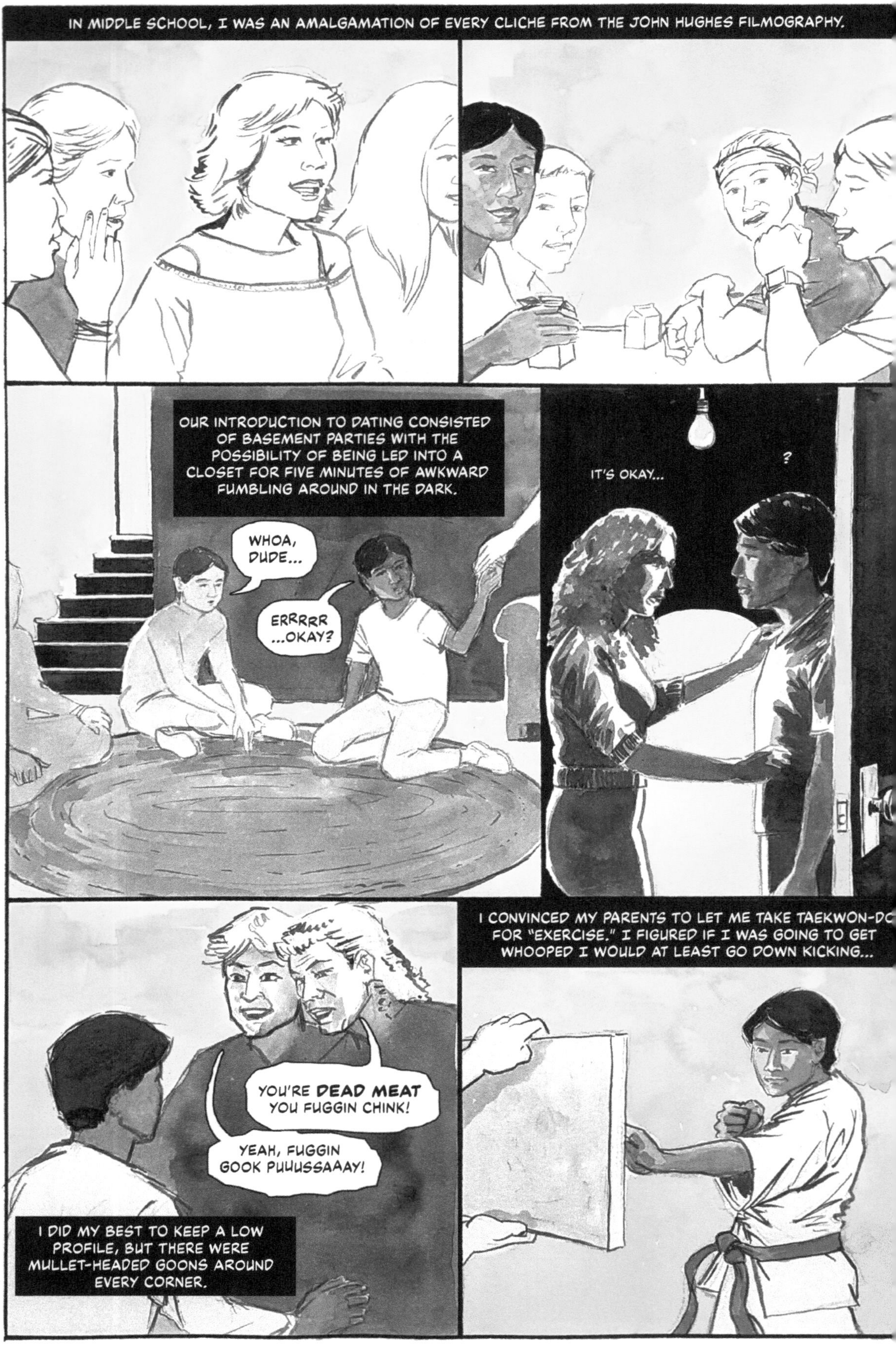
IN MIDDLE SCHOOL, I WAS AN AMALGAMATION OF EVERY CLICHE FROM THE JOHN HUGHES FILMOGRAPHY.
OUR INTRODUCTION TO DATING CONSISTED OF BASEMENT PARTIES WITH THE POSSIBILITY OF BEING LED INTO A CLOSET FOR FIVE MINUTES OF AWKWARD FUMBLING AROUND IN THE DARK.
WHOA, DUDE...
ERRRRR ...OKAY?
IT'S OKAY...
?
YOU'RE **DEAD MEAT** YOU FUGGIN CHINK!
YEAH, FUGGIN GOOK PUUUSSAAAY!
I DID MY BEST TO KEEP A LOW PROFILE, BUT THERE WERE MULLET-HEADED GOONS AROUND EVERY CORNER.
I CONVINCED MY PARENTS TO LET ME TAKE TAEKWON-DO FOR "EXERCISE." I FIGURED IF I WAS GOING TO GET WHOOPED I WOULD AT LEAST GO DOWN KICKING...

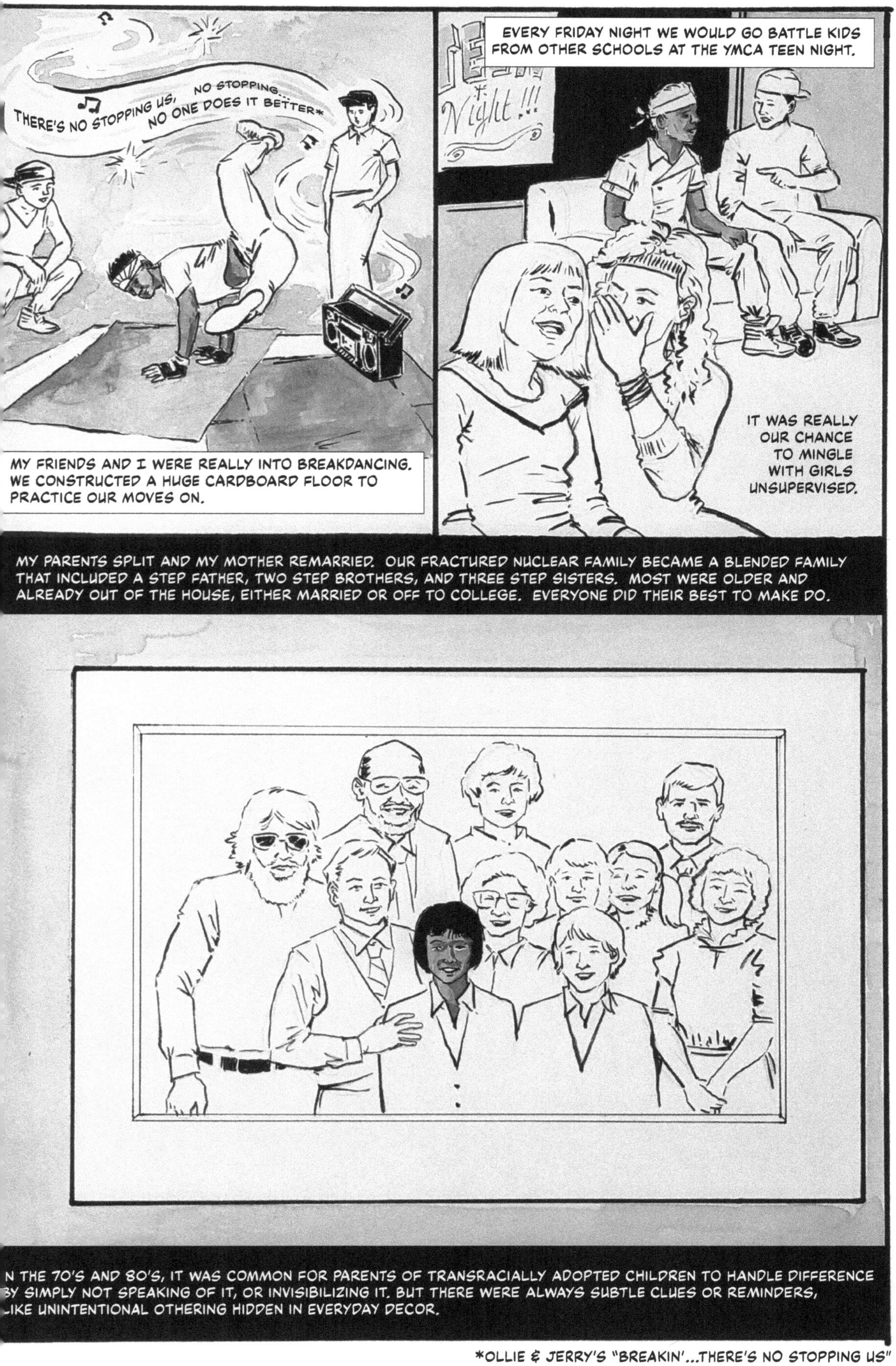

THERE'S NO STOPPING US, NO STOPPING... NO ONE DOES IT BETTER*
MY FRIENDS AND I WERE REALLY INTO BREAKDANCING. WE CONSTRUCTED A HUGE CARDBOARD FLOOR TO PRACTICE OUR MOVES ON.
EVERY FRIDAY NIGHT WE WOULD GO BATTLE KIDS FROM OTHER SCHOOLS AT THE YMCA TEEN NIGHT.
Night!!!
IT WAS REALLY OUR CHANCE TO MINGLE WITH GIRLS UNSUPERVISED.
MY PARENTS SPLIT AND MY MOTHER REMARRIED. OUR FRACTURED NUCLEAR FAMILY BECAME A BLENDED FAMILY THAT INCLUDED A STEP FATHER, TWO STEP BROTHERS, AND THREE STEP SISTERS. MOST WERE OLDER AND ALREADY OUT OF THE HOUSE, EITHER MARRIED OR OFF TO COLLEGE. EVERYONE DID THEIR BEST TO MAKE DO.
N THE 70'S AND 80'S, IT WAS COMMON FOR PARENTS OF TRANSRACIALLY ADOPTED CHILDREN TO HANDLE DIFFERENCE Y SIMPLY NOT SPEAKING OF IT, OR INVISIBILIZING IT. BUT THERE WERE ALWAYS SUBTLE CLUES OR REMINDERS, IKE UNINTENTIONAL OTHERING HIDDEN IN EVERYDAY DECOR.

*OLLIE & JERRY'S "BREAKIN'...THERE'S NO STOPPING US"

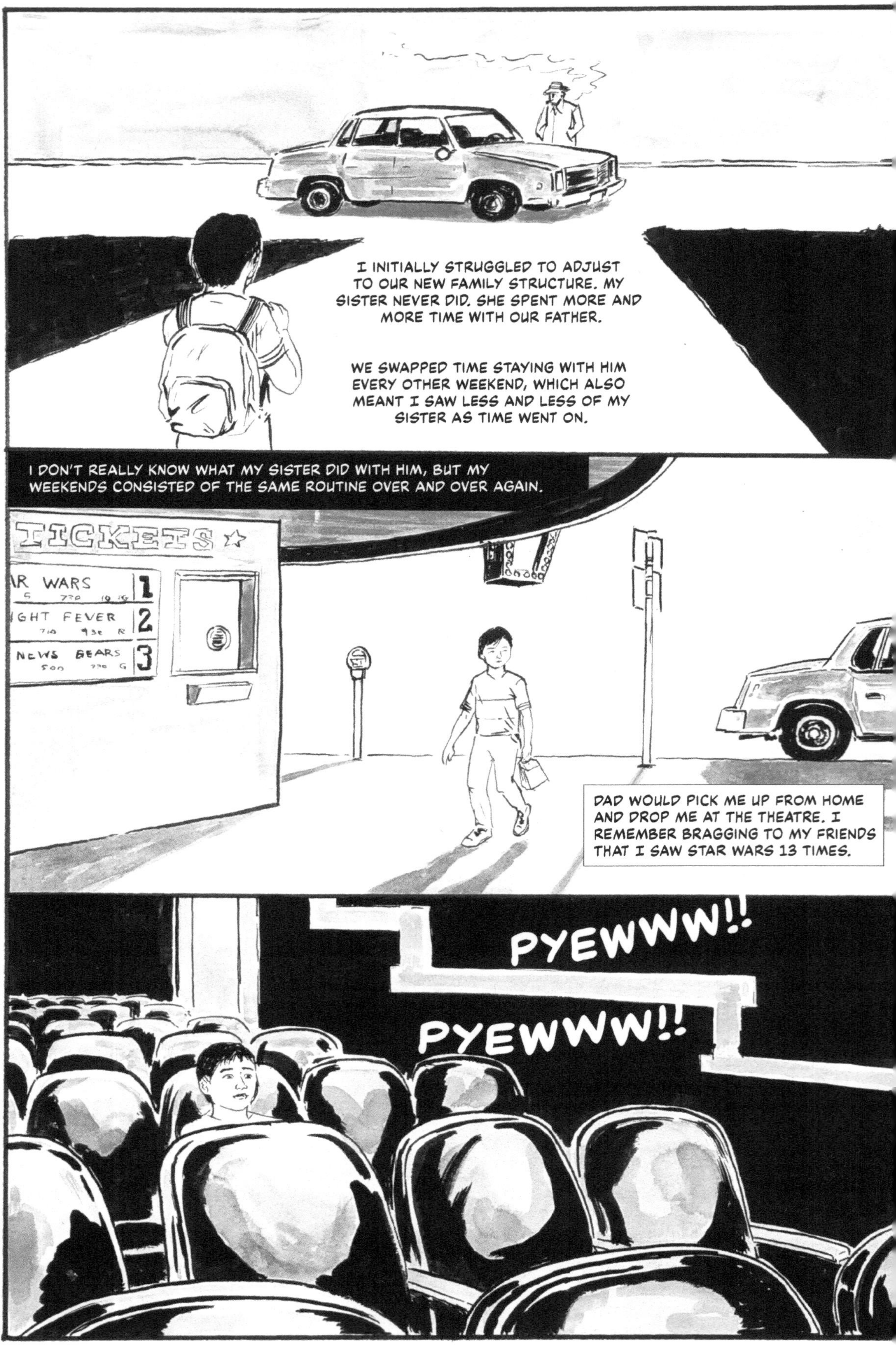
I INITIALLY STRUGGLED TO ADJUST TO OUR NEW FAMILY STRUCTURE. MY SISTER NEVER DID. SHE SPENT MORE AND MORE TIME WITH OUR FATHER.
WE SWAPPED TIME STAYING WITH HIM EVERY OTHER WEEKEND, WHICH ALSO MEANT I SAW LESS AND LESS OF MY SISTER AS TIME WENT ON.
I DON'T REALLY KNOW WHAT MY SISTER DID WITH HIM, BUT MY WEEKENDS CONSISTED OF THE SAME ROUTINE OVER AND OVER AGAIN.
AR WARS 1
GHT FEVER 2
NEWS BEARS 3
DAD WOULD PICK ME UP FROM HOME AND DROP ME AT THE THEATRE. I REMEMBER BRAGGING TO MY FRIENDS THAT I SAW STAR WARS 13 TIMES.
PYEWWW!!
PYEWWW!!

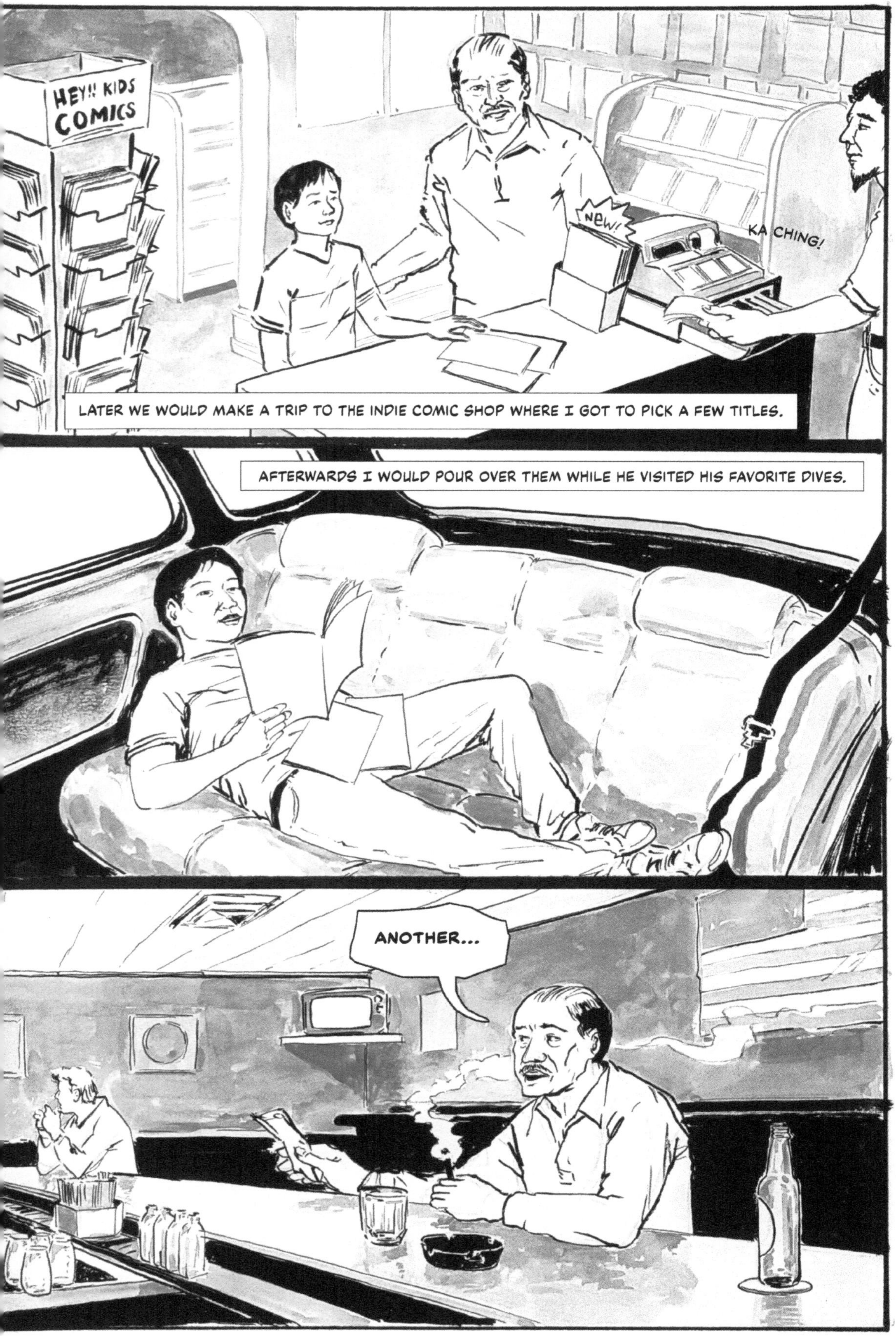
HEY!! KIDS COMICS
NEW!
KA CHING!
LATER WE WOULD MAKE A TRIP TO THE INDIE COMIC SHOP WHERE I GOT TO PICK A FEW TITLES.
AFTERWARDS I WOULD POUR OVER THEM WHILE HE VISITED HIS FAVORITE DIVES.
ANOTHER...

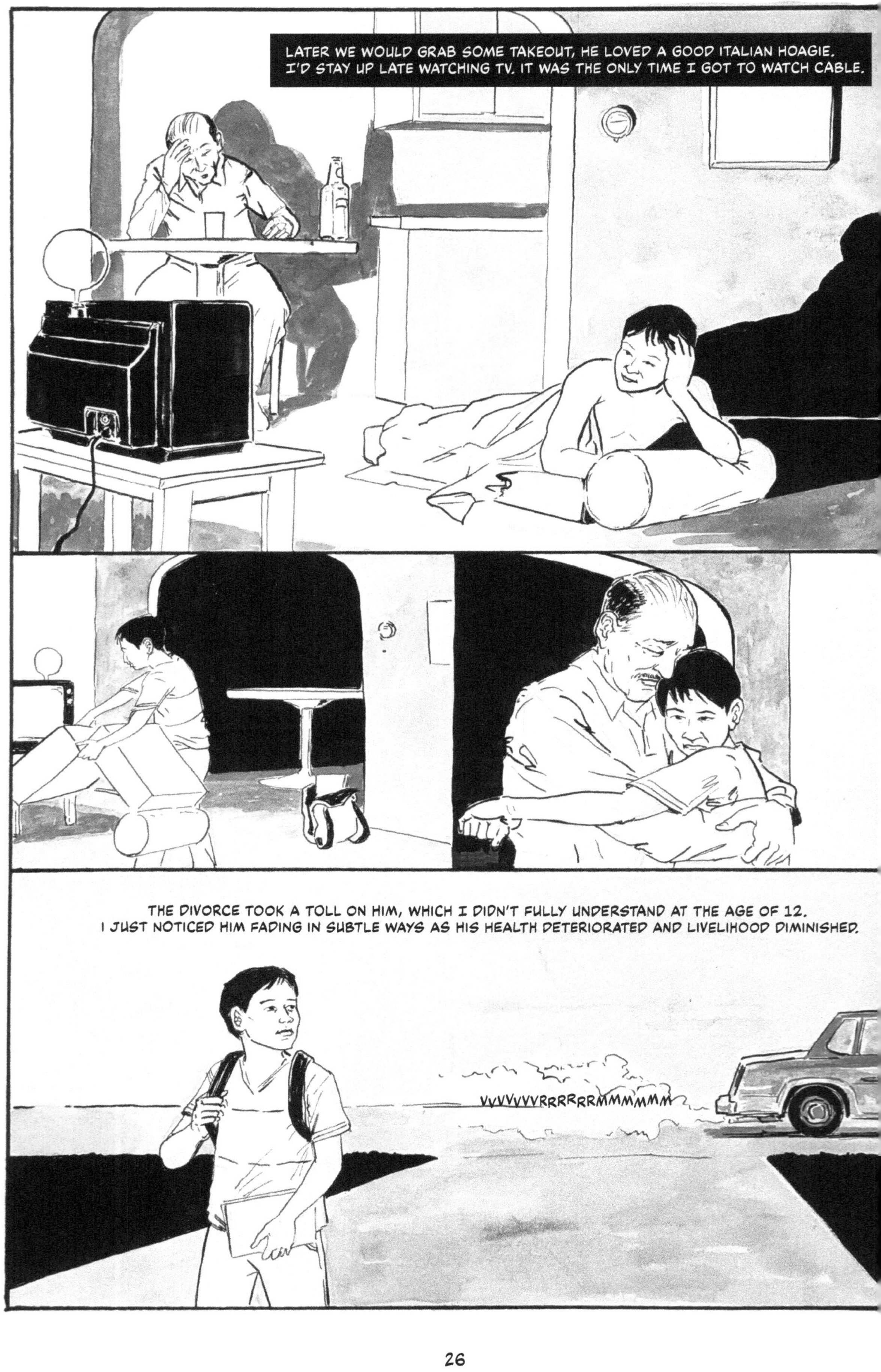
LATER WE WOULD GRAB SOME TAKEOUT, HE LOVED A GOOD ITALIAN HOAGIE.
I'D STAY UP LATE WATCHING TV. IT WAS THE ONLY TIME I GOT TO WATCH CABLE.
THE DIVORCE TOOK A TOLL ON HIM, WHICH I DIDN'T FULLY UNDERSTAND AT THE AGE OF 12.
I JUST NOTICED HIM FADING IN SUBTLE WAYS AS HIS HEALTH DETERIORATED AND LIVELIHOOD DIMINISHED.
VVVVVVVRRRRRRMMMMMM

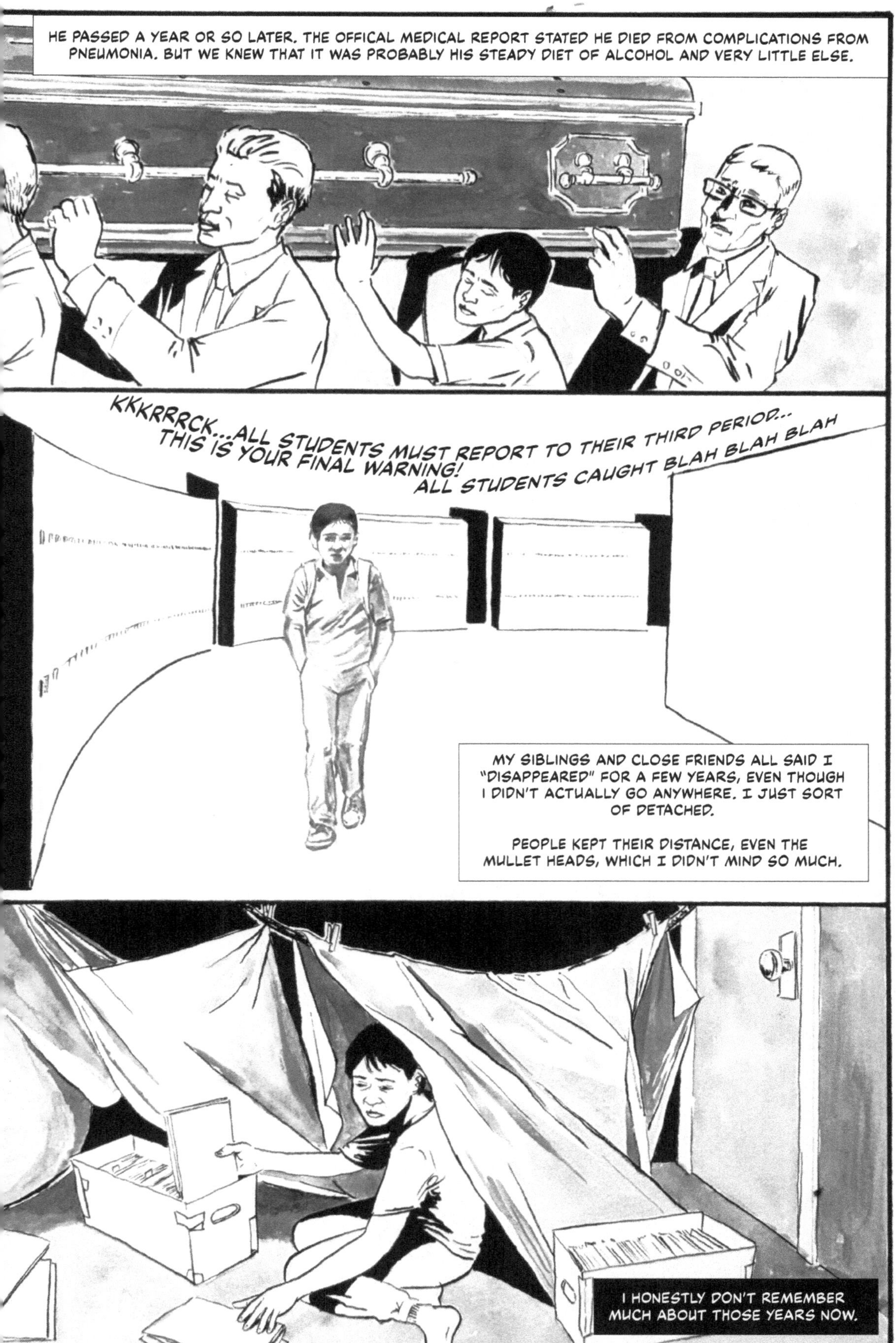
HE PASSED A YEAR OR SO LATER. THE OFFICAL MEDICAL REPORT STATED HE DIED FROM COMPLICATIONS FROM PNEUMONIA. BUT WE KNEW THAT IT WAS PROBABLY HIS STEADY DIET OF ALCOHOL AND VERY LITTLE ELSE.
KKKRRRCK...ALL STUDENTS MUST REPORT TO THEIR THIRD PERIOD... THIS IS YOUR FINAL WARNING!
ALL STUDENTS CAUGHT BLAH BLAH BLAH
MY SIBLINGS AND CLOSE FRIENDS ALL SAID I "DISAPPEARED" FOR A FEW YEARS, EVEN THOUGH I DIDN'T ACTUALLY GO ANYWHERE. I JUST SORT OF DETACHED.
PEOPLE KEPT THEIR DISTANCE, EVEN THE MULLET HEADS, WHICH I DIDN'T MIND SO MUCH.
I HONESTLY DON'T REMEMBER MUCH ABOUT THOSE YEARS NOW.

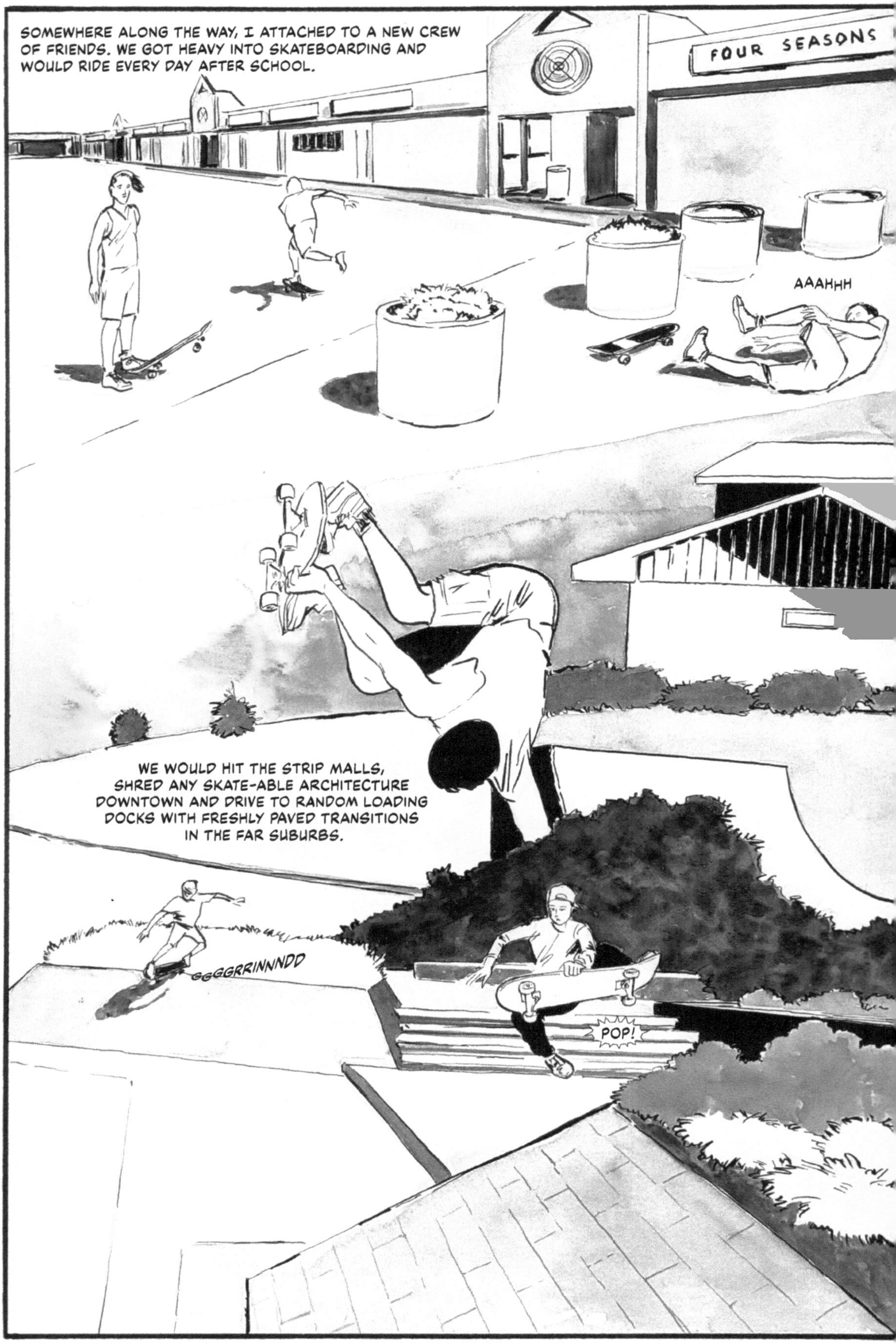
SOMEWHERE ALONG THE WAY, I ATTACHED TO A NEW CREW OF FRIENDS. WE GOT HEAVY INTO SKATEBOARDING AND WOULD RIDE EVERY DAY AFTER SCHOOL.
FOUR SEASONS
AAAHHH
WE WOULD HIT THE STRIP MALLS, SHRED ANY SKATE-ABLE ARCHITECTURE DOWNTOWN AND DRIVE TO RANDOM LOADING DOCKS WITH FRESHLY PAVED TRANSITIONS IN THE FAR SUBURBS.
GGGGRRINNNDD
POP!

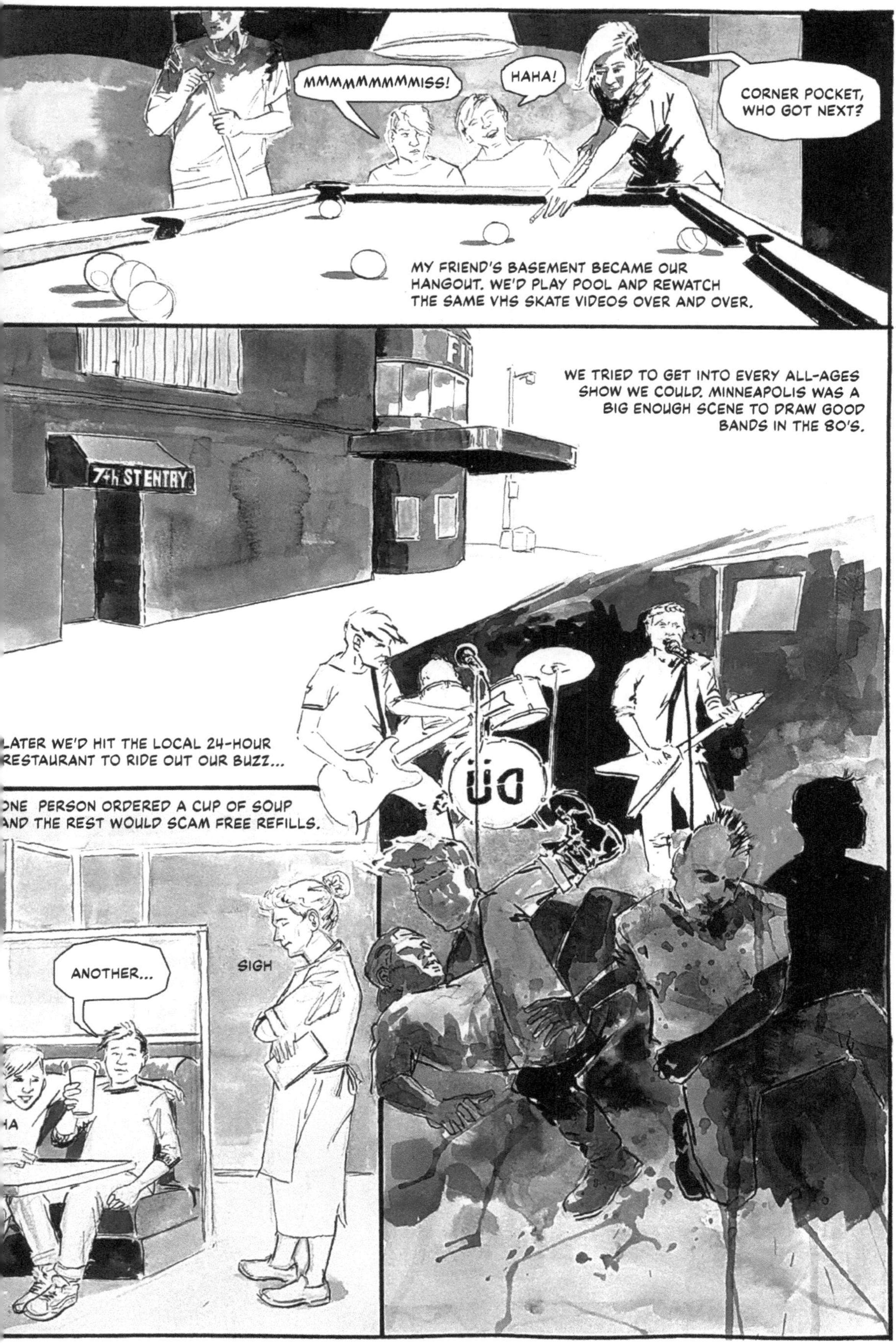
MMMMMMMMMMISS!
HAHA!
CORNER POCKET, WHO GOT NEXT?
MY FRIEND'S BASEMENT BECAME OUR HANGOUT. WE'D PLAY POOL AND REWATCH THE SAME VHS SKATE VIDEOS OVER AND OVER.
7th ST ENTRY
WE TRIED TO GET INTO EVERY ALL-AGES SHOW WE COULD. MINNEAPOLIS WAS A BIG ENOUGH SCENE TO DRAW GOOD BANDS IN THE 80'S.
LATER WE'D HIT THE LOCAL 24-HOUR RESTAURANT TO RIDE OUT OUR BUZZ...
ONE PERSON ORDERED A CUP OF SOUP AND THE REST WOULD SCAM FREE REFILLS.
ANOTHER...
SIGH
HA

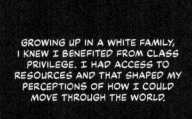

GROWING UP IN A WHITE FAMILY, I KNEW I BENEFITED FROM CLASS PRIVILEGE. I HAD ACCESS TO RESOURCES AND THAT SHAPED MY PERCEPTIONS OF HOW I COULD MOVE THROUGH THE WORLD.

BUT I WAS OFTEN REMINDED THAT MY PERCEPTIONS, FORMED THROUGHOUT A CHILDHOOD OF ASSIMILATION, WERE NOT HOW MY BODY WAS PERCEIVED.

DO YOU KNOW HOW FAST YOU WERE GOING?

MA'AM, OFFICER. MAYBE THIRTY FIVE?

SIGH. THIS SEEMS A BIT EXCESSIVE FOR A SPEEDING TICKET...

SHUT IT! UNLESS YOU'D PREFER WE GO DOWN TO THE STATION...

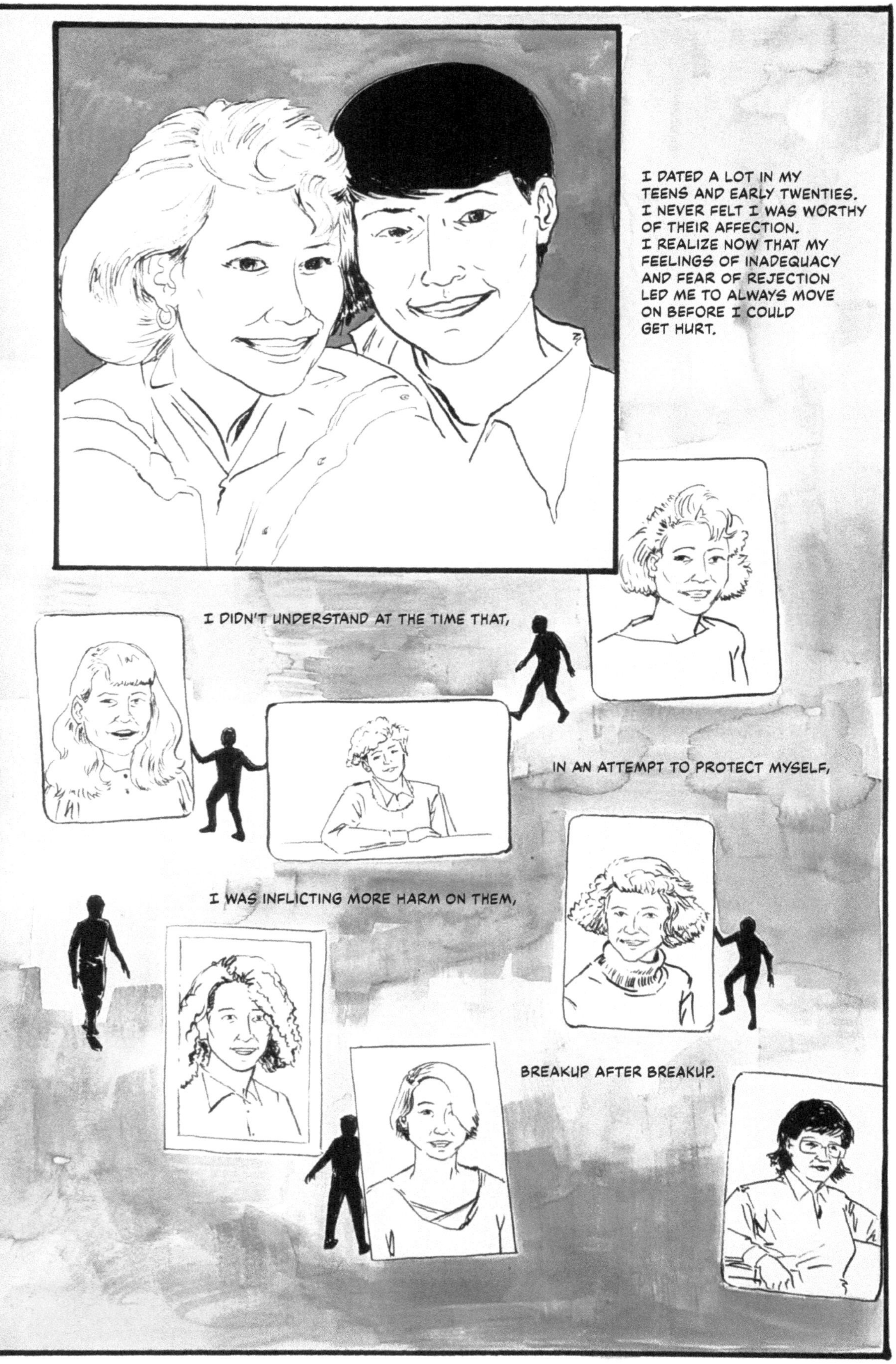

I DATED A LOT IN MY TEENS AND EARLY TWENTIES. I NEVER FELT I WAS WORTHY OF THEIR AFFECTION. I REALIZE NOW THAT MY FEELINGS OF INADEQUACY AND FEAR OF REJECTION LED ME TO ALWAYS MOVE ON BEFORE I COULD GET HURT.
I DIDN'T UNDERSTAND AT THE TIME THAT,
IN AN ATTEMPT TO PROTECT MYSELF,
I WAS INFLICTING MORE HARM ON THEM,
BREAKUP AFTER BREAKUP.

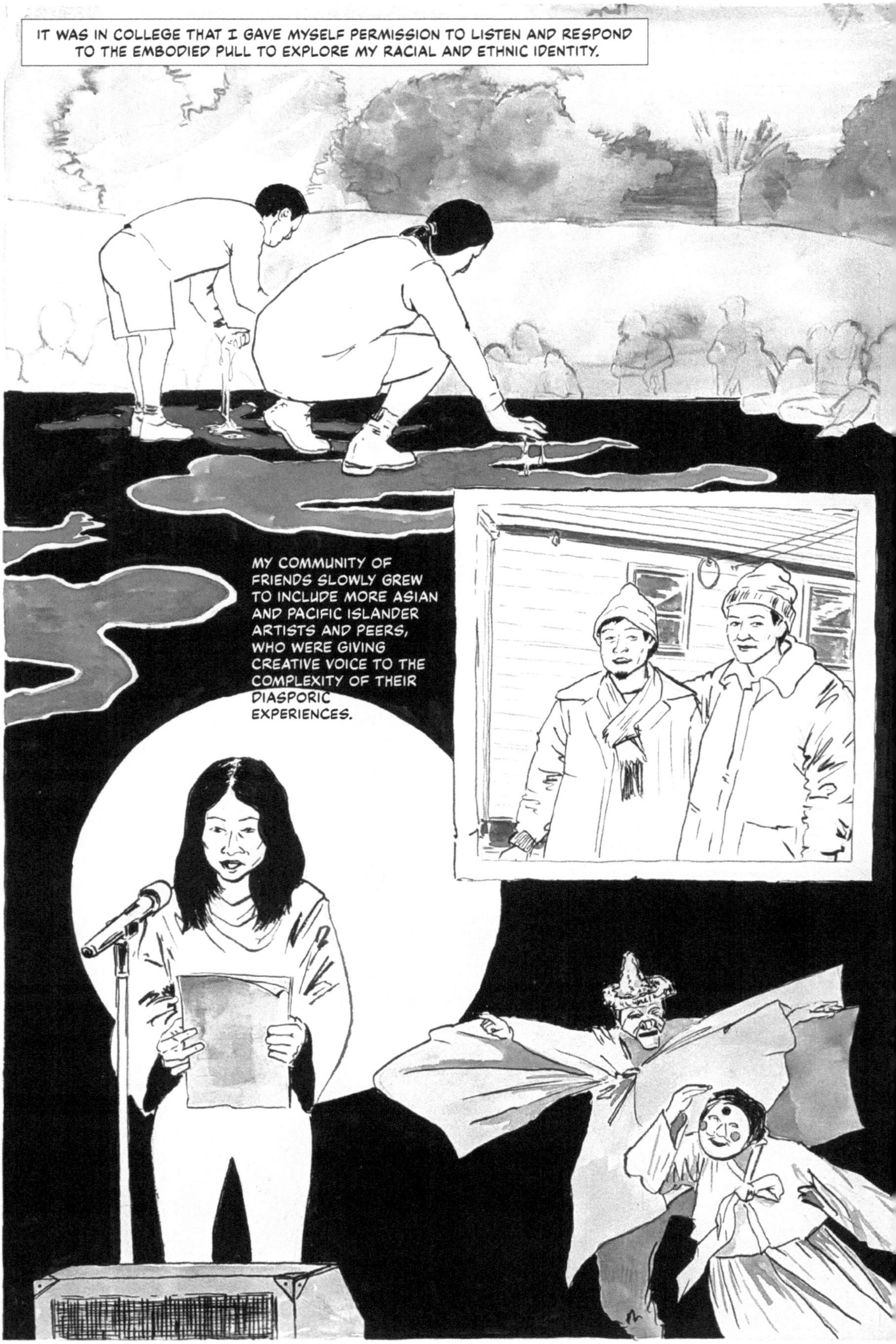
IT WAS IN COLLEGE THAT I GAVE MYSELF PERMISSION TO LISTEN AND RESPOND TO THE EMBODIED PULL TO EXPLORE MY RACIAL AND ETHNIC IDENTITY.
MY COMMUNITY OF FRIENDS SLOWLY GREW TO INCLUDE MORE ASIAN AND PACIFIC ISLANDER ARTISTS AND PEERS, WHO WERE GIVING CREATIVE VOICE TO THE COMPLEXITY OF THEIR DIASPORIC EXPERIENCES.

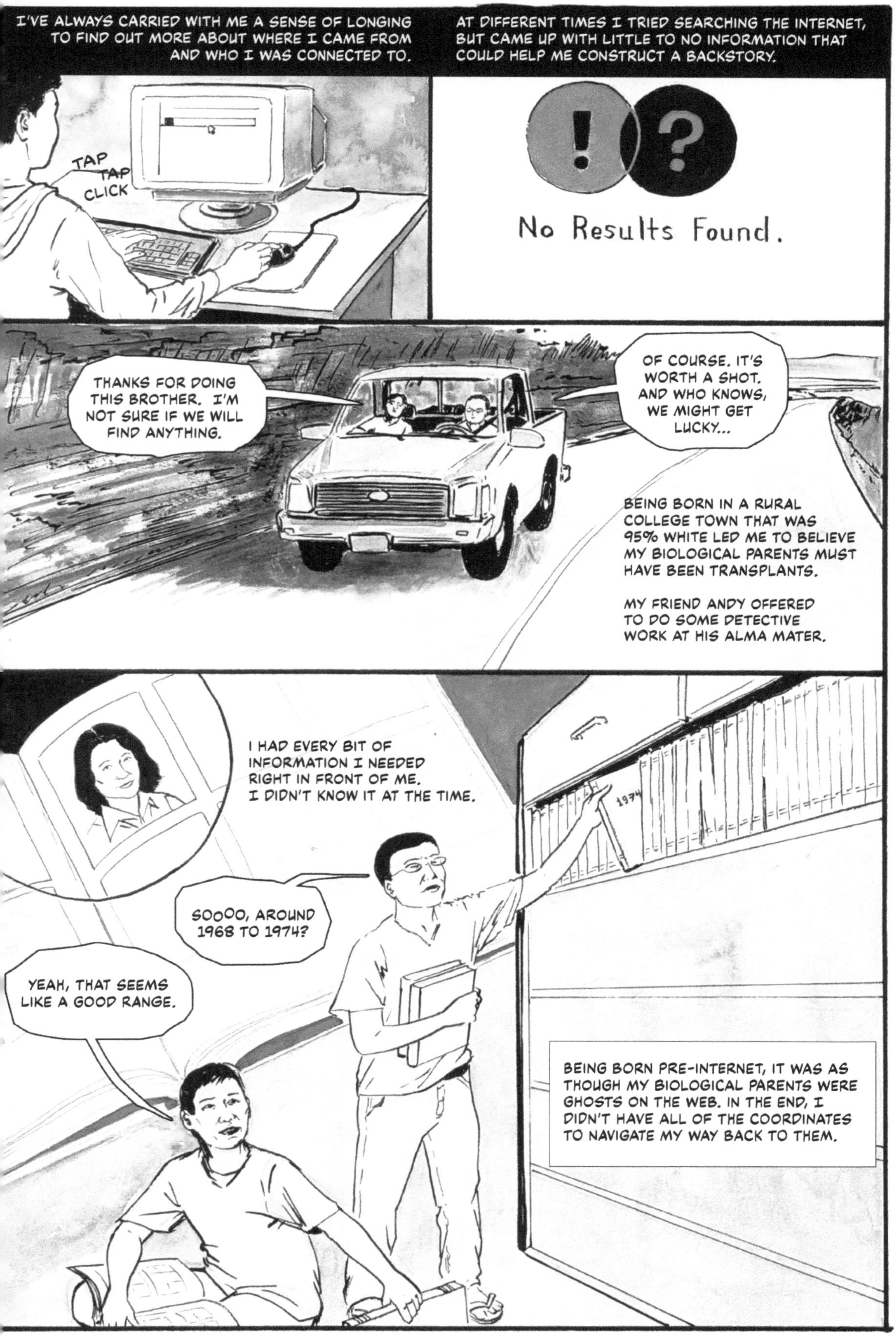
I'VE ALWAYS CARRIED WITH ME A SENSE OF LONGING TO FIND OUT MORE ABOUT WHERE I CAME FROM AND WHO I WAS CONNECTED TO.
AT DIFFERENT TIMES I TRIED SEARCHING THE INTERNET, BUT CAME UP WITH LITTLE TO NO INFORMATION THAT COULD HELP ME CONSTRUCT A BACKSTORY.
TAP TAP CLICK
!?
No Results Found.
THANKS FOR DOING THIS BROTHER. I'M NOT SURE IF WE WILL FIND ANYTHING.
OF COURSE. IT'S WORTH A SHOT. AND WHO KNOWS, WE MIGHT GET LUCKY...
BEING BORN IN A RURAL COLLEGE TOWN THAT WAS 95% WHITE LED ME TO BELIEVE MY BIOLOGICAL PARENTS MUST HAVE BEEN TRANSPLANTS.
MY FRIEND ANDY OFFERED TO DO SOME DETECTIVE WORK AT HIS ALMA MATER.
I HAD EVERY BIT OF INFORMATION I NEEDED RIGHT IN FRONT OF ME. I DIDN'T KNOW IT AT THE TIME.
1974
SOOOO, AROUND 1968 TO 1974?
YEAH, THAT SEEMS LIKE A GOOD RANGE.
BEING BORN PRE-INTERNET, IT WAS AS THOUGH MY BIOLOGICAL PARENTS WERE GHOSTS ON THE WEB. IN THE END, I DIDN'T HAVE ALL OF THE COORDINATES TO NAVIGATE MY WAY BACK TO THEM.

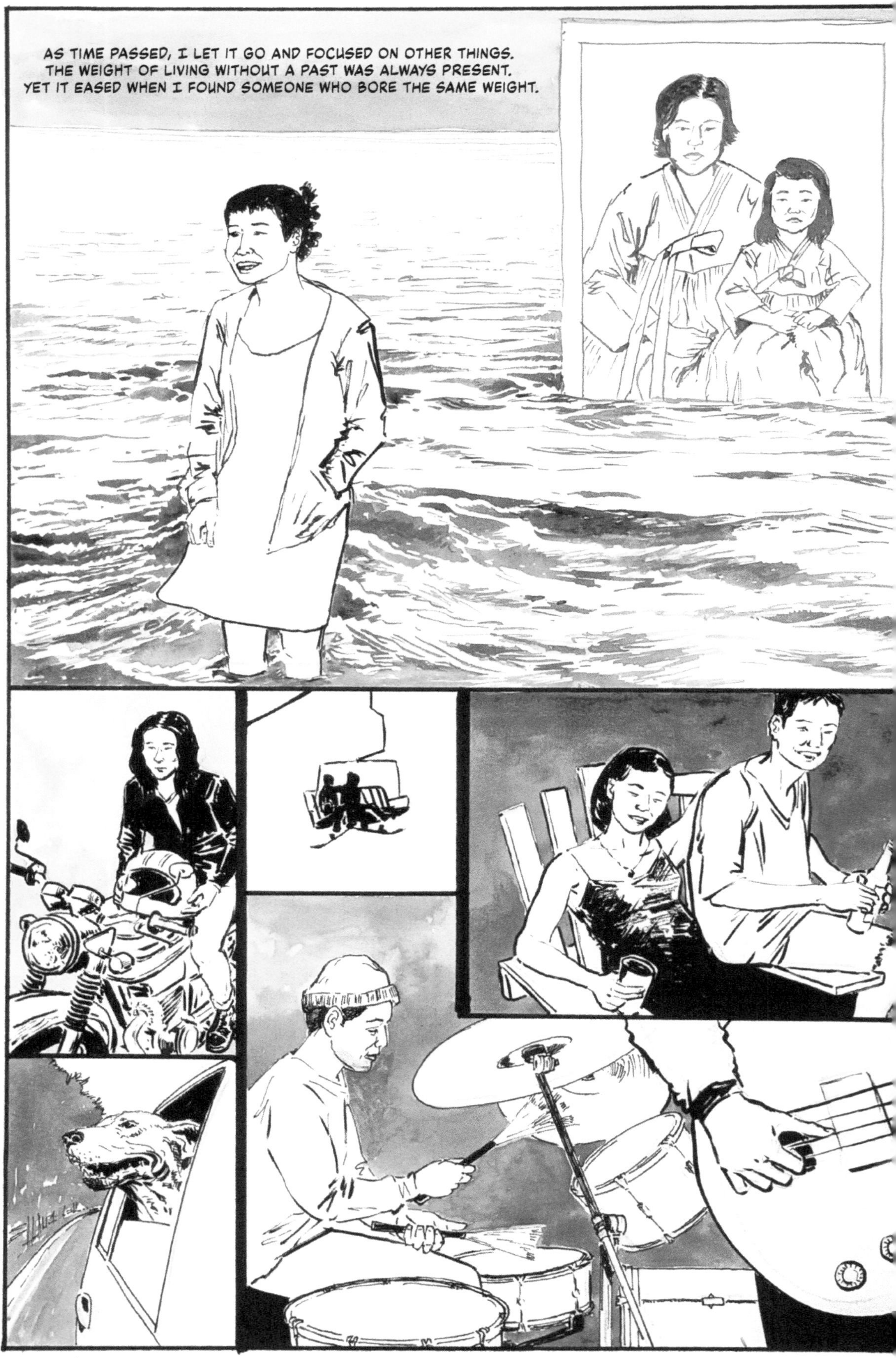
AS TIME PASSED, I LET IT GO AND FOCUSED ON OTHER THINGS. THE WEIGHT OF LIVING WITHOUT A PAST WAS ALWAYS PRESENT. YET IT EASED WHEN I FOUND SOMEONE WHO BORE THE SAME WEIGHT.

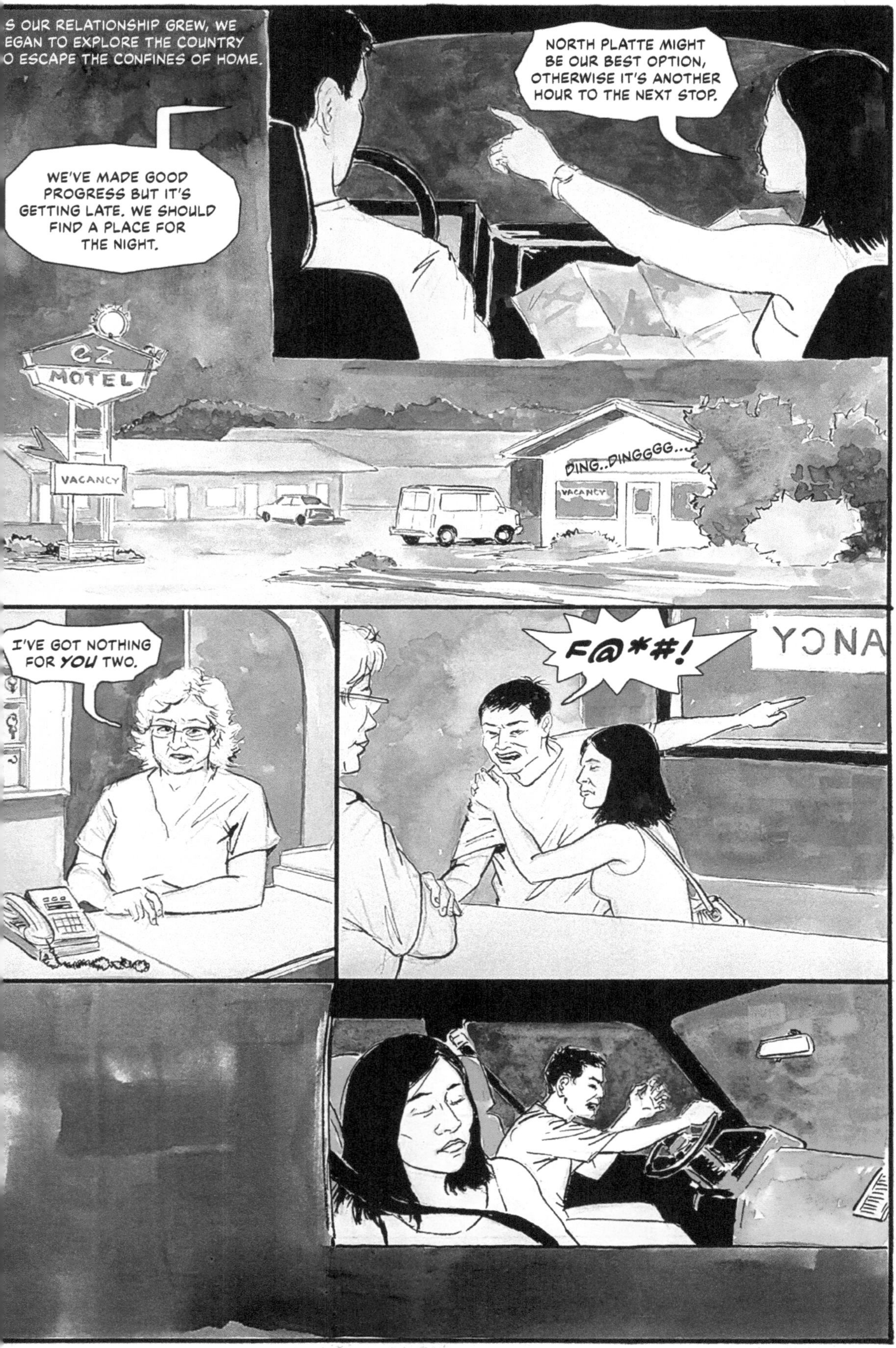
S OUR RELATIONSHIP GREW, WE EGAN TO EXPLORE THE COUNTRY O ESCAPE THE CONFINES OF HOME.
WE'VE MADE GOOD PROGRESS BUT IT'S GETTING LATE. WE SHOULD FIND A PLACE FOR THE NIGHT.
NORTH PLATTE MIGHT BE OUR BEST OPTION, OTHERWISE IT'S ANOTHER HOUR TO THE NEXT STOP.
EZ MOTEL
VACANCY
DING..DINGGGG...
VACANCY
I'VE GOT NOTHING FOR YOU TWO.
F@*#!
ANCY

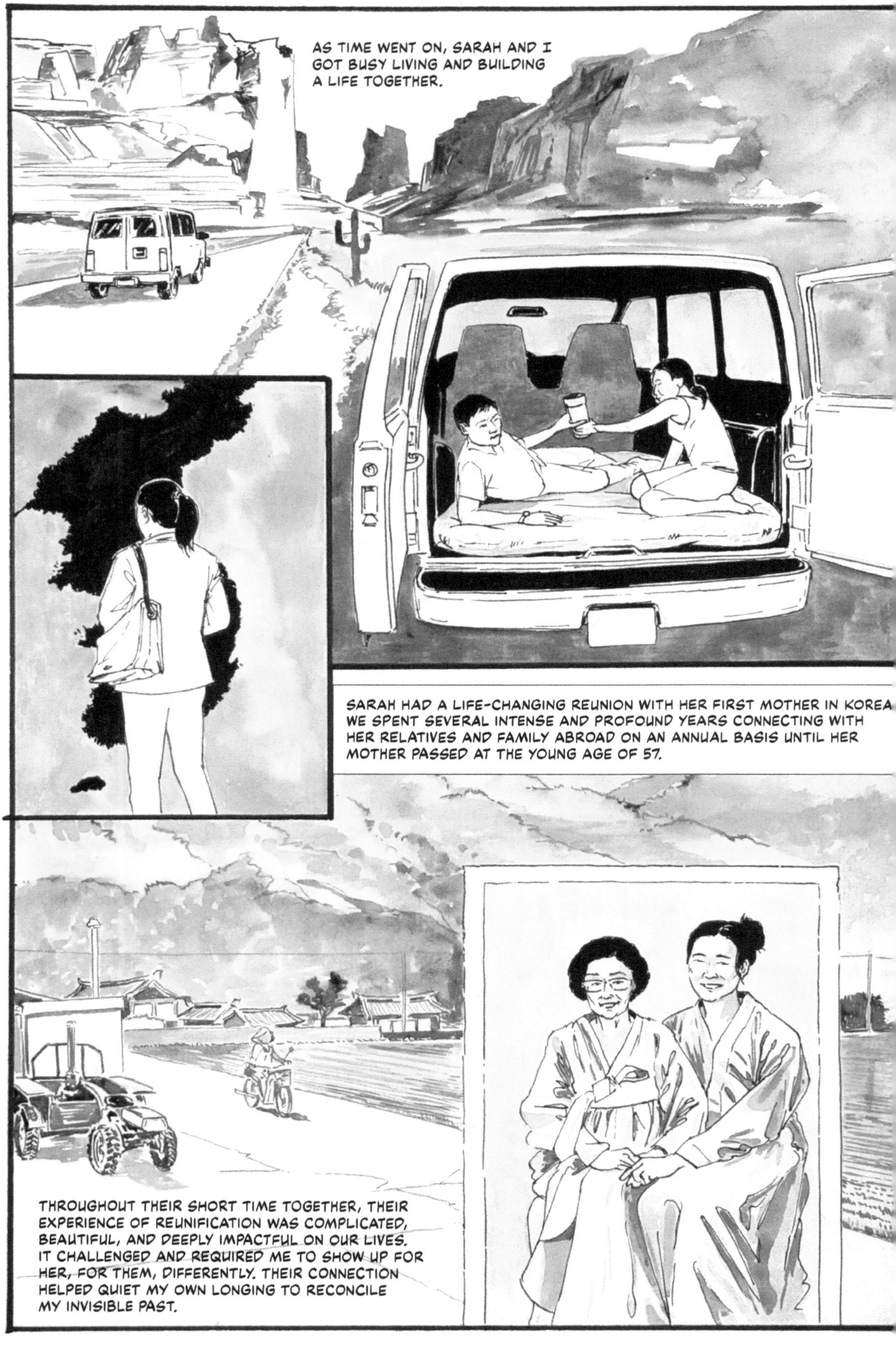
AS TIME WENT ON, SARAH AND I GOT BUSY LIVING AND BUILDING A LIFE TOGETHER.
SARAH HAD A LIFE-CHANGING REUNION WITH HER FIRST MOTHER IN KOREA. WE SPENT SEVERAL INTENSE AND PROFOUND YEARS CONNECTING WITH HER RELATIVES AND FAMILY ABROAD ON AN ANNUAL BASIS UNTIL HER MOTHER PASSED AT THE YOUNG AGE OF 57.
THROUGHOUT THEIR SHORT TIME TOGETHER, THEIR EXPERIENCE OF REUNIFICATION WAS COMPLICATED, BEAUTIFUL, AND DEEPLY IMPACTFUL ON OUR LIVES. IT CHALLENGED AND REQUIRED ME TO SHOW UP FOR HER, FOR THEM, DIFFERENTLY. THEIR CONNECTION HELPED QUIET MY OWN LONGING TO RECONCILE MY INVISIBLE PAST.

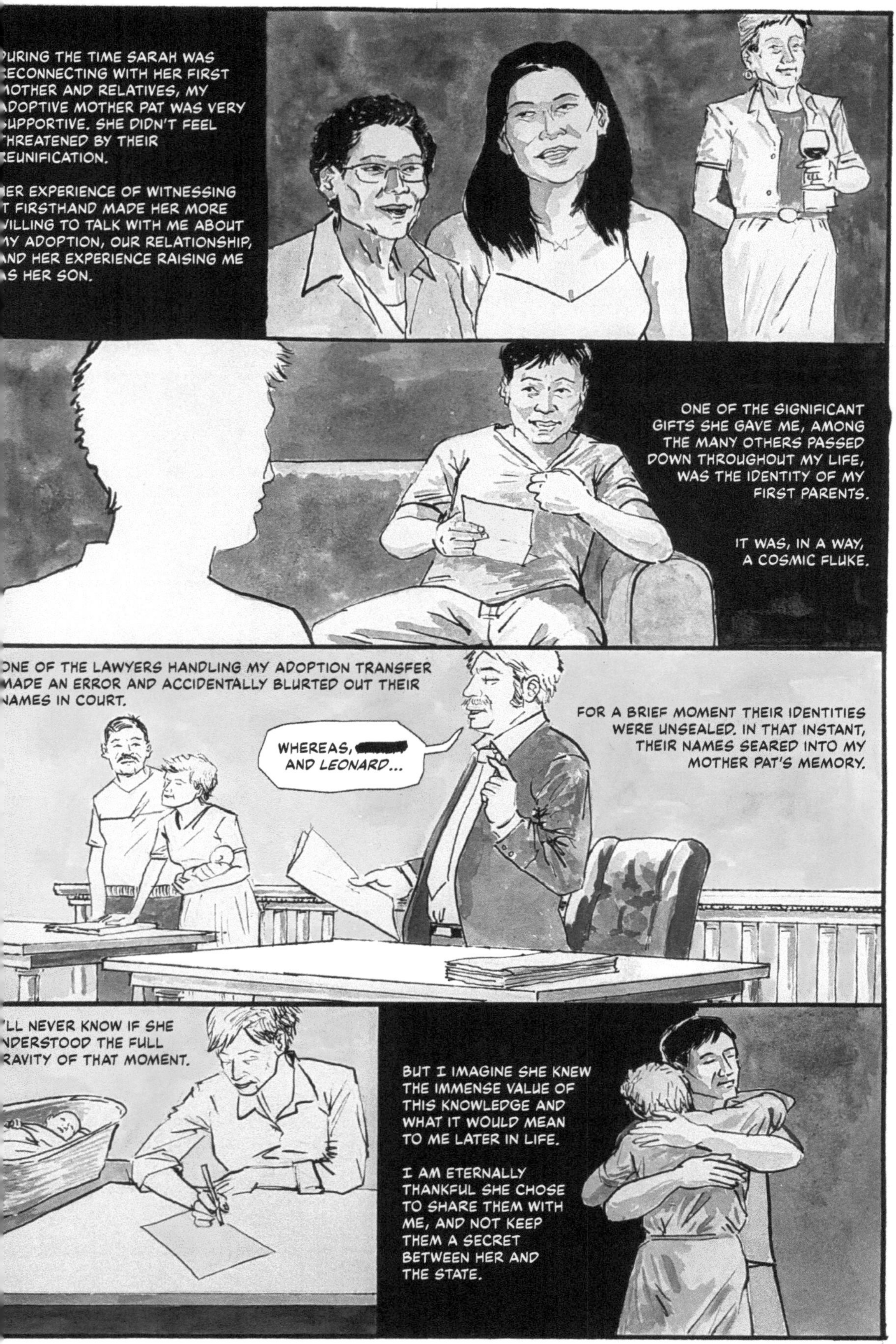
DURING THE TIME SARAH WAS RECONNECTING WITH HER FIRST MOTHER AND RELATIVES, MY ADOPTIVE MOTHER PAT WAS VERY SUPPORTIVE. SHE DIDN'T FEEL THREATENED BY THEIR REUNIFICATION.
HER EXPERIENCE OF WITNESSING IT FIRSTHAND MADE HER MORE WILLING TO TALK WITH ME ABOUT MY ADOPTION, OUR RELATIONSHIP, AND HER EXPERIENCE RAISING ME AS HER SON.
ONE OF THE SIGNIFICANT GIFTS SHE GAVE ME, AMONG THE MANY OTHERS PASSED DOWN THROUGHOUT MY LIFE, WAS THE IDENTITY OF MY FIRST PARENTS.
IT WAS, IN A WAY, A COSMIC FLUKE.
ONE OF THE LAWYERS HANDLING MY ADOPTION TRANSFER MADE AN ERROR AND ACCIDENTALLY BLURTED OUT THEIR NAMES IN COURT.
WHEREAS, [redacted] AND *LEONARD*...
FOR A BRIEF MOMENT THEIR IDENTITIES WERE UNSEALED. IN THAT INSTANT, THEIR NAMES SEARED INTO MY MOTHER PAT'S MEMORY.
I'LL NEVER KNOW IF SHE UNDERSTOOD THE FULL GRAVITY OF THAT MOMENT.
BUT I IMAGINE SHE KNEW THE IMMENSE VALUE OF THIS KNOWLEDGE AND WHAT IT WOULD MEAN TO ME LATER IN LIFE.
I AM ETERNALLY THANKFUL SHE CHOSE TO SHARE THEM WITH ME, AND NOT KEEP THEM A SECRET BETWEEN HER AND THE STATE.

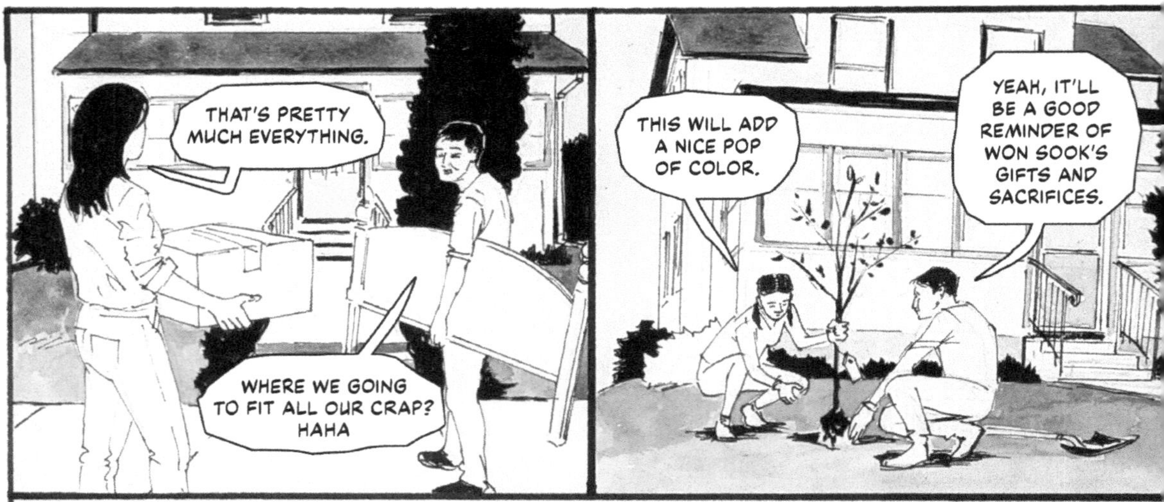
THAT'S PRETTY MUCH EVERYTHING.
WHERE WE GOING TO FIT ALL OUR CRAP? HAHA
THIS WILL ADD A NICE POP OF COLOR.
YEAH, IT'LL BE A GOOD REMINDER OF WON SOOK'S GIFTS AND SACRIFICES.

AFTER THE PASSING OF SARAH'S BIOLOGICAL MOTHER WON SOOK, OUR 30'S CONTINUED TO BE A TIME OF LARGE-SCALE CHANGE.

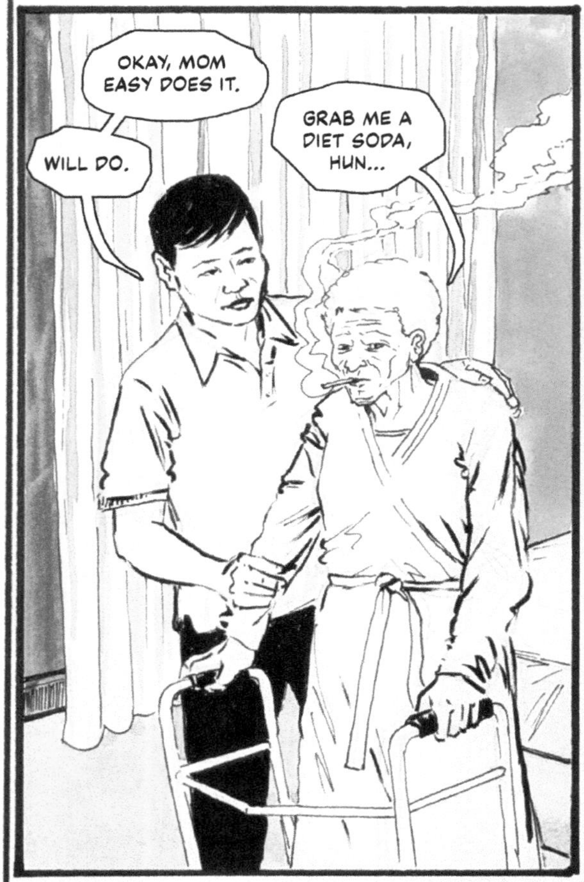
OKAY, MOM EASY DOES IT.
GRAB ME A DIET SODA, HUN...
WILL DO.

WE FINALLY GOT MARRIED AND WERE ABLE TO PURCHASE A SMALL HOUSE WITH THE HELP OF WON SOOK.

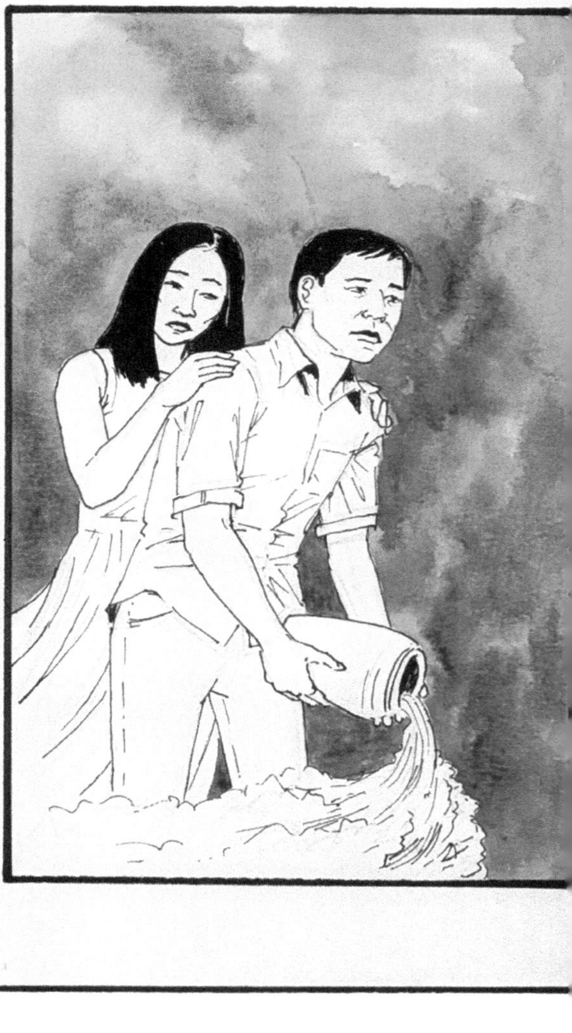

WE ENTERED THE AGE WHERE OUR FAMILY ROLES SHIFTED, AND WE BEGAN CARING FOR MY AGING MOTHER. EVENTUALLY SHE TOO TRANSITIONED. IN THE ABSENCE OF HER STEADY PRESENCE, OUR FAMILY STRUCTURE BEGAN TO FEEL MORE FRACTURED AS TIME WENT ON.

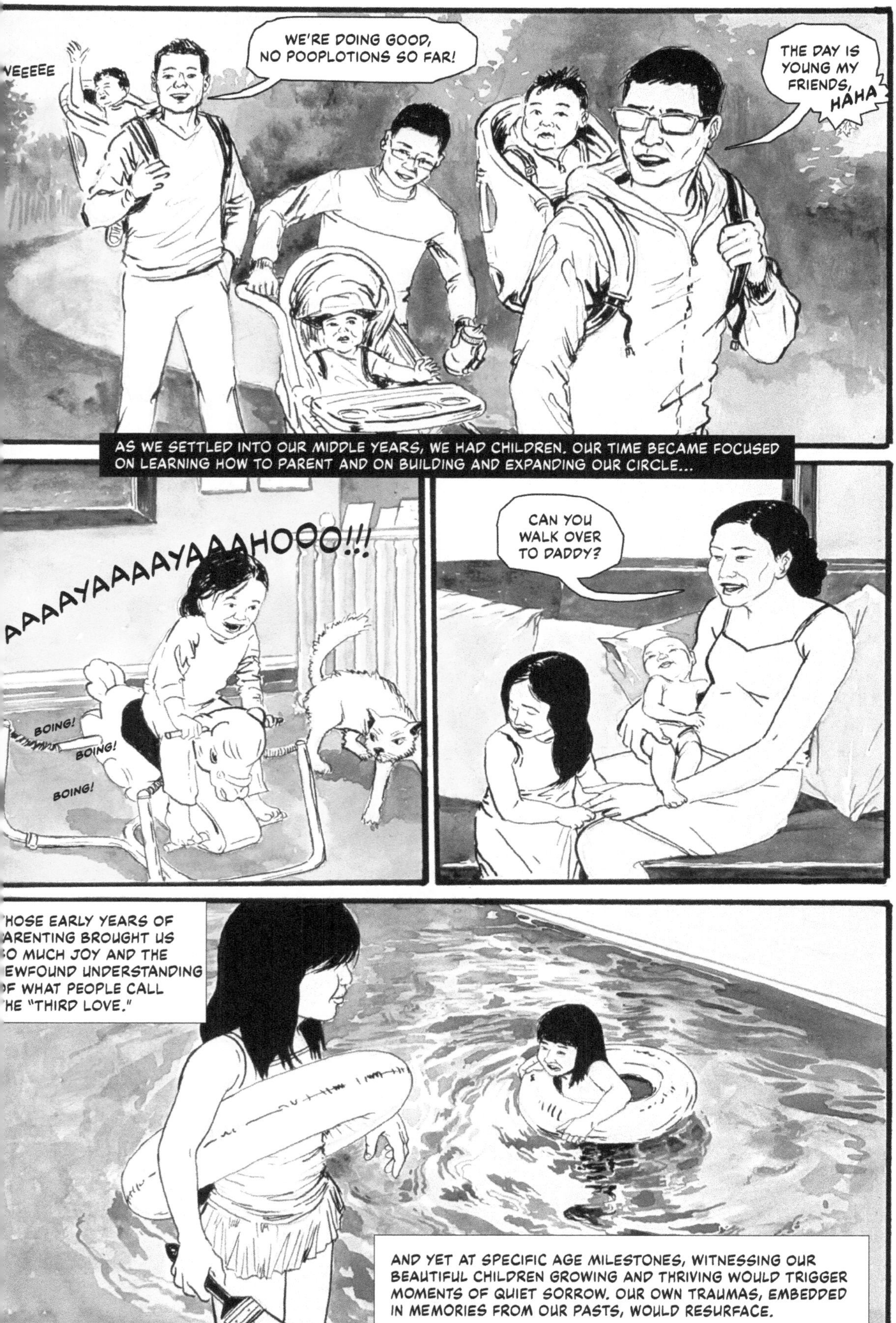

WEEEEE
WE'RE DOING GOOD, NO POOPLOTIONS SO FAR!
THE DAY IS YOUNG MY FRIENDS, HAHA
AS WE SETTLED INTO OUR MIDDLE YEARS, WE HAD CHILDREN. OUR TIME BECAME FOCUSED ON LEARNING HOW TO PARENT AND ON BUILDING AND EXPANDING OUR CIRCLE...
AAAAYAAAAYAAAHOOO!!!
BOING!
BOING!
BOING!
CAN YOU WALK OVER TO DADDY?
THOSE EARLY YEARS OF PARENTING BROUGHT US SO MUCH JOY AND THE NEWFOUND UNDERSTANDING OF WHAT PEOPLE CALL THE "THIRD LOVE."
AND YET AT SPECIFIC AGE MILESTONES, WITNESSING OUR BEAUTIFUL CHILDREN GROWING AND THRIVING WOULD TRIGGER MOMENTS OF QUIET SORROW. OUR OWN TRAUMAS, EMBEDDED IN MEMORIES FROM OUR PASTS, WOULD RESURFACE.

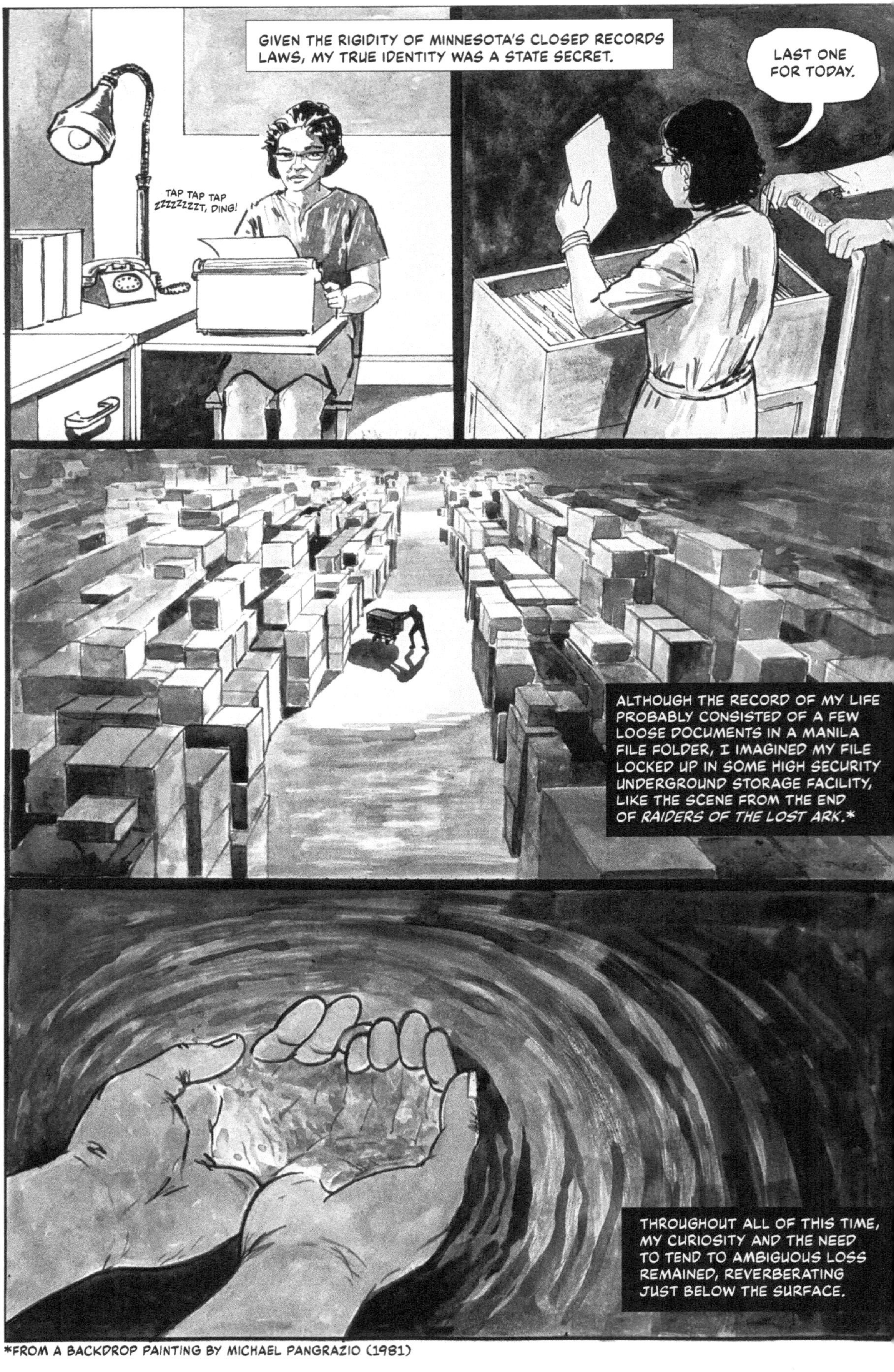
GIVEN THE RIGIDITY OF MINNESOTA'S CLOSED RECORDS LAWS, MY TRUE IDENTITY WAS A STATE SECRET.
TAP TAP TAP ZZZZZZZZT, DING!
LAST ONE FOR TODAY.
ALTHOUGH THE RECORD OF MY LIFE PROBABLY CONSISTED OF A FEW LOOSE DOCUMENTS IN A MANILA FILE FOLDER, I IMAGINED MY FILE LOCKED UP IN SOME HIGH SECURITY UNDERGROUND STORAGE FACILITY, LIKE THE SCENE FROM THE END OF *RAIDERS OF THE LOST ARK.**
THROUGHOUT ALL OF THIS TIME, MY CURIOSITY AND THE NEED TO TEND TO AMBIGUOUS LOSS REMAINED, REVERBERATING JUST BELOW THE SURFACE.

*FROM A BACKDROP PAINTING BY MICHAEL PANGRAZIO (1981)

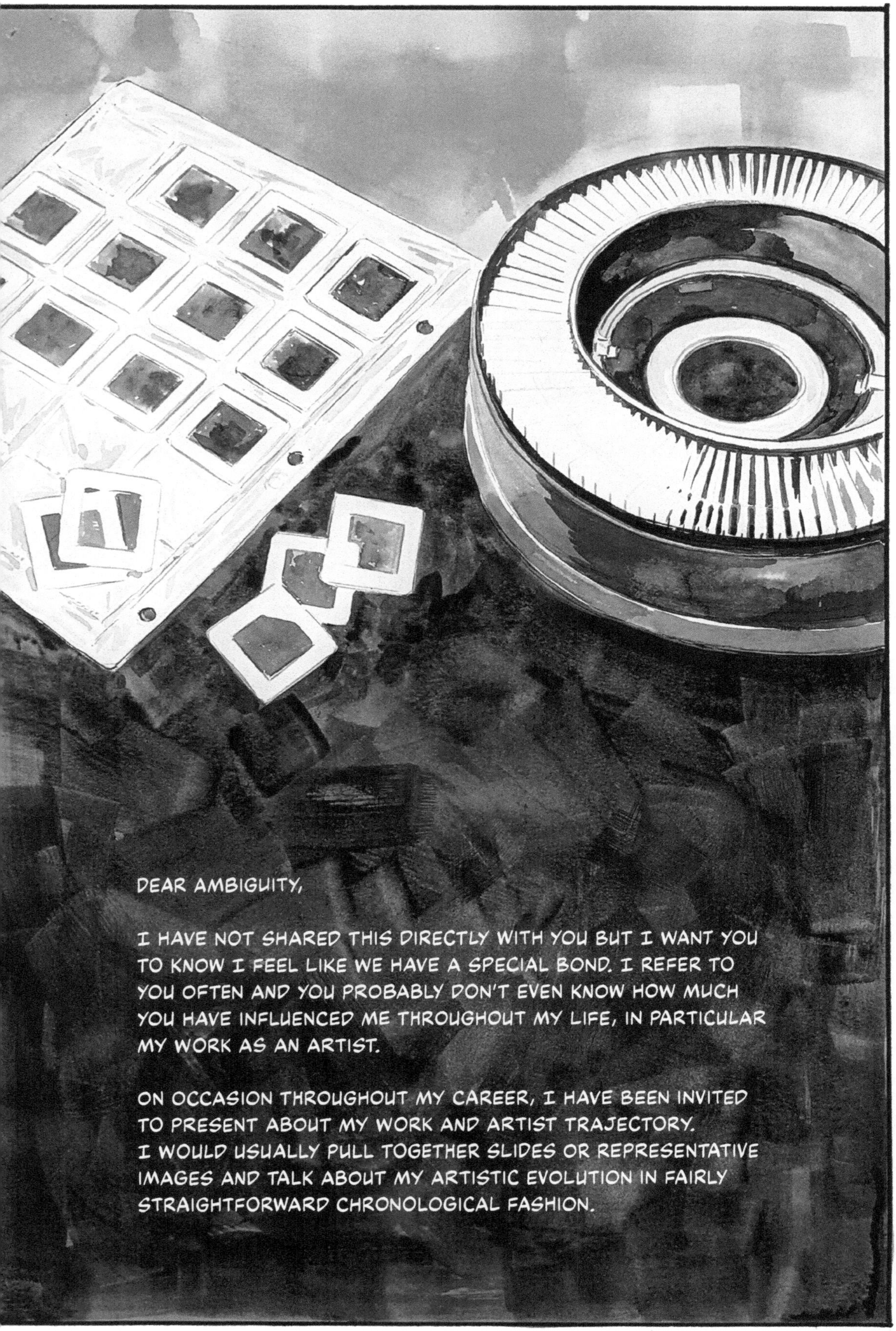
DEAR AMBIGUITY,
I HAVE NOT SHARED THIS DIRECTLY WITH YOU BUT I WANT YOU TO KNOW I FEEL LIKE WE HAVE A SPECIAL BOND. I REFER TO YOU OFTEN AND YOU PROBABLY DON'T EVEN KNOW HOW MUCH YOU HAVE INFLUENCED ME THROUGHOUT MY LIFE, IN PARTICULAR MY WORK AS AN ARTIST.
ON OCCASION THROUGHOUT MY CAREER, I HAVE BEEN INVITED TO PRESENT ABOUT MY WORK AND ARTIST TRAJECTORY. I WOULD USUALLY PULL TOGETHER SLIDES OR REPRESENTATIVE IMAGES AND TALK ABOUT MY ARTISTIC EVOLUTION IN FAIRLY STRAIGHTFORWARD CHRONOLOGICAL FASHION.

"I STUDIED THESE THINGS... LEARNED THESE SKILLS, EXPLORED THESE MATERIALS... WAS CURIOUS ABOUT THESE SOCIAL OR POLITICAL THEMES, WHICH LED TO THESE NEW MATERIAL CURIOSITIES OR ADAPTATIONS, BLAH BLAH BLAH," AND SO ON.

IT WAS YAAAAWN... PRETTY STANDARD STUFF.

WHEN IN MY 30'S I WAS INTRODUCED TO THE WORK OF DR. PAULINE BOSS AND HER RESEARCH AND CLINICAL WORK AROUND "AMBIGUOUS LOSS," I HAD A SMALL EPIPHANY. THERE YOU WERE! YOU HAD A SHAPE, A FORM TO GO ALONG WITH YOUR PERSISTENT PRESENCE.

MORE SHOCKING WAS THE REALIZATION THAT HER FRAMEWORK, "SIX GUIDELINES FOR BUILDING RESILIENCY TO LIVE WELL DESPITE AMBIGUOUS LOSS," TRACKED ALONG THE TRAJECTORY OF MY ARTISTIC PRODUCTION AND EVOLUTION IN THE MOST UNCANNY WAY.

I HAD UNKNOWINGLY BEEN ON A PATH OF EMOTIONAL RECKONING MOST OF MY ADULT LIFE, AND I HAD NOT RECOGNIZED HOW VISIBLE IT WAS THROUGHOUT MY ARTISTIC DEVELOPMENT.

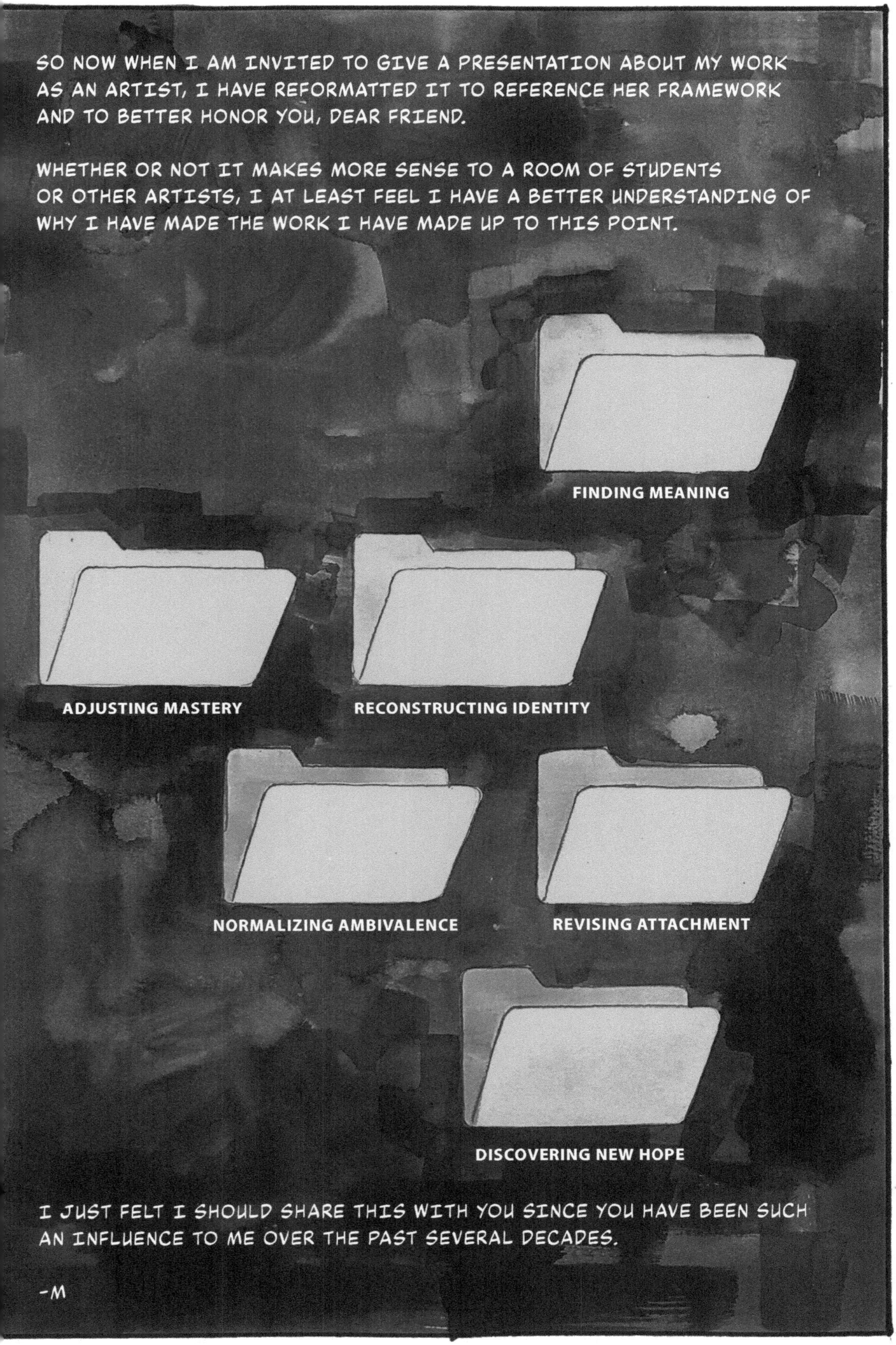
SO NOW WHEN I AM INVITED TO GIVE A PRESENTATION ABOUT MY WORK AS AN ARTIST, I HAVE REFORMATTED IT TO REFERENCE HER FRAMEWORK AND TO BETTER HONOR YOU, DEAR FRIEND.
WHETHER OR NOT IT MAKES MORE SENSE TO A ROOM OF STUDENTS OR OTHER ARTISTS, I AT LEAST FEEL I HAVE A BETTER UNDERSTANDING OF WHY I HAVE MADE THE WORK I HAVE MADE UP TO THIS POINT.
FINDING MEANING
ADJUSTING MASTERY
RECONSTRUCTING IDENTITY
NORMALIZING AMBIVALENCE
REVISING ATTACHMENT
DISCOVERING NEW HOPE
I JUST FELT I SHOULD SHARE THIS WITH YOU SINCE YOU HAVE BEEN SUCH AN INFLUENCE TO ME OVER THE PAST SEVERAL DECADES.
-M

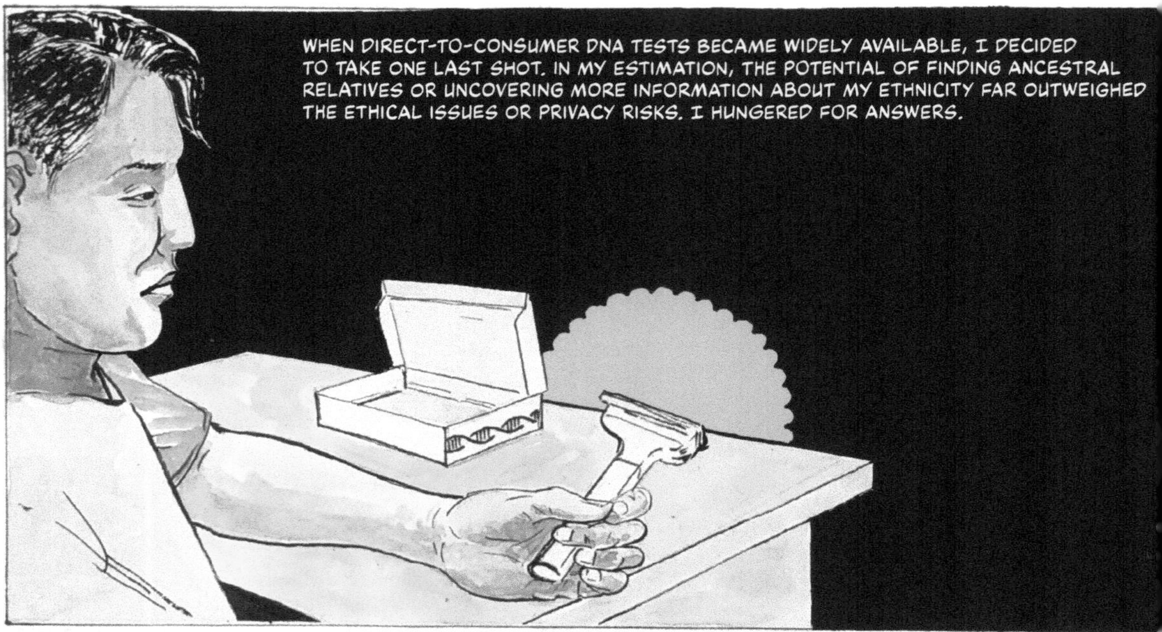
WHEN DIRECT-TO-CONSUMER DNA TESTS BECAME WIDELY AVAILABLE, I DECIDED TO TAKE ONE LAST SHOT. IN MY ESTIMATION, THE POTENTIAL OF FINDING ANCESTRAL RELATIVES OR UNCOVERING MORE INFORMATION ABOUT MY ETHNICITY FAR OUTWEIGHED THE ETHICAL ISSUES OR PRIVACY RISKS. I HUNGERED FOR ANSWERS.

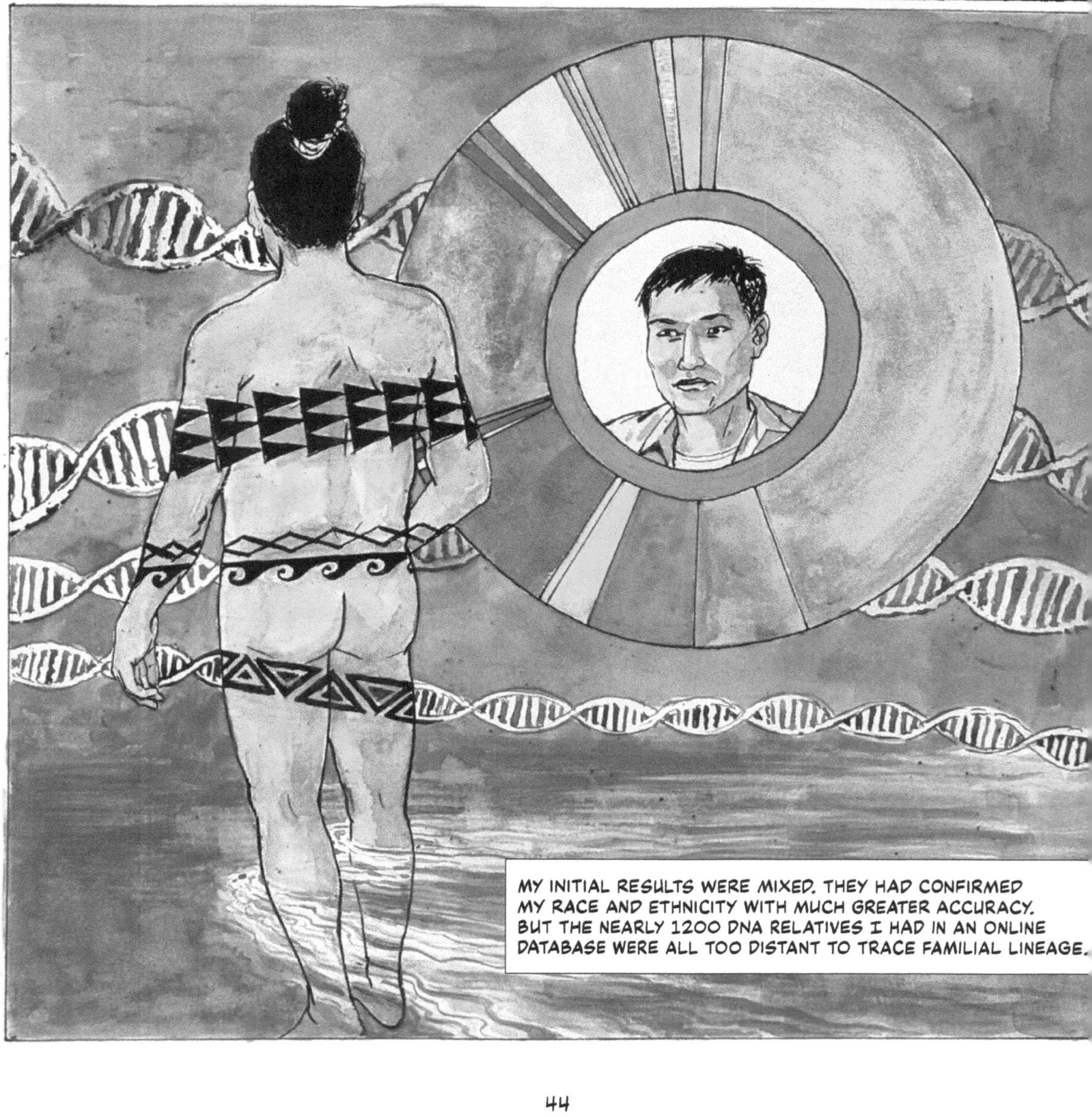
MY INITIAL RESULTS WERE MIXED. THEY HAD CONFIRMED MY RACE AND ETHNICITY WITH MUCH GREATER ACCURACY. BUT THE NEARLY 1200 DNA RELATIVES I HAD IN AN ONLINE DATABASE WERE ALL TOO DISTANT TO TRACE FAMILIAL LINEAGE.

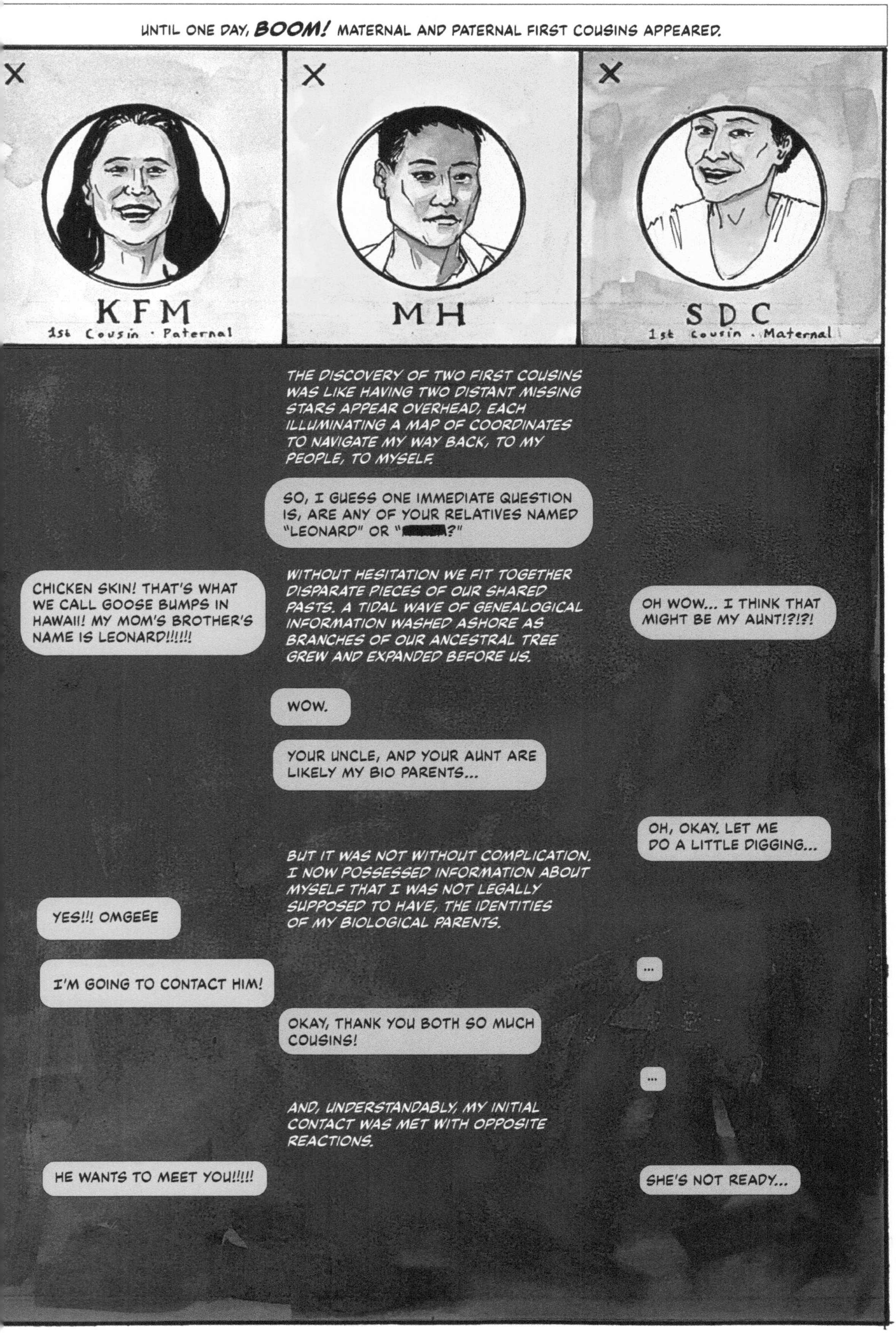
UNTIL ONE DAY, BOOM! MATERNAL AND PATERNAL FIRST COUSINS APPEARED.
X
KFM
1st Cousin · Paternal
X
MH
X
SDC
1st Cousin · Maternal
THE DISCOVERY OF TWO FIRST COUSINS WAS LIKE HAVING TWO DISTANT MISSING STARS APPEAR OVERHEAD, EACH ILLUMINATING A MAP OF COORDINATES TO NAVIGATE MY WAY BACK, TO MY PEOPLE, TO MYSELF.
SO, I GUESS ONE IMMEDIATE QUESTION IS, ARE ANY OF YOUR RELATIVES NAMED "LEONARD" OR "[redacted]?"
CHICKEN SKIN! THAT'S WHAT WE CALL GOOSE BUMPS IN HAWAII! MY MOM'S BROTHER'S NAME IS LEONARD!!!!!!
WITHOUT HESITATION WE FIT TOGETHER DISPARATE PIECES OF OUR SHARED PASTS. A TIDAL WAVE OF GENEALOGICAL INFORMATION WASHED ASHORE AS BRANCHES OF OUR ANCESTRAL TREE GREW AND EXPANDED BEFORE US.
OH WOW... I THINK THAT MIGHT BE MY AUNT!?!?!
WOW.
YOUR UNCLE, AND YOUR AUNT ARE LIKELY MY BIO PARENTS...
OH, OKAY. LET ME DO A LITTLE DIGGING...
BUT IT WAS NOT WITHOUT COMPLICATION. I NOW POSSESSED INFORMATION ABOUT MYSELF THAT I WAS NOT LEGALLY SUPPOSED TO HAVE, THE IDENTITIES OF MY BIOLOGICAL PARENTS.
YES!!! OMGEEE
I'M GOING TO CONTACT HIM!
...
OKAY, THANK YOU BOTH SO MUCH COUSINS!
...
AND, UNDERSTANDABLY, MY INITIAL CONTACT WAS MET WITH OPPOSITE REACTIONS.
HE WANTS TO MEET YOU!!!!!
SHE'S NOT READY...

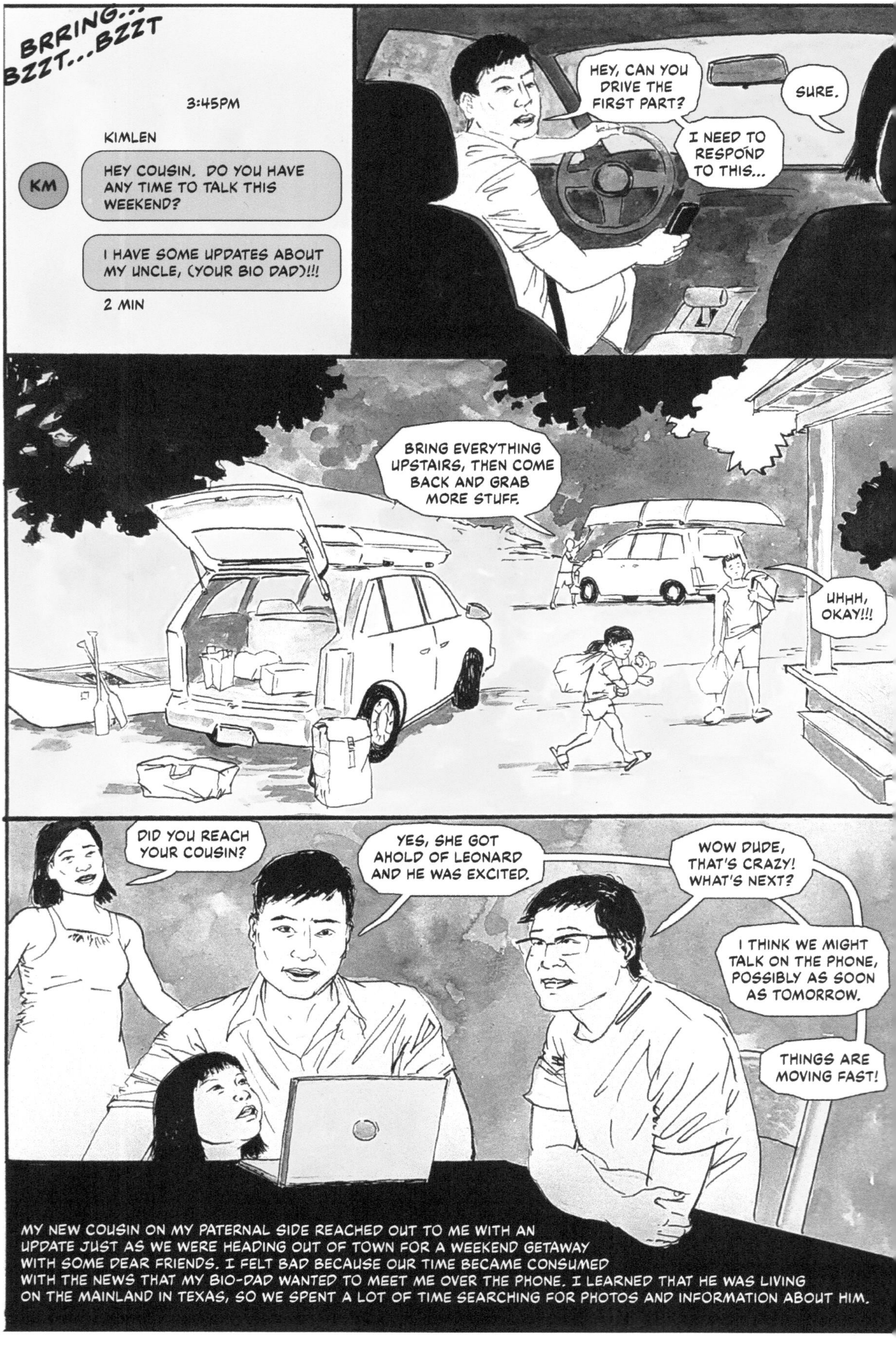
BRRING... BZZT...BZZT
3:45PM
KIMLEN
KM
HEY COUSIN. DO YOU HAVE ANY TIME TO TALK THIS WEEKEND?
I HAVE SOME UPDATES ABOUT MY UNCLE, (YOUR BIO DAD)!!!
2 MIN
HEY, CAN YOU DRIVE THE FIRST PART?
SURE.
I NEED TO RESPOND TO THIS...
BRING EVERYTHING UPSTAIRS, THEN COME BACK AND GRAB MORE STUFF.
UHHH, OKAY!!!
DID YOU REACH YOUR COUSIN?
YES, SHE GOT AHOLD OF LEONARD AND HE WAS EXCITED.
WOW DUDE, THAT'S CRAZY! WHAT'S NEXT?
I THINK WE MIGHT TALK ON THE PHONE, POSSIBLY AS SOON AS TOMORROW.
THINGS ARE MOVING FAST!
MY NEW COUSIN ON MY PATERNAL SIDE REACHED OUT TO ME WITH AN UPDATE JUST AS WE WERE HEADING OUT OF TOWN FOR A WEEKEND GETAWAY WITH SOME DEAR FRIENDS. I FELT BAD BECAUSE OUR TIME BECAME CONSUMED WITH THE NEWS THAT MY BIO-DAD WANTED TO MEET ME OVER THE PHONE. I LEARNED THAT HE WAS LIVING ON THE MAINLAND IN TEXAS, SO WE SPENT A LOT OF TIME SEARCHING FOR PHOTOS AND INFORMATION ABOUT HIM.

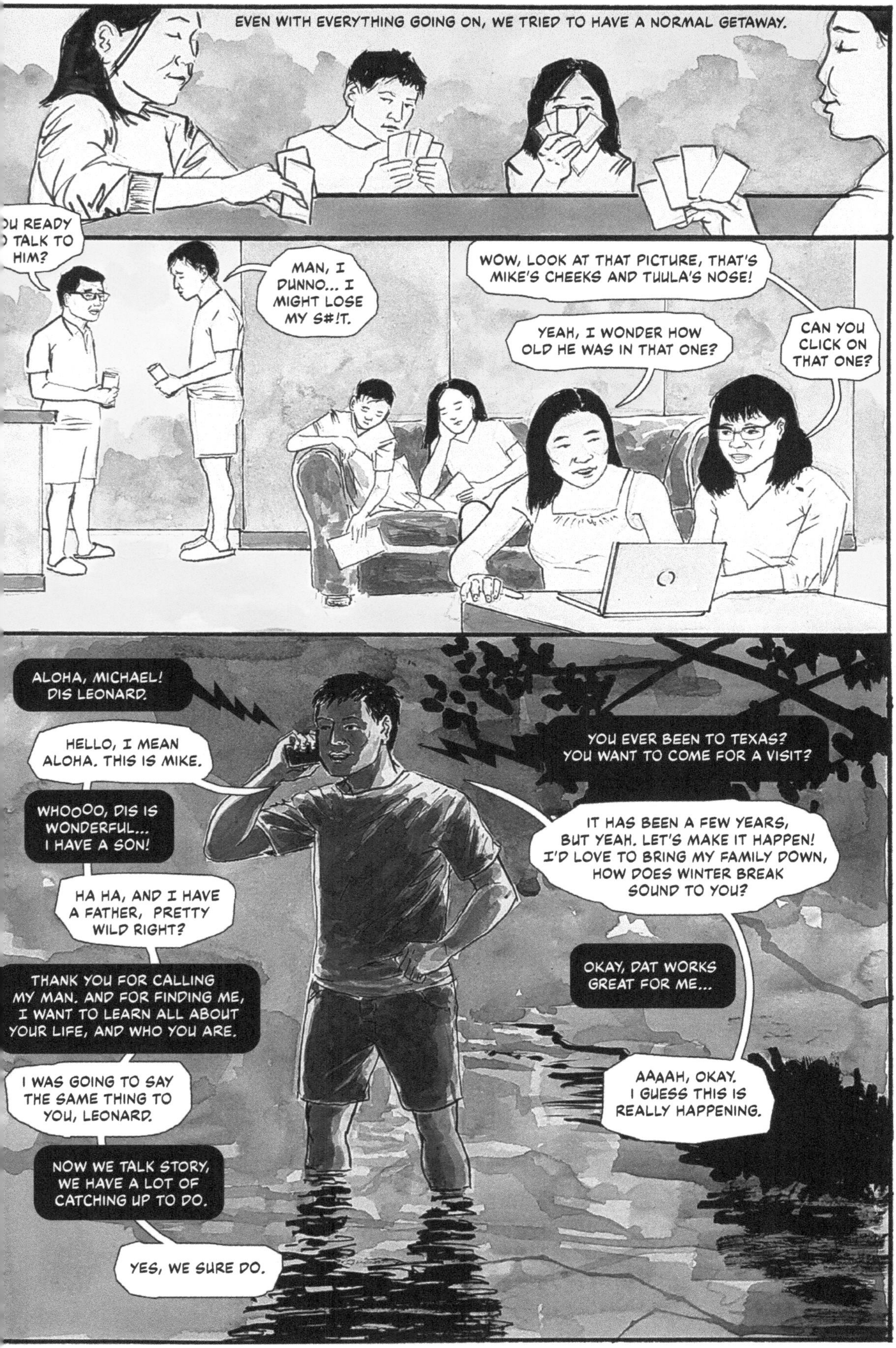
EVEN WITH EVERYTHING GOING ON, WE TRIED TO HAVE A NORMAL GETAWAY.
OU READY TO TALK TO HIM?
MAN, I DUNNO... I MIGHT LOSE MY S#!T.
WOW, LOOK AT THAT PICTURE, THAT'S MIKE'S CHEEKS AND TUULA'S NOSE!
YEAH, I WONDER HOW OLD HE WAS IN THAT ONE?
CAN YOU CLICK ON THAT ONE?
ALOHA, MICHAEL! DIS LEONARD.
HELLO, I MEAN ALOHA. THIS IS MIKE.
WHOOOO, DIS IS WONDERFUL... I HAVE A SON!
HA HA, AND I HAVE A FATHER, PRETTY WILD RIGHT?
THANK YOU FOR CALLING MY MAN. AND FOR FINDING ME, I WANT TO LEARN ALL ABOUT YOUR LIFE, AND WHO YOU ARE.
I WAS GOING TO SAY THE SAME THING TO YOU, LEONARD.
NOW WE TALK STORY, WE HAVE A LOT OF CATCHING UP TO DO.
YES, WE SURE DO.
YOU EVER BEEN TO TEXAS? YOU WANT TO COME FOR A VISIT?
IT HAS BEEN A FEW YEARS, BUT YEAH. LET'S MAKE IT HAPPEN! I'D LOVE TO BRING MY FAMILY DOWN, HOW DOES WINTER BREAK SOUND TO YOU?
OKAY, DAT WORKS GREAT FOR ME...
AAAAH, OKAY. I GUESS THIS IS REALLY HAPPENING.

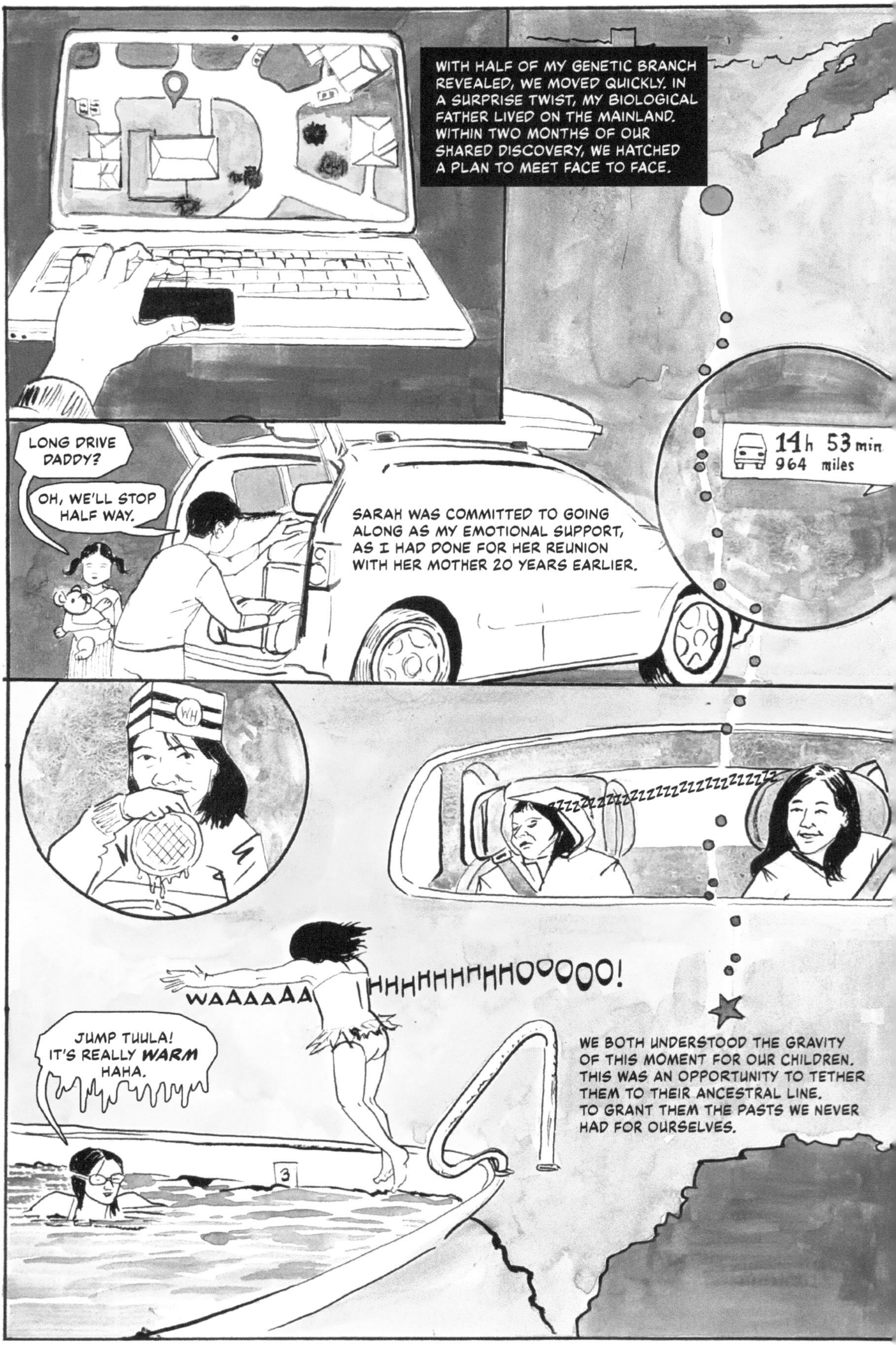

WITH HALF OF MY GENETIC BRANCH REVEALED, WE MOVED QUICKLY. IN A SURPRISE TWIST, MY BIOLOGICAL FATHER LIVED ON THE MAINLAND. WITHIN TWO MONTHS OF OUR SHARED DISCOVERY, WE HATCHED A PLAN TO MEET FACE TO FACE.
LONG DRIVE DADDY?
OH, WE'LL STOP HALF WAY.
SARAH WAS COMMITTED TO GOING ALONG AS MY EMOTIONAL SUPPORT, AS I HAD DONE FOR HER REUNION WITH HER MOTHER 20 YEARS EARLIER.
14h 53min
964 miles
WH
ZZZZZZZZZZZZZZZZZZZZZZZZZZZZZZ
WAAAAAAHHHHHHHHHOOOOOO!
JUMP TUULA! IT'S REALLY **WARM** HAHA.
3
WE BOTH UNDERSTOOD THE GRAVITY OF THIS MOMENT FOR OUR CHILDREN. THIS WAS AN OPPORTUNITY TO TETHER THEM TO THEIR ANCESTRAL LINE. TO GRANT THEM THE PASTS WE NEVER HAD FOR OURSELVES.

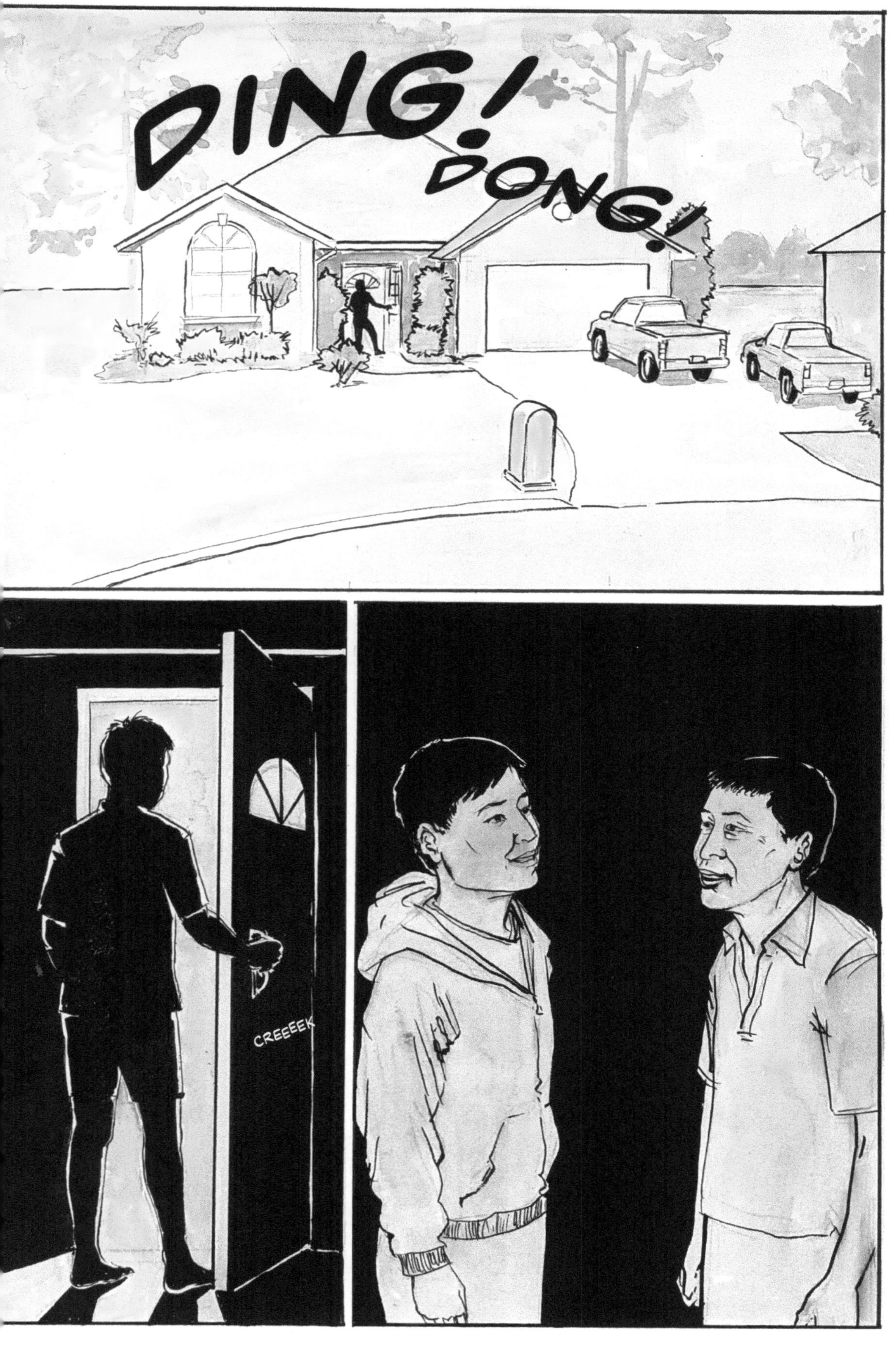
DING!
DONG!
CREEEEK

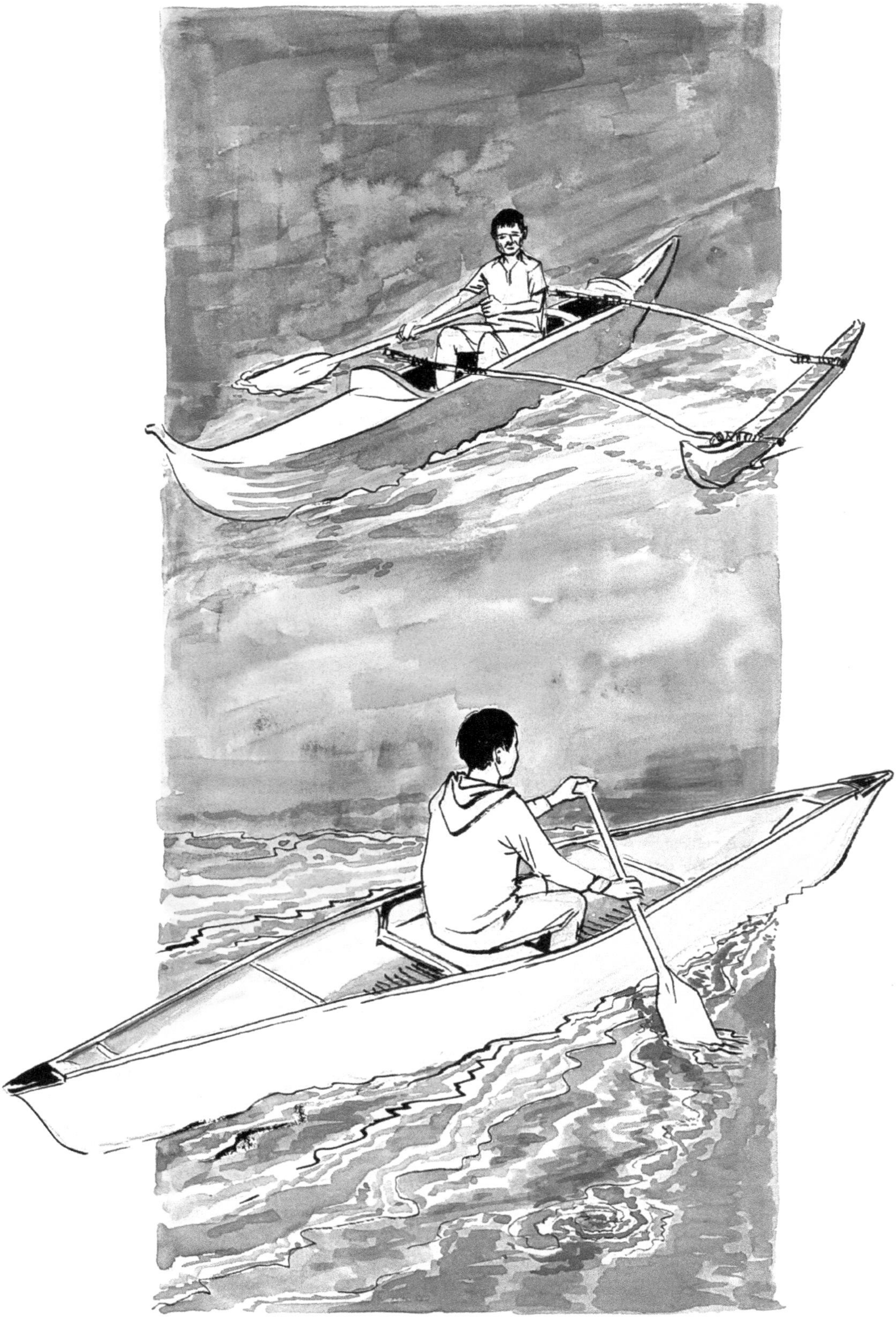

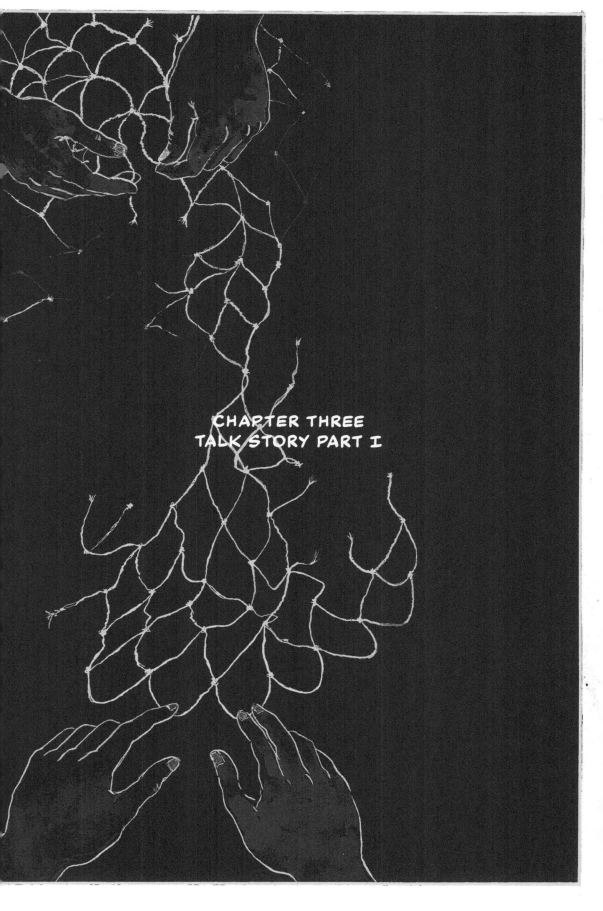

CHAPTER THREE
TALK STORY PART I

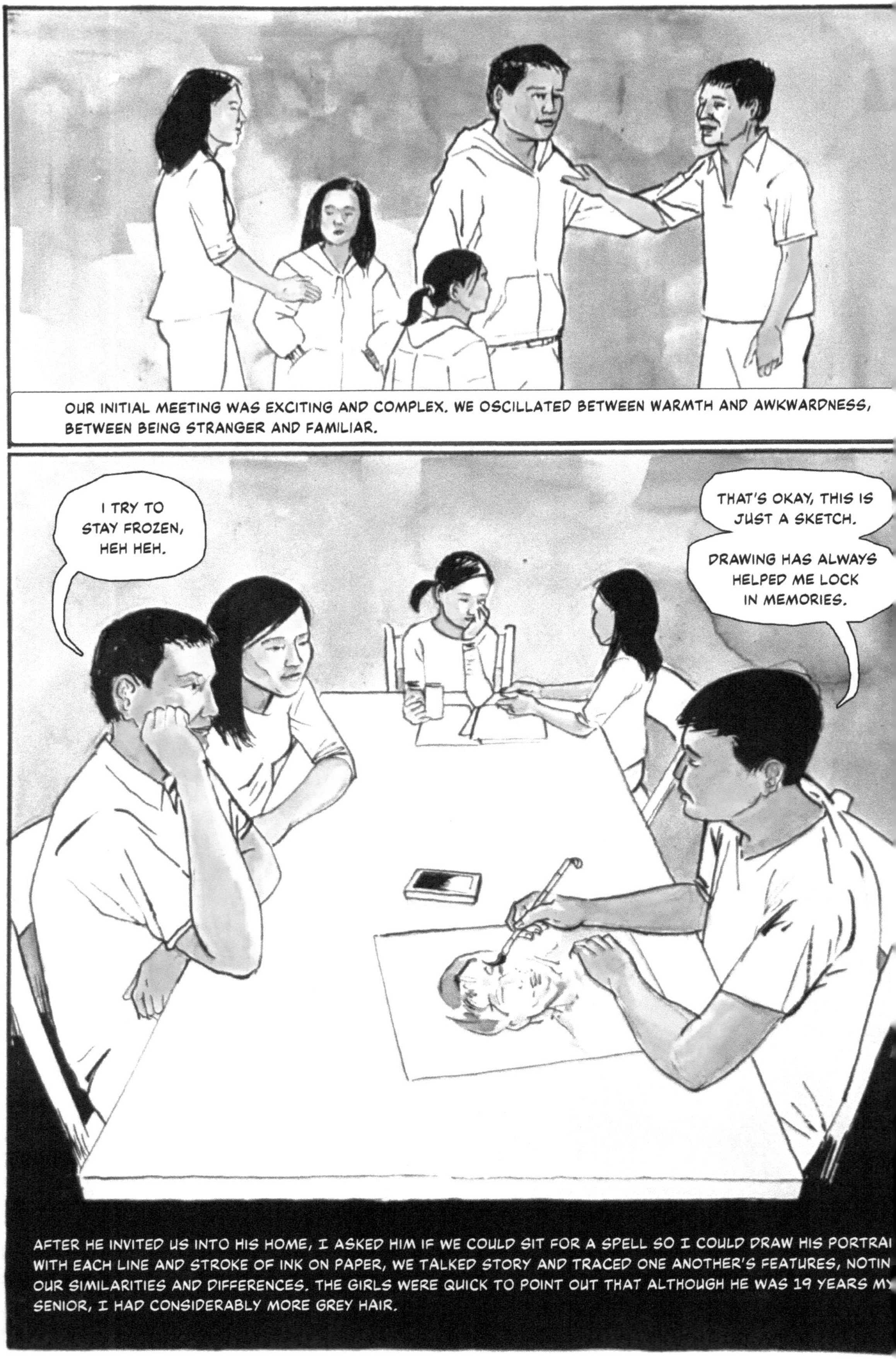

OUR INITIAL MEETING WAS EXCITING AND COMPLEX. WE OSCILLATED BETWEEN WARMTH AND AWKWARDNESS, BETWEEN BEING STRANGER AND FAMILIAR.
I TRY TO STAY FROZEN, HEH HEH.
THAT'S OKAY, THIS IS JUST A SKETCH.
DRAWING HAS ALWAYS HELPED ME LOCK IN MEMORIES.
AFTER HE INVITED US INTO HIS HOME, I ASKED HIM IF WE COULD SIT FOR A SPELL SO I COULD DRAW HIS PORTRAI WITH EACH LINE AND STROKE OF INK ON PAPER, WE TALKED STORY AND TRACED ONE ANOTHER'S FEATURES, NOTIN OUR SIMILARITIES AND DIFFERENCES. THE GIRLS WERE QUICK TO POINT OUT THAT ALTHOUGH HE WAS 19 YEARS MY SENIOR, I HAD CONSIDERABLY MORE GREY HAIR.

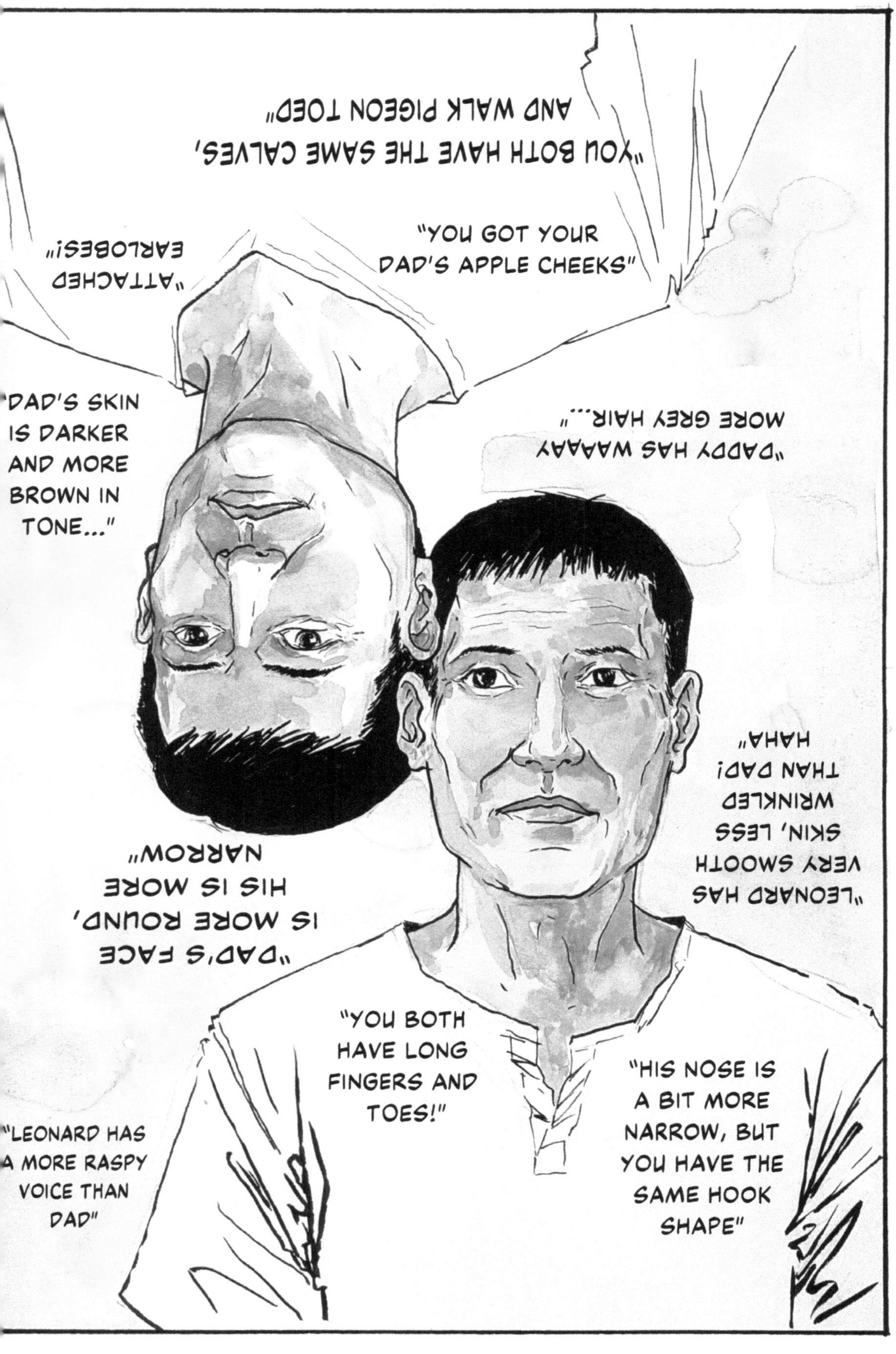
"YOU BOTH HAVE THE SAME CALVES, AND WALK PIGEON TOED"
"ATTACHED EARLOBES!"
"YOU GOT YOUR DAD'S APPLE CHEEKS"
"DAD'S SKIN IS DARKER AND MORE BROWN IN TONE..."
"DADDY HAS WAAAAY MORE GREY HAIR...."
"LEONARD HAS VERY SMOOTH SKIN, LESS WRINKLED THAN DAD! HAHA"
"DAD'S FACE IS MORE ROUND, HIS IS MORE NARROW"
"YOU BOTH HAVE LONG FINGERS AND TOES!"
"HIS NOSE IS A BIT MORE NARROW, BUT YOU HAVE THE SAME HOOK SHAPE"
"LEONARD HAS A MORE RASPY VOICE THAN DAD"

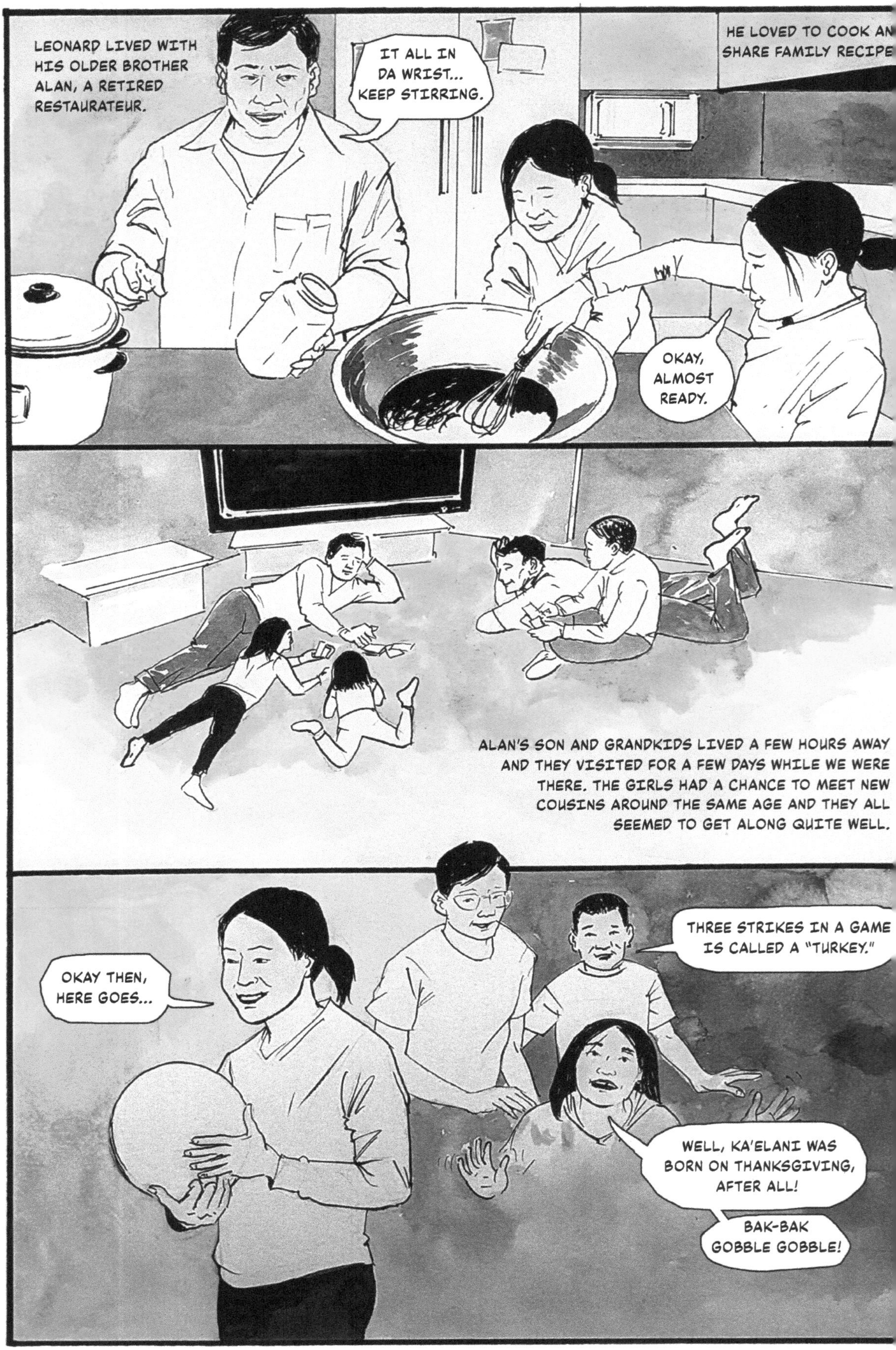
LEONARD LIVED WITH HIS OLDER BROTHER ALAN, A RETIRED RESTAURATEUR.
IT ALL IN DA WRIST... KEEP STIRRING.
HE LOVED TO COOK AN SHARE FAMILY RECIPE
OKAY, ALMOST READY.
ALAN'S SON AND GRANDKIDS LIVED A FEW HOURS AWAY AND THEY VISITED FOR A FEW DAYS WHILE WE WERE THERE. THE GIRLS HAD A CHANCE TO MEET NEW COUSINS AROUND THE SAME AGE AND THEY ALL SEEMED TO GET ALONG QUITE WELL.
OKAY THEN, HERE GOES...
THREE STRIKES IN A GAME IS CALLED A "TURKEY."
WELL, KA'ELANI WAS BORN ON THANKSGIVING, AFTER ALL!
BAK-BAK GOBBLE GOBBLE!

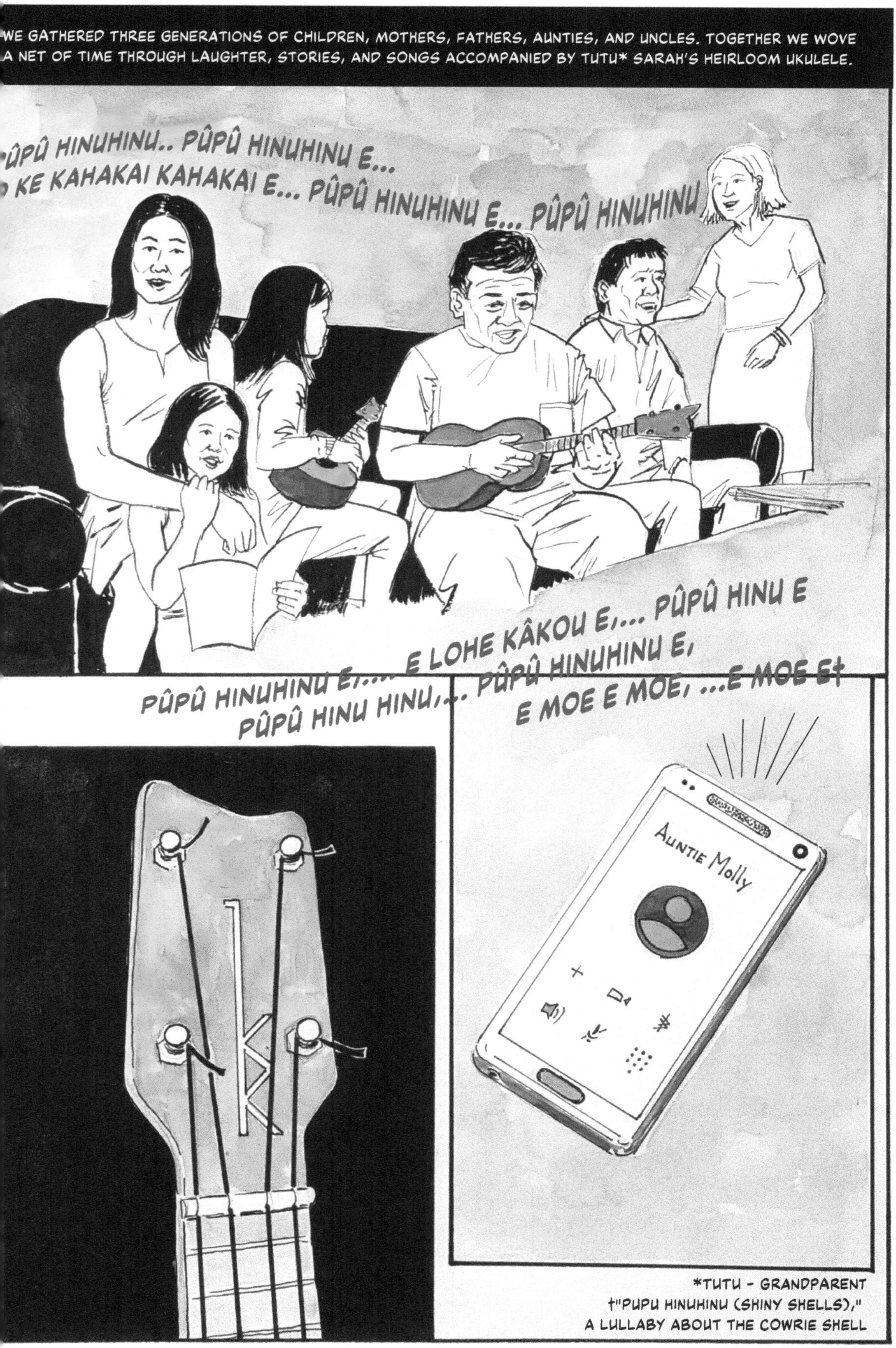
WE GATHERED THREE GENERATIONS OF CHILDREN, MOTHERS, FATHERS, AUNTIES, AND UNCLES. TOGETHER WE WOVE A NET OF TIME THROUGH LAUGHTER, STORIES, AND SONGS ACCOMPANIED BY TUTU* SARAH'S HEIRLOOM UKULELE.
ÛPÛ HINUHINU.. PÛPÛ HINUHINU E...
KE KAHAKAI KAHAKAI E... PÛPÛ HINUHINU E... PÛPÛ HINUHINU
E LOHE KÂKOU E,... PÛPÛ HINU E
PÛPÛ HINUHINU E,.... PÛPÛ HINUHINU E,
PÛPÛ HINU HINU,... E MOE E MOE, ...E MOE E†
Auntie Molly
*TUTU - GRANDPARENT
†"PUPU HINUHINU (SHINY SHELLS),"
A LULLABY ABOUT THE COWRIE SHELL

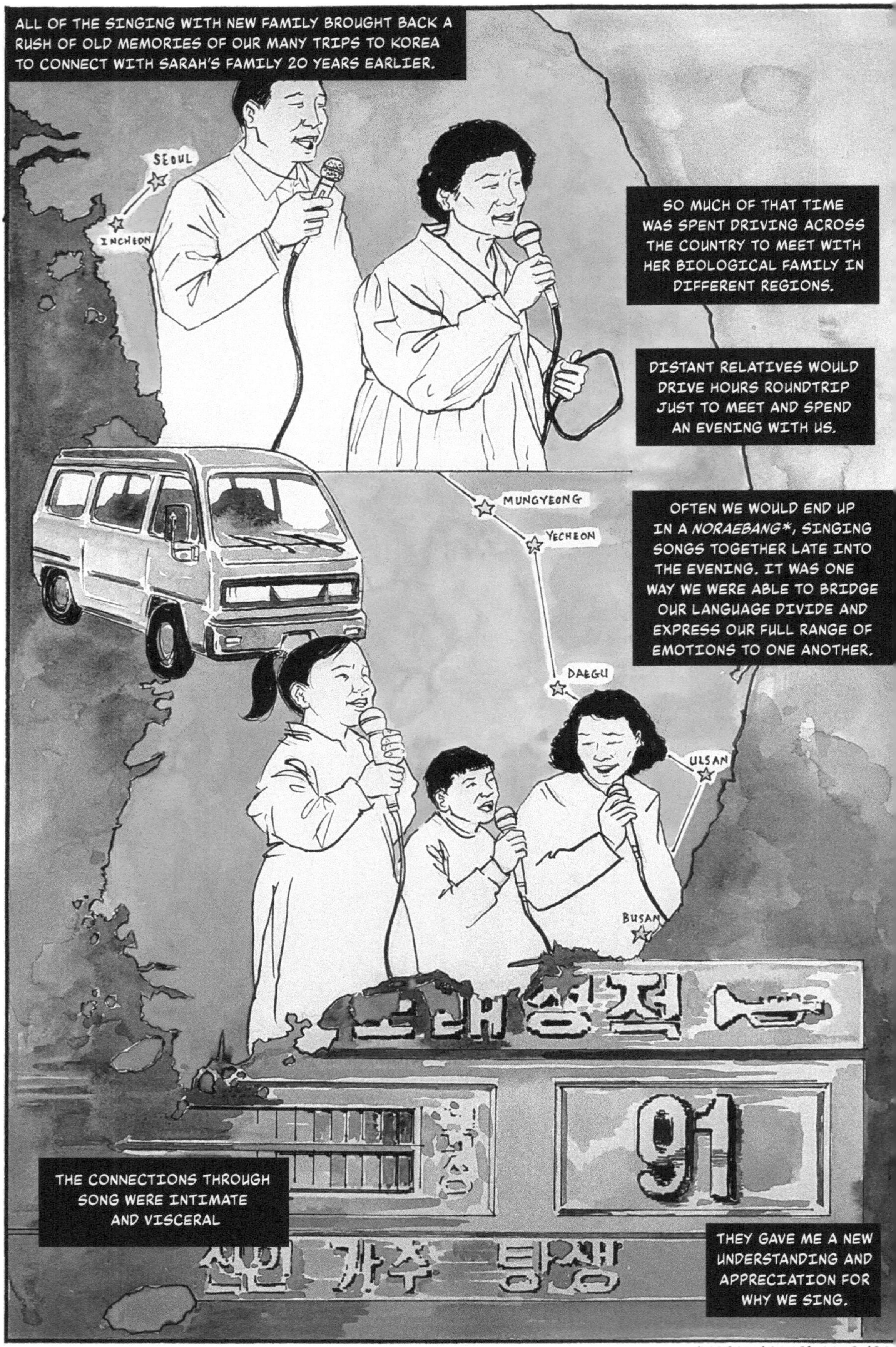
ALL OF THE SINGING WITH NEW FAMILY BROUGHT BACK A RUSH OF OLD MEMORIES OF OUR MANY TRIPS TO KOREA TO CONNECT WITH SARAH'S FAMILY 20 YEARS EARLIER.
SEOUL
INCHEON
SO MUCH OF THAT TIME WAS SPENT DRIVING ACROSS THE COUNTRY TO MEET WITH HER BIOLOGICAL FAMILY IN DIFFERENT REGIONS.
DISTANT RELATIVES WOULD DRIVE HOURS ROUNDTRIP JUST TO MEET AND SPEND AN EVENING WITH US.
MUNGYEONG
YECHEON
OFTEN WE WOULD END UP IN A *NORAEBANG**, SINGING SONGS TOGETHER LATE INTO THE EVENING. IT WAS ONE WAY WE WERE ABLE TO BRIDGE OUR LANGUAGE DIVIDE AND EXPRESS OUR FULL RANGE OF EMOTIONS TO ONE ANOTHER.
DAEGU
ULSAN
BUSAN
91
THE CONNECTIONS THROUGH SONG WERE INTIMATE AND VISCERAL
THEY GAVE ME A NEW UNDERSTANDING AND APPRECIATION FOR WHY WE SING.

*NORAE (SONG) BANG (RO

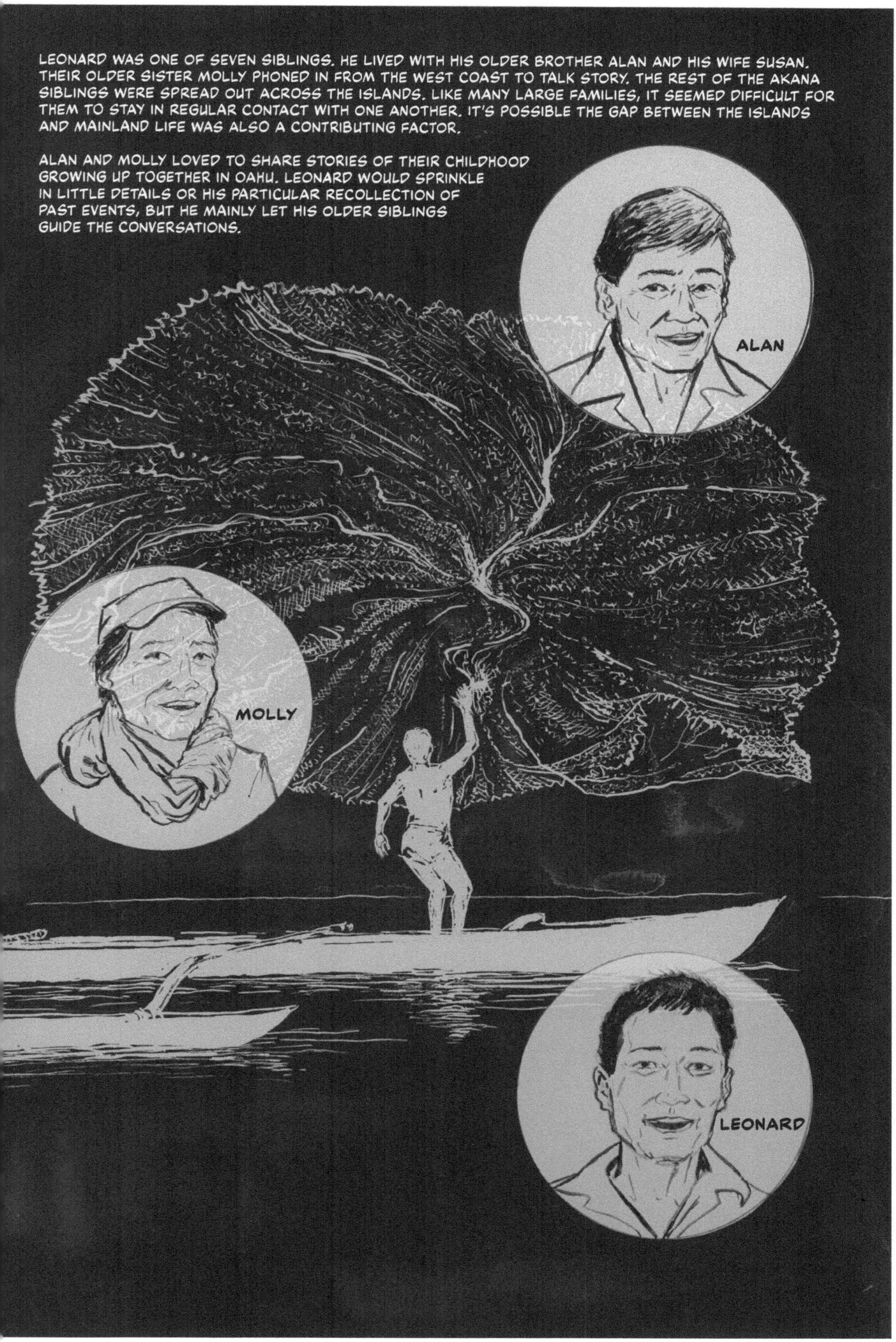
LEONARD WAS ONE OF SEVEN SIBLINGS. HE LIVED WITH HIS OLDER BROTHER ALAN AND HIS WIFE SUSAN. THEIR OLDER SISTER MOLLY PHONED IN FROM THE WEST COAST TO TALK STORY. THE REST OF THE AKANA SIBLINGS WERE SPREAD OUT ACROSS THE ISLANDS. LIKE MANY LARGE FAMILIES, IT SEEMED DIFFICULT FOR THEM TO STAY IN REGULAR CONTACT WITH ONE ANOTHER. IT'S POSSIBLE THE GAP BETWEEN THE ISLANDS AND MAINLAND LIFE WAS ALSO A CONTRIBUTING FACTOR.
ALAN AND MOLLY LOVED TO SHARE STORIES OF THEIR CHILDHOOD GROWING UP TOGETHER IN OAHU. LEONARD WOULD SPRINKLE IN LITTLE DETAILS OR HIS PARTICULAR RECOLLECTION OF PAST EVENTS, BUT HE MAINLY LET HIS OLDER SIBLINGS GUIDE THE CONVERSATIONS.
ALAN
MOLLY
LEONARD

OUR PROPERTY WAS IN THE LILIHA AREA OF OAHU, ORIGINALLY FROM THE CHINESE SIDE OF THE FAMILY. IT HIDDEN AWAY OFF DA ROAD AND ONLY ACCESSIBLE BY TAKING A NARROW PATH BETWEEN THE NEIGHBOR HOUSES. YOU CROSS DA BRIDGE OVER WAOLANI STREAM TO GET THERE.
—ALAN

WE HAD AN INTERESTING GROWING UP DAYS, WE LIVED IN A TINY HOUSE WITH ALL OF US, OH MY GOSH. GROWING UP I NEVER HAD A BED, I HAD A COUCH TO SLEEP ON. WE NEVER THOUGHT WE WERE POOR THOUGH.
—MOLLY

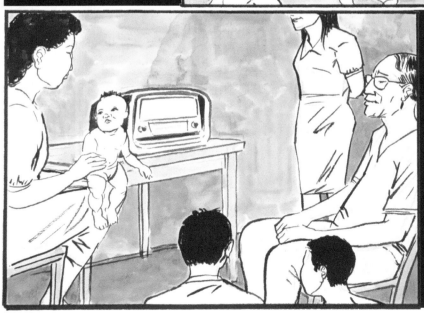

MONDAY NIGHTS WERE HOT BREAD AND DETECTIVE "BOSTON BLACKIE" RADIO SHOW.

WE HAD NO TV. YOU SIT DOWN, YOU CANNOT TALK, WE HAVE A ROUND OF HOT BREAD (FRESH BAKE) AND JUST BE TOGETHER.
—LEONARD

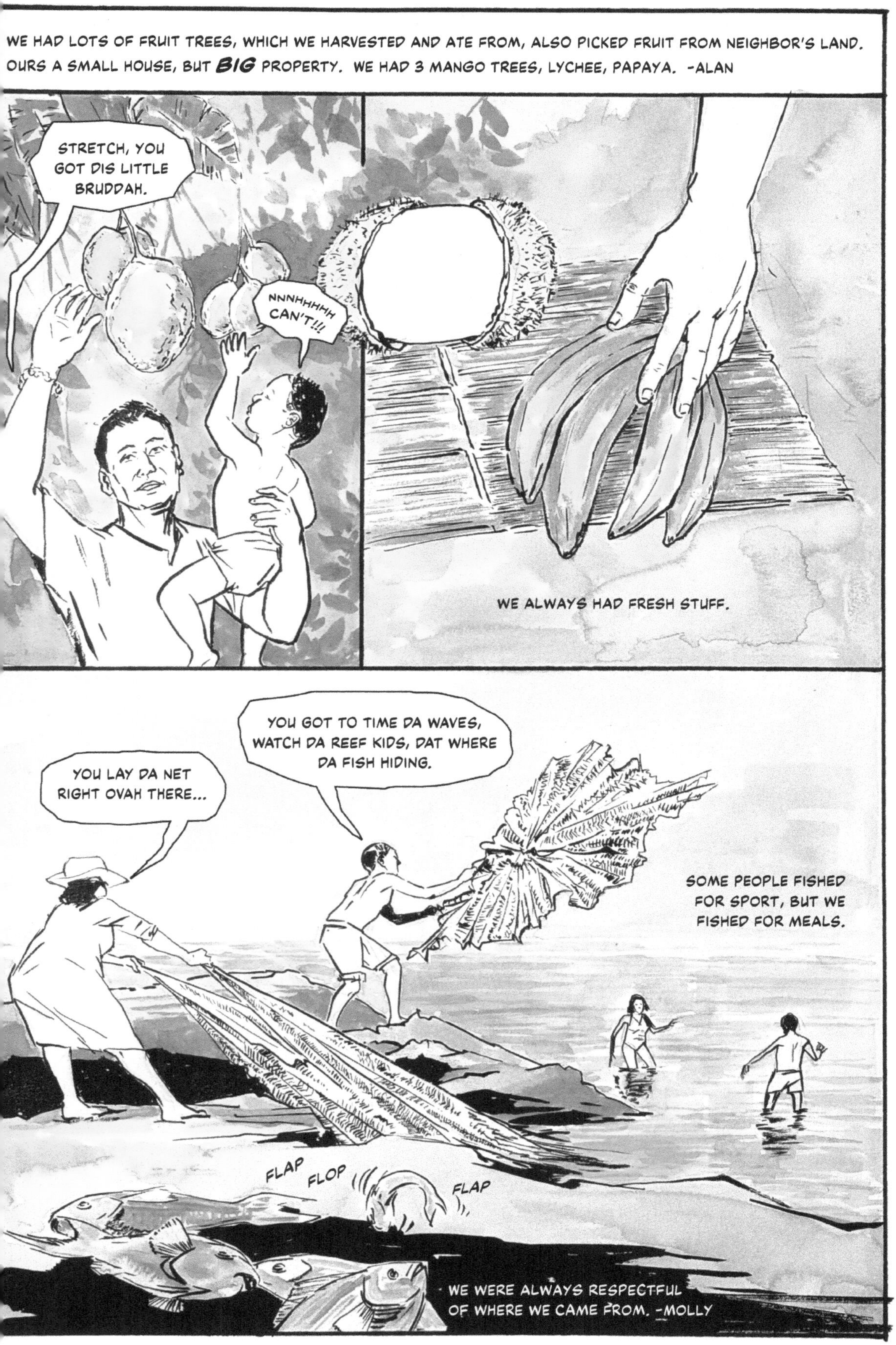
WE HAD LOTS OF FRUIT TREES, WHICH WE HARVESTED AND ATE FROM, ALSO PICKED FRUIT FROM NEIGHBOR'S LAND. OURS A SMALL HOUSE, BUT BIG PROPERTY. WE HAD 3 MANGO TREES, LYCHEE, PAPAYA. -ALAN
STRETCH, YOU GOT DIS LITTLE BRUDDAH.
NNNHHHHH CAN'T!!!
WE ALWAYS HAD FRESH STUFF.
YOU LAY DA NET RIGHT OVAH THERE...
YOU GOT TO TIME DA WAVES, WATCH DA REEF KIDS, DAT WHERE DA FISH HIDING.
SOME PEOPLE FISHED FOR SPORT, BUT WE FISHED FOR MEALS.
FLAP
FLOP
FLAP
WE WERE ALWAYS RESPECTFUL OF WHERE WE CAME FROM. -MOLLY

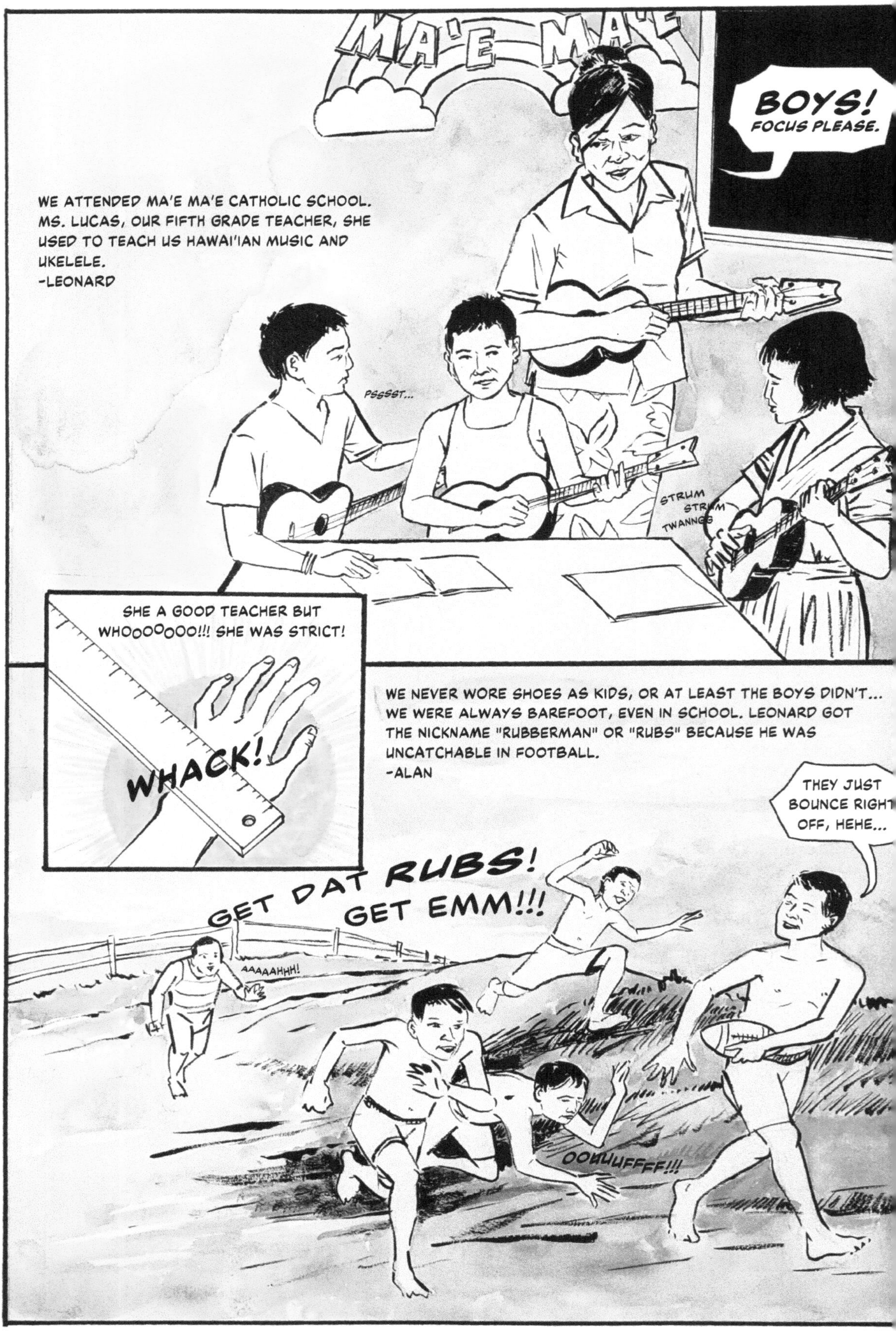
MA'E MA'E
BOYS! FOCUS PLEASE.
WE ATTENDED MA'E MA'E CATHOLIC SCHOOL. MS. LUCAS, OUR FIFTH GRADE TEACHER, SHE USED TO TEACH US HAWAI'IAN MUSIC AND UKELELE.
-LEONARD
PSSSST...
STRUM STRUM TWANNGG
SHE A GOOD TEACHER BUT WHOOOOOOO!!! SHE WAS STRICT!
WHACK!
WE NEVER WORE SHOES AS KIDS, OR AT LEAST THE BOYS DIDN'T... WE WERE ALWAYS BAREFOOT, EVEN IN SCHOOL. LEONARD GOT THE NICKNAME "RUBBERMAN" OR "RUBS" BECAUSE HE WAS UNCATCHABLE IN FOOTBALL.
-ALAN
THEY JUST BOUNCE RIGHT OFF, HEHE...
GET DAT RUBS! GET EMM!!!
AAAAAHHH!
OOUUUFFFF!!!

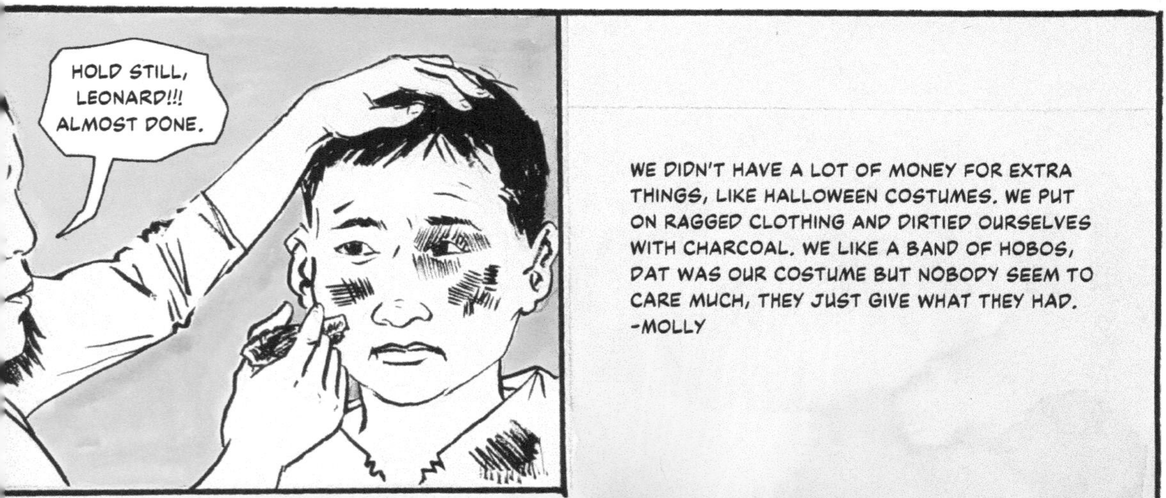
HOLD STILL, LEONARD!!! ALMOST DONE.
WE DIDN'T HAVE A LOT OF MONEY FOR EXTRA THINGS, LIKE HALLOWEEN COSTUMES. WE PUT ON RAGGED CLOTHING AND DIRTIED OURSELVES WITH CHARCOAL. WE LIKE A BAND OF HOBOS, DAT WAS OUR COSTUME BUT NOBODY SEEM TO CARE MUCH, THEY JUST GIVE WHAT THEY HAD.
-MOLLY

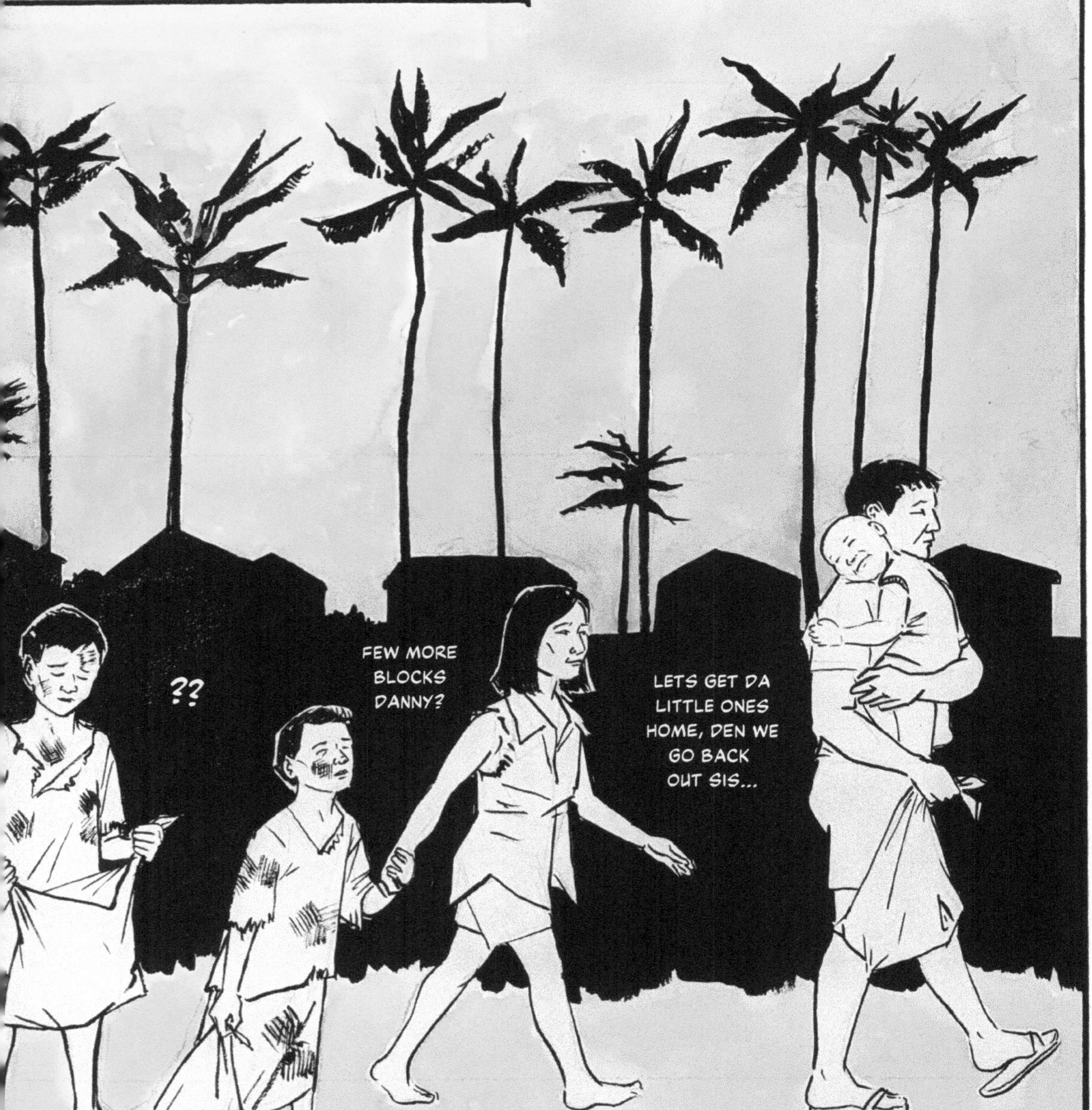
??
FEW MORE BLOCKS DANNY?
LETS GET DA LITTLE ONES HOME, DEN WE GO BACK OUT SIS...

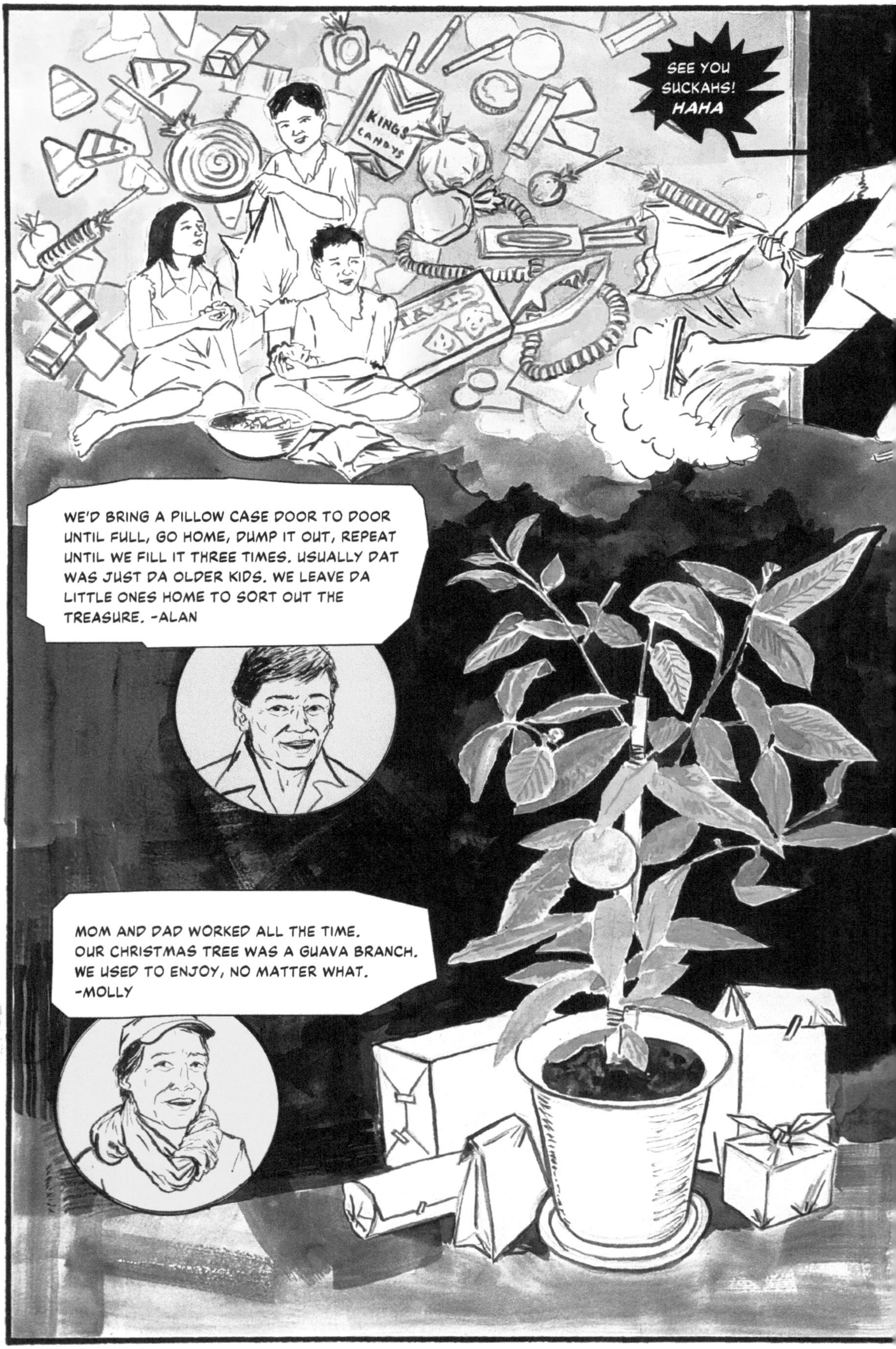
KINGS CANDYS
TARTS
SEE YOU SUCKAHS! HAHA
WE'D BRING A PILLOW CASE DOOR TO DOOR UNTIL FULL, GO HOME, DUMP IT OUT, REPEAT UNTIL WE FILL IT THREE TIMES. USUALLY DAT WAS JUST DA OLDER KIDS. WE LEAVE DA LITTLE ONES HOME TO SORT OUT THE TREASURE. -ALAN
MOM AND DAD WORKED ALL THE TIME. OUR CHRISTMAS TREE WAS A GUAVA BRANCH. WE USED TO ENJOY, NO MATTER WHAT. -MOLLY

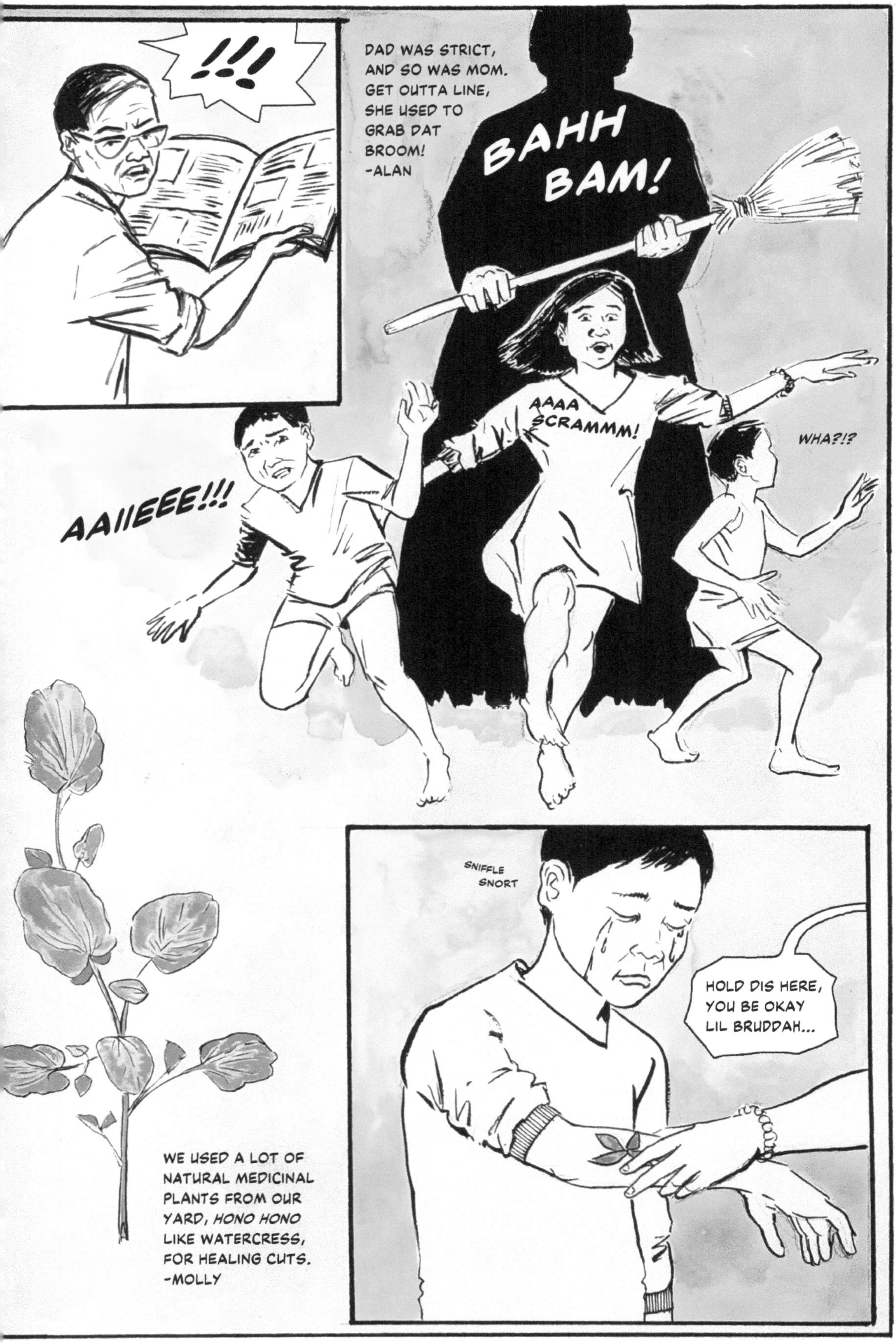

!!!
DAD WAS STRICT, AND SO WAS MOM. GET OUTTA LINE, SHE USED TO GRAB DAT BROOM! -ALAN
BAHH BAM!
AAAA SCRAMMM!
WHA?!?
AAIIEEE!!!
SNIFFLE SNORT
HOLD DIS HERE, YOU BE OKAY LIL BRUDDAH...
WE USED A LOT OF NATURAL MEDICINAL PLANTS FROM OUR YARD, *HONO HONO* LIKE WATERCRESS, FOR HEALING CUTS. -MOLLY

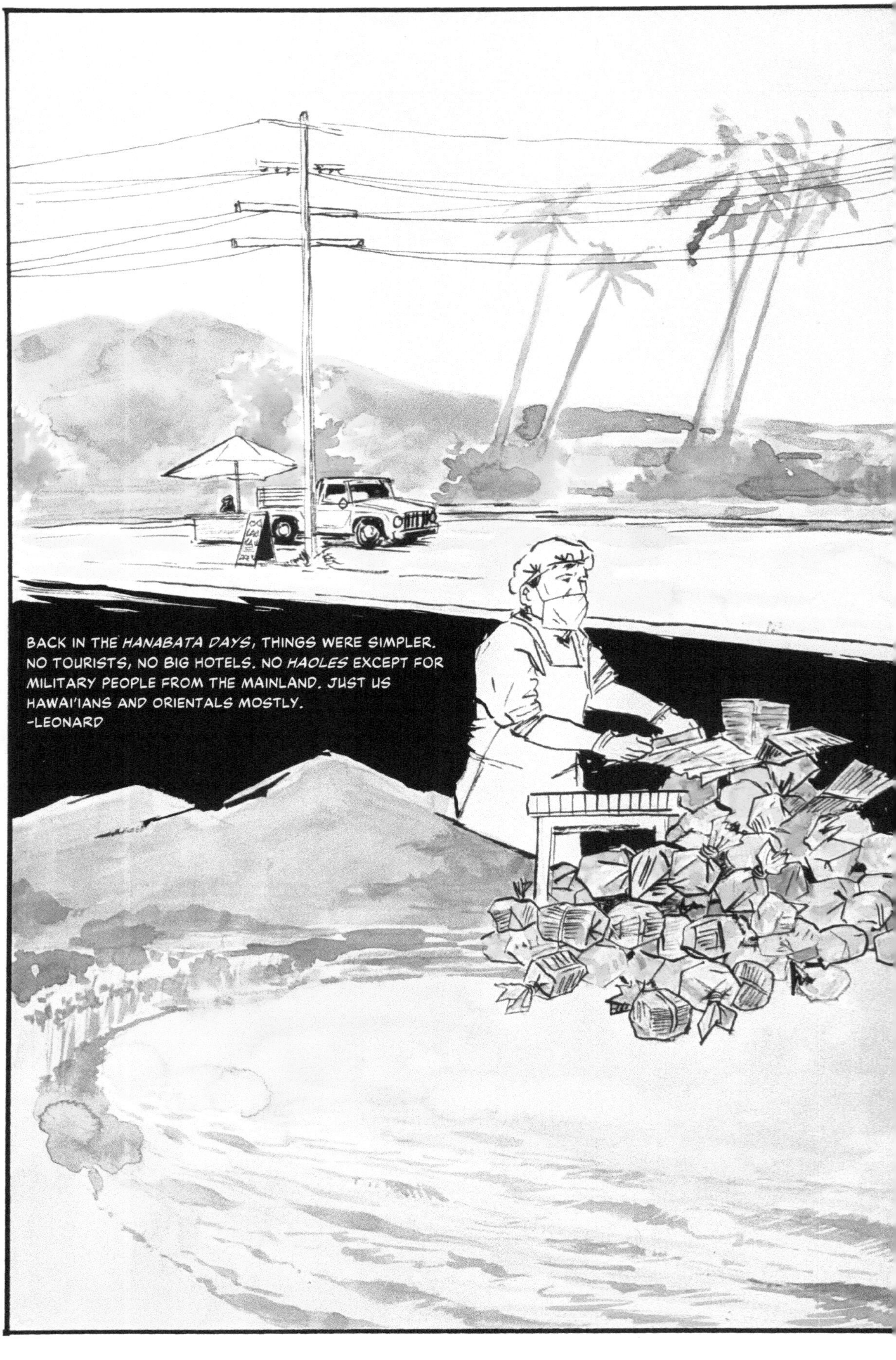
BACK IN THE *HANABATA DAYS*, THINGS WERE SIMPLER. NO TOURISTS, NO BIG HOTELS. NO *HAOLES* EXCEPT FOR MILITARY PEOPLE FROM THE MAINLAND. JUST US HAWAI'IANS AND ORIENTALS MOSTLY.
-LEONARD

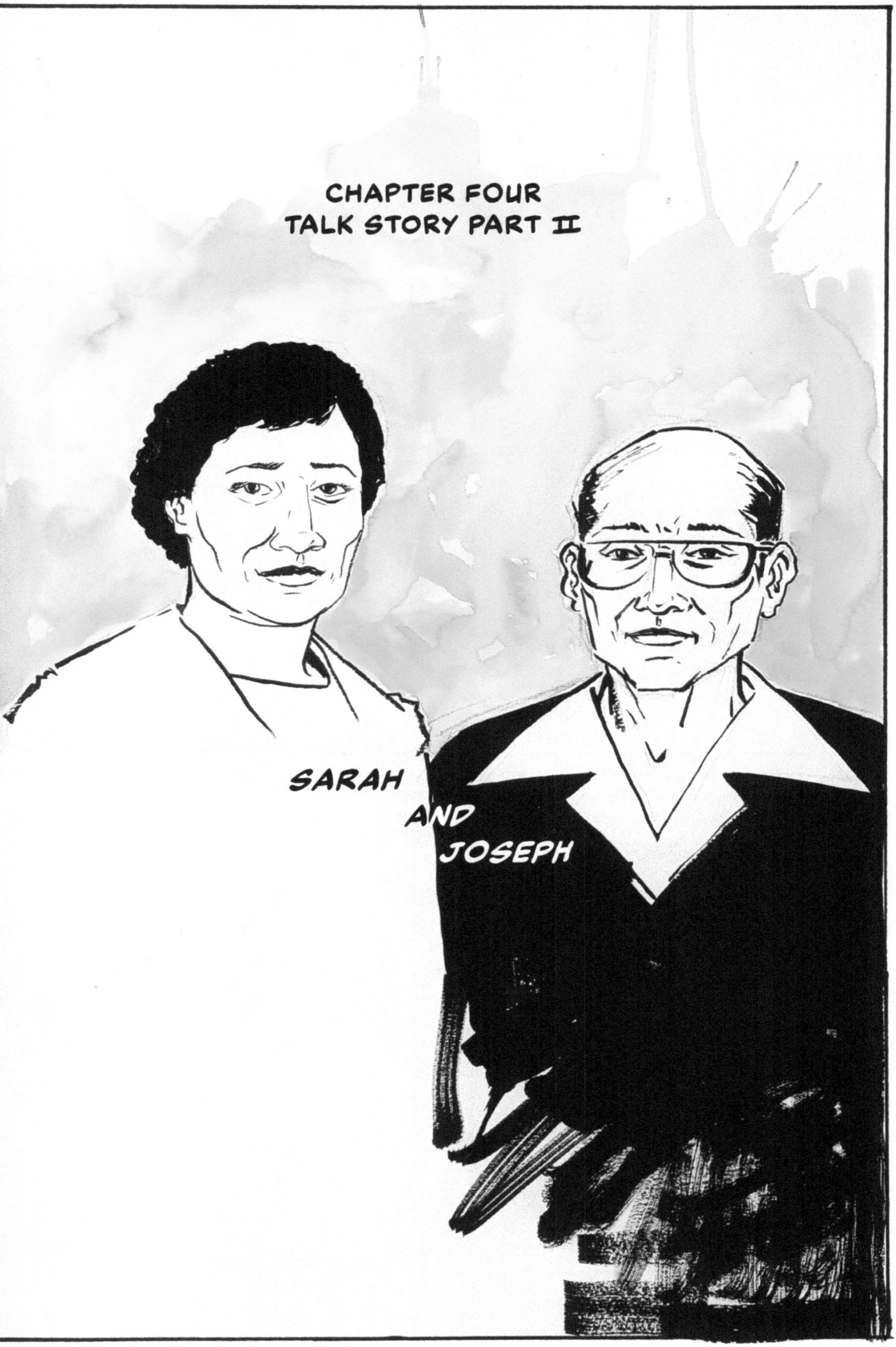
CHAPTER FOUR
TALK STORY PART II
SARAH
AND
JOSEPH

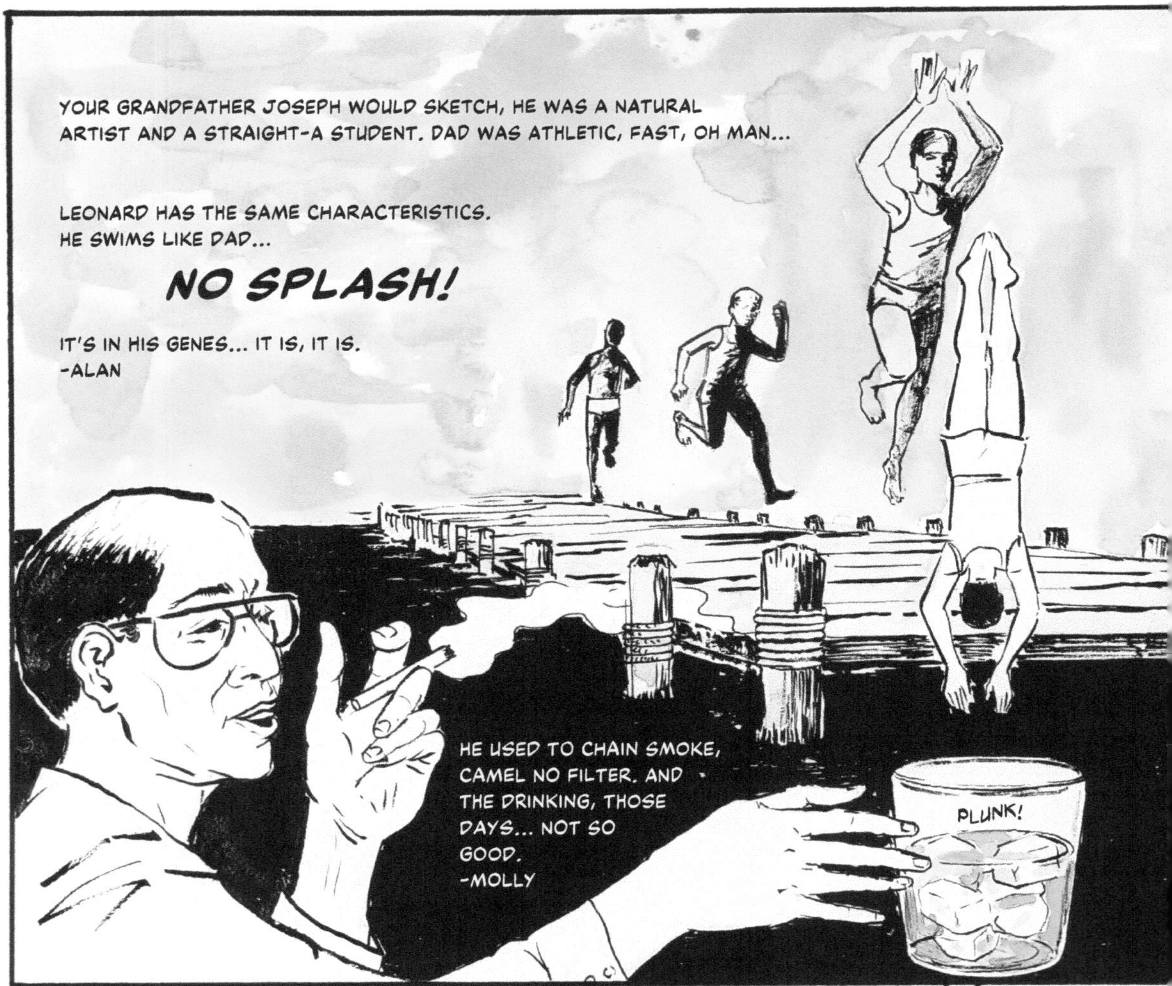
YOUR GRANDFATHER JOSEPH WOULD SKETCH, HE WAS A NATURAL ARTIST AND A STRAIGHT-A STUDENT. DAD WAS ATHLETIC, FAST, OH MAN...
LEONARD HAS THE SAME CHARACTERISTICS. HE SWIMS LIKE DAD...
NO SPLASH!
IT'S IN HIS GENES... IT IS, IT IS.
-ALAN
HE USED TO CHAIN SMOKE, CAMEL NO FILTER. AND THE DRINKING, THOSE DAYS... NOT SO GOOD.
-MOLLY
PLUNK!

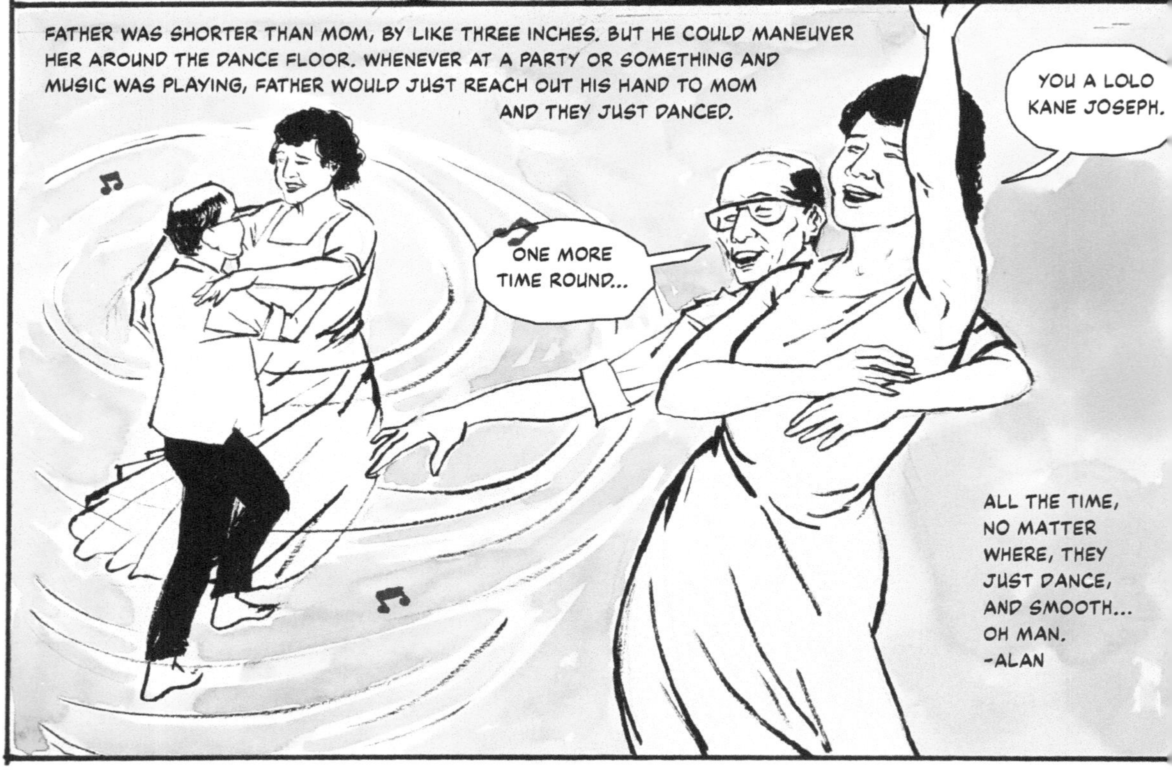
FATHER WAS SHORTER THAN MOM, BY LIKE THREE INCHES. BUT HE COULD MANEUVER HER AROUND THE DANCE FLOOR. WHENEVER AT A PARTY OR SOMETHING AND MUSIC WAS PLAYING, FATHER WOULD JUST REACH OUT HIS HAND TO MOM AND THEY JUST DANCED.
YOU A LOLO KANE JOSEPH.
ONE MORE TIME ROUND...
ALL THE TIME, NO MATTER WHERE, THEY JUST DANCE, AND SMOOTH... OH MAN.
-ALAN

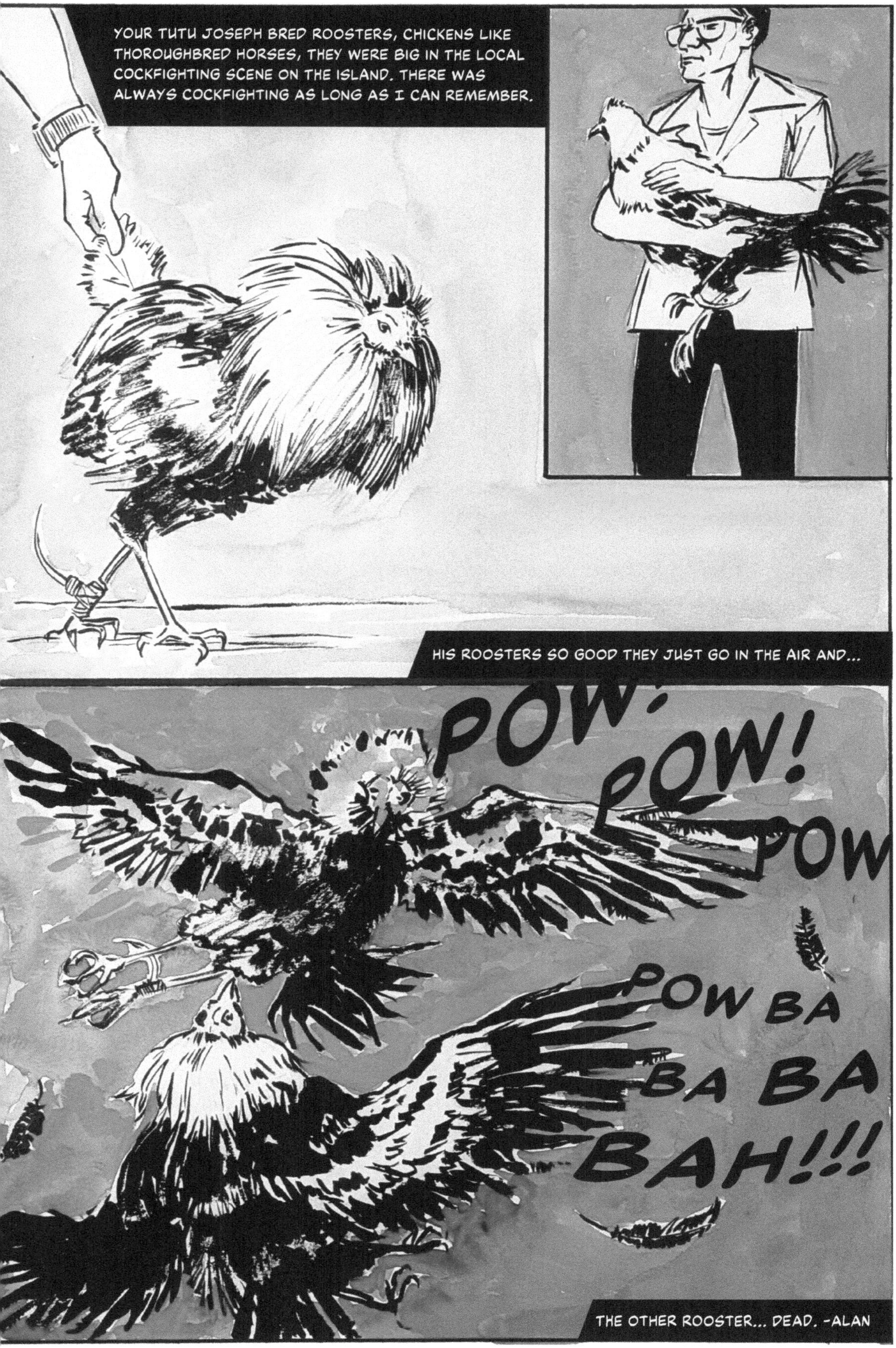
YOUR TUTU JOSEPH BRED ROOSTERS, CHICKENS LIKE THOROUGHBRED HORSES, THEY WERE BIG IN THE LOCAL COCKFIGHTING SCENE ON THE ISLAND. THERE WAS ALWAYS COCKFIGHTING AS LONG AS I CAN REMEMBER.
HIS ROOSTERS SO GOOD THEY JUST GO IN THE AIR AND...
POW!
POW!
POW
POW BA
BA BA
BAH!!!
THE OTHER ROOSTER... DEAD. -ALAN

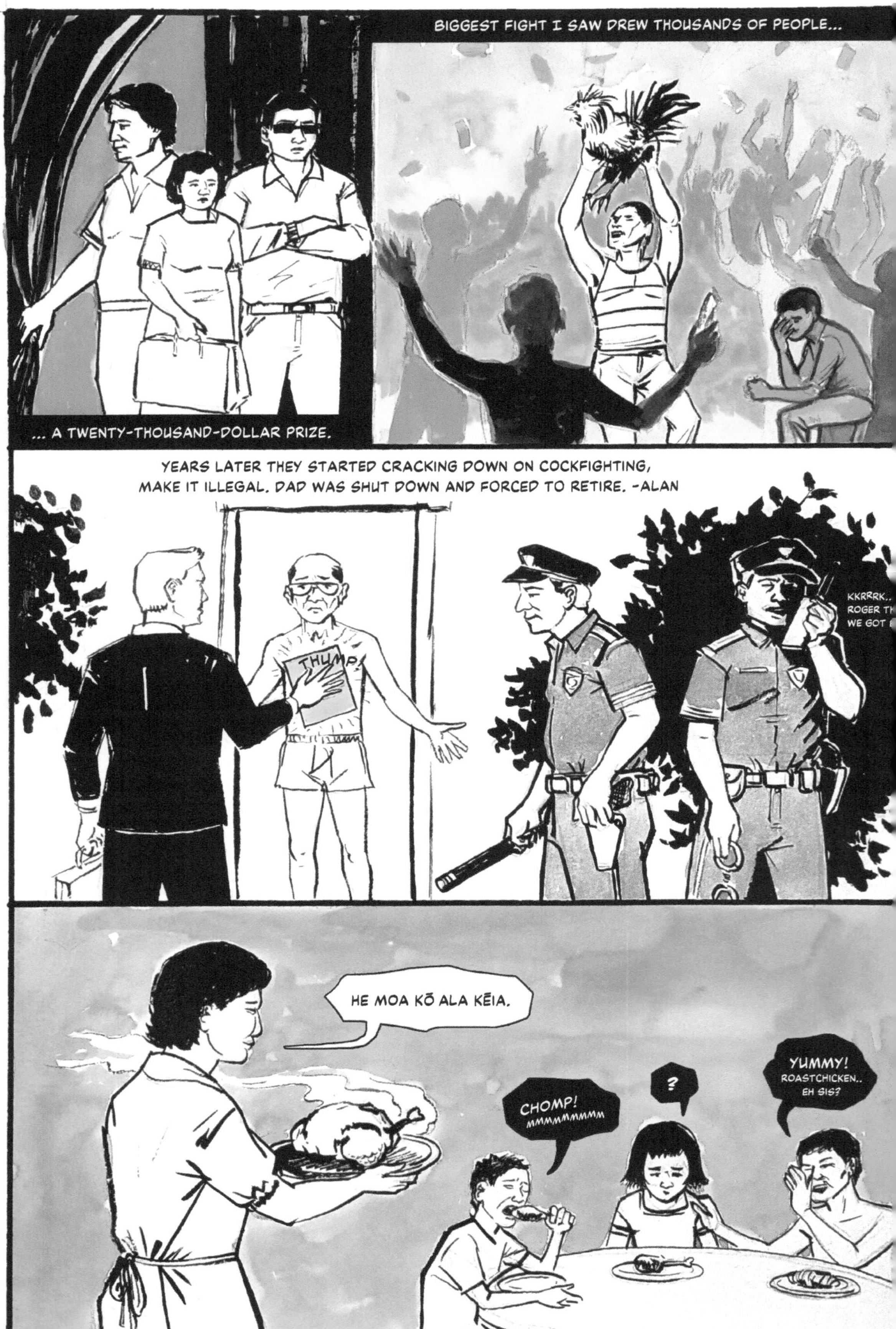

BIGGEST FIGHT I SAW DREW THOUSANDS OF PEOPLE...
... A TWENTY-THOUSAND-DOLLAR PRIZE.
YEARS LATER THEY STARTED CRACKING DOWN ON COCKFIGHTING, MAKE IT ILLEGAL. DAD WAS SHUT DOWN AND FORCED TO RETIRE. -ALAN
THUMP
KKRRRK..
ROGER TH
WE GOT
HE MOA KŌ ALA KĒIA.
CHOMP! MMMMMMMMM
?
YUMMY! ROASTCHICKEN.. EH SIS?

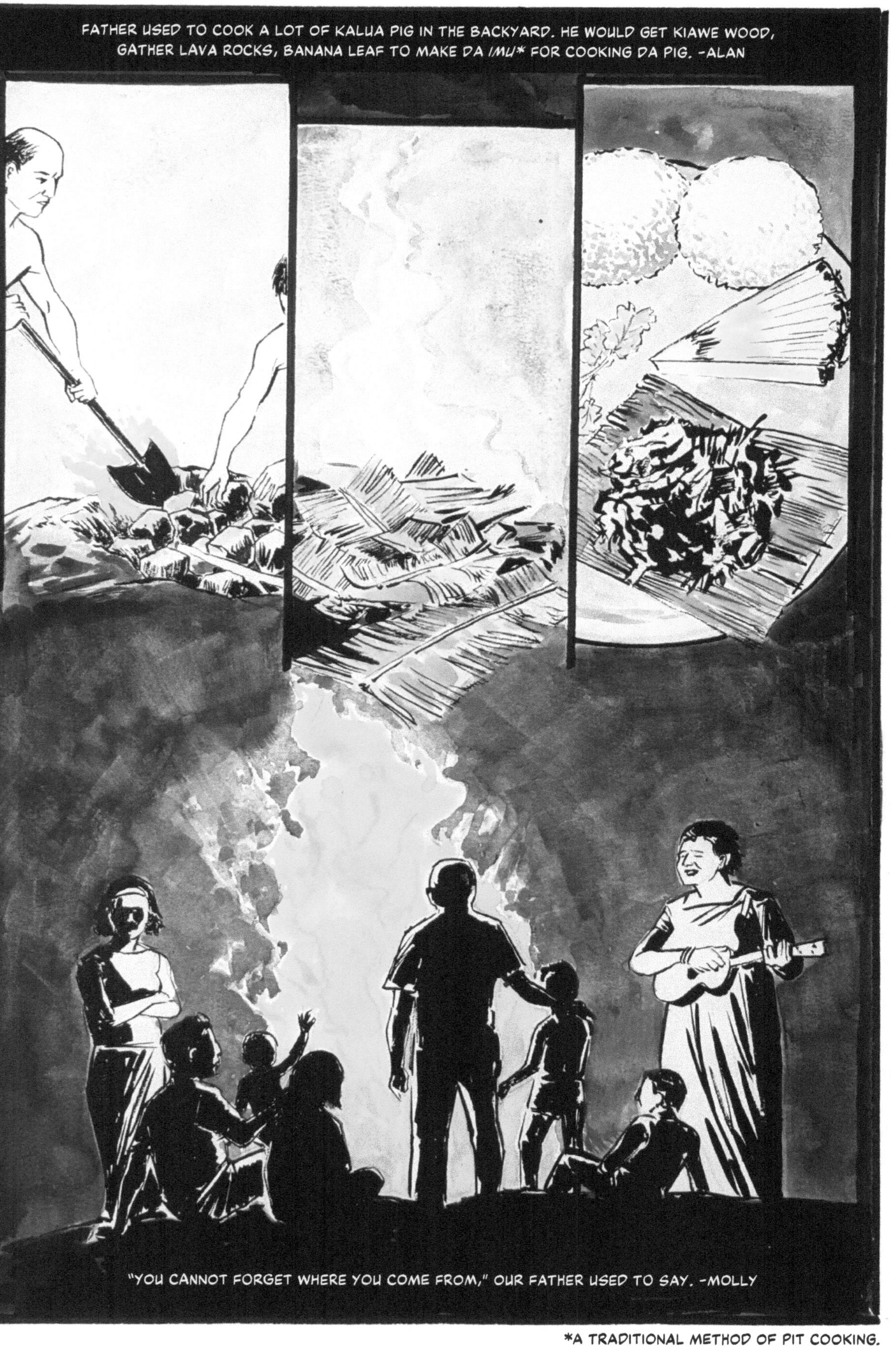
FATHER USED TO COOK A LOT OF KALUA PIG IN THE BACKYARD. HE WOULD GET KIAWE WOOD, GATHER LAVA ROCKS, BANANA LEAF TO MAKE DA *IMU** FOR COOKING DA PIG. -ALAN
"YOU CANNOT FORGET WHERE YOU COME FROM," OUR FATHER USED TO SAY. -MOLLY

*A TRADITIONAL METHOD OF PIT COOKING.

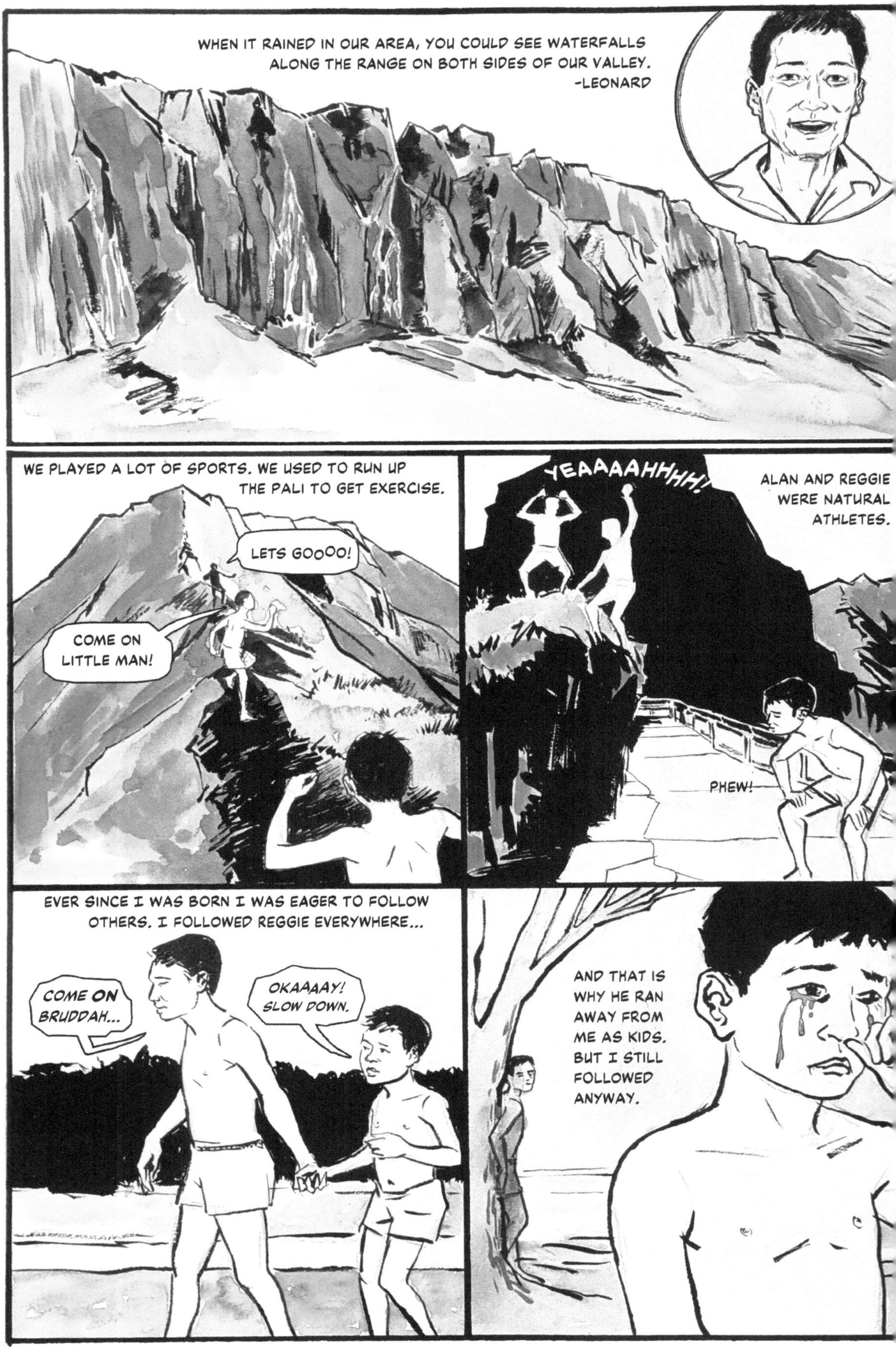
WHEN IT RAINED IN OUR AREA, YOU COULD SEE WATERFALLS ALONG THE RANGE ON BOTH SIDES OF OUR VALLEY.
-LEONARD
WE PLAYED A LOT OF SPORTS. WE USED TO RUN UP THE PALI TO GET EXERCISE.
LETS GOOOO!
COME ON LITTLE MAN!
YEAAAAHHHH!
ALAN AND REGGIE WERE NATURAL ATHLETES.
PHEW!
EVER SINCE I WAS BORN I WAS EAGER TO FOLLOW OTHERS. I FOLLOWED REGGIE EVERYWHERE...
COME ON BRUDDAH...
OKAAAAY! SLOW DOWN.
AND THAT IS WHY HE RAN AWAY FROM ME AS KIDS. BUT I STILL FOLLOWED ANYWAY.

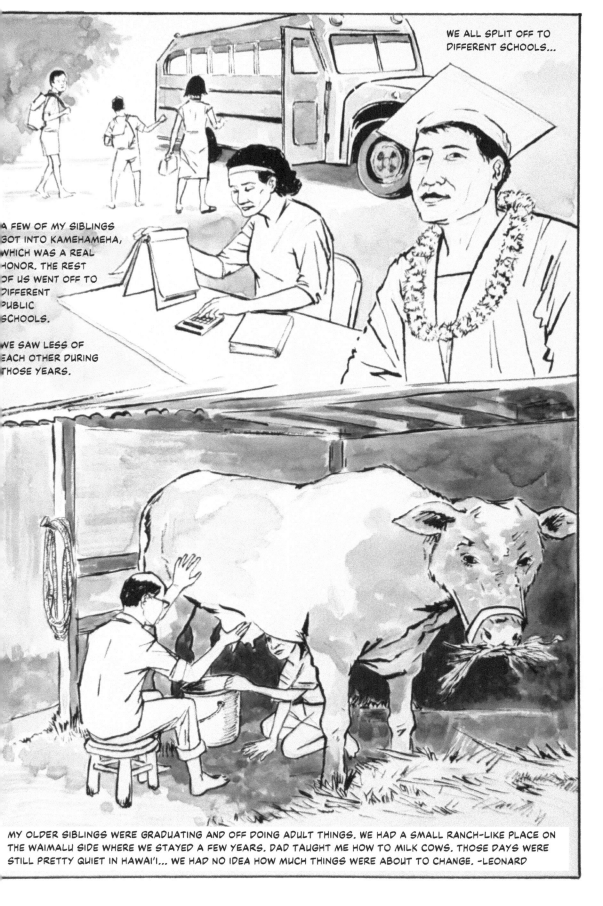

WE ALL SPLIT OFF TO DIFFERENT SCHOOLS...

A FEW OF MY SIBLINGS GOT INTO KAMEHAMEHA, WHICH WAS A REAL HONOR. THE REST OF US WENT OFF TO DIFFERENT PUBLIC SCHOOLS.

WE SAW LESS OF EACH OTHER DURING THOSE YEARS.

MY OLDER SIBLINGS WERE GRADUATING AND OFF DOING ADULT THINGS. WE HAD A SMALL RANCH-LIKE PLACE ON THE WAIMALU SIDE WHERE WE STAYED A FEW YEARS. DAD TAUGHT ME HOW TO MILK COWS. THOSE DAYS WERE STILL PRETTY QUIET IN HAWAI'I... WE HAD NO IDEA HOW MUCH THINGS WERE ABOUT TO CHANGE. -LEONARD

71

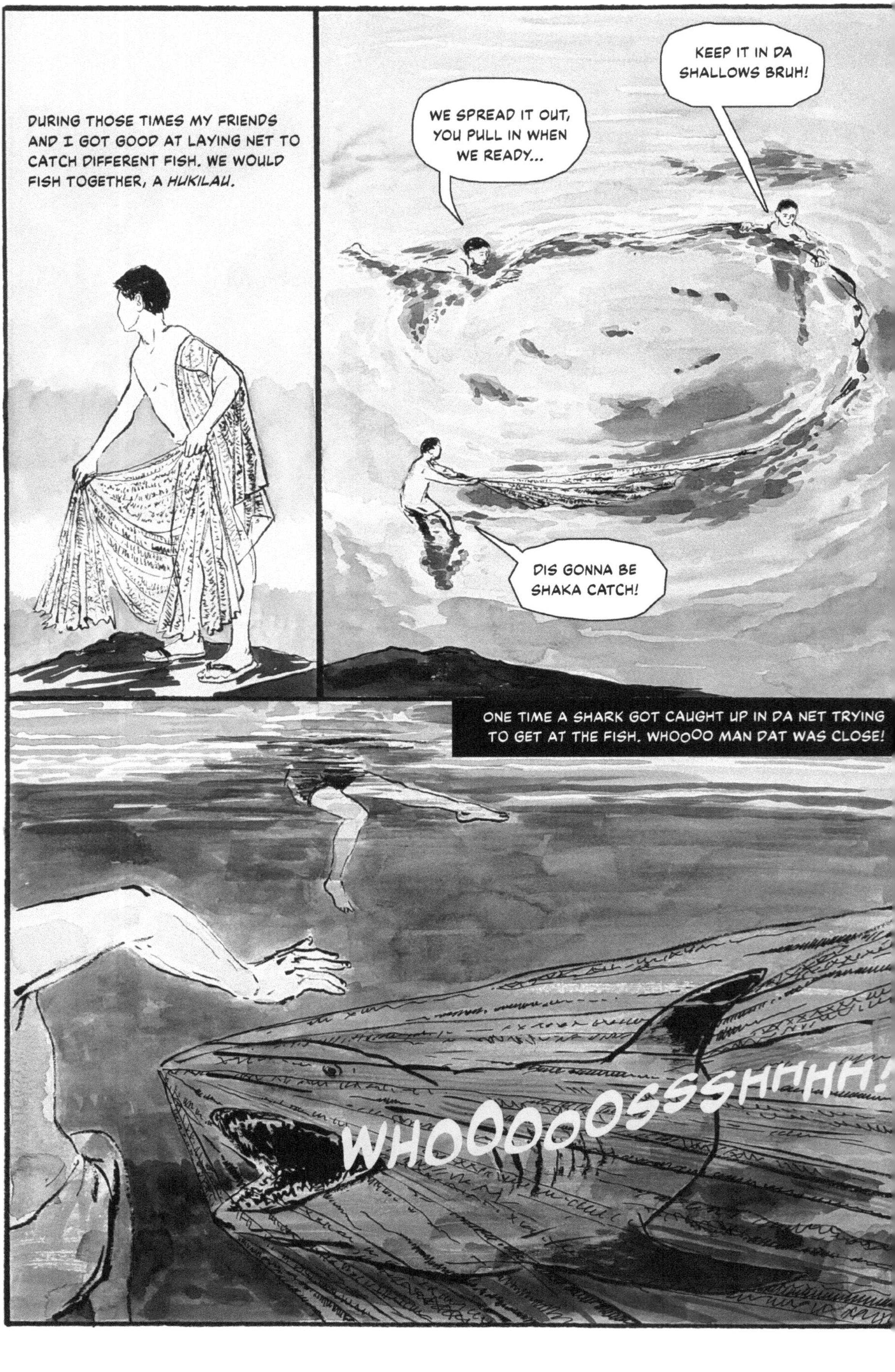
DURING THOSE TIMES MY FRIENDS AND I GOT GOOD AT LAYING NET TO CATCH DIFFERENT FISH. WE WOULD FISH TOGETHER, A *HUKILAU*.
WE SPREAD IT OUT, YOU PULL IN WHEN WE READY...
KEEP IT IN DA SHALLOWS BRUH!
DIS GONNA BE SHAKA CATCH!
ONE TIME A SHARK GOT CAUGHT UP IN DA NET TRYING TO GET AT THE FISH. WHOOOO MAN DAT WAS CLOSE!
WHOOOOOSSSHHHH!

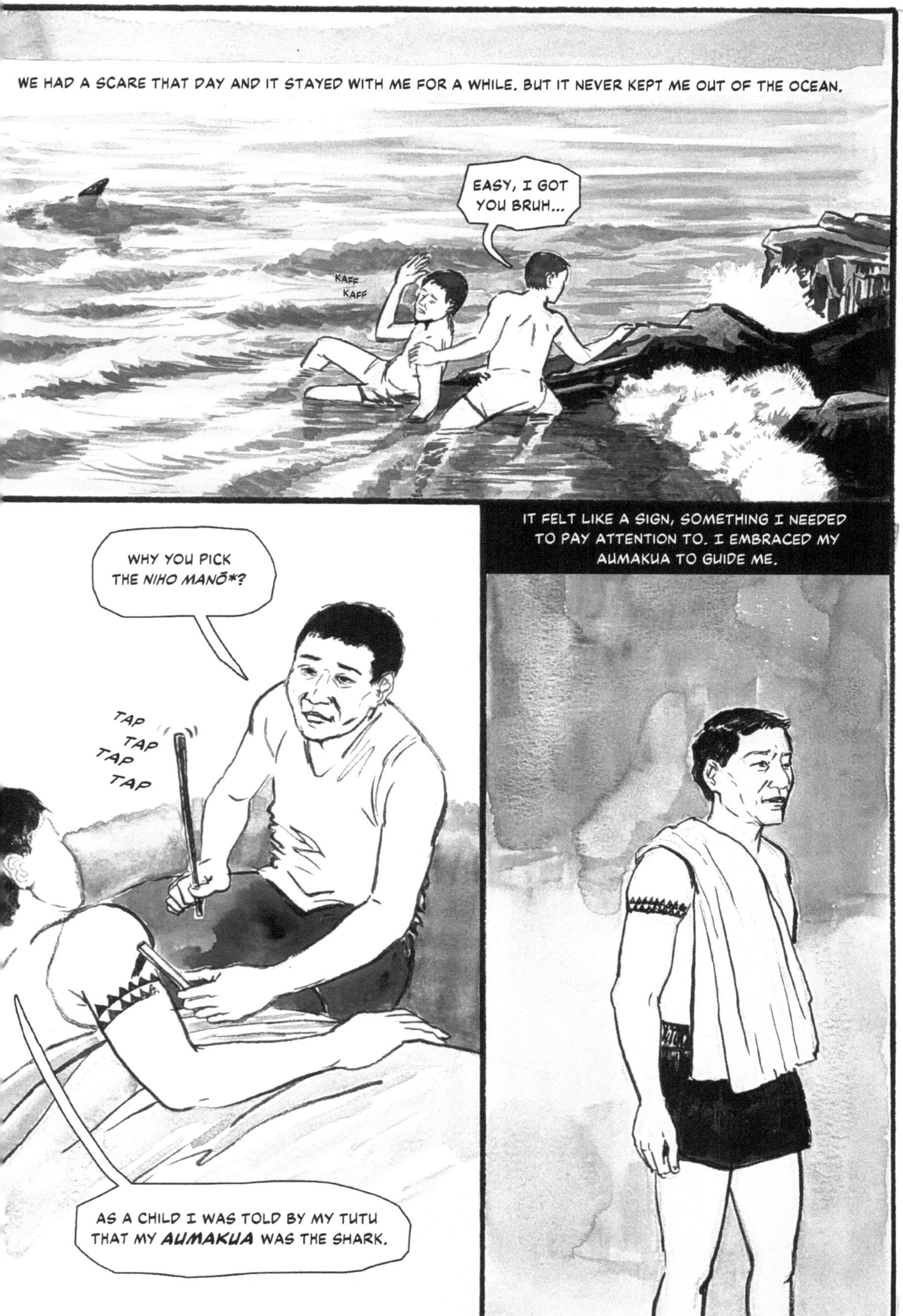
WE HAD A SCARE THAT DAY AND IT STAYED WITH ME FOR A WHILE. BUT IT NEVER KEPT ME OUT OF THE OCEAN.
EASY, I GOT YOU BRUH...
KAFF KAFF
WHY YOU PICK THE *NIHO MANŌ**?
TAP TAP TAP TAP
AS A CHILD I WAS TOLD BY MY TUTU THAT MY ***AUMAKUA*** WAS THE SHARK.
IT FELT LIKE A SIGN, SOMETHING I NEEDED TO PAY ATTENTION TO. I EMBRACED MY AUMAKUA TO GUIDE ME.

*SHARK TOOTH TAPA DESIGN

CHAPTER FIVE
ADULTING

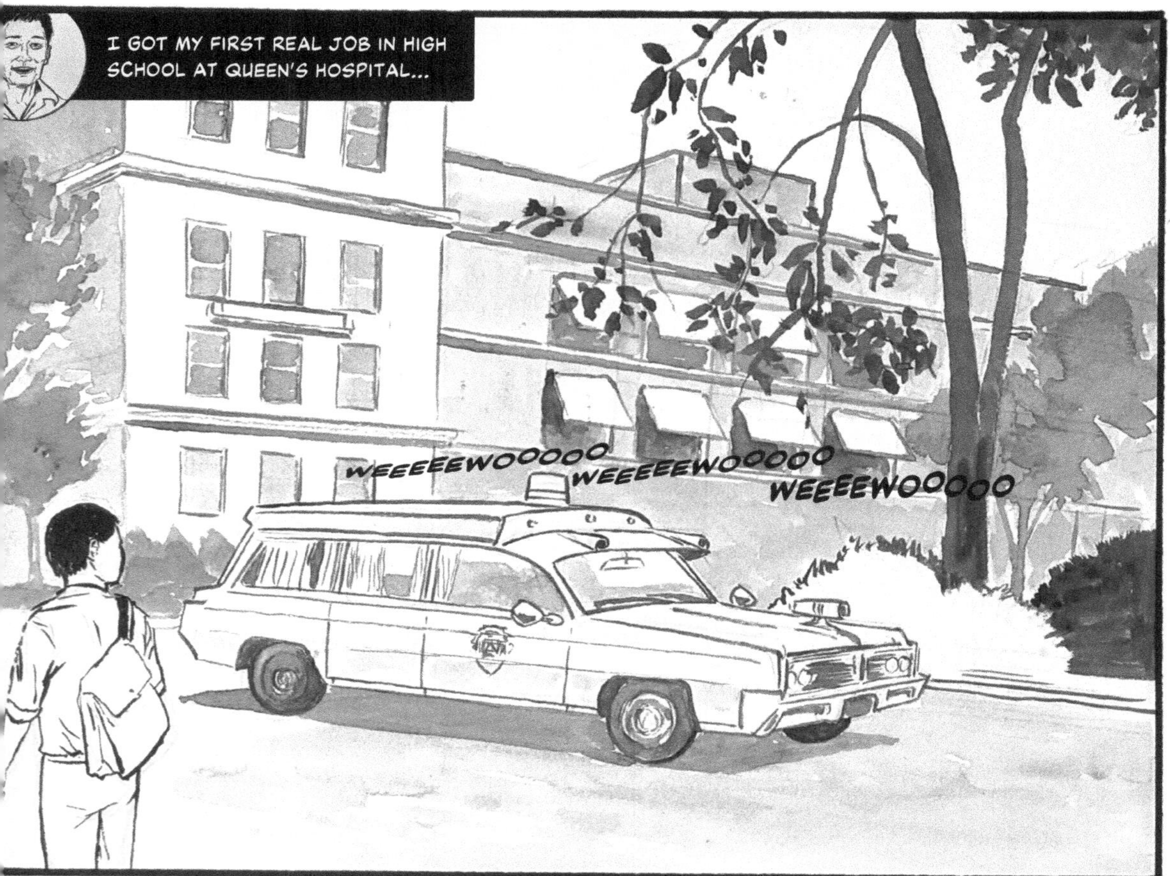
I GOT MY FIRST REAL JOB IN HIGH SCHOOL AT QUEEN'S HOSPITAL...
WEEEEEWOOOOO
WEEEEEWOOOOO
WEEEEWOOOOO

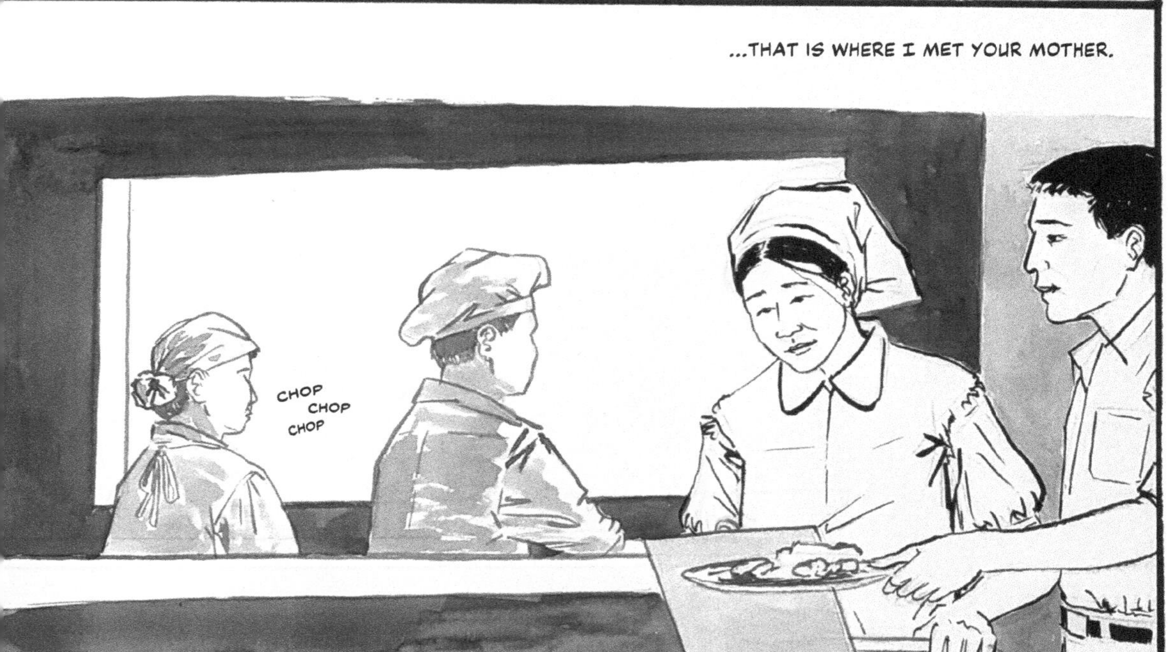
...THAT IS WHERE I MET YOUR MOTHER.
CHOP
CHOP
CHOP

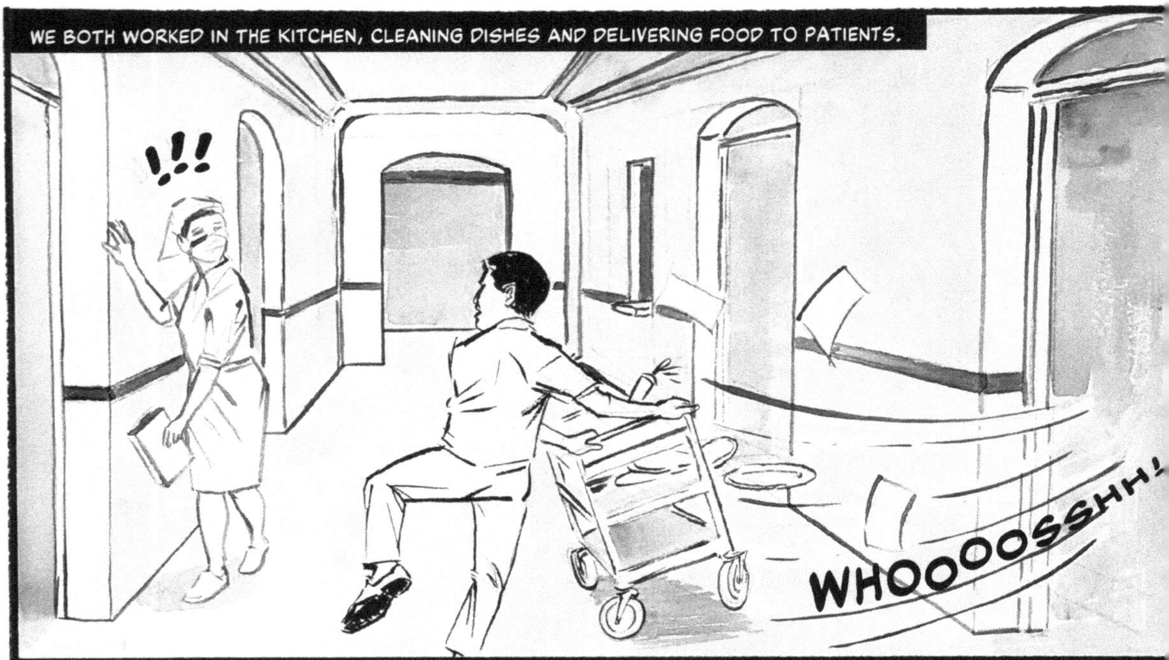
WE BOTH WORKED IN THE KITCHEN, CLEANING DISHES AND DELIVERING FOOD TO PATIENTS.
!!!
WHOOOOSSHH!

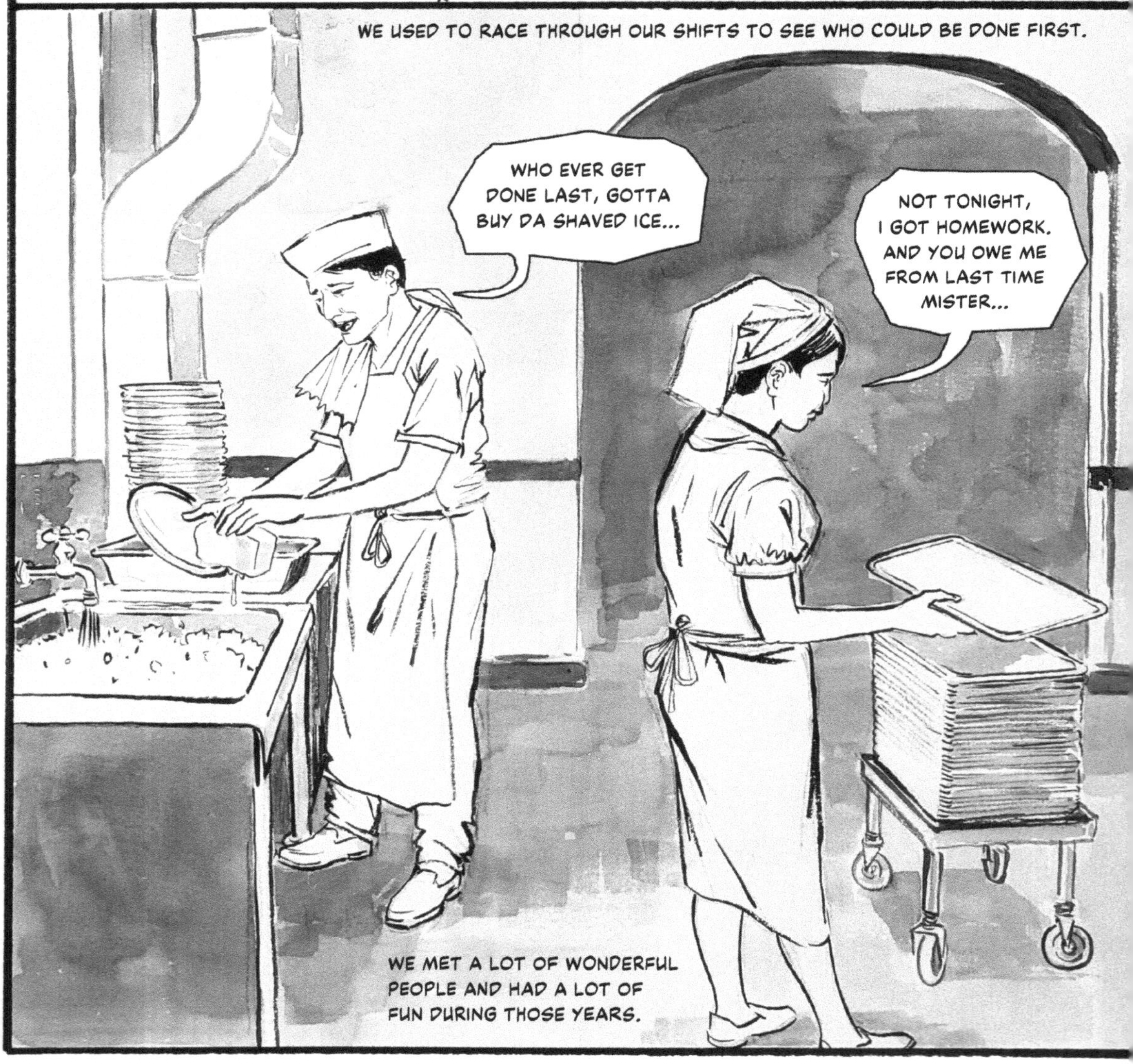
WE USED TO RACE THROUGH OUR SHIFTS TO SEE WHO COULD BE DONE FIRST.
WHO EVER GET DONE LAST, GOTTA BUY DA SHAVED ICE...
NOT TONIGHT, I GOT HOMEWORK. AND YOU OWE ME FROM LAST TIME MISTER...
WE MET A LOT OF WONDERFUL PEOPLE AND HAD A LOT OF FUN DURING THOSE YEARS.

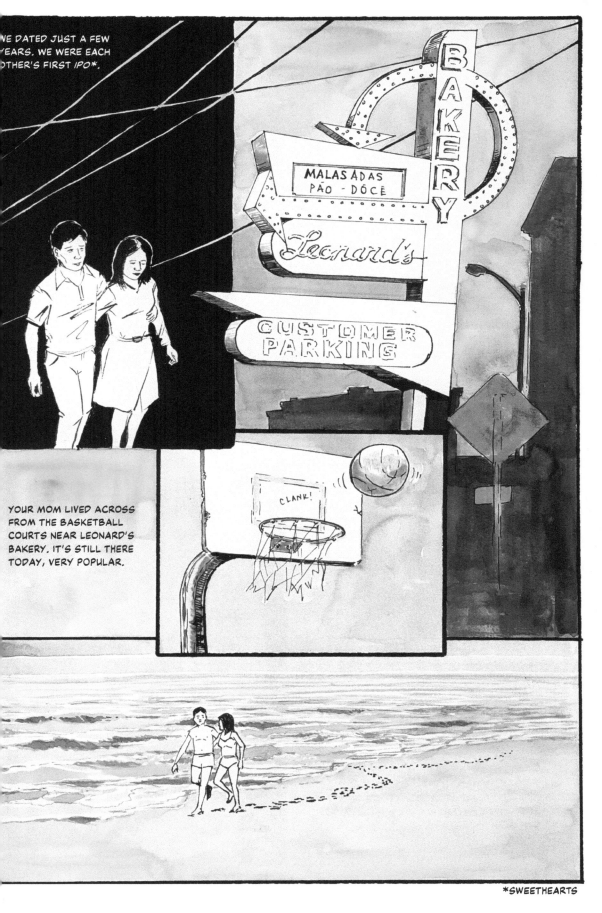

WE DATED JUST A FEW YEARS. WE WERE EACH OTHER'S FIRST *IPO**.

MALASADAS
PÃO - DÔCE

Leonard's

BAKERY

CUSTOMER PARKING

CLANK!

YOUR MOM LIVED ACROSS FROM THE BASKETBALL COURTS NEAR LEONARD'S BAKERY. IT'S STILL THERE TODAY, VERY POPULAR.

*SWEETHEARTS

77

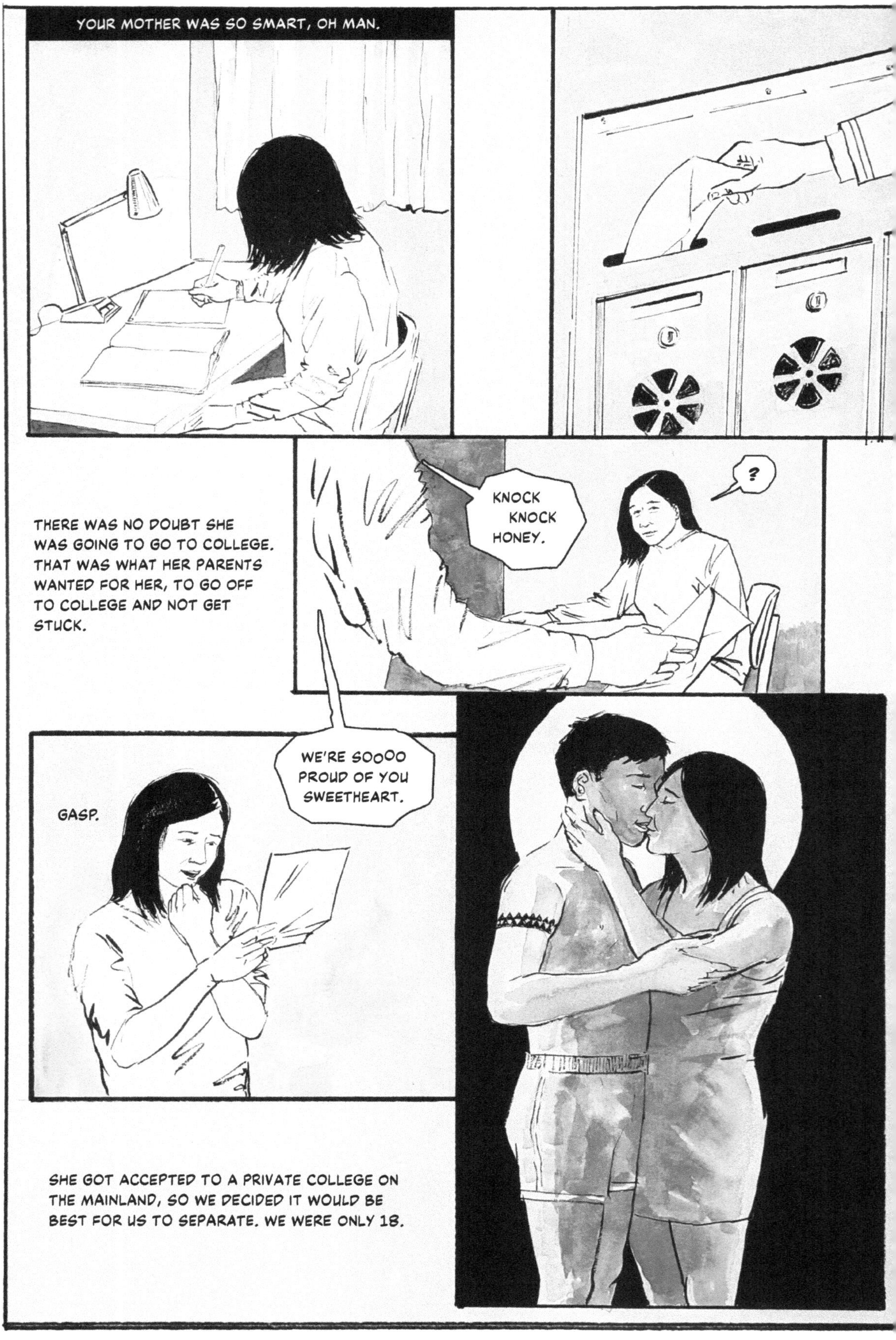
YOUR MOTHER WAS SO SMART, OH MAN.
THERE WAS NO DOUBT SHE WAS GOING TO GO TO COLLEGE. THAT WAS WHAT HER PARENTS WANTED FOR HER, TO GO OFF TO COLLEGE AND NOT GET STUCK.
KNOCK KNOCK HONEY.
?
GASP.
WE'RE SOOOO PROUD OF YOU SWEETHEART.
SHE GOT ACCEPTED TO A PRIVATE COLLEGE ON THE MAINLAND, SO WE DECIDED IT WOULD BE BEST FOR US TO SEPARATE. WE WERE ONLY 18.

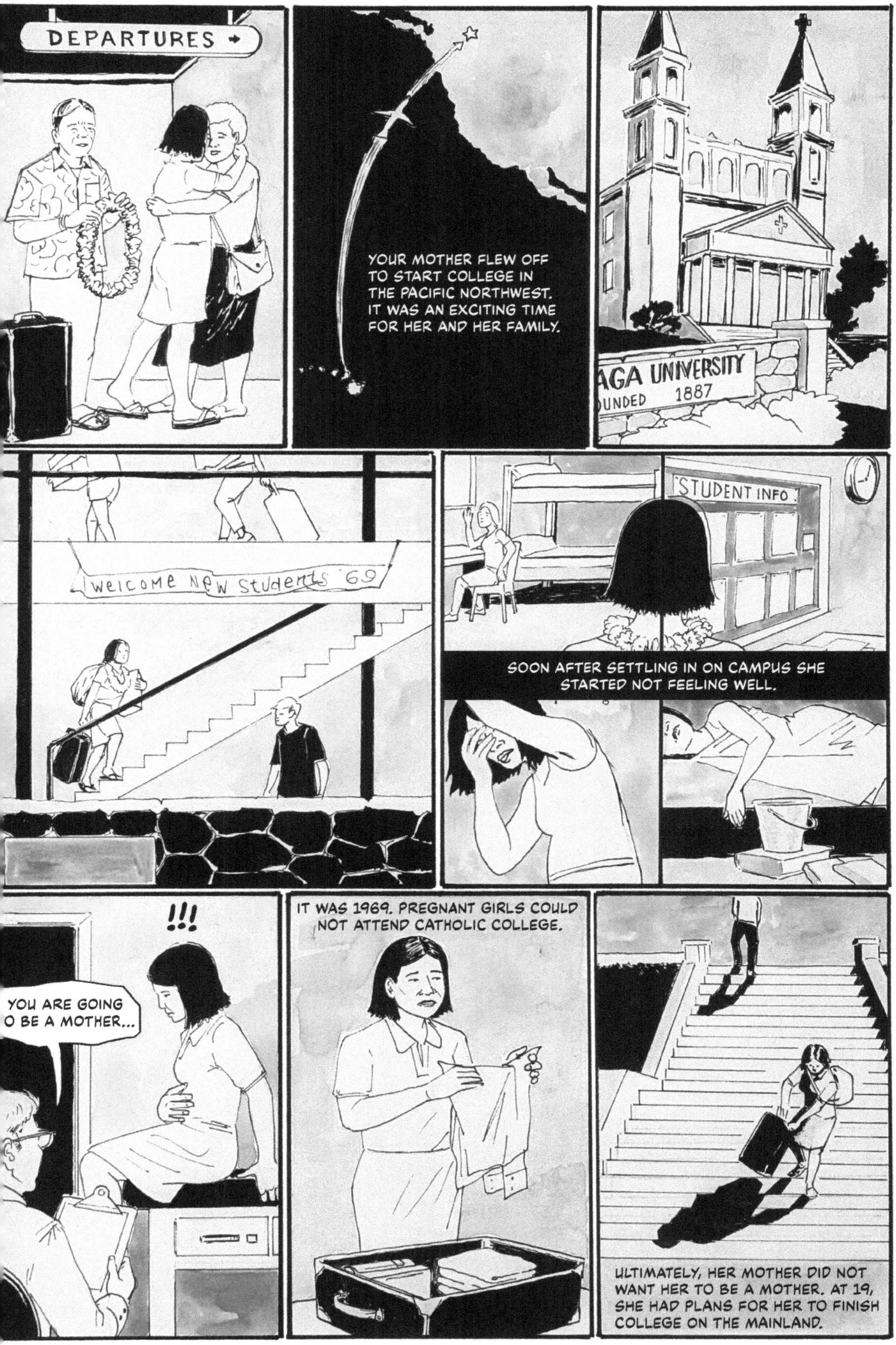
DEPARTURES
YOUR MOTHER FLEW OFF TO START COLLEGE IN THE PACIFIC NORTHWEST. IT WAS AN EXCITING TIME FOR HER AND HER FAMILY.
AGA UNIVERSITY
UNDED 1887
welcome New Students 69
STUDENT INFO
SOON AFTER SETTLING IN ON CAMPUS SHE STARTED NOT FEELING WELL.
!!!
YOU ARE GOING O BE A MOTHER...
IT WAS 1969. PREGNANT GIRLS COULD NOT ATTEND CATHOLIC COLLEGE.
ULTIMATELY, HER MOTHER DID NOT WANT HER TO BE A MOTHER. AT 19, SHE HAD PLANS FOR HER TO FINISH COLLEGE ON THE MAINLAND.

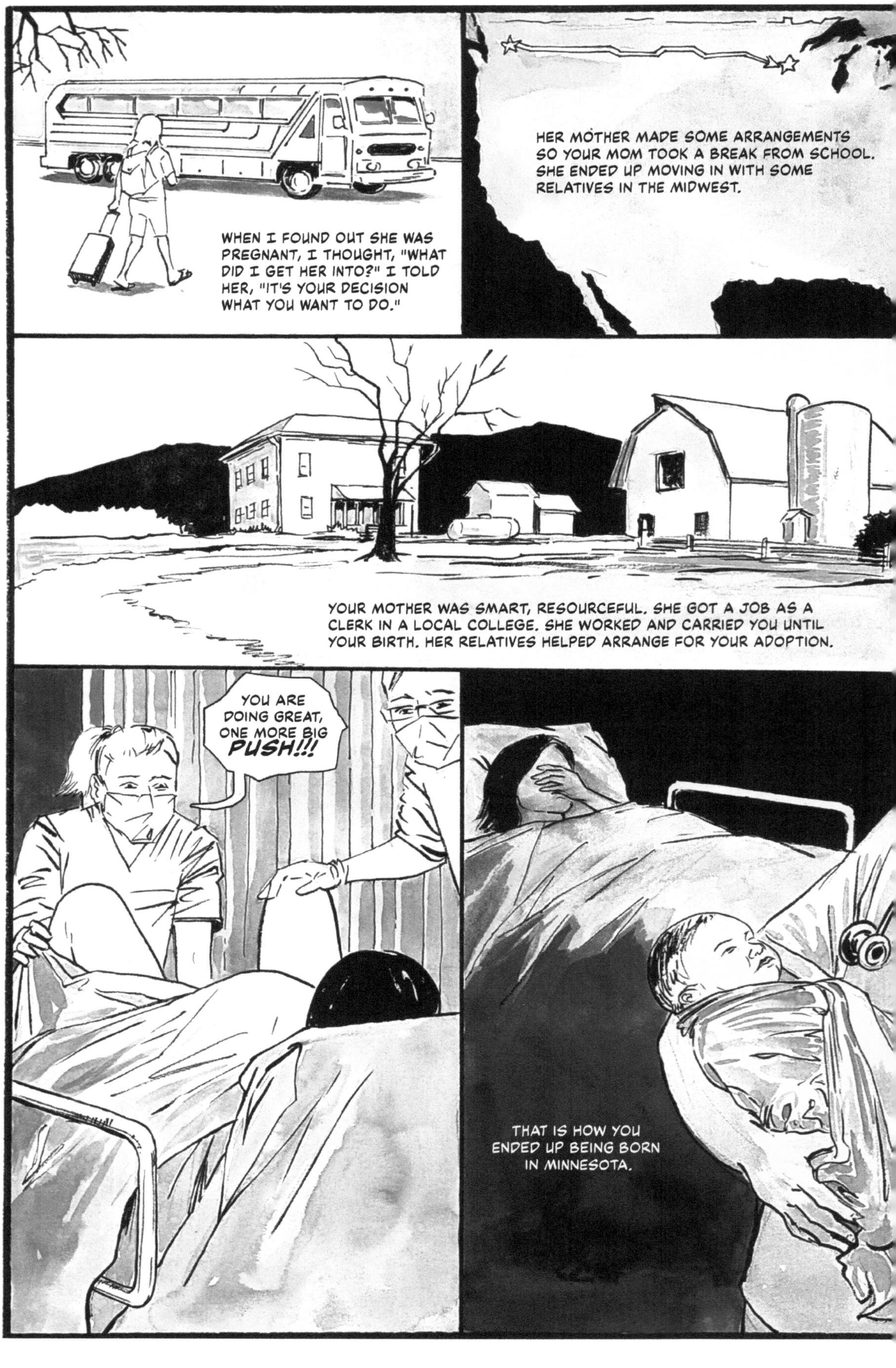
WHEN I FOUND OUT SHE WAS PREGNANT, I THOUGHT, "WHAT DID I GET HER INTO?" I TOLD HER, "IT'S YOUR DECISION WHAT YOU WANT TO DO."
HER MOTHER MADE SOME ARRANGEMENTS SO YOUR MOM TOOK A BREAK FROM SCHOOL. SHE ENDED UP MOVING IN WITH SOME RELATIVES IN THE MIDWEST.
YOUR MOTHER WAS SMART, RESOURCEFUL. SHE GOT A JOB AS A CLERK IN A LOCAL COLLEGE. SHE WORKED AND CARRIED YOU UNTIL YOUR BIRTH. HER RELATIVES HELPED ARRANGE FOR YOUR ADOPTION.
YOU ARE DOING GREAT, ONE MORE BIG PUSH!!!
THAT IS HOW YOU ENDED UP BEING BORN IN MINNESOTA.

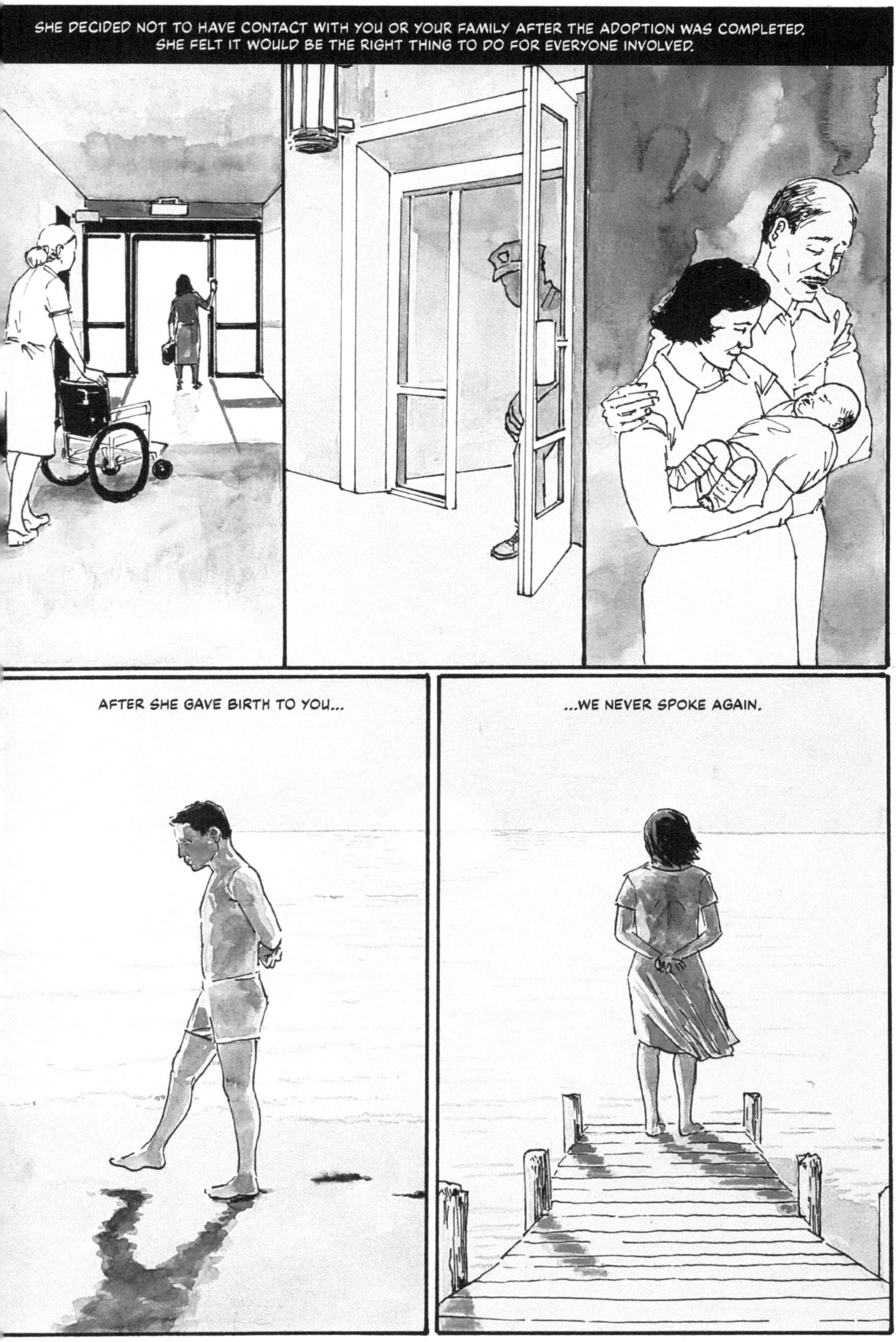
SHE DECIDED NOT TO HAVE CONTACT WITH YOU OR YOUR FAMILY AFTER THE ADOPTION WAS COMPLETED. SHE FELT IT WOULD BE THE RIGHT THING TO DO FOR EVERYONE INVOLVED.
AFTER SHE GAVE BIRTH TO YOU...
...WE NEVER SPOKE AGAIN.

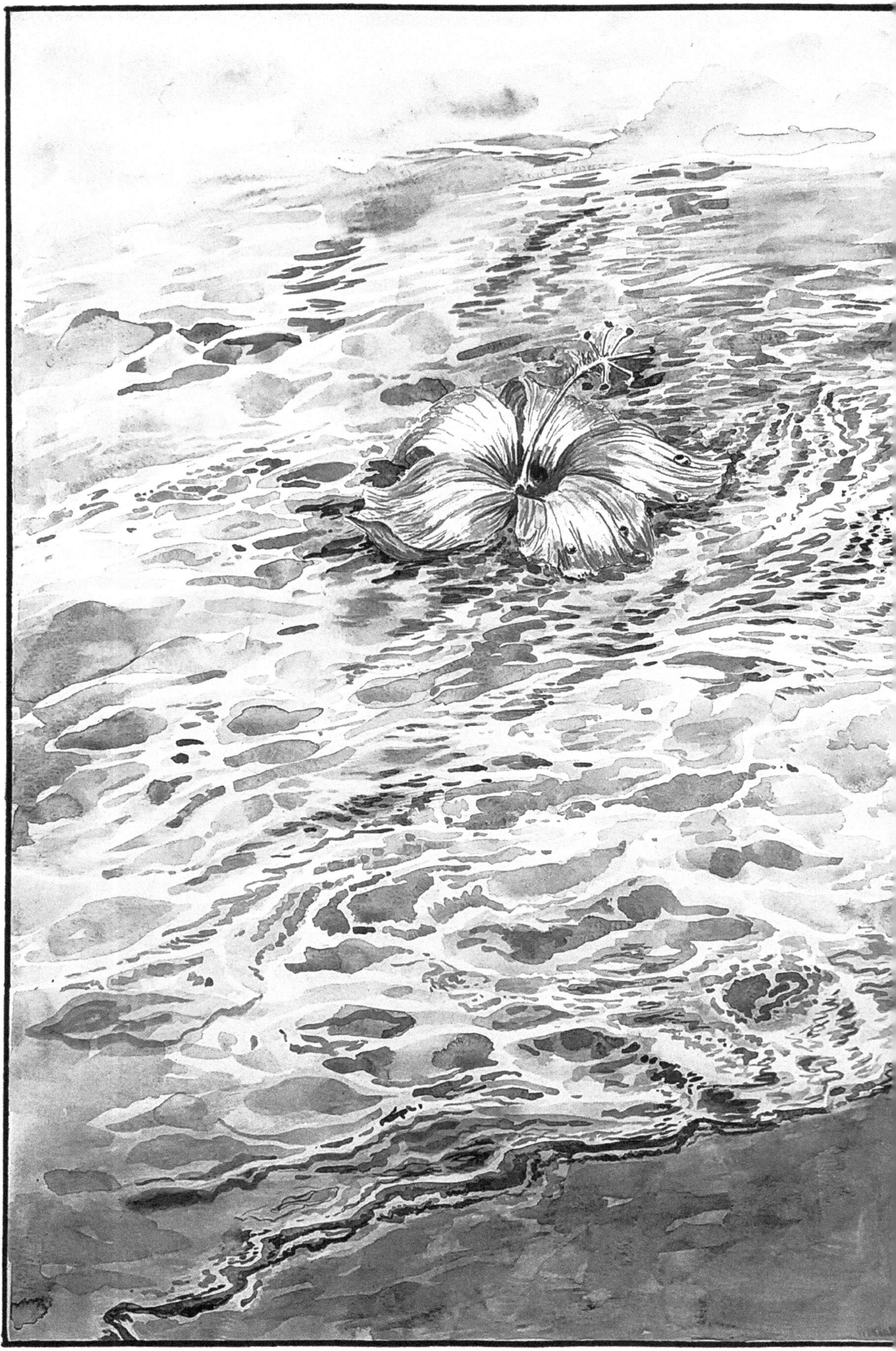

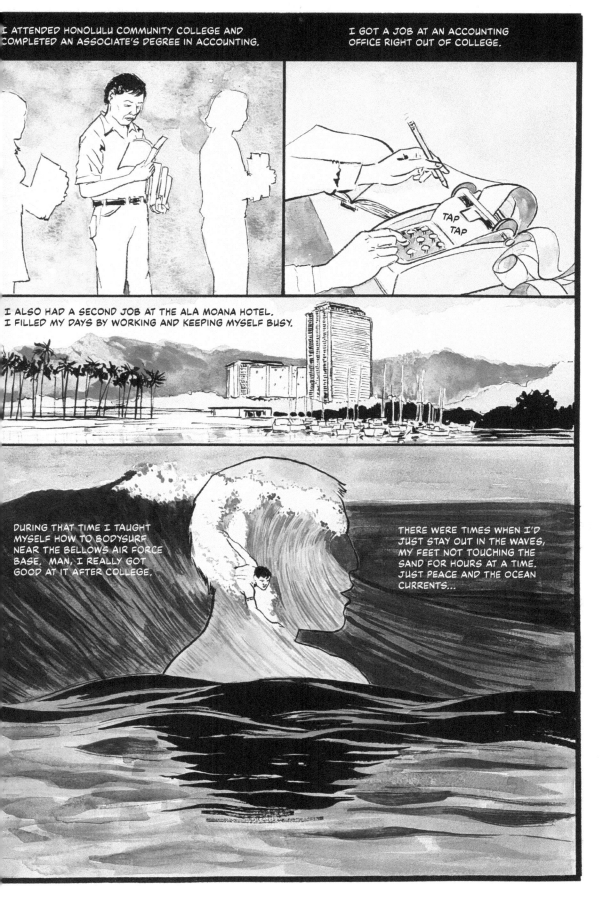

I ATTENDED HONOLULU COMMUNITY COLLEGE AND COMPLETED AN ASSOCIATE'S DEGREE IN ACCOUNTING.

I GOT A JOB AT AN ACCOUNTING OFFICE RIGHT OUT OF COLLEGE.

TAP TAP

I ALSO HAD A SECOND JOB AT THE ALA MOANA HOTEL. I FILLED MY DAYS BY WORKING AND KEEPING MYSELF BUSY.

DURING THAT TIME I TAUGHT MYSELF HOW TO BODYSURF NEAR THE BELLOWS AIR FORCE BASE. MAN, I REALLY GOT GOOD AT IT AFTER COLLEGE.

THERE WERE TIMES WHEN I'D JUST STAY OUT IN THE WAVES, MY FEET NOT TOUCHING THE SAND FOR HOURS AT A TIME. JUST PEACE AND THE OCEAN CURRENTS...

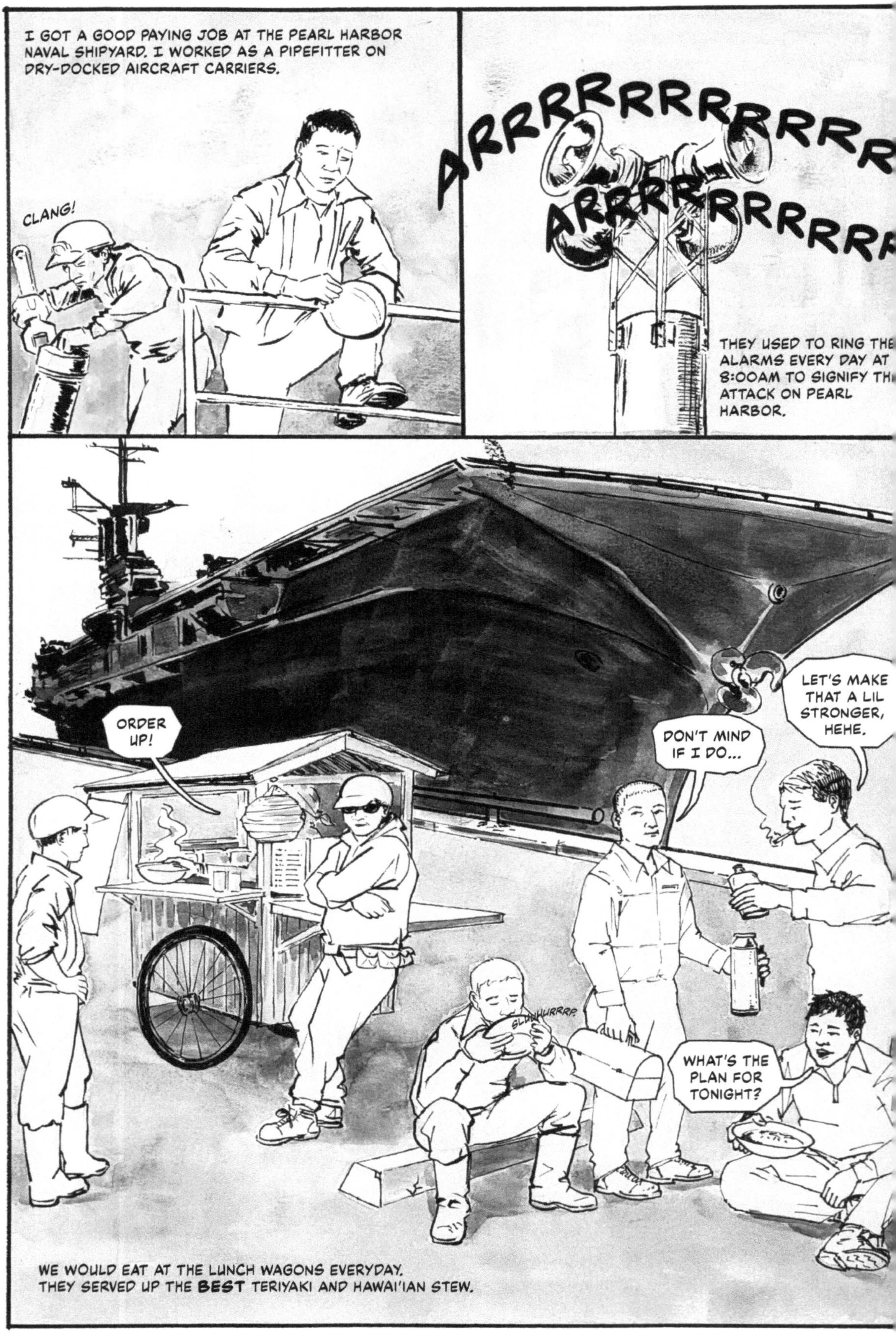
I GOT A GOOD PAYING JOB AT THE PEARL HARBOR NAVAL SHIPYARD. I WORKED AS A PIPEFITTER ON DRY-DOCKED AIRCRAFT CARRIERS.
CLANG!
ARRRRRRRRRRRR
ARRRRRRRRRR
THEY USED TO RING THE ALARMS EVERY DAY AT 8:00AM TO SIGNIFY TH ATTACK ON PEARL HARBOR.
ORDER UP!
DON'T MIND IF I DO...
LET'S MAKE THAT A LIL STRONGER, HEHE.
WHAT'S THE PLAN FOR TONIGHT?
WE WOULD EAT AT THE LUNCH WAGONS EVERYDAY. THEY SERVED UP THE BEST TERIYAKI AND HAWAI'IAN STEW.

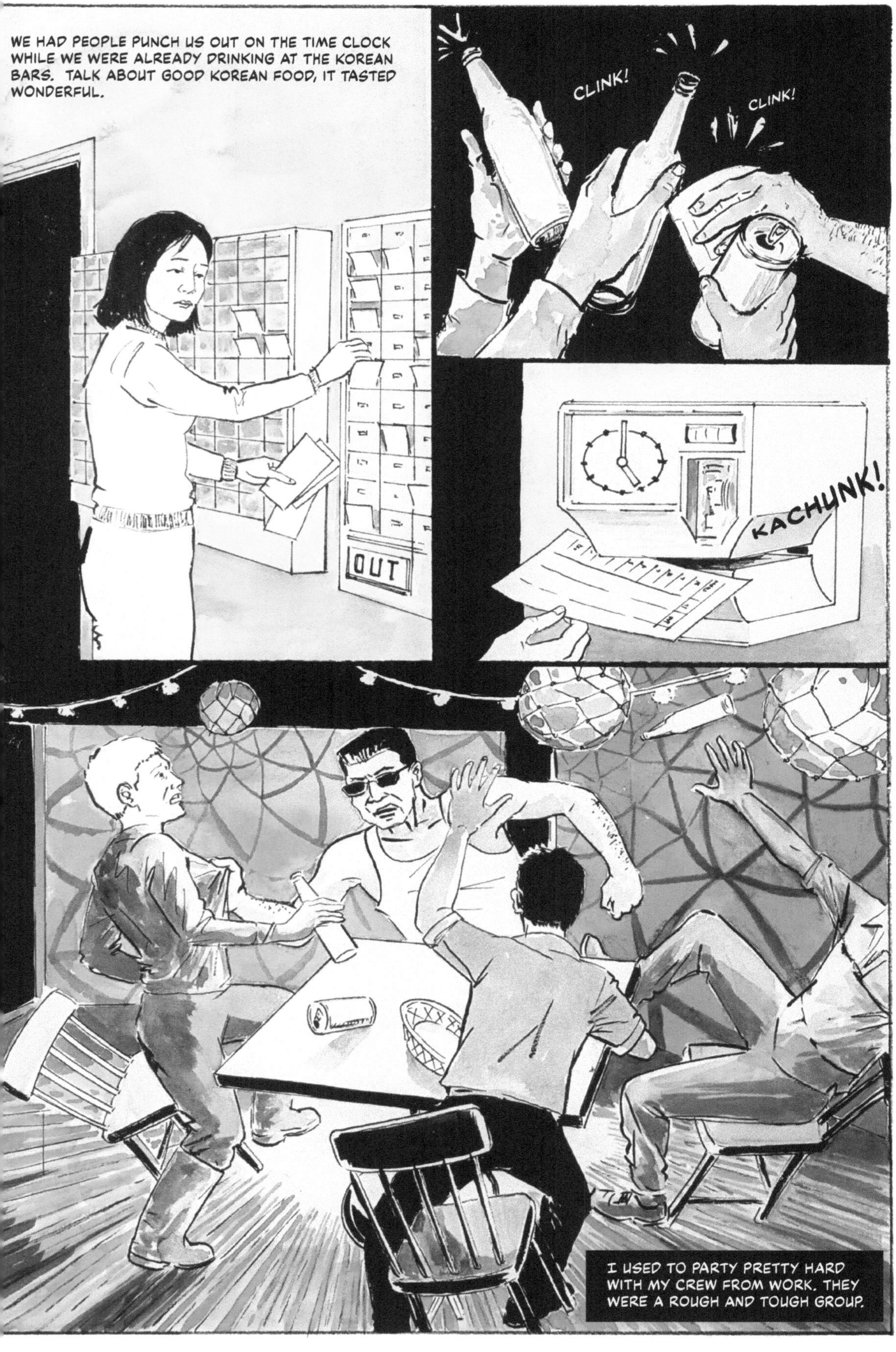
WE HAD PEOPLE PUNCH US OUT ON THE TIME CLOCK WHILE WE WERE ALREADY DRINKING AT THE KOREAN BARS. TALK ABOUT GOOD KOREAN FOOD, IT TASTED WONDERFUL.
OUT
CLINK!
CLINK!
KACHUNK!
I USED TO PARTY PRETTY HARD WITH MY CREW FROM WORK. THEY WERE A ROUGH AND TOUGH GROUP.

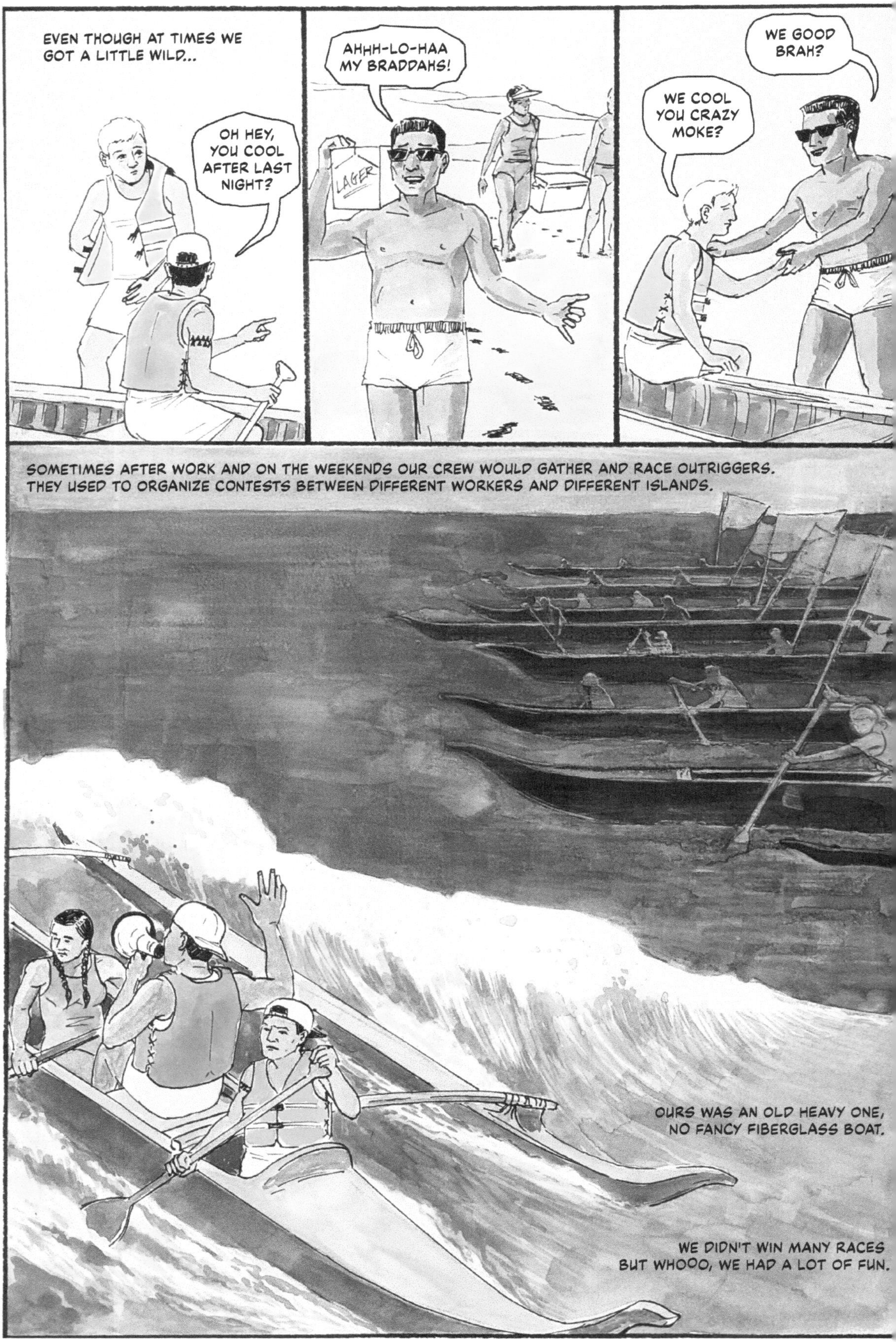
EVEN THOUGH AT TIMES WE GOT A LITTLE WILD...
OH HEY, YOU COOL AFTER LAST NIGHT?
AHHH-LO-HAA MY BRADDAHS!
LAGER
WE GOOD BRAH?
WE COOL YOU CRAZY MOKE?
SOMETIMES AFTER WORK AND ON THE WEEKENDS OUR CREW WOULD GATHER AND RACE OUTRIGGERS. THEY USED TO ORGANIZE CONTESTS BETWEEN DIFFERENT WORKERS AND DIFFERENT ISLANDS.
OURS WAS AN OLD HEAVY ONE, NO FANCY FIBERGLASS BOAT.
WE DIDN'T WIN MANY RACES BUT WHOOO, WE HAD A LOT OF FUN.

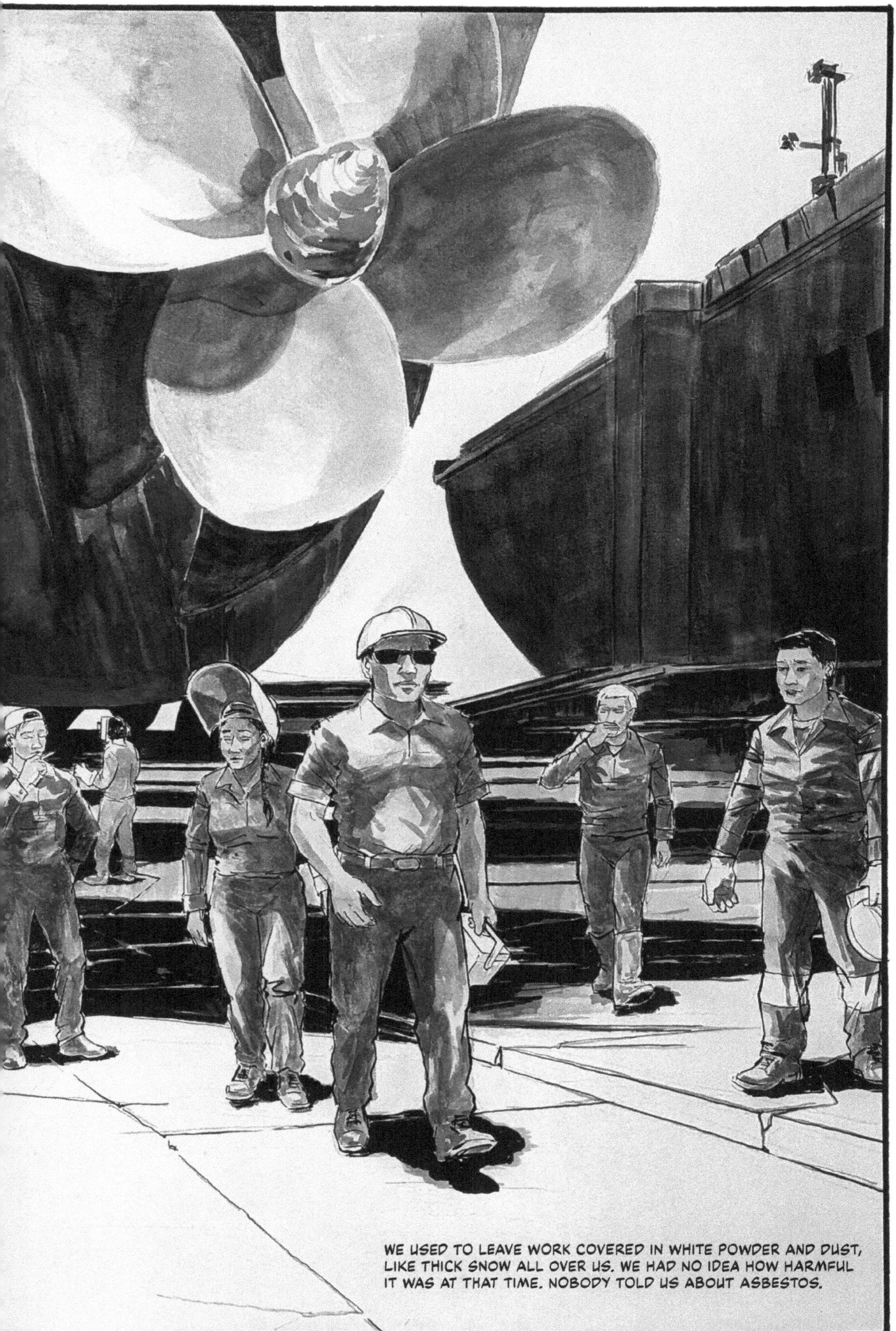
WE USED TO LEAVE WORK COVERED IN WHITE POWDER AND DUST, LIKE THICK SNOW ALL OVER US. WE HAD NO IDEA HOW HARMFUL IT WAS AT THAT TIME. NOBODY TOLD US ABOUT ASBESTOS.

PEOPLE IN OUR CREW STARTED GETTING REALLY SICK.

OKAY NOW, SLOWLY EXHALE.

KAF KAF

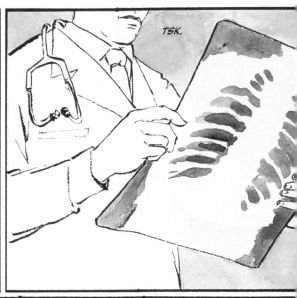

TSK.

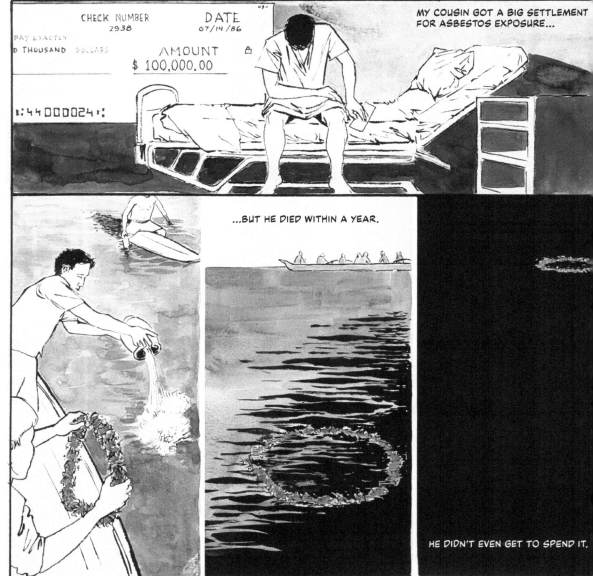

CHECK NUMBER 2938

DATE 07/14/86

PAY EXACTLY D THOUSAND DOLLARS

AMOUNT $ 100,000.00

1:44000024:

MY COUSIN GOT A BIG SETTLEMENT FOR ASBESTOS EXPOSURE...

...BUT HE DIED WITHIN A YEAR.

HE DIDN'T EVEN GET TO SPEND IT.

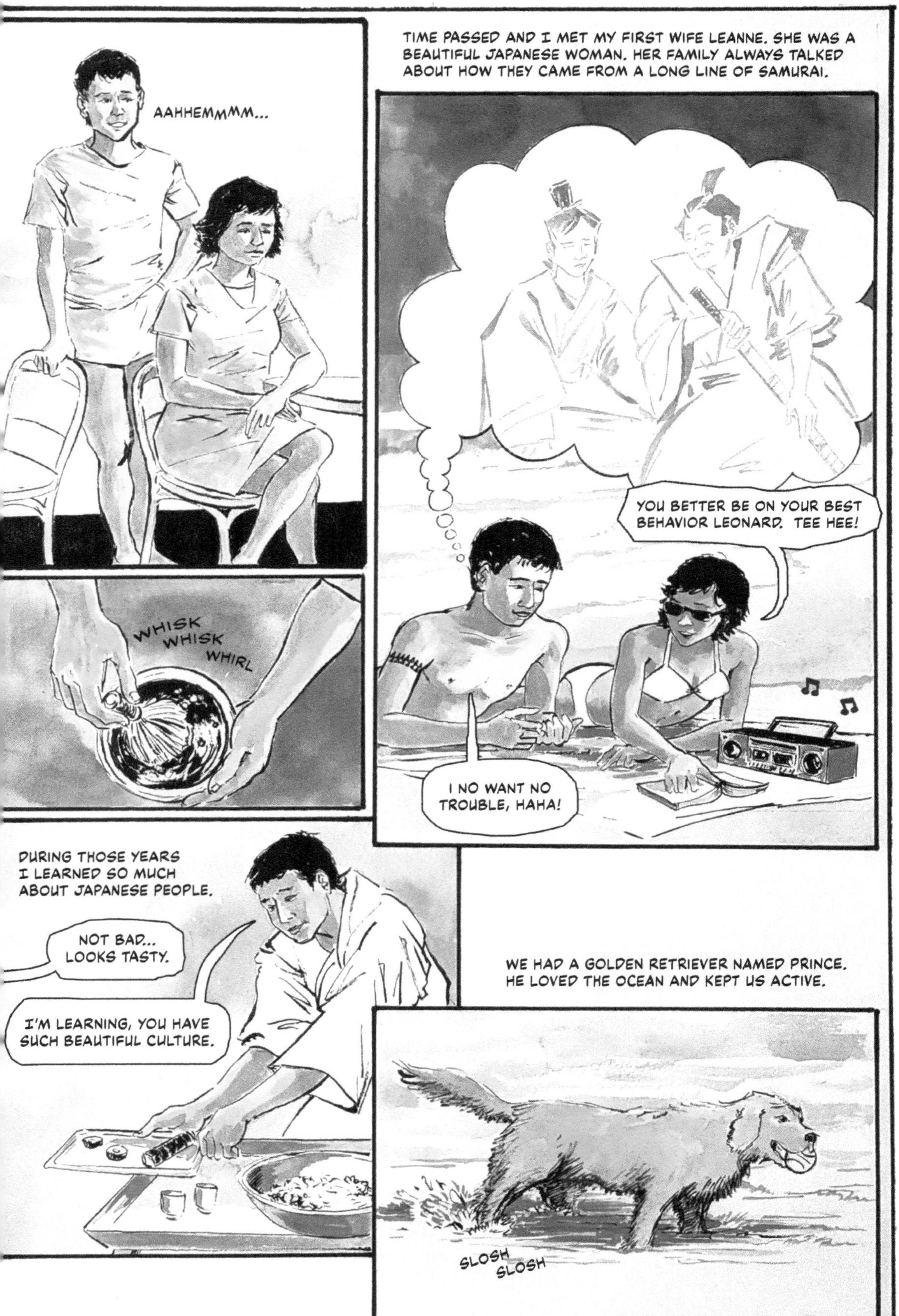
AAHHEMMMM...
TIME PASSED AND I MET MY FIRST WIFE LEANNE. SHE WAS A BEAUTIFUL JAPANESE WOMAN. HER FAMILY ALWAYS TALKED ABOUT HOW THEY CAME FROM A LONG LINE OF SAMURAI.
YOU BETTER BE ON YOUR BEST BEHAVIOR LEONARD. TEE HEE!
I NO WANT NO TROUBLE, HAHA!
WHISK WHISK WHIRL
DURING THOSE YEARS I LEARNED SO MUCH ABOUT JAPANESE PEOPLE.
NOT BAD... LOOKS TASTY.
I'M LEARNING, YOU HAVE SUCH BEAUTIFUL CULTURE.
WE HAD A GOLDEN RETRIEVER NAMED PRINCE. HE LOVED THE OCEAN AND KEPT US ACTIVE.
SLOSH SLOSH

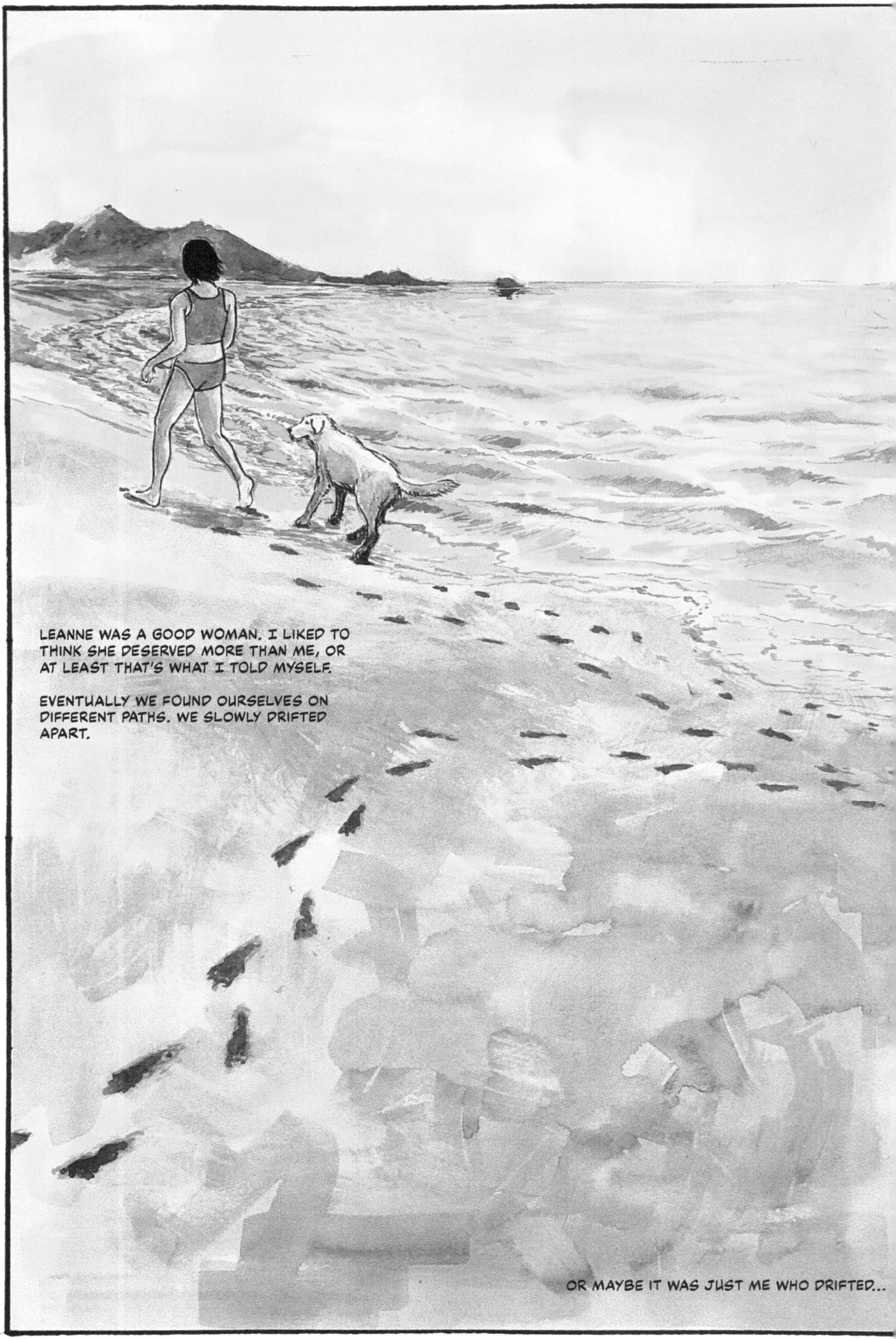
LEANNE WAS A GOOD WOMAN. I LIKED TO THINK SHE DESERVED MORE THAN ME, OR AT LEAST THAT'S WHAT I TOLD MYSELF.
EVENTUALLY WE FOUND OURSELVES ON DIFFERENT PATHS. WE SLOWLY DRIFTED APART.
OR MAYBE IT WAS JUST ME WHO DRIFTED...

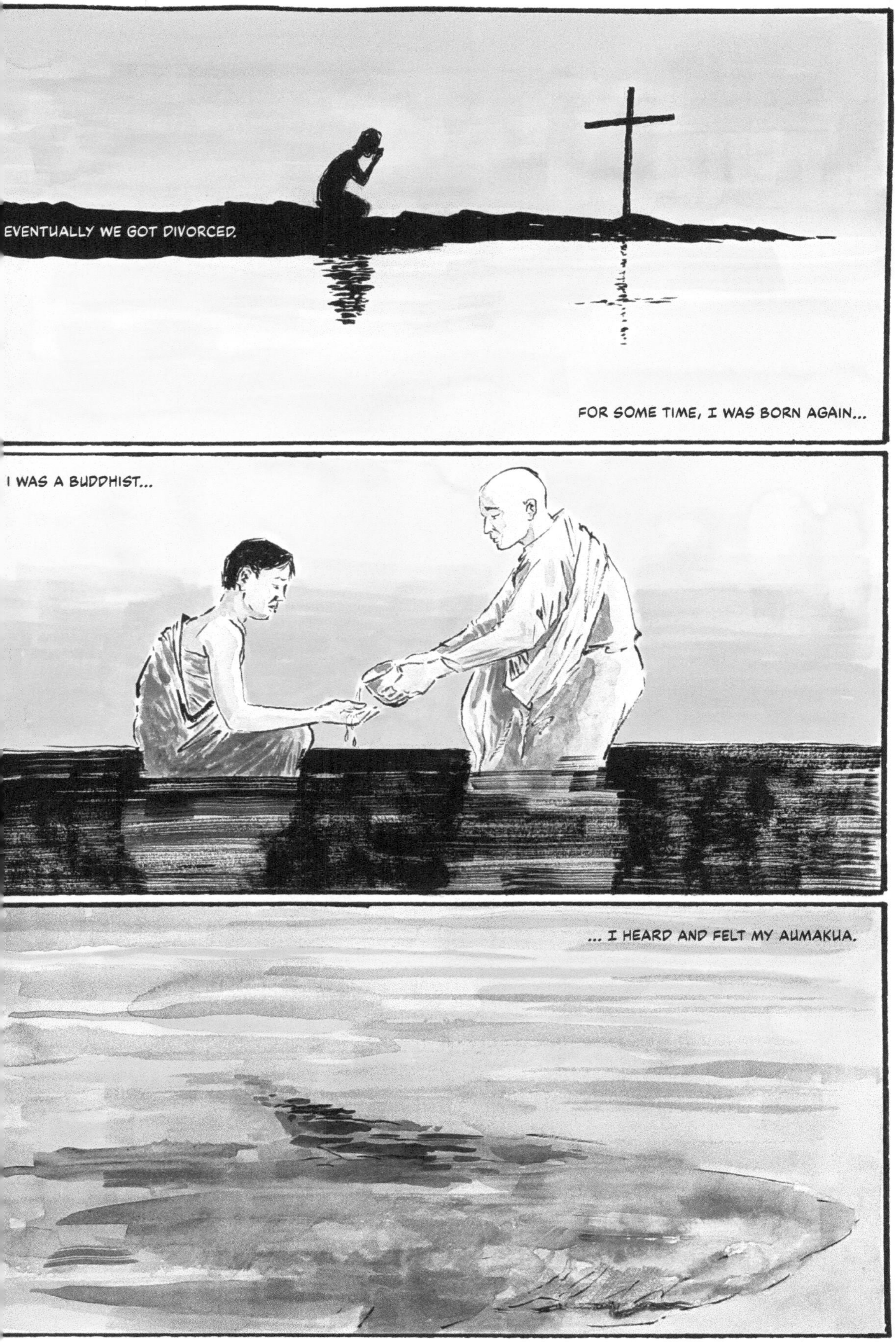
EVENTUALLY WE GOT DIVORCED.
FOR SOME TIME, I WAS BORN AGAIN...
I WAS A BUDDHIST...
... I HEARD AND FELT MY AUMAKUA.

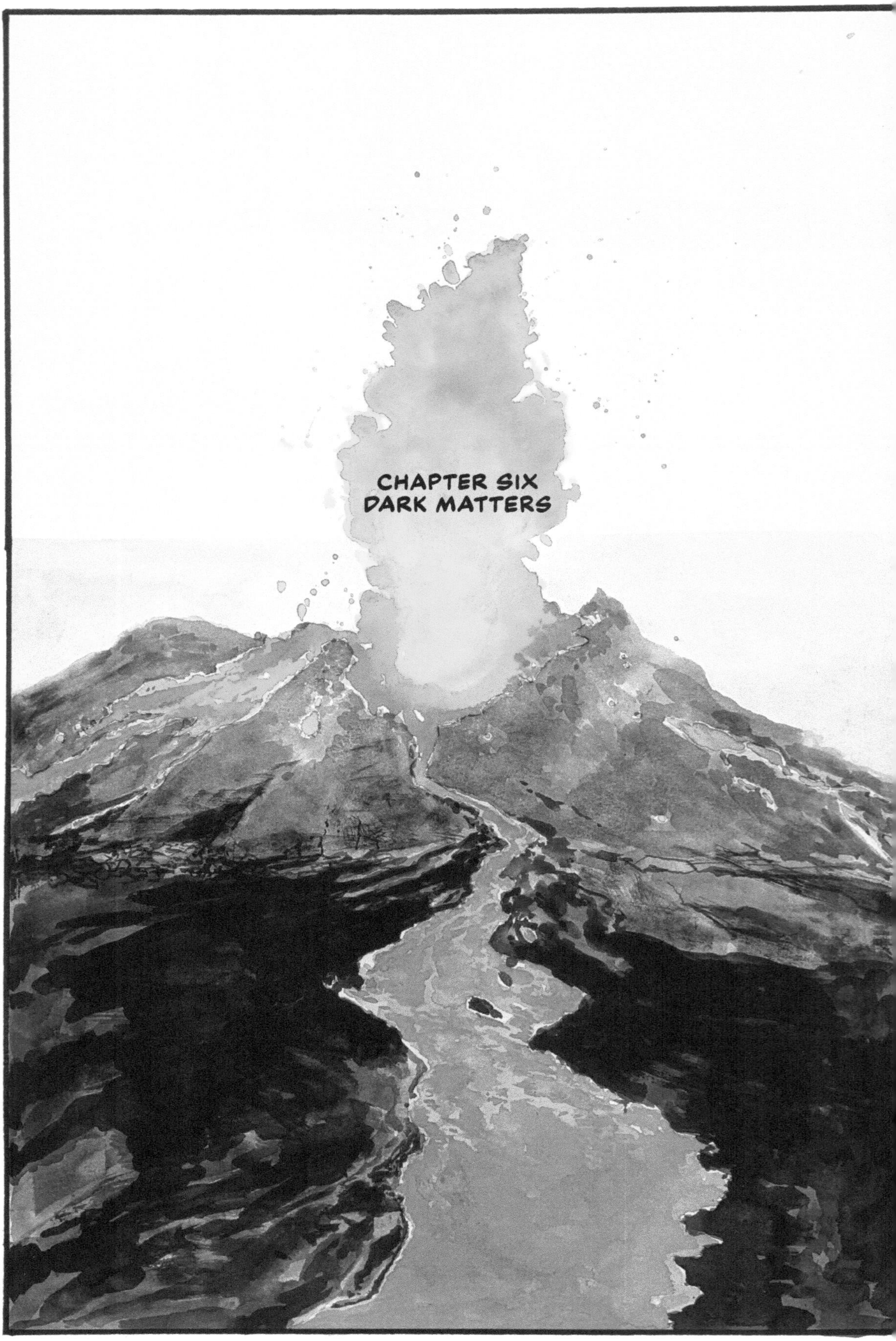
CHAPTER SIX
DARK MATTERS

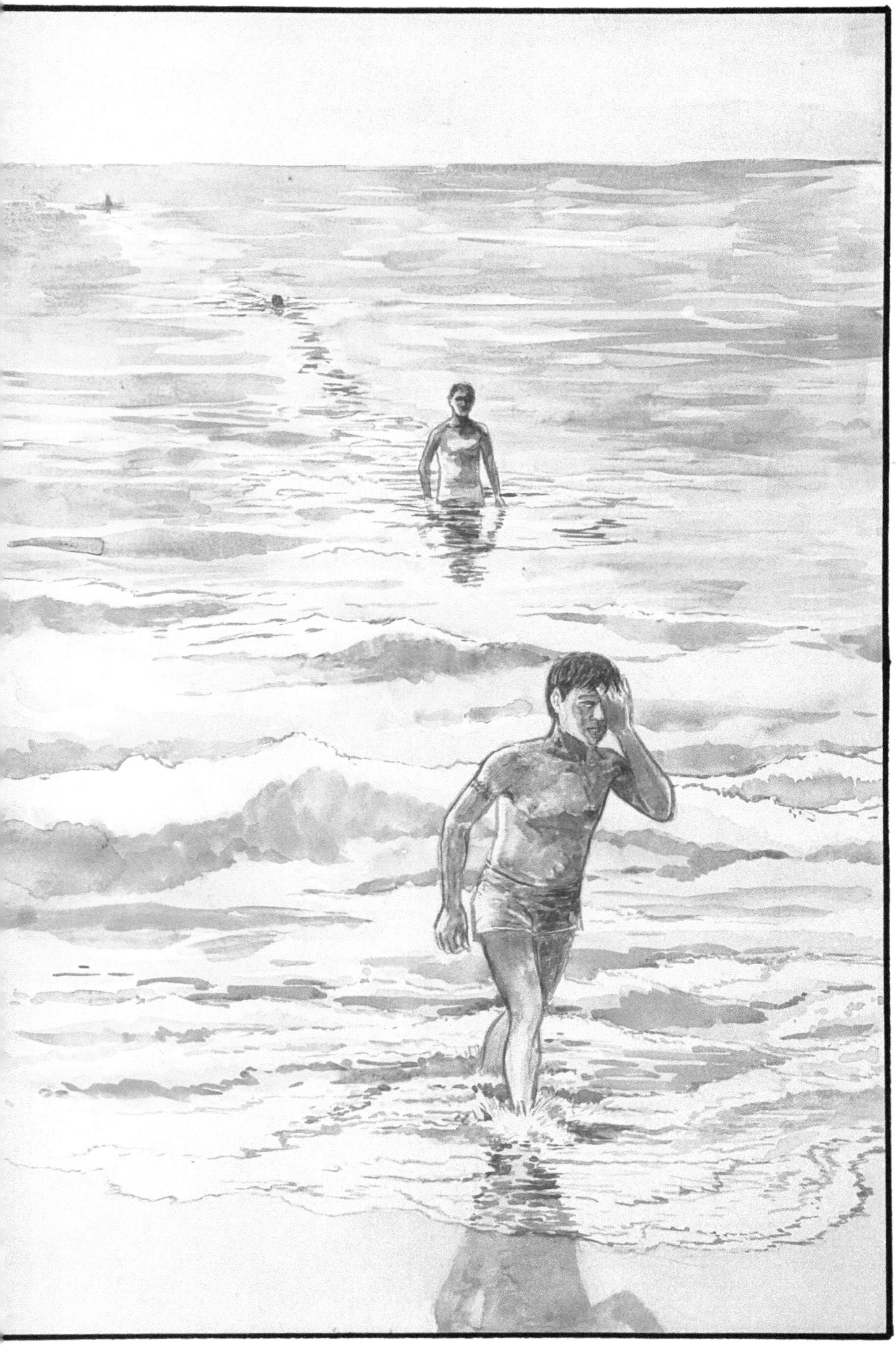

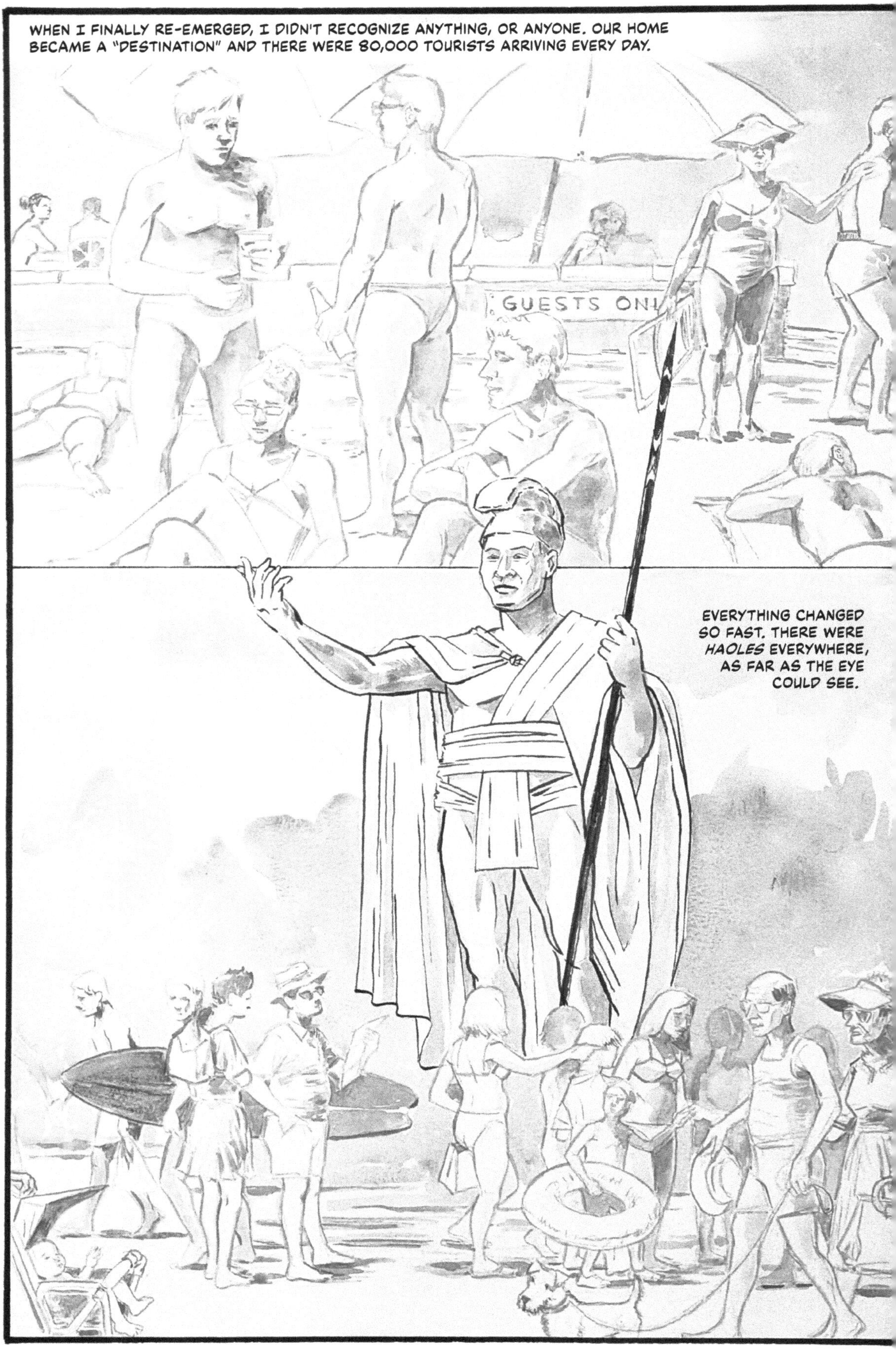
WHEN I FINALLY RE-EMERGED, I DIDN'T RECOGNIZE ANYTHING, OR ANYONE. OUR HOME BECAME A "DESTINATION" AND THERE WERE 80,000 TOURISTS ARRIVING EVERY DAY.
GUESTS ONL
EVERYTHING CHANGED SO FAST. THERE WERE *HAOLES* EVERYWHERE, AS FAR AS THE EYE COULD SEE.

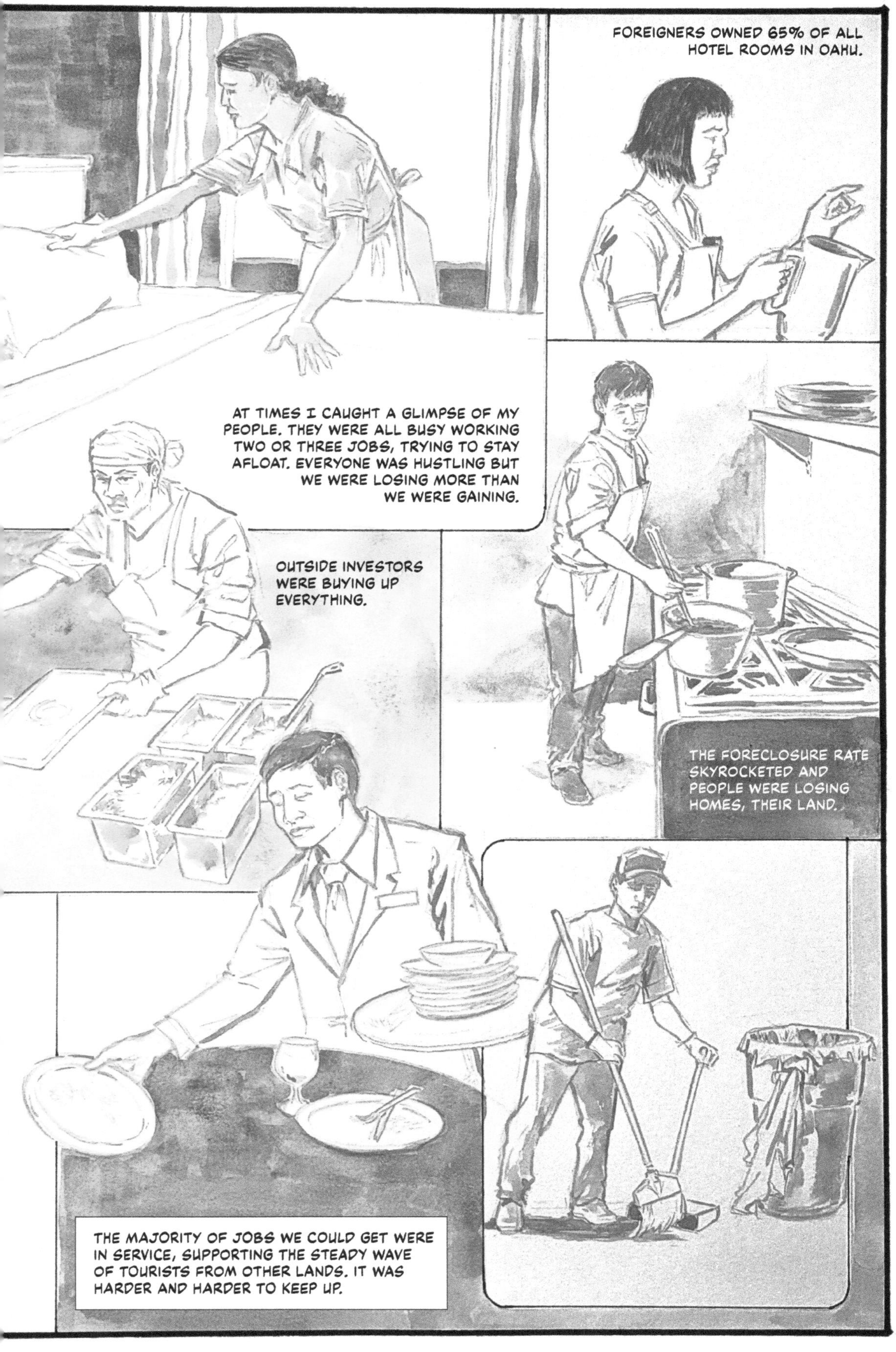
FOREIGNERS OWNED 65% OF ALL HOTEL ROOMS IN OAHU.
AT TIMES I CAUGHT A GLIMPSE OF MY PEOPLE. THEY WERE ALL BUSY WORKING TWO OR THREE JOBS, TRYING TO STAY AFLOAT. EVERYONE WAS HUSTLING BUT WE WERE LOSING MORE THAN WE WERE GAINING.
OUTSIDE INVESTORS WERE BUYING UP EVERYTHING.
THE FORECLOSURE RATE SKYROCKETED AND PEOPLE WERE LOSING HOMES, THEIR LAND.
THE MAJORITY OF JOBS WE COULD GET WERE IN SERVICE, SUPPORTING THE STEADY WAVE OF TOURISTS FROM OTHER LANDS. IT WAS HARDER AND HARDER TO KEEP UP.

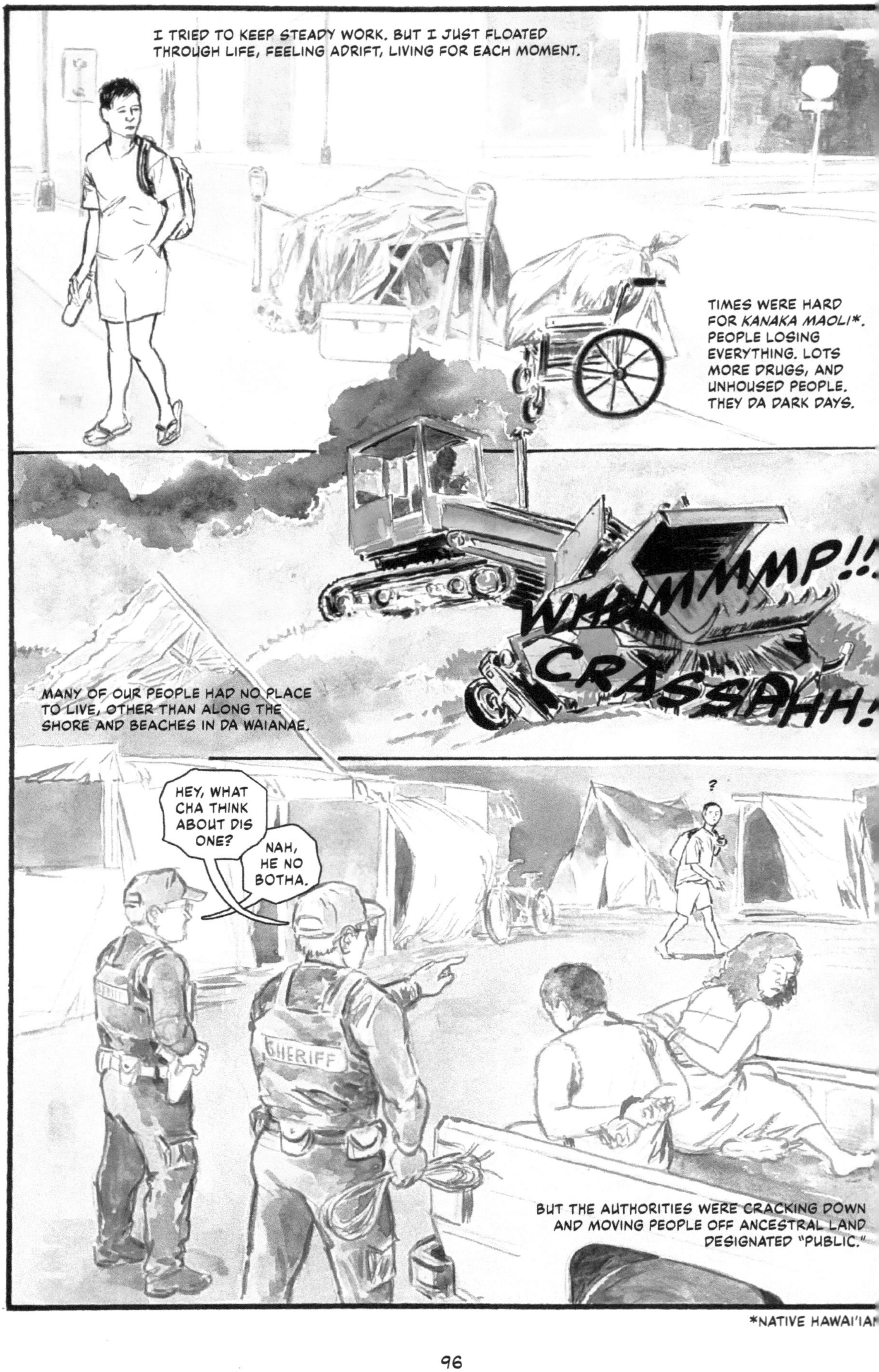
I TRIED TO KEEP STEADY WORK. BUT I JUST FLOATED THROUGH LIFE, FEELING ADRIFT, LIVING FOR EACH MOMENT.
TIMES WERE HARD FOR *KANAKA MAOLI**. PEOPLE LOSING EVERYTHING. LOTS MORE DRUGS, AND UNHOUSED PEOPLE. THEY DA DARK DAYS.
MANY OF OUR PEOPLE HAD NO PLACE TO LIVE, OTHER THAN ALONG THE SHORE AND BEACHES IN DA WAIANAE.
WHAMMMMP!!
CRASSHHH!
HEY, WHAT CHA THINK ABOUT DIS ONE?
NAH, HE NO BOTHA.
?
SHERIFF
BUT THE AUTHORITIES WERE CRACKING DOWN AND MOVING PEOPLE OFF ANCESTRAL LAND DESIGNATED "PUBLIC."

*NATIVE HAWAI'IAN

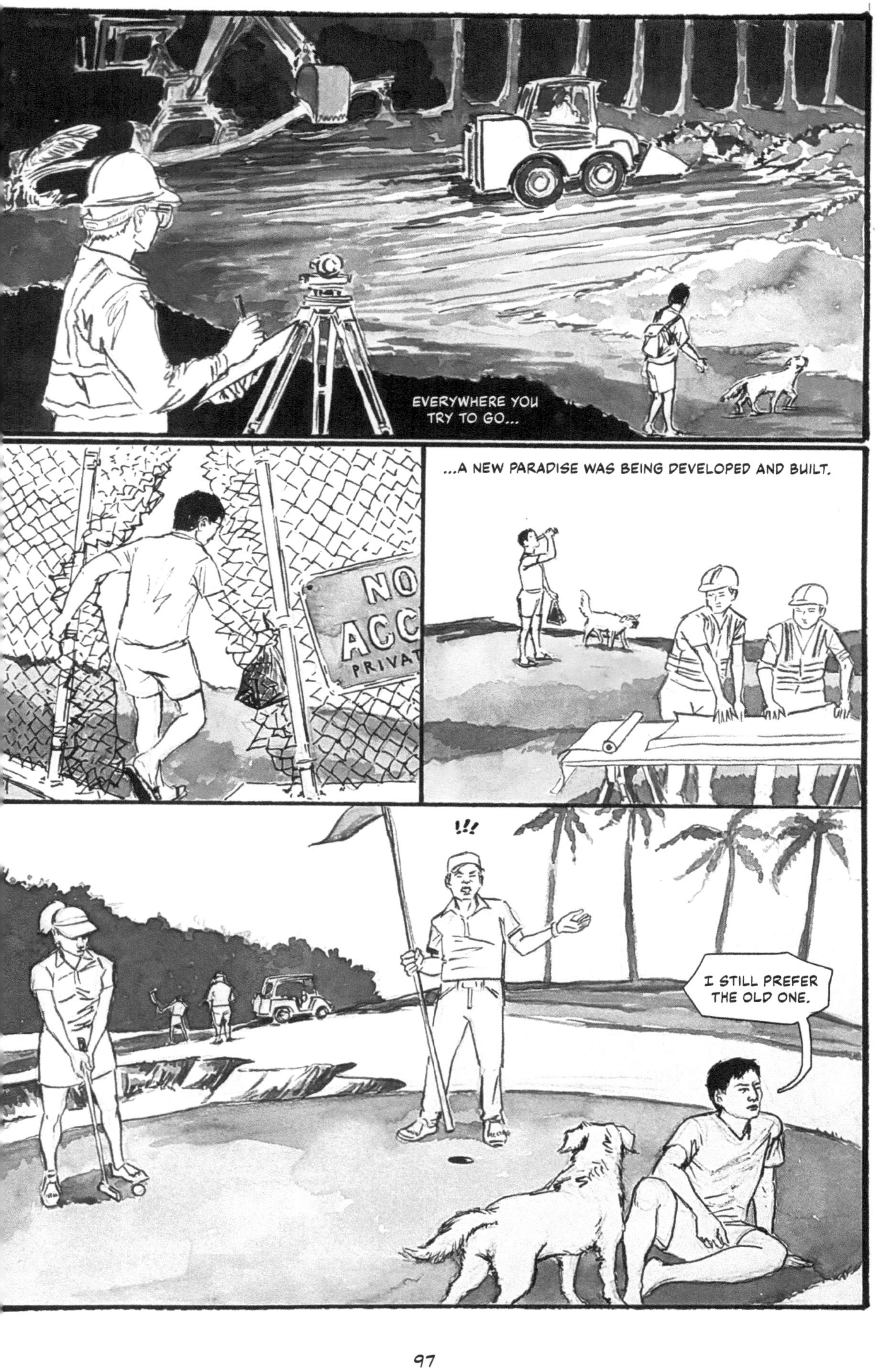
EVERYWHERE YOU TRY TO GO...
NO
ACC
PRIVAT
...A NEW PARADISE WAS BEING DEVELOPED AND BUILT.
!!!
I STILL PREFER THE OLD ONE.

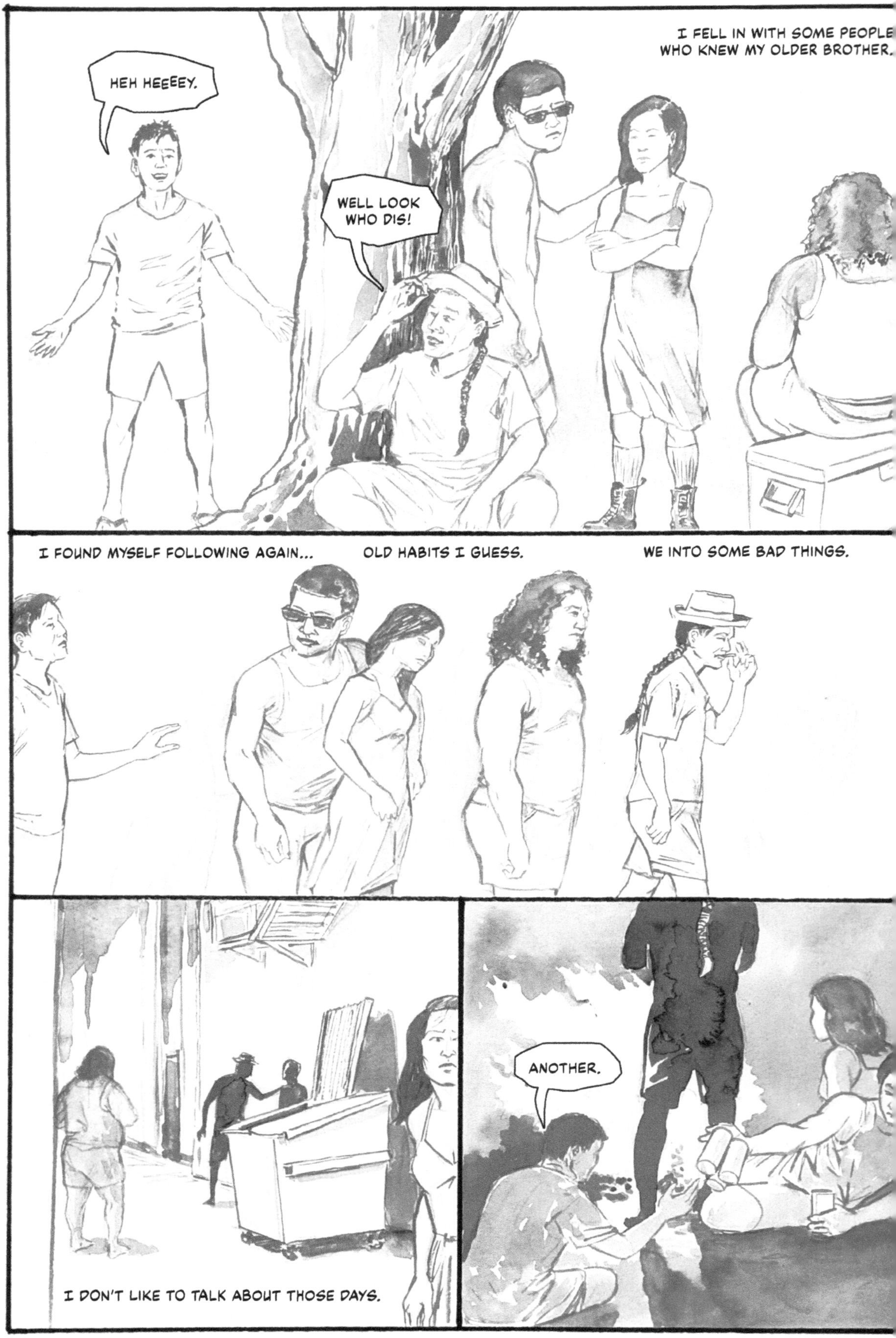

I FELL IN WITH SOME PEOPLE WHO KNEW MY OLDER BROTHER.
HEH HEEEEY.
WELL LOOK WHO DIS!
I FOUND MYSELF FOLLOWING AGAIN...
OLD HABITS I GUESS.
WE INTO SOME BAD THINGS.
I DON'T LIKE TO TALK ABOUT THOSE DAYS.
ANOTHER.

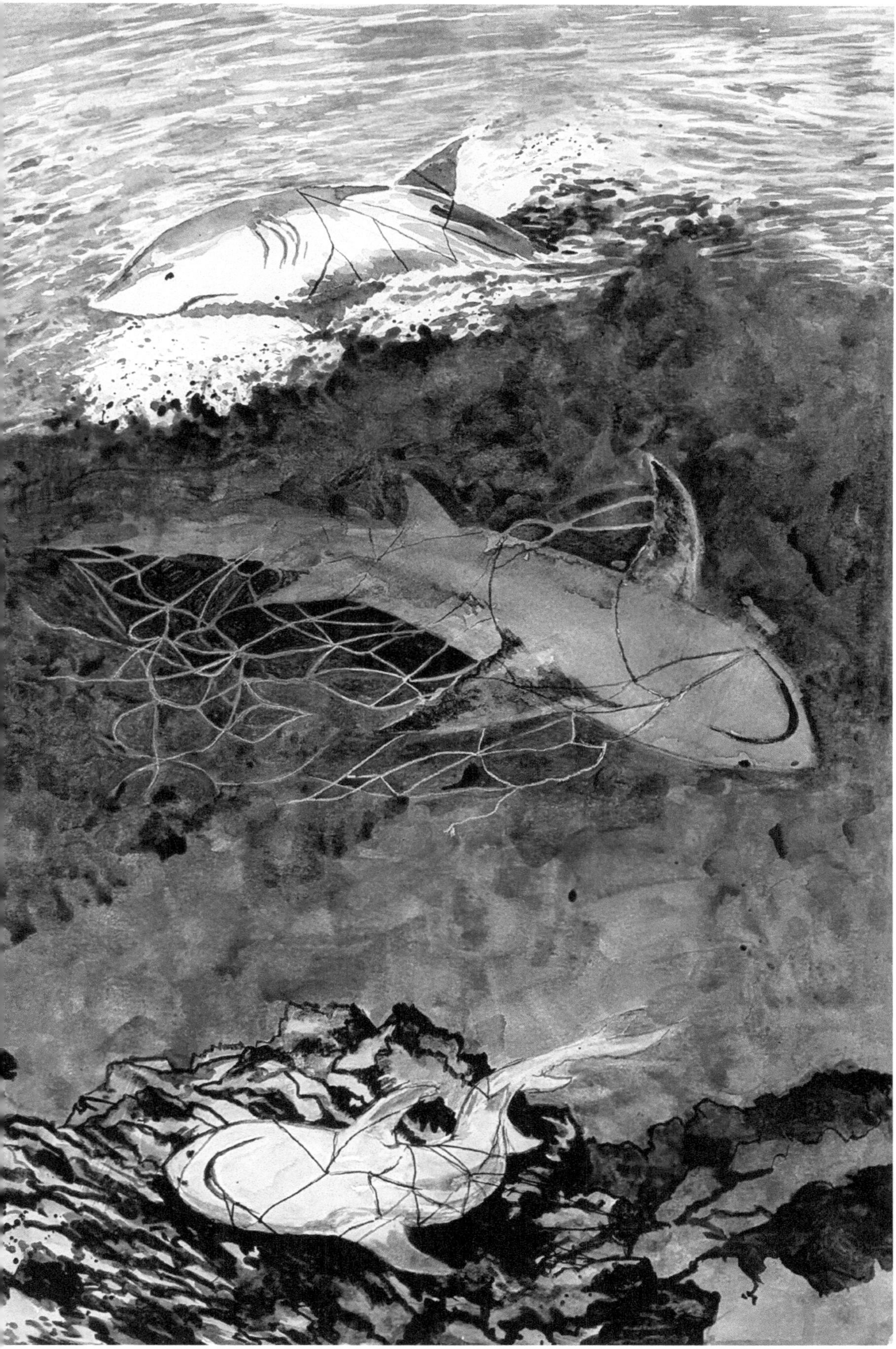

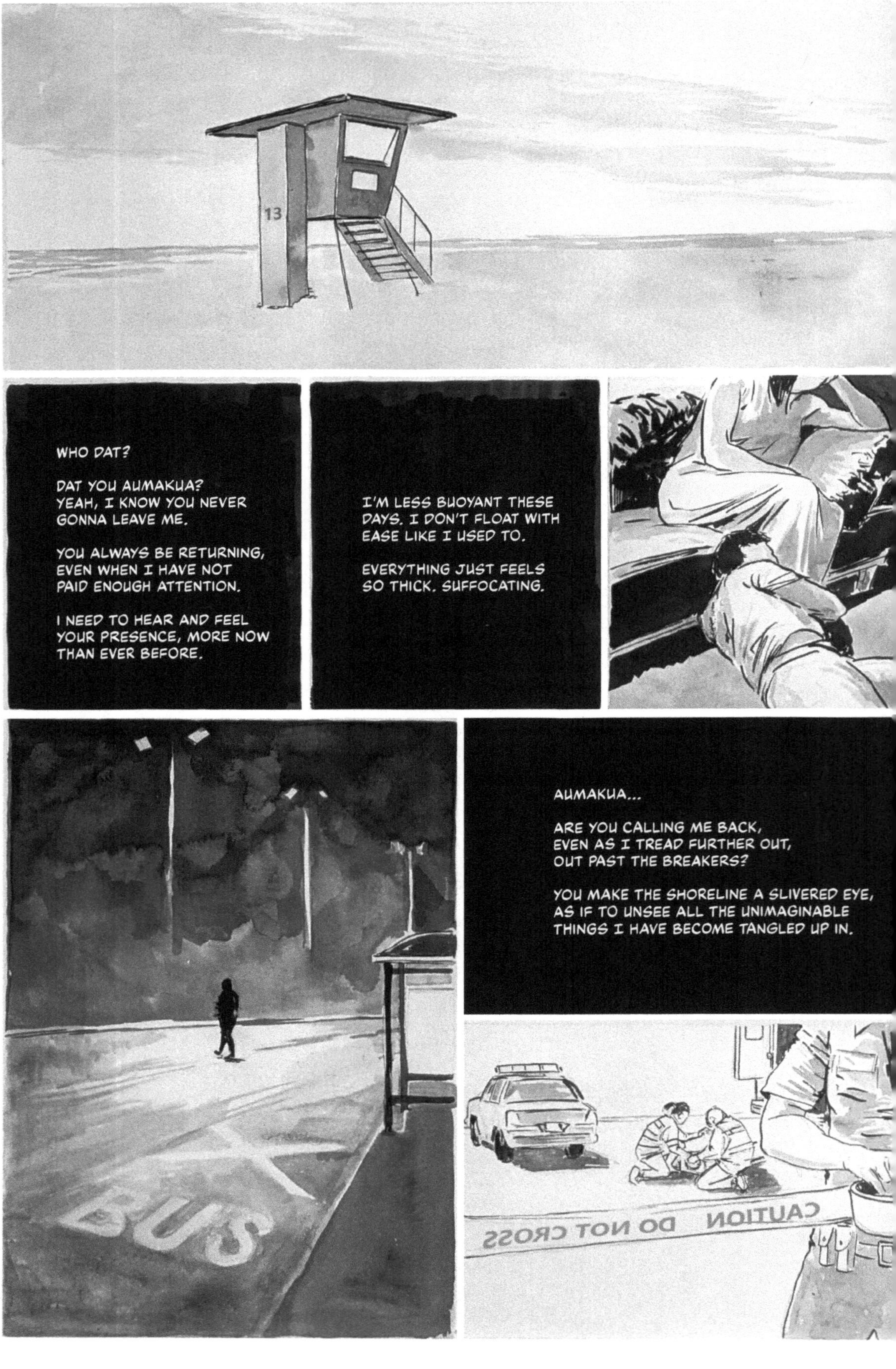
13
WHO DAT?
DAT YOU AUMAKUA? YEAH, I KNOW YOU NEVER GONNA LEAVE ME.
YOU ALWAYS BE RETURNING, EVEN WHEN I HAVE NOT PAID ENOUGH ATTENTION.
I NEED TO HEAR AND FEEL YOUR PRESENCE, MORE NOW THAN EVER BEFORE.
I'M LESS BUOYANT THESE DAYS. I DON'T FLOAT WITH EASE LIKE I USED TO.
EVERYTHING JUST FEELS SO THICK. SUFFOCATING.
BUS
AUMAKUA...
ARE YOU CALLING ME BACK, EVEN AS I TREAD FURTHER OUT, OUT PAST THE BREAKERS?
YOU MAKE THE SHORELINE A SLIVERED EYE, AS IF TO UNSEE ALL THE UNIMAGINABLE THINGS I HAVE BECOME TANGLED UP IN.
CAUTION DO NOT CROSS

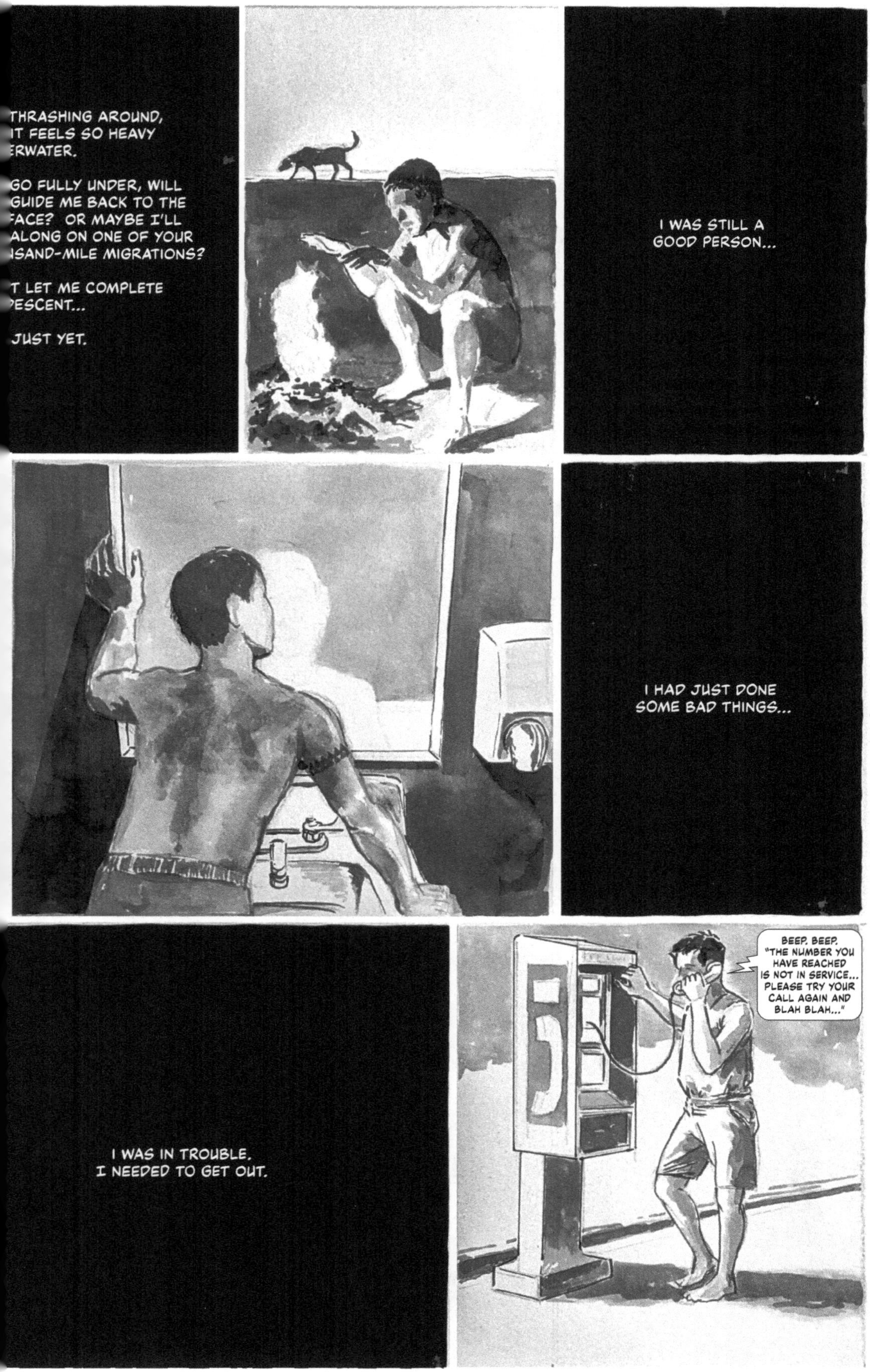

THRASHING AROUND,
IT FEELS SO HEAVY
ERWATER.
GO FULLY UNDER, WILL
GUIDE ME BACK TO THE
FACE? OR MAYBE I'LL
ALONG ON ONE OF YOUR
USAND-MILE MIGRATIONS?
T LET ME COMPLETE
ESCENT...
JUST YET.
I WAS STILL A GOOD PERSON...
I HAD JUST DONE SOME BAD THINGS...
I WAS IN TROUBLE. I NEEDED TO GET OUT.
BEEP. BEEP. "THE NUMBER YOU HAVE REACHED IS NOT IN SERVICE... PLEASE TRY YOUR CALL AGAIN AND BLAH BLAH..."

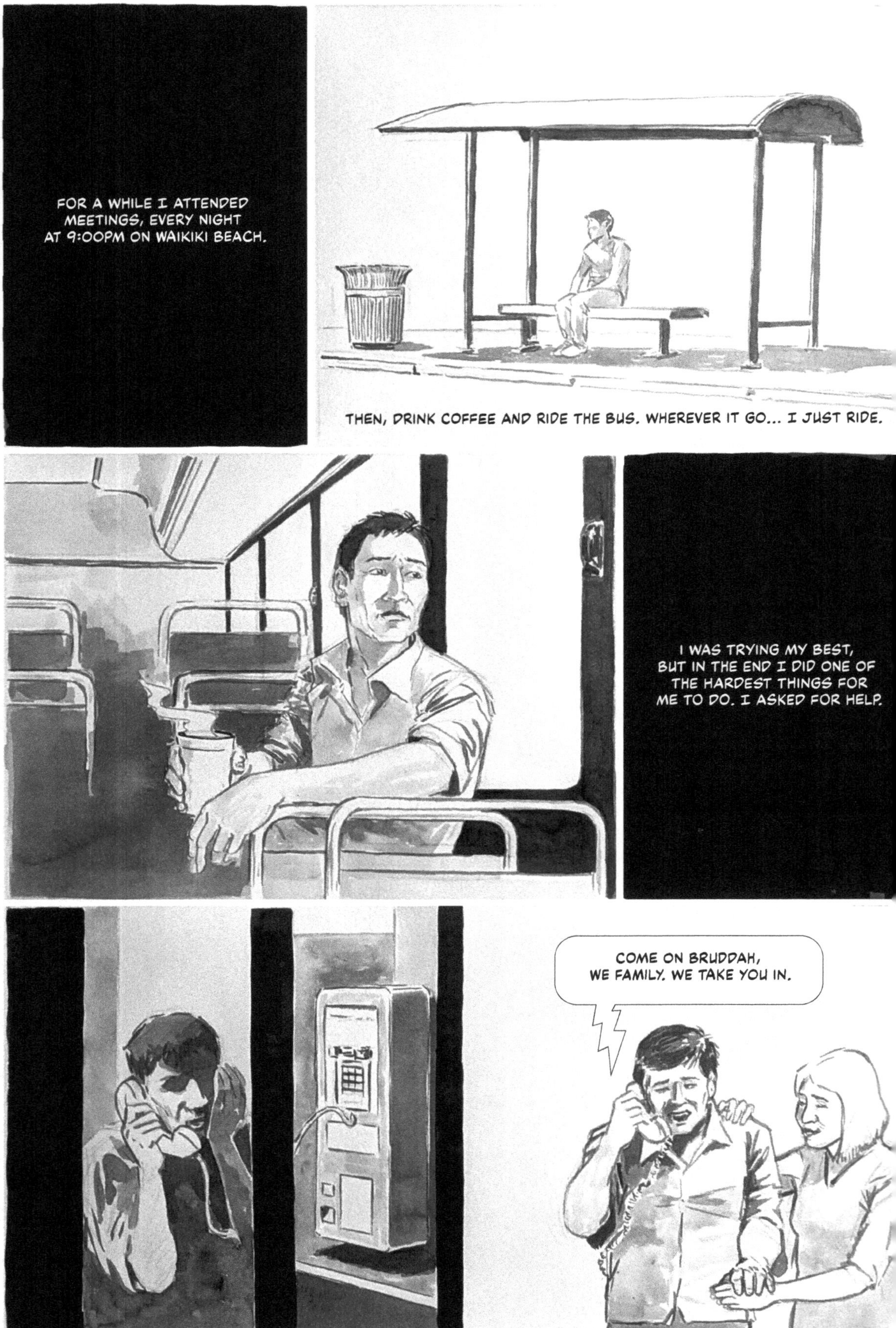
FOR A WHILE I ATTENDED MEETINGS, EVERY NIGHT AT 9:00PM ON WAIKIKI BEACH.
THEN, DRINK COFFEE AND RIDE THE BUS. WHEREVER IT GO... I JUST RIDE.
I WAS TRYING MY BEST, BUT IN THE END I DID ONE OF THE HARDEST THINGS FOR ME TO DO. I ASKED FOR HELP.
COME ON BRUDDAH, WE FAMILY. WE TAKE YOU IN.

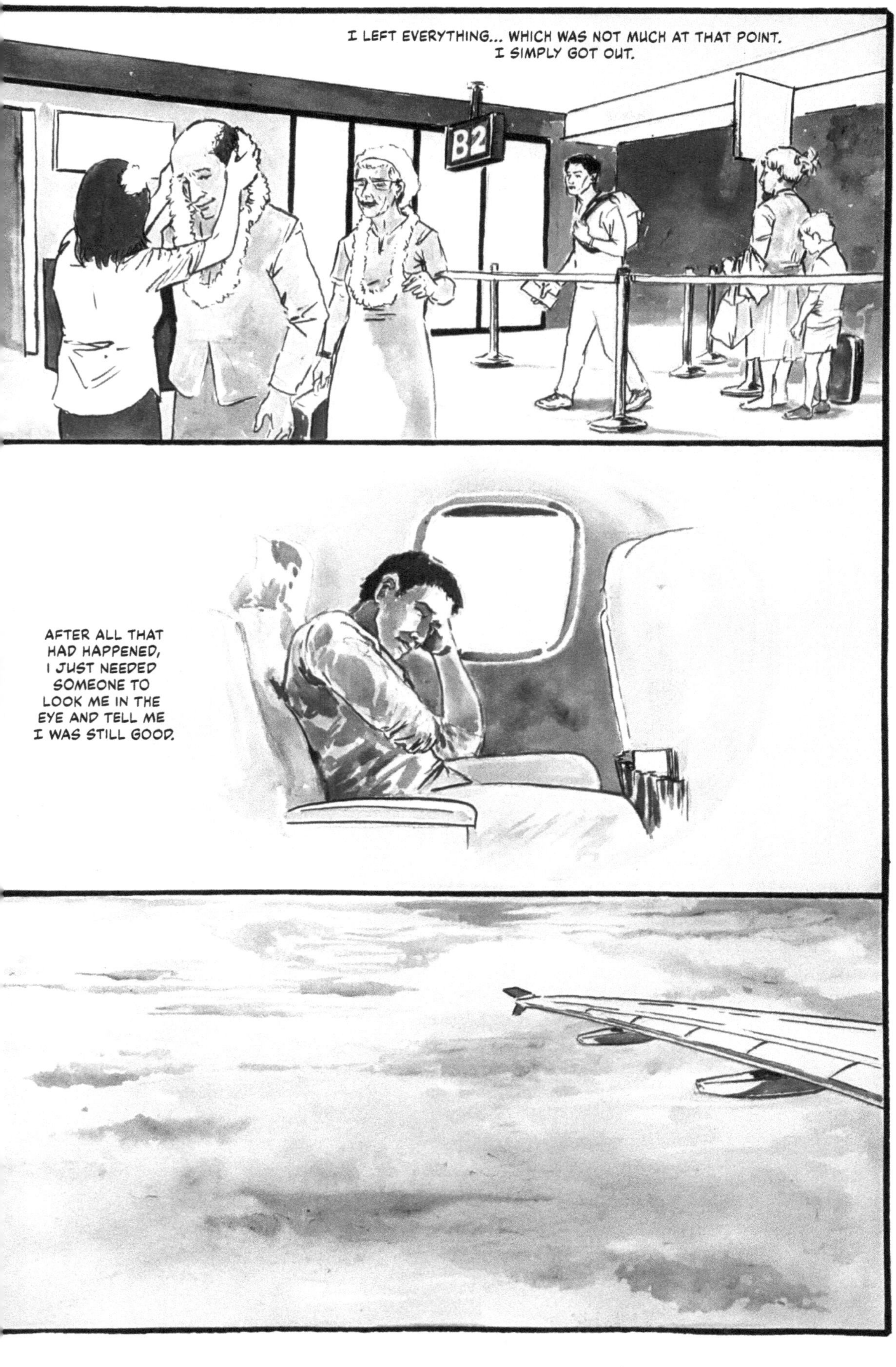
I LEFT EVERYTHING... WHICH WAS NOT MUCH AT THAT POINT.
I SIMPLY GOT OUT.
B2
AFTER ALL THAT HAD HAPPENED, I JUST NEEDED SOMEONE TO LOOK ME IN THE EYE AND TELL ME I WAS STILL GOOD.

AHHH, BRING IT IN BRUDDAH!

WELCOME *HOME*.

THANK YOU "BOSS" LADY...

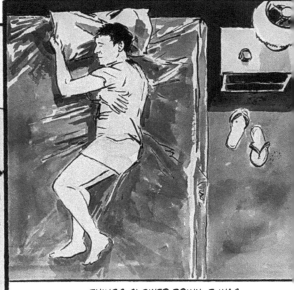

THINGS SLOWED DOWN. I WAS HEALTHIER, AND STAYING SOBER.

HAPPY AND CONTENT FOR THE FIRST TIME IN A LONG WHILE, I FINALLY FELT LIKE I WAS IN CONTROL AGAIN.

I WORKED AT MY BROTHER'S PAINT AND BODY SHOP. WE DID REPAIRS FOR DEALERSHIPS. HE COULD MATCH ANY COLOR, HE WAS A MASTER!

I GOT REALLY GOOD AT BODY WORK. I THINK I GOT BETTER THAN MY BROTHER, BUT HE WILL DENY THAT TO THIS DAY. HEHE.

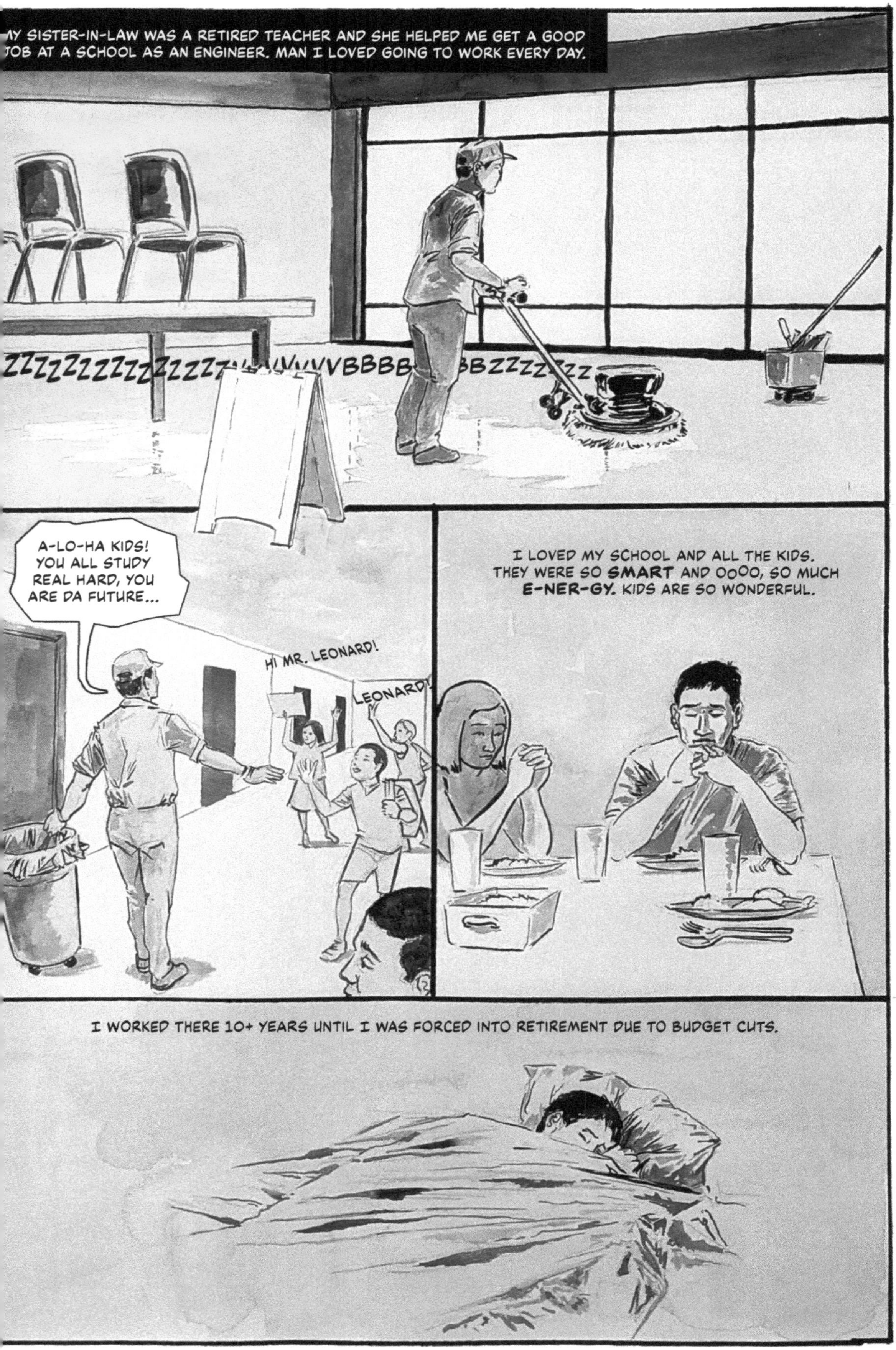
MY SISTER-IN-LAW WAS A RETIRED TEACHER AND SHE HELPED ME GET A GOOD JOB AT A SCHOOL AS AN ENGINEER. MAN I LOVED GOING TO WORK EVERY DAY.
ZZZZZZZZZZZZZZZZ VVVVBBBB BBZZZZZZZ
A-LO-HA KIDS! YOU ALL STUDY REAL HARD, YOU ARE DA FUTURE...
HI MR. LEONARD!
LEONARD!
I LOVED MY SCHOOL AND ALL THE KIDS. THEY WERE SO SMART AND OOOO, SO MUCH E-NER-GY. KIDS ARE SO WONDERFUL.
I WORKED THERE 10+ YEARS UNTIL I WAS FORCED INTO RETIREMENT DUE TO BUDGET CUTS.

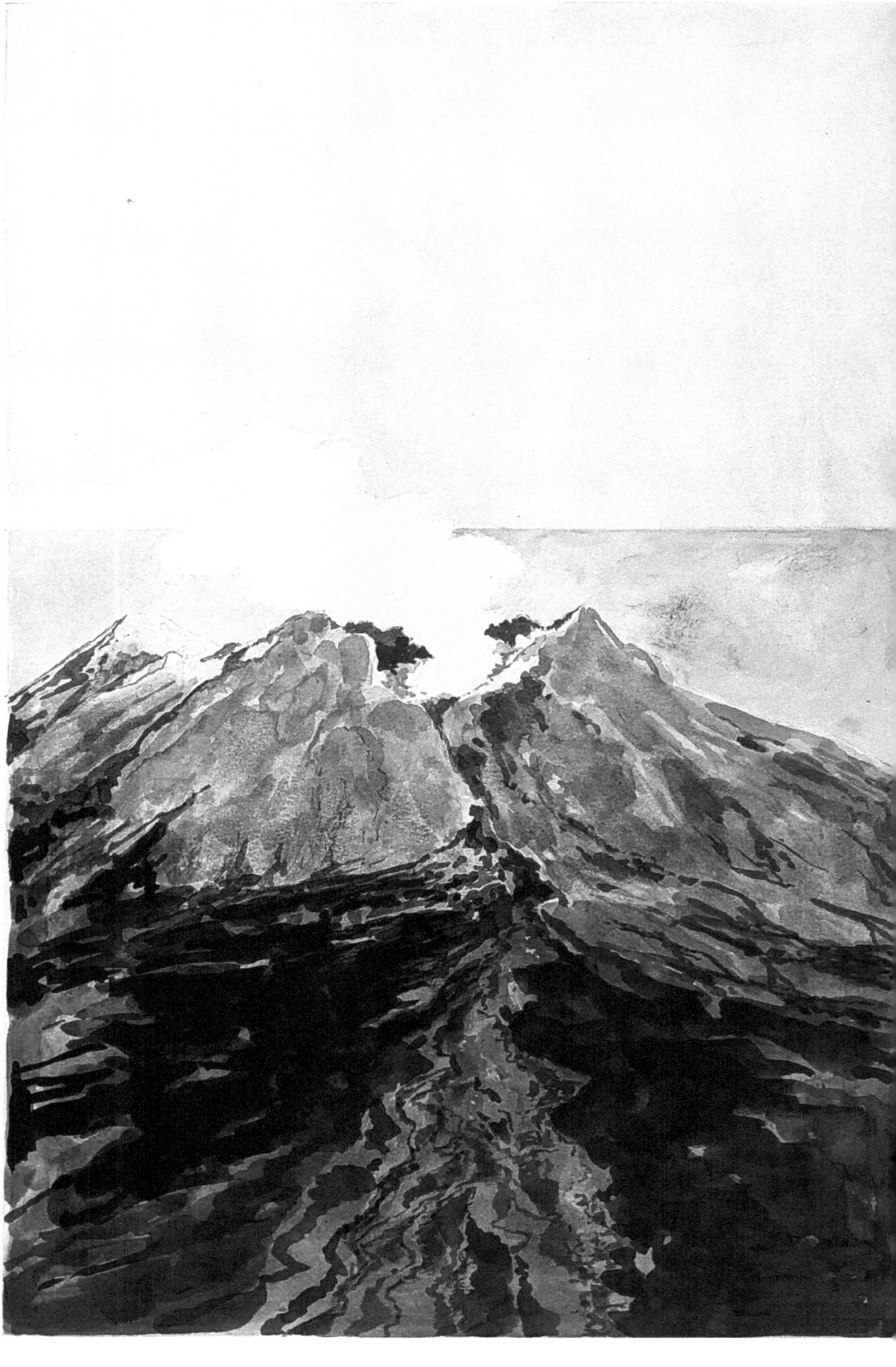

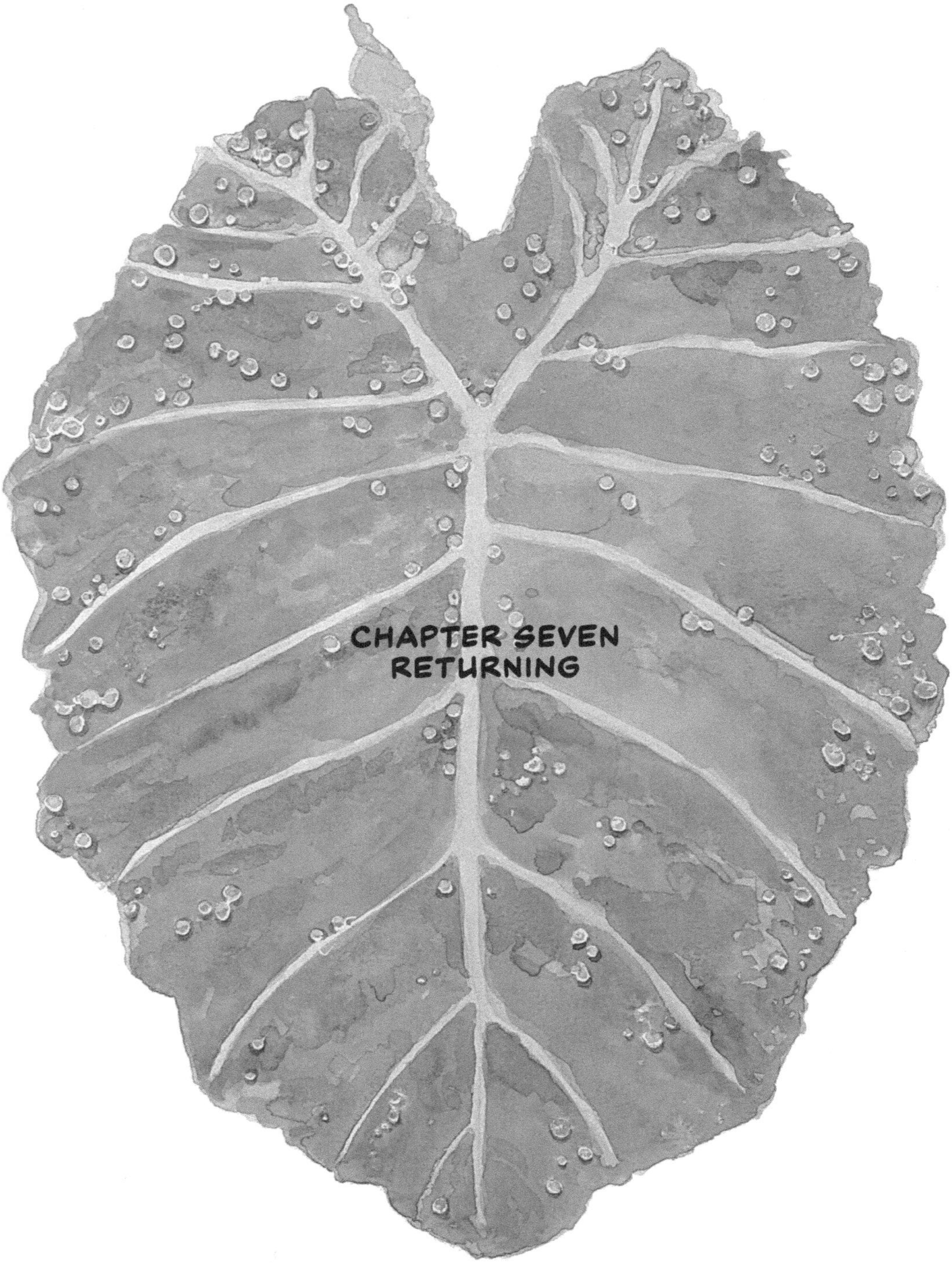

CHAPTER SEVEN
RETURNING

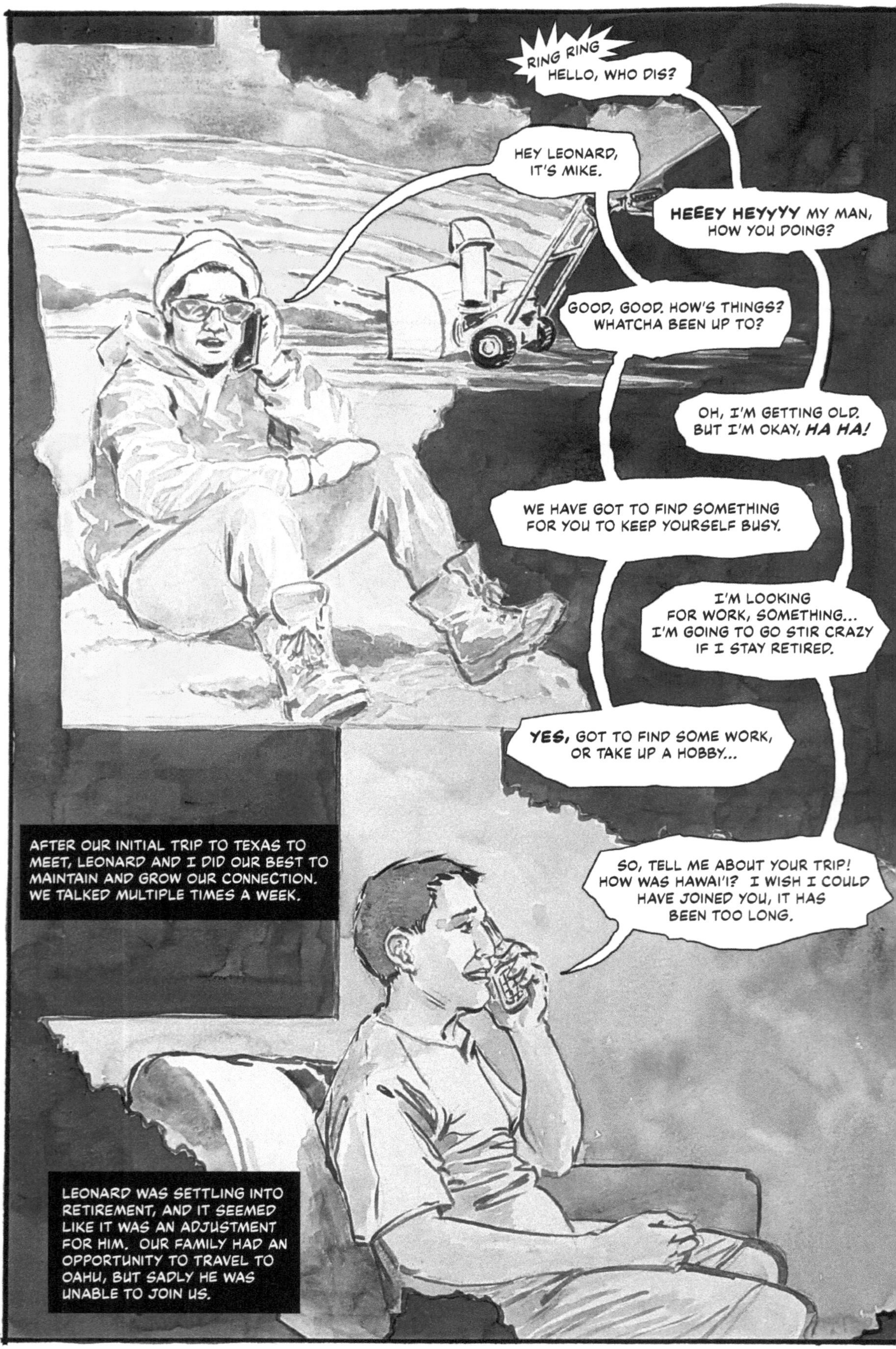
RING RING
HELLO, WHO DIS?
HEY LEONARD, IT'S MIKE.
HEEEY HEYYYY MY MAN, HOW YOU DOING?
GOOD, GOOD. HOW'S THINGS? WHATCHA BEEN UP TO?
OH, I'M GETTING OLD. BUT I'M OKAY, HA HA!
WE HAVE GOT TO FIND SOMETHING FOR YOU TO KEEP YOURSELF BUSY.
I'M LOOKING FOR WORK, SOMETHING... I'M GOING TO GO STIR CRAZY IF I STAY RETIRED.
YES, GOT TO FIND SOME WORK, OR TAKE UP A HOBBY...
AFTER OUR INITIAL TRIP TO TEXAS TO MEET, LEONARD AND I DID OUR BEST TO MAINTAIN AND GROW OUR CONNECTION. WE TALKED MULTIPLE TIMES A WEEK.
SO, TELL ME ABOUT YOUR TRIP! HOW WAS HAWAI'I? I WISH I COULD HAVE JOINED YOU, IT HAS BEEN TOO LONG.
LEONARD WAS SETTLING INTO RETIREMENT, AND IT SEEMED LIKE IT WAS AN ADJUSTMENT FOR HIM. OUR FAMILY HAD AN OPPORTUNITY TO TRAVEL TO OAHU, BUT SADLY HE WAS UNABLE TO JOIN US.

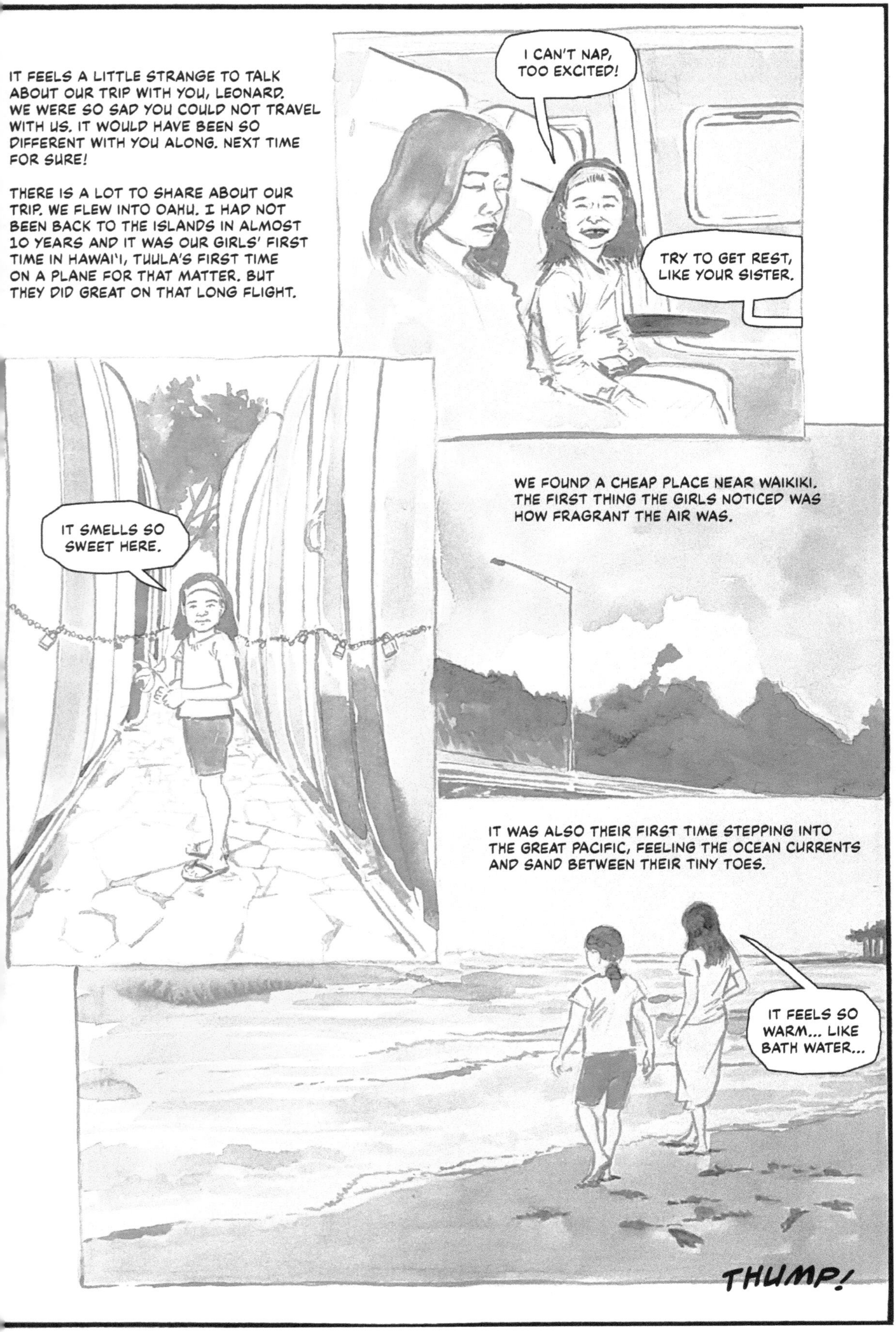
IT FEELS A LITTLE STRANGE TO TALK ABOUT OUR TRIP WITH YOU, LEONARD. WE WERE SO SAD YOU COULD NOT TRAVEL WITH US. IT WOULD HAVE BEEN SO DIFFERENT WITH YOU ALONG. NEXT TIME FOR SURE!
THERE IS A LOT TO SHARE ABOUT OUR TRIP. WE FLEW INTO OAHU. I HAD NOT BEEN BACK TO THE ISLANDS IN ALMOST 10 YEARS AND IT WAS OUR GIRLS' FIRST TIME IN HAWAI'I, TUULA'S FIRST TIME ON A PLANE FOR THAT MATTER. BUT THEY DID GREAT ON THAT LONG FLIGHT.
I CAN'T NAP, TOO EXCITED!
TRY TO GET REST, LIKE YOUR SISTER.
WE FOUND A CHEAP PLACE NEAR WAIKIKI. THE FIRST THING THE GIRLS NOTICED WAS HOW FRAGRANT THE AIR WAS.
IT SMELLS SO SWEET HERE.
IT WAS ALSO THEIR FIRST TIME STEPPING INTO THE GREAT PACIFIC, FEELING THE OCEAN CURRENTS AND SAND BETWEEN THEIR TINY TOES.
IT FEELS SO WARM... LIKE BATH WATER...
THUMP!

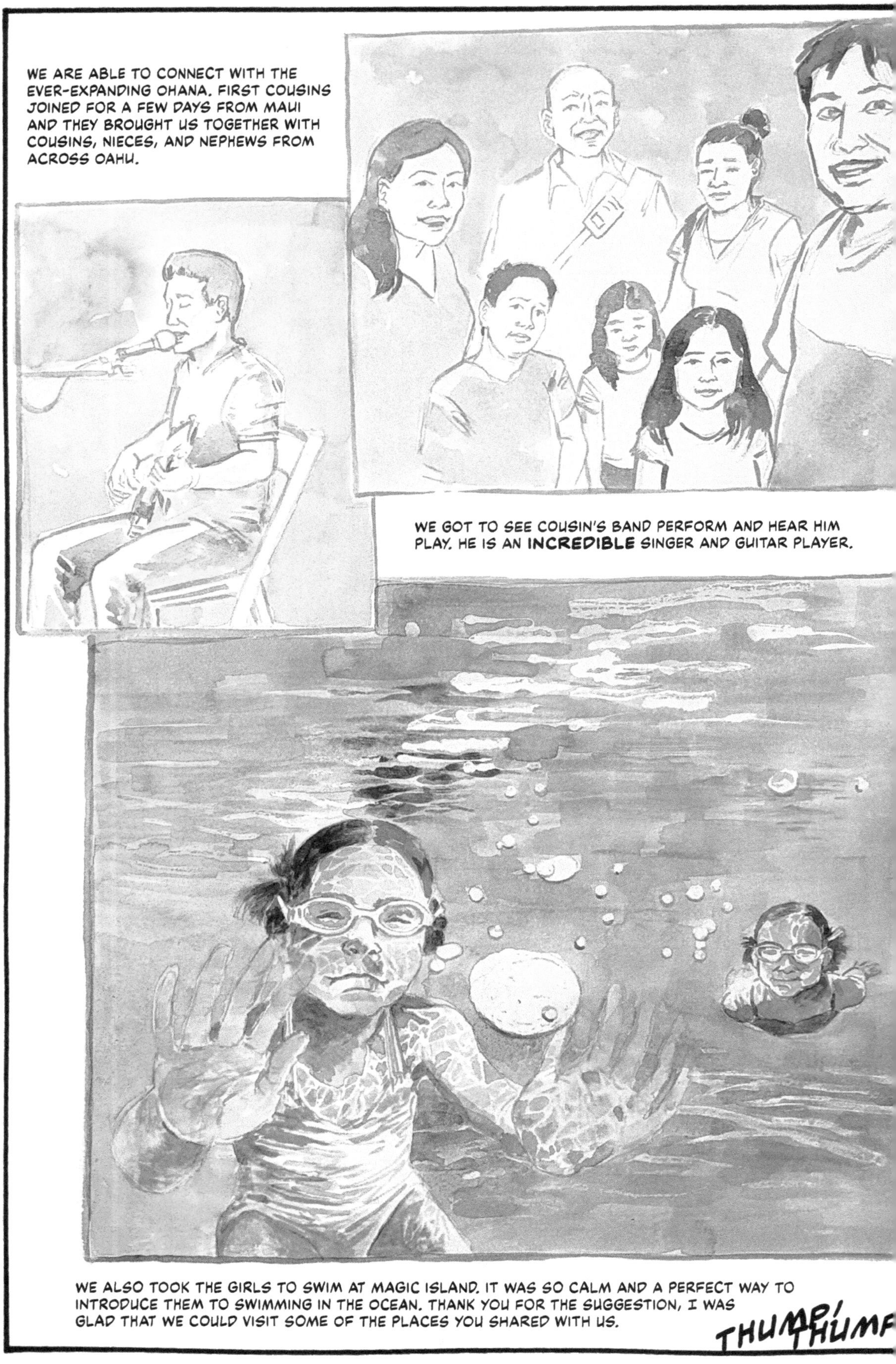
WE ARE ABLE TO CONNECT WITH THE EVER-EXPANDING OHANA. FIRST COUSINS JOINED FOR A FEW DAYS FROM MAUI AND THEY BROUGHT US TOGETHER WITH COUSINS, NIECES, AND NEPHEWS FROM ACROSS OAHU.
WE GOT TO SEE COUSIN'S BAND PERFORM AND HEAR HIM PLAY. HE IS AN **INCREDIBLE** SINGER AND GUITAR PLAYER.
WE ALSO TOOK THE GIRLS TO SWIM AT MAGIC ISLAND. IT WAS SO CALM AND A PERFECT WAY TO INTRODUCE THEM TO SWIMMING IN THE OCEAN. THANK YOU FOR THE SUGGESTION, I WAS GLAD THAT WE COULD VISIT SOME OF THE PLACES YOU SHARED WITH US.
THUMP! THUMP

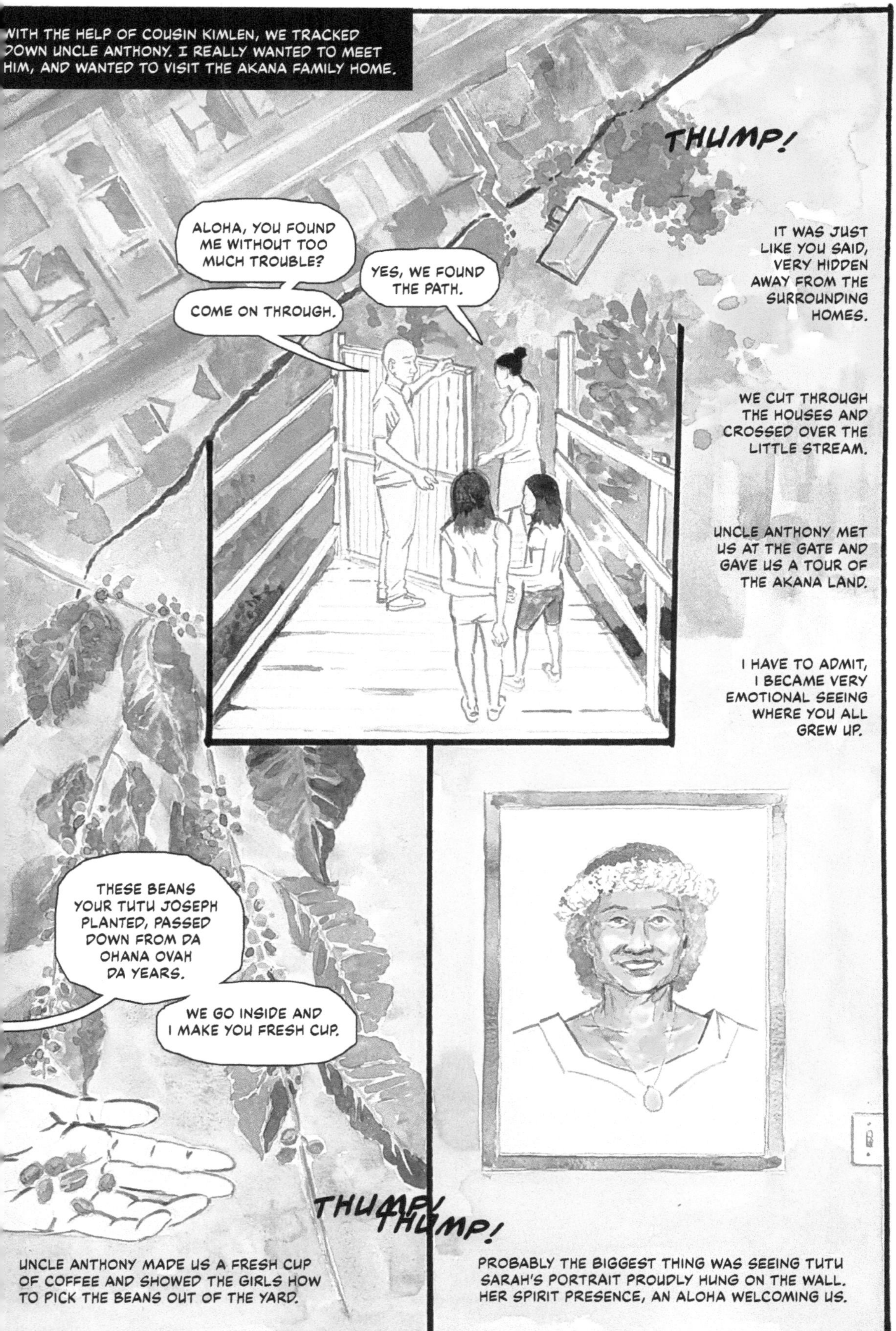
WITH THE HELP OF COUSIN KIMLEN, WE TRACKED DOWN UNCLE ANTHONY. I REALLY WANTED TO MEET HIM, AND WANTED TO VISIT THE AKANA FAMILY HOME.
THUMP!
ALOHA, YOU FOUND ME WITHOUT TOO MUCH TROUBLE?
YES, WE FOUND THE PATH.
COME ON THROUGH.
IT WAS JUST LIKE YOU SAID, VERY HIDDEN AWAY FROM THE SURROUNDING HOMES.
WE CUT THROUGH THE HOUSES AND CROSSED OVER THE LITTLE STREAM.
UNCLE ANTHONY MET US AT THE GATE AND GAVE US A TOUR OF THE AKANA LAND.
I HAVE TO ADMIT, I BECAME VERY EMOTIONAL SEEING WHERE YOU ALL GREW UP.
THESE BEANS YOUR TUTU JOSEPH PLANTED, PASSED DOWN FROM DA OHANA OVAH DA YEARS.
WE GO INSIDE AND I MAKE YOU FRESH CUP.
THUMP! THUMP!
UNCLE ANTHONY MADE US A FRESH CUP OF COFFEE AND SHOWED THE GIRLS HOW TO PICK THE BEANS OUT OF THE YARD.
PROBABLY THE BIGGEST THING WAS SEEING TUTU SARAH'S PORTRAIT PROUDLY HUNG ON THE WALL. HER SPIRIT PRESENCE, AN ALOHA WELCOMING US.

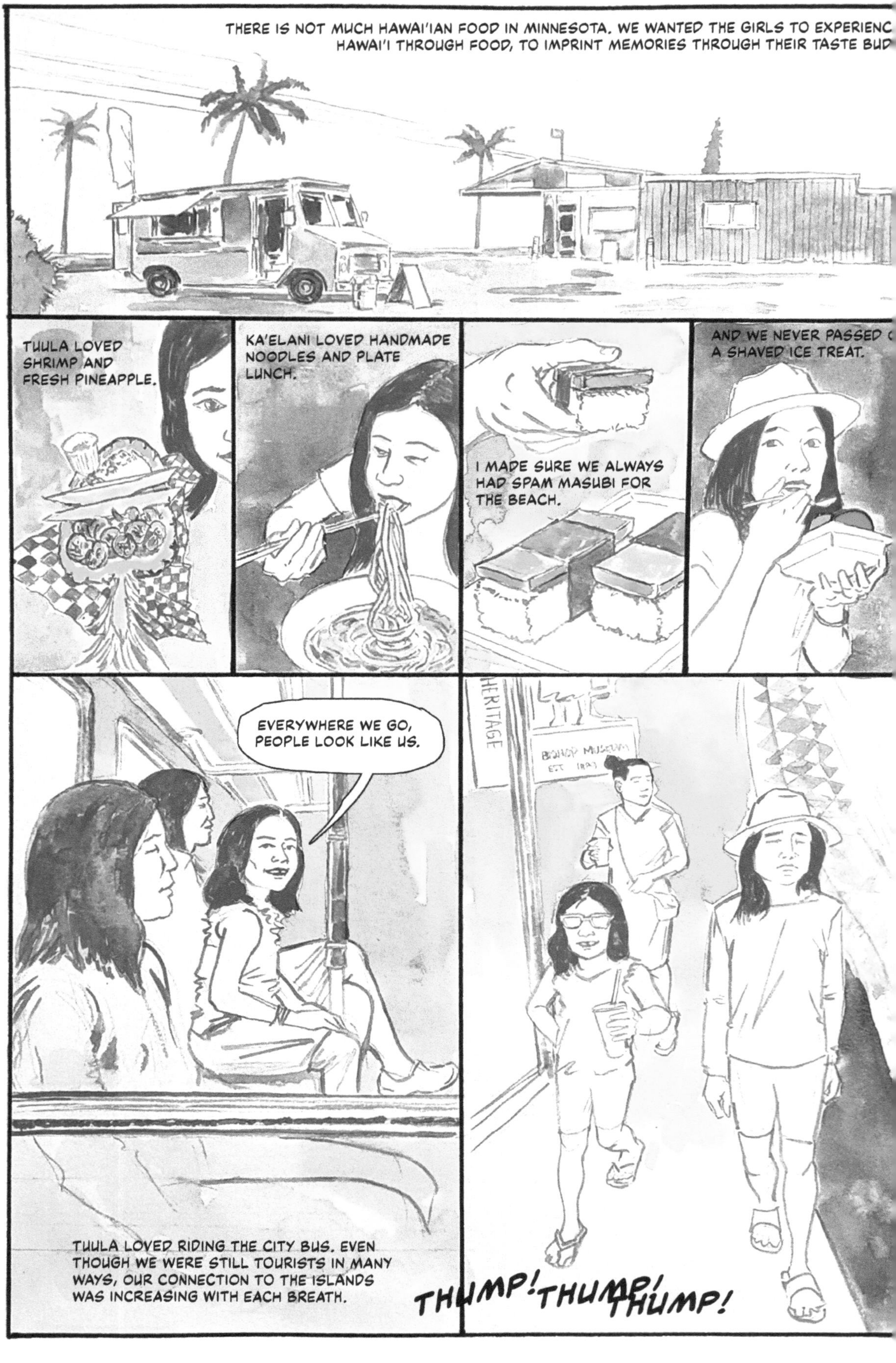

THERE IS NOT MUCH HAWAI'IAN FOOD IN MINNESOTA. WE WANTED THE GIRLS TO EXPERIENC
HAWAI'I THROUGH FOOD, TO IMPRINT MEMORIES THROUGH THEIR TASTE BUD
TUULA LOVED SHRIMP AND FRESH PINEAPPLE.
KA'ELANI LOVED HANDMADE NOODLES AND PLATE LUNCH.
I MADE SURE WE ALWAYS HAD SPAM MASUBI FOR THE BEACH.
AND WE NEVER PASSED
A SHAVED ICE TREAT.
EVERYWHERE WE GO, PEOPLE LOOK LIKE US.
TUULA LOVED RIDING THE CITY BUS. EVEN THOUGH WE WERE STILL TOURISTS IN MANY WAYS, OUR CONNECTION TO THE ISLANDS WAS INCREASING WITH EACH BREATH.
HERITAGE
BISHOP MUSEUM
THUMP! THUMP! THUMP!

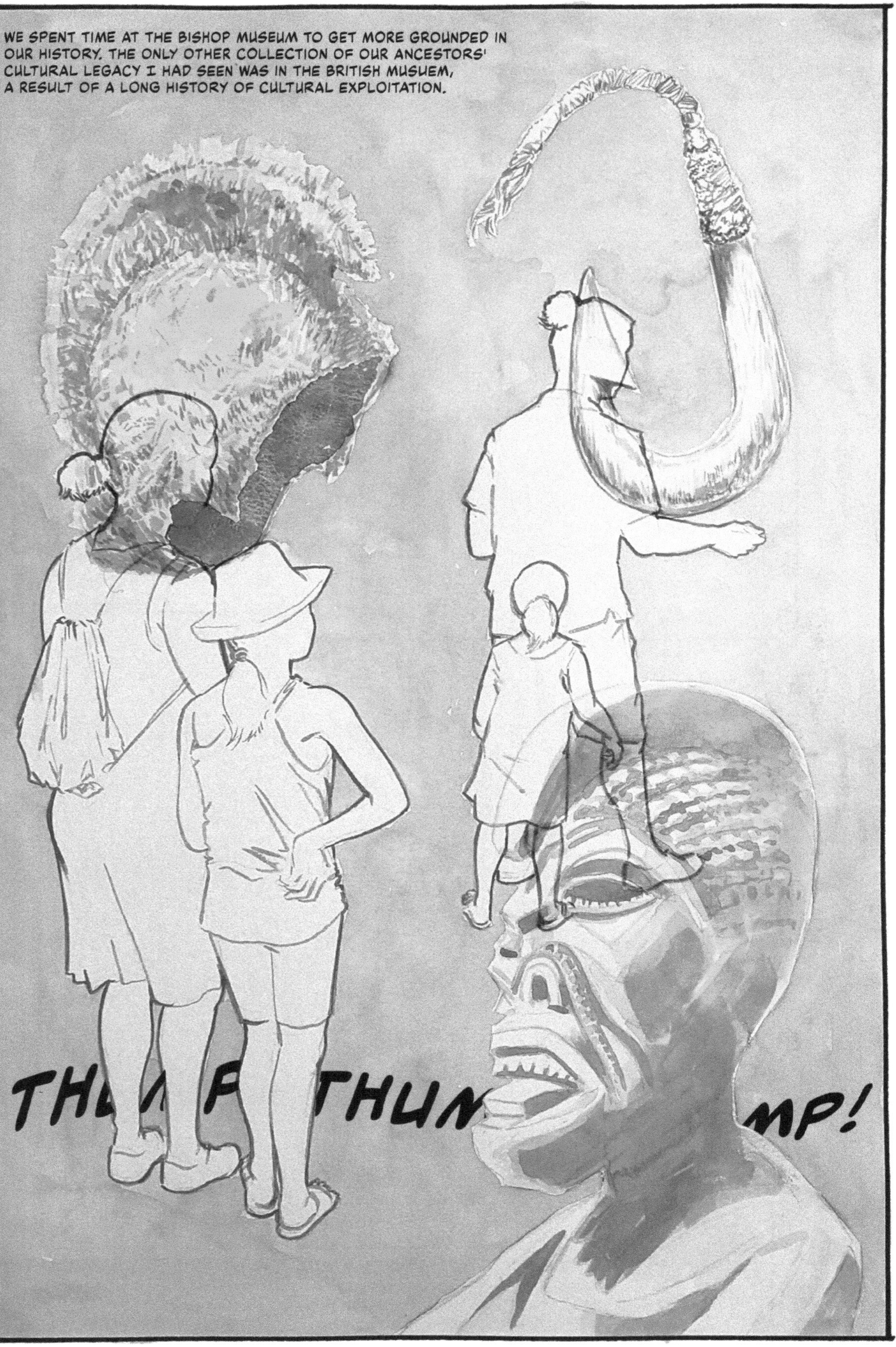
WE SPENT TIME AT THE BISHOP MUSEUM TO GET MORE GROUNDED IN OUR HISTORY. THE ONLY OTHER COLLECTION OF OUR ANCESTORS' CULTURAL LEGACY I HAD SEEN WAS IN THE BRITISH MUSUEM, A RESULT OF A LONG HISTORY OF CULTURAL EXPLOITATION.
THUN
MP!

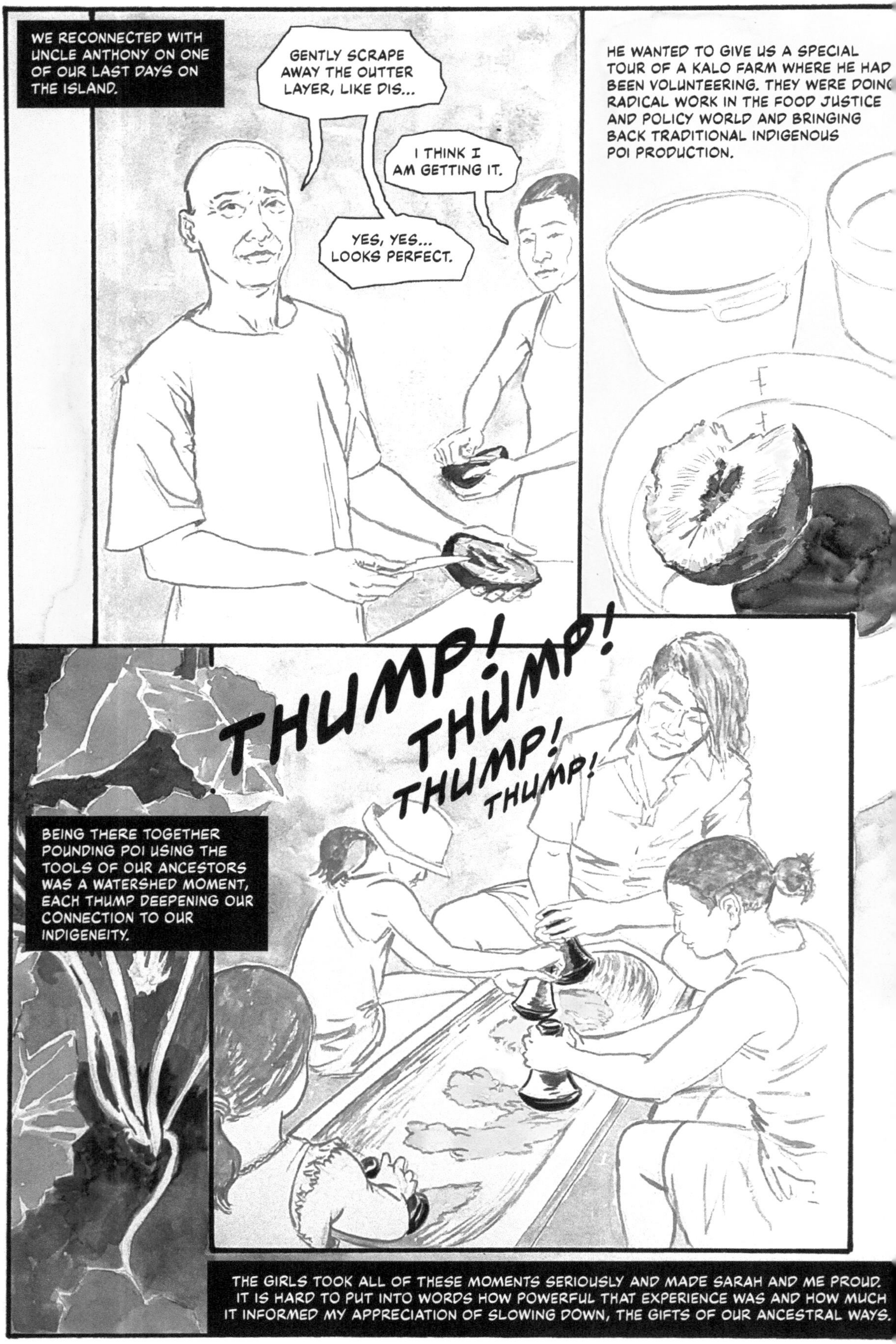
WE RECONNECTED WITH UNCLE ANTHONY ON ONE OF OUR LAST DAYS ON THE ISLAND.
GENTLY SCRAPE AWAY THE OUTTER LAYER, LIKE DIS...
I THINK I AM GETTING IT.
YES, YES... LOOKS PERFECT.
HE WANTED TO GIVE US A SPECIAL TOUR OF A KALO FARM WHERE HE HAD BEEN VOLUNTEERING. THEY WERE DOING RADICAL WORK IN THE FOOD JUSTICE AND POLICY WORLD AND BRINGING BACK TRADITIONAL INDIGENOUS POI PRODUCTION.
THUMP! THUMP! THUMP! THUMP!
BEING THERE TOGETHER POUNDING POI USING THE TOOLS OF OUR ANCESTORS WAS A WATERSHED MOMENT, EACH THUMP DEEPENING OUR CONNECTION TO OUR INDIGENEITY.
THE GIRLS TOOK ALL OF THESE MOMENTS SERIOUSLY AND MADE SARAH AND ME PROUD. IT IS HARD TO PUT INTO WORDS HOW POWERFUL THAT EXPERIENCE WAS AND HOW MUCH IT INFORMED MY APPRECIATION OF SLOWING DOWN, THE GIFTS OF OUR ANCESTRAL WAYS.

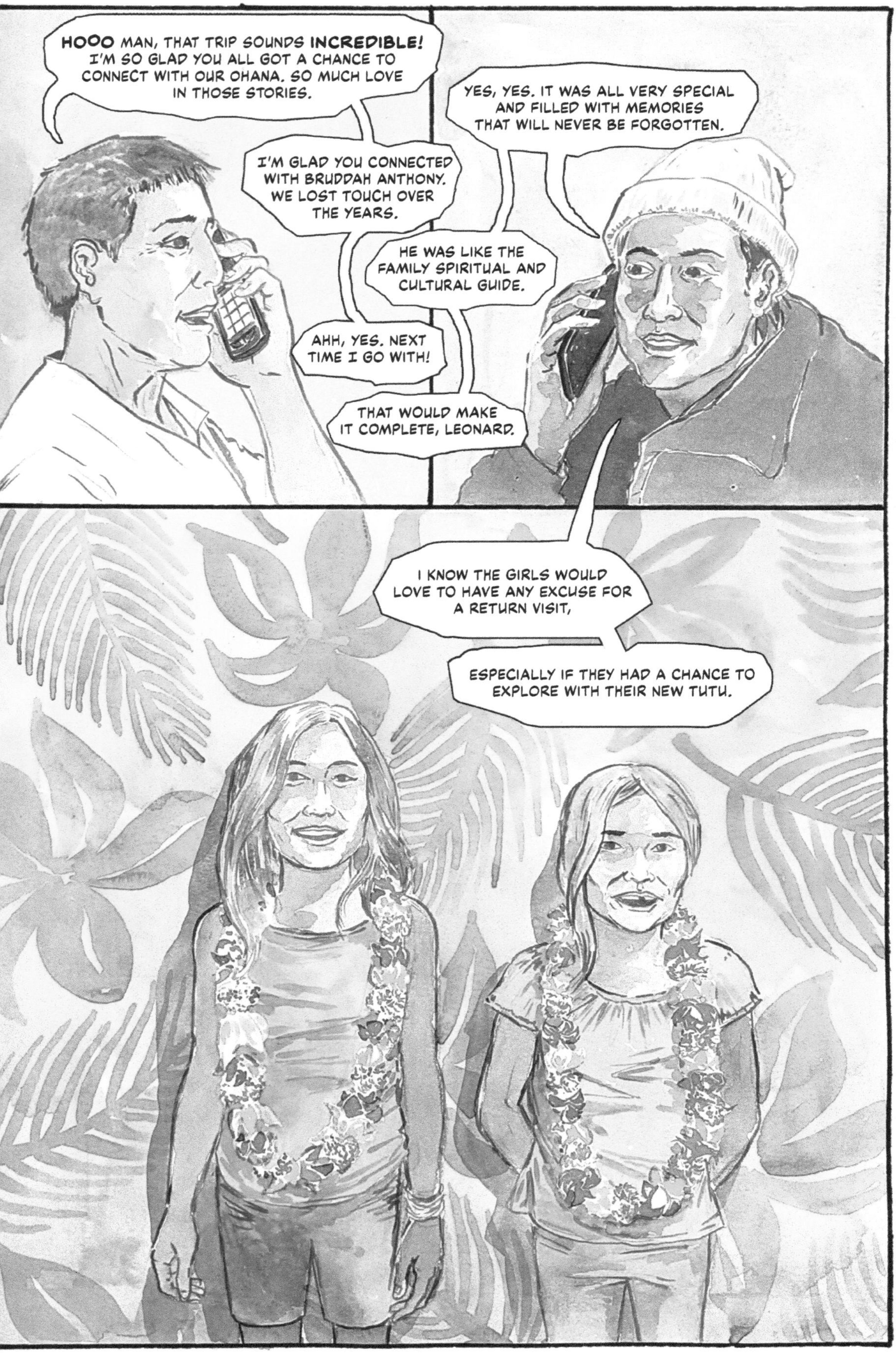

HOOO MAN, THAT TRIP SOUNDS INCREDIBLE! I'M SO GLAD YOU ALL GOT A CHANCE TO CONNECT WITH OUR OHANA. SO MUCH LOVE IN THOSE STORIES.
YES, YES. IT WAS ALL VERY SPECIAL AND FILLED WITH MEMORIES THAT WILL NEVER BE FORGOTTEN.
I'M GLAD YOU CONNECTED WITH BRUDDAH ANTHONY. WE LOST TOUCH OVER THE YEARS.
HE WAS LIKE THE FAMILY SPIRITUAL AND CULTURAL GUIDE.
AHH, YES. NEXT TIME I GO WITH!
THAT WOULD MAKE IT COMPLETE, LEONARD.
I KNOW THE GIRLS WOULD LOVE TO HAVE ANY EXCUSE FOR A RETURN VISIT,
ESPECIALLY IF THEY HAD A CHANCE TO EXPLORE WITH THEIR NEW TUTU.

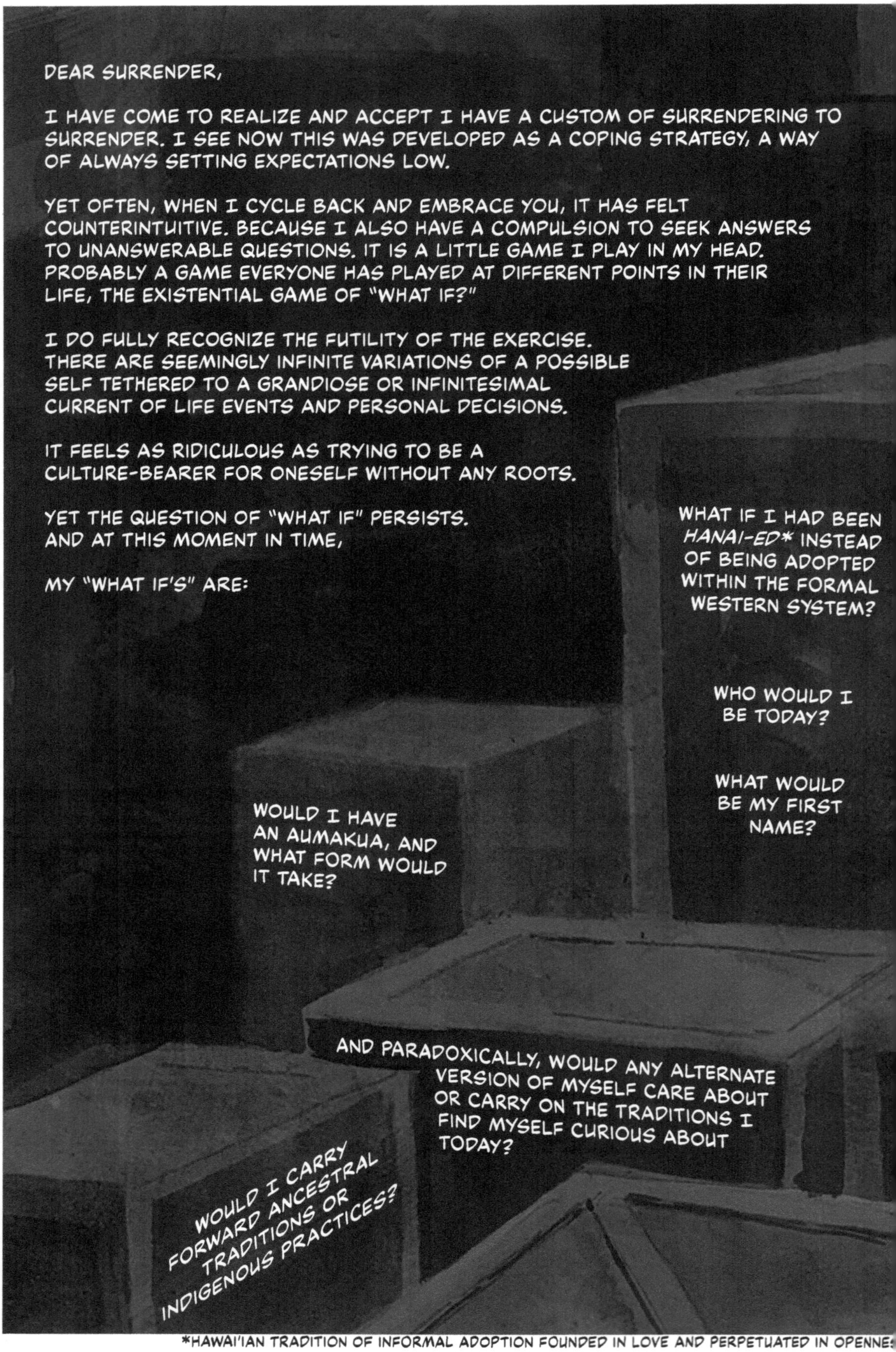
DEAR SURRENDER,
I HAVE COME TO REALIZE AND ACCEPT I HAVE A CUSTOM OF SURRENDERING TO SURRENDER. I SEE NOW THIS WAS DEVELOPED AS A COPING STRATEGY, A WAY OF ALWAYS SETTING EXPECTATIONS LOW.
YET OFTEN, WHEN I CYCLE BACK AND EMBRACE YOU, IT HAS FELT COUNTERINTUITIVE. BECAUSE I ALSO HAVE A COMPULSION TO SEEK ANSWERS TO UNANSWERABLE QUESTIONS. IT IS A LITTLE GAME I PLAY IN MY HEAD. PROBABLY A GAME EVERYONE HAS PLAYED AT DIFFERENT POINTS IN THEIR LIFE, THE EXISTENTIAL GAME OF "WHAT IF?"
I DO FULLY RECOGNIZE THE FUTILITY OF THE EXERCISE. THERE ARE SEEMINGLY INFINITE VARIATIONS OF A POSSIBLE SELF TETHERED TO A GRANDIOSE OR INFINITESIMAL CURRENT OF LIFE EVENTS AND PERSONAL DECISIONS.
IT FEELS AS RIDICULOUS AS TRYING TO BE A CULTURE-BEARER FOR ONESELF WITHOUT ANY ROOTS.
YET THE QUESTION OF "WHAT IF" PERSISTS. AND AT THIS MOMENT IN TIME,
MY "WHAT IF'S" ARE:
WHAT IF I HAD BEEN *HANAI-ED** INSTEAD OF BEING ADOPTED WITHIN THE FORMAL WESTERN SYSTEM?
WHO WOULD I BE TODAY?
WHAT WOULD BE MY FIRST NAME?
WOULD I HAVE AN AUMAKUA, AND WHAT FORM WOULD IT TAKE?
AND PARADOXICALLY, WOULD ANY ALTERNATE VERSION OF MYSELF CARE ABOUT OR CARRY ON THE TRADITIONS I FIND MYSELF CURIOUS ABOUT TODAY?
WOULD I CARRY FORWARD ANCESTRAL TRADITIONS OR INDIGENOUS PRACTICES?

*HAWAI'IAN TRADITION OF INFORMAL ADOPTION FOUNDED IN LOVE AND PERPETUATED IN OPENNE

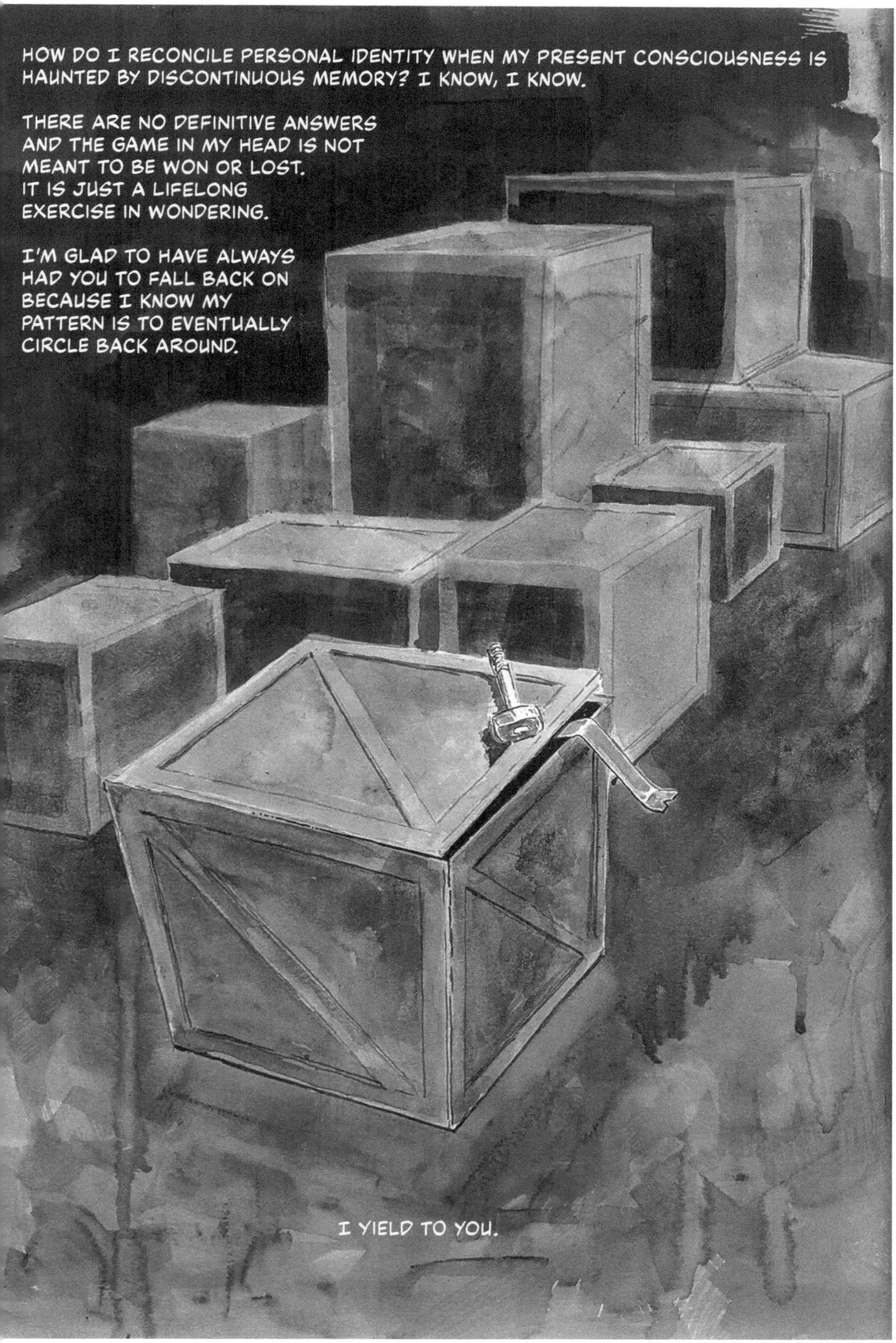
HOW DO I RECONCILE PERSONAL IDENTITY WHEN MY PRESENT CONSCIOUSNESS IS HAUNTED BY DISCONTINUOUS MEMORY? I KNOW, I KNOW.
THERE ARE NO DEFINITIVE ANSWERS AND THE GAME IN MY HEAD IS NOT MEANT TO BE WON OR LOST. IT IS JUST A LIFELONG EXERCISE IN WONDERING.
I'M GLAD TO HAVE ALWAYS HAD YOU TO FALL BACK ON BECAUSE I KNOW MY PATTERN IS TO EVENTUALLY CIRCLE BACK AROUND.
I YIELD TO YOU.

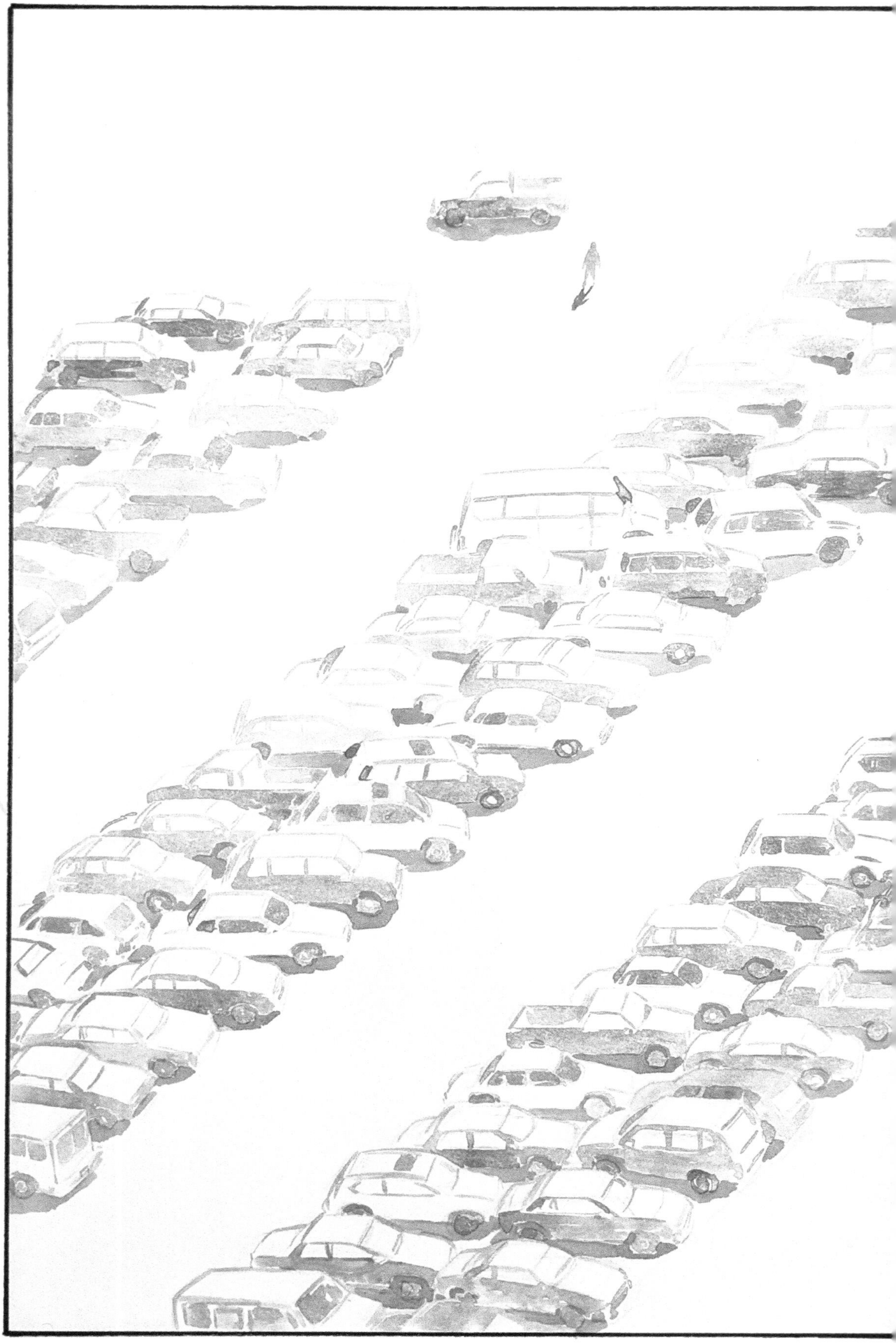

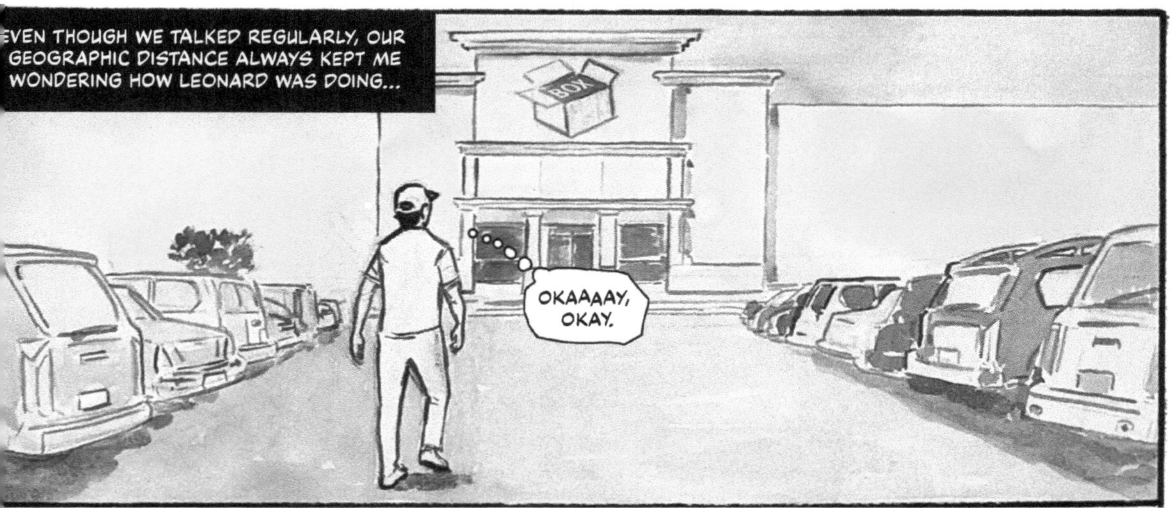
EVEN THOUGH WE TALKED REGULARLY, OUR GEOGRAPHIC DISTANCE ALWAYS KEPT ME WONDERING HOW LEONARD WAS DOING...
BOX
OKAAAAY, OKAY.

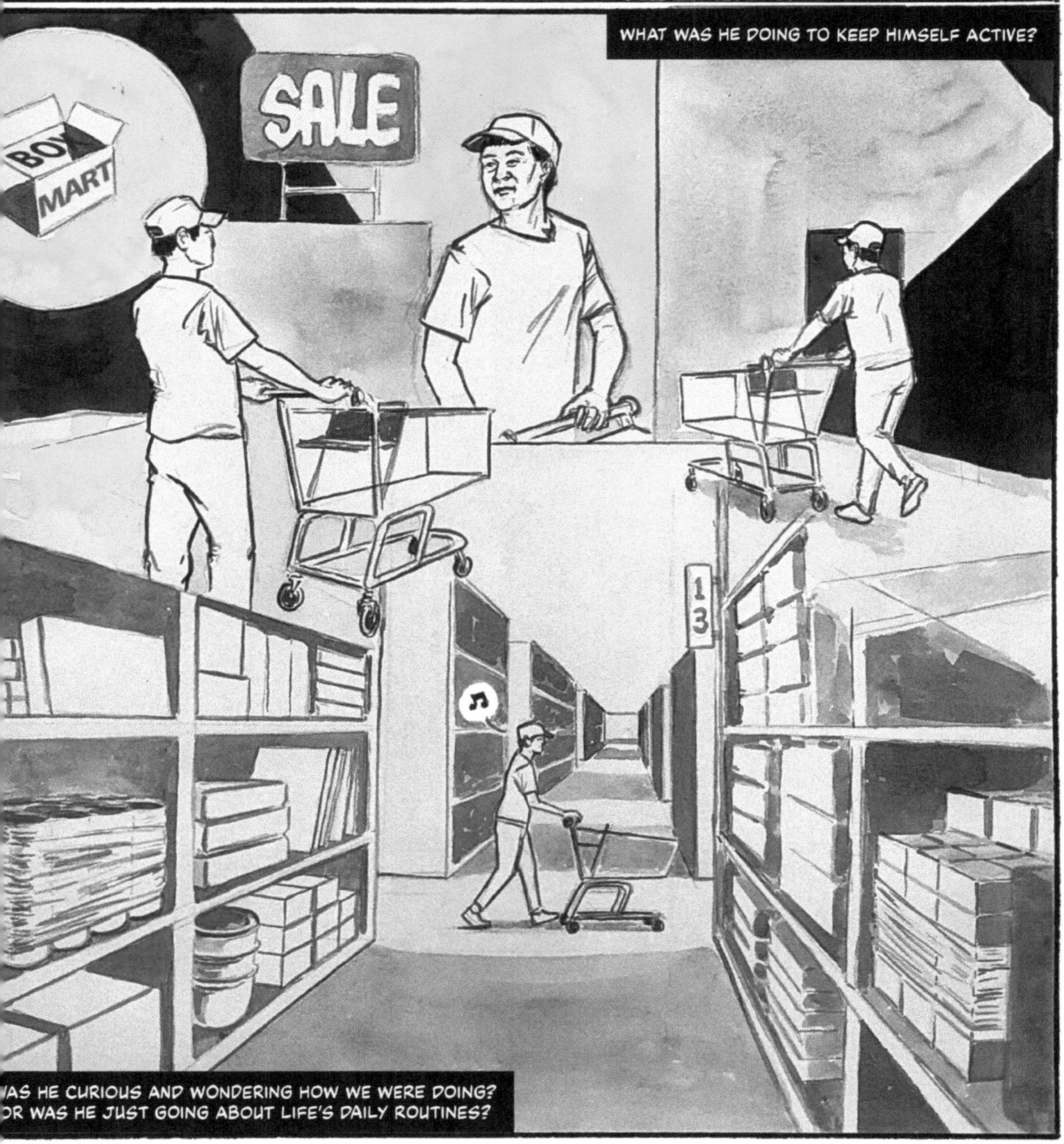
WHAT WAS HE DOING TO KEEP HIMSELF ACTIVE?
BOX MART
SALE
13
WAS HE CURIOUS AND WONDERING HOW WE WERE DOING? OR WAS HE JUST GOING ABOUT LIFE'S DAILY ROUTINES?

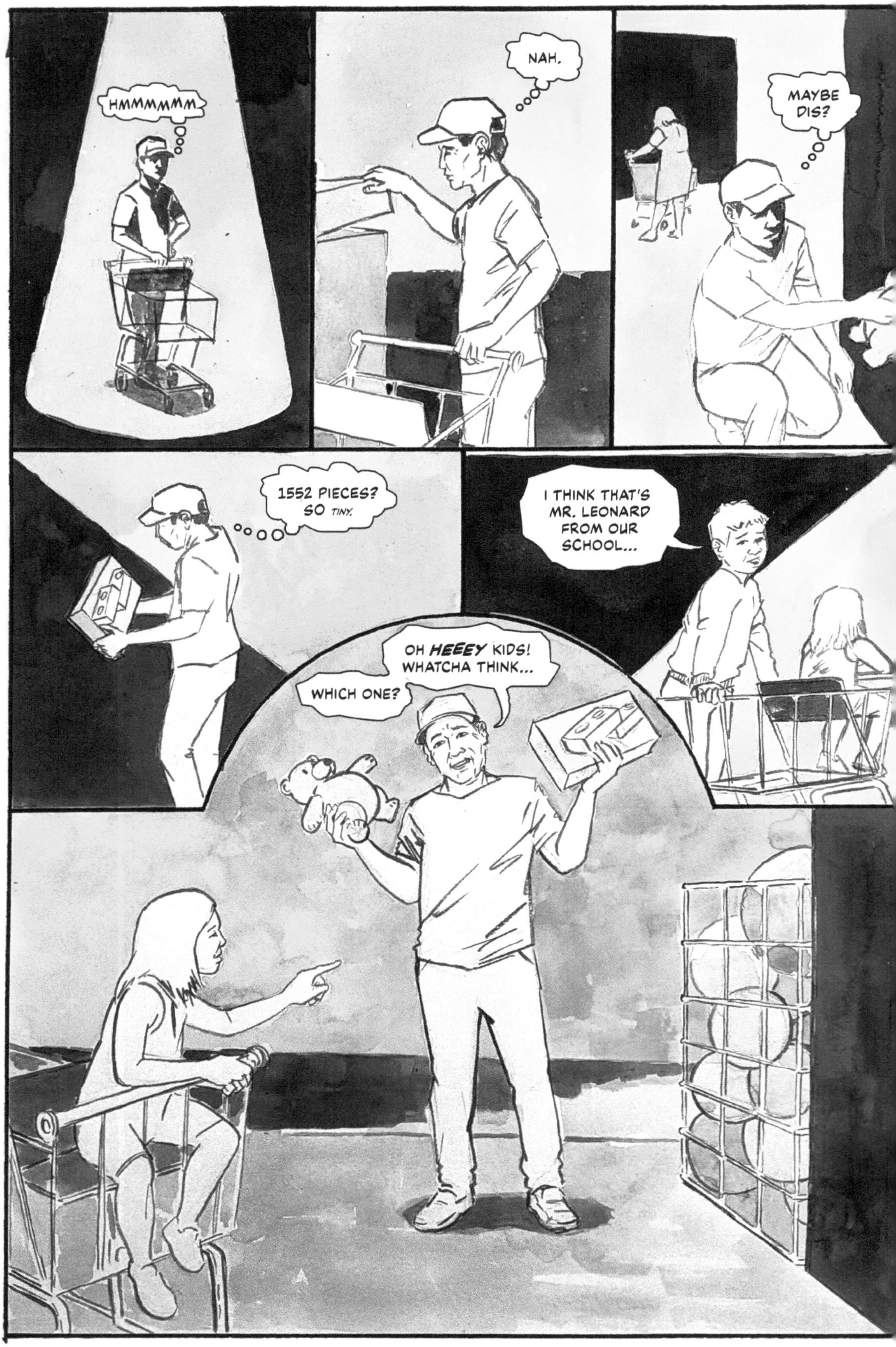
HMMMMMM
NAH.
MAYBE DIS?
1552 PIECES? SO TINY.
I THINK THAT'S MR. LEONARD FROM OUR SCHOOL...
OH HEEEY KIDS! WHATCHA THINK...
WHICH ONE?

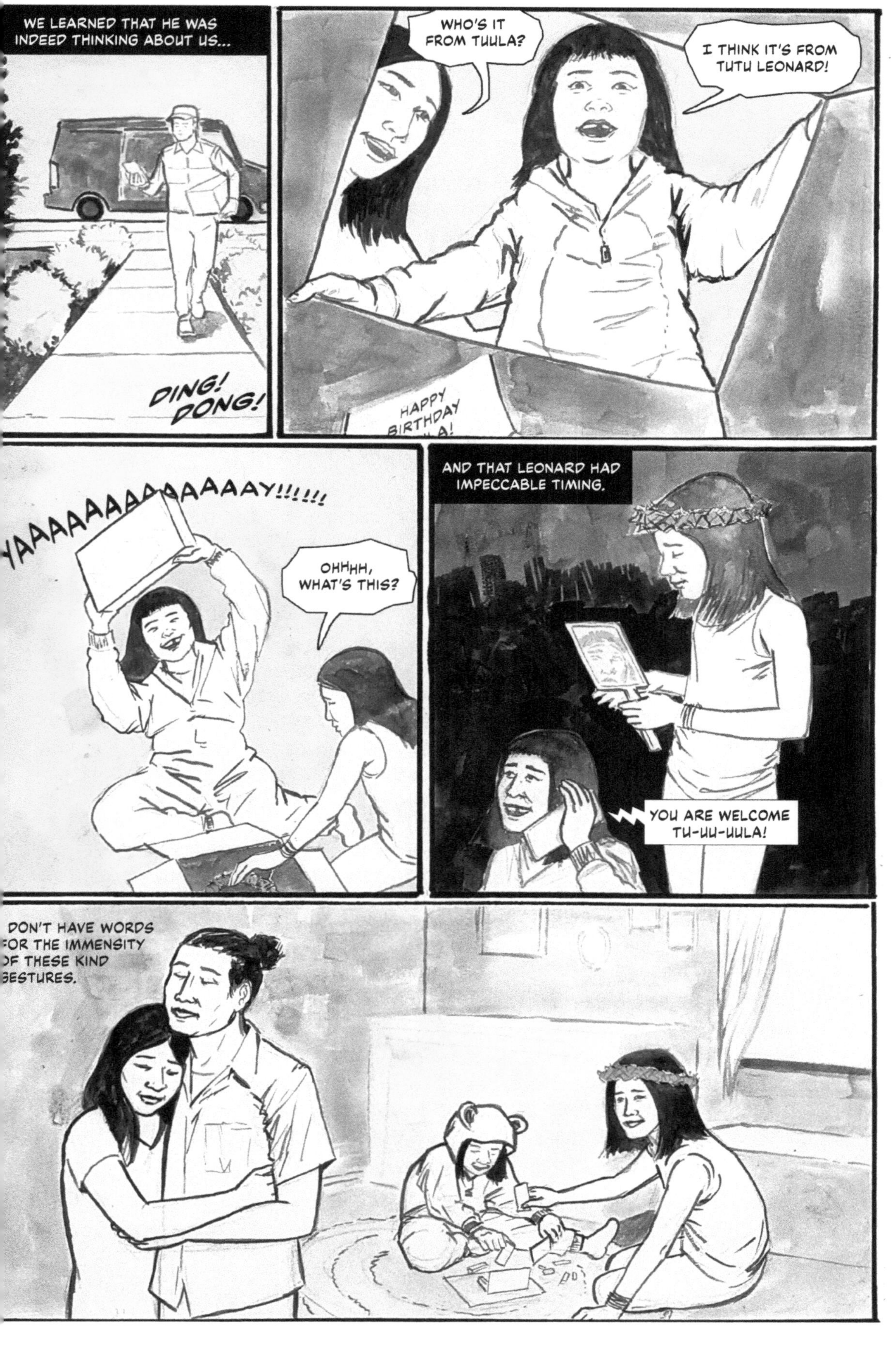
WE LEARNED THAT HE WAS INDEED THINKING ABOUT US...
DING! DONG!
WHO'S IT FROM TUULA?
I THINK IT'S FROM TUTU LEONARD!
HAPPY BIRTHDAY
YAAAAAAAAAAAAAY!!!!!!
OHHHH, WHAT'S THIS?
AND THAT LEONARD HAD IMPECCABLE TIMING.
YOU ARE WELCOME TU-UU-UULA!
DON'T HAVE WORDS FOR THE IMMENSITY OF THESE KIND GESTURES.

DEAR LEONARD,

THROUGHOUT MY LIFE I'VE COME TO KNOW LOVE IN A PLURAL SENSE.
A FIRST LOVE BOUND TO FAMILY AND GUARDIANS. A SECOND LOVE FOR INTIMATE
PARTNERS. AND, AS A DEAR FRIEND NEAL EXPLAINED TO ME PRIOR TO OUR
FIRST DAUGHTER'S BIRTH, A THIRD UNDERSTANDING OF LOVE THAT COMES WITH
CARING FOR A CHILD. THESE WAYS OF KNOWING LOVE ARE NOT STACKED, OR
WEIGHTED, BUT COMMINGLE OVER A LIFETIME. ALL LOVE, BUT UNIQUE IN
DIMENSION AND REQUEST.

MY CHILDREN EMBRACE LOVE WHEN THEY SPEAK TO YOU, THEIR NEW TUTU, ON
THE PHONE. THEY TELL YOU THEY "LOVE" YOU AS THEY PASS THE PHONE BACK TO
ME, AND I BELIEVE THEY DO WITH A FULLNESS AND SINCERITY. I HEAR THEM
EXPRESS THEIR LOVE TO YOU AND IT MAKES MY HEART SWELL AND MOMENTARILY
STOPS MY BREATH. BUT I REALIZE I MAY HAVE NEVER SAID IT MYSELF,
CALLED LOVE OUT BY NAME FOR YOU, FIRST FATHER. I CARE FOR YOU AND THAT
CARE GROWS INCREMENTALLY WITH EACH DAY AND LONG DISTANCE INTERACTION,
YET I DON'T KNOW HOW TO SITUATE IT AS A LOVE THAT I HAVE KNOWN BEFORE.
SO IT HAS BEEN FELT, YET... UNSPOKEN.

WHAT IS THE LOVE BETWEEN FAMILIAL STRANGERS? HOW DOES LOVE SPAN A
47-YEAR INTERRUPTION? WE ARE SIMULTANEOUSLY COMPLICATED AND
UNCOMPLICATED. WE HAVE LITTLE HISTORY, BUT WE ALSO HAVE NEVER
SQUABBLED OR CARRIED WITH US DECADES OF PARENT-CHILD INTERPERSONAL
BAGGAGE. I WONDER IF YOU ASK YOURSELF IF YOU WOULD HAVE BEEN A GOOD
FATHER IN THE WAYS I PONDER IF I WOULD HAVE BEEN A GOOD SON? IN WHAT
WAYS DO WE CHOOSE TO NOW BE ACCOUNTABLE TO ONE ANOTHER?

IT ALL MAKES ME WONDER IF THERE IS YET ANOTHER VERSION OF LOVE,
PERHAPS A FOURTH LOVE THAT IS STILL SOMEWHAT UNDEFINED. MAYBE YOU
DON'T THINK ABOUT LOVE AS COMPARTMENTALIZED OR RIGIDLY DEFINED, BUT I
CURRENTLY FEEL CONFUSED. MAYBE TRYING TO CREATE A CATEGORY OF
FOURTH LOVE IS A FALSE PREMISE I AM CONSTRUCTING FOR MY OWN NECESSITY.

CAN IT BE THAT EASY, TO JUST SAY IT? IF NOT NOW, WHEN? IS THERE
SOMETHING BROKEN WITHIN ME? I DON'T KNOW HOW TO COMPLETE THIS RITE.
FOR THE MOMENT I KNOW YOU AND I ARE COMMITTED TO THIS PATH OF
KNOWING ONE ANOTHER FORWARD. AND IN THAT PROCESS I AM COMING TO
UNDERSTAND THAT IF THERE IS A FOURTH VERSION OF LOVE, IT IS ONE THAT
PULLS WITH THE TRANSITORY GRAVITY OF OUR COMBINED SORROW AND JOY.

-M

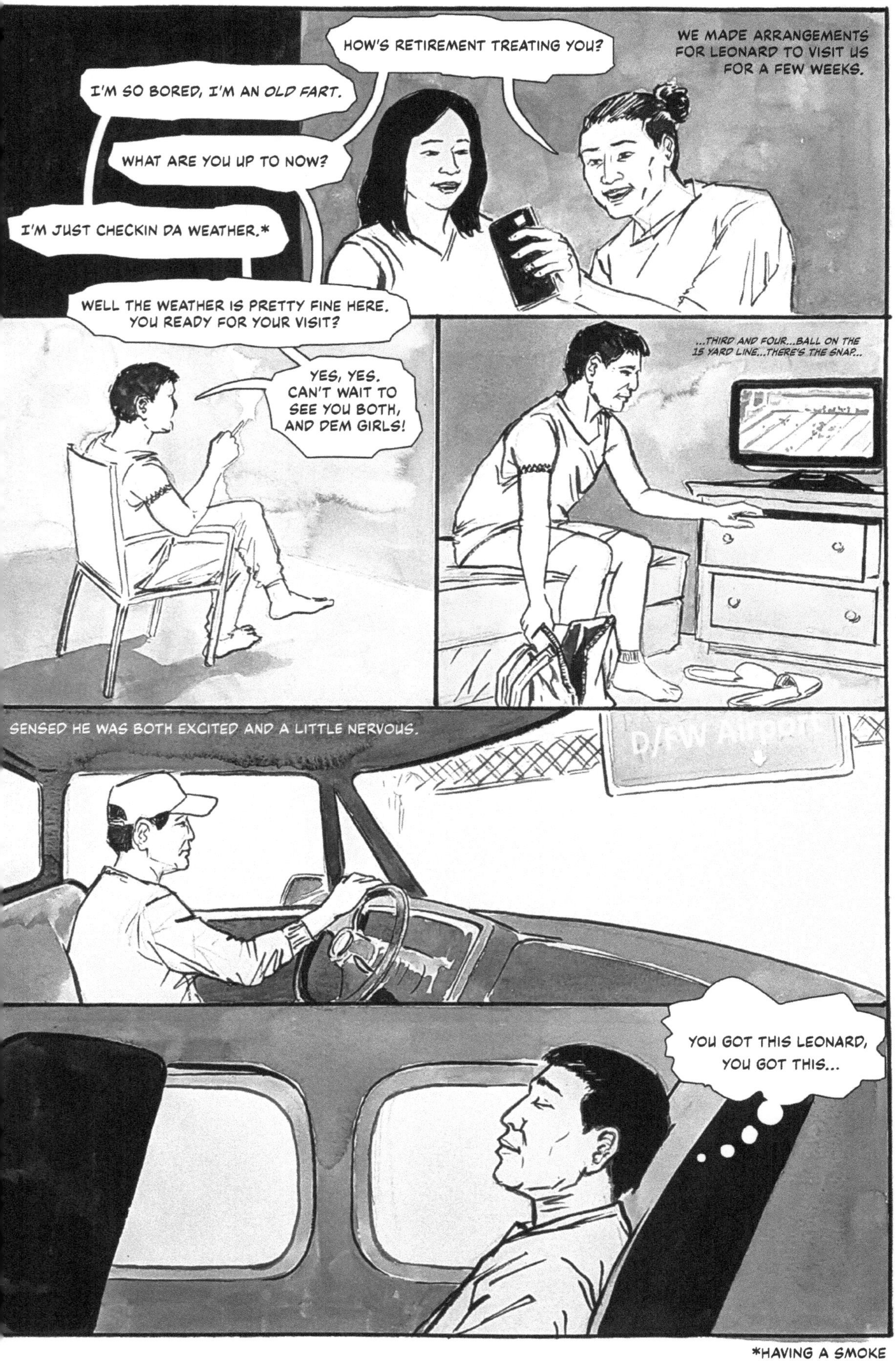
WE MADE ARRANGEMENTS FOR LEONARD TO VISIT US FOR A FEW WEEKS.
HOW'S RETIREMENT TREATING YOU?
I'M SO BORED, I'M AN *OLD FART*.
WHAT ARE YOU UP TO NOW?
I'M JUST CHECKIN DA WEATHER.*
WELL THE WEATHER IS PRETTY FINE HERE. YOU READY FOR YOUR VISIT?
YES, YES. CAN'T WAIT TO SEE YOU BOTH, AND DEM GIRLS!
...THIRD AND FOUR...BALL ON THE 15 YARD LINE...THERE'S THE SNAP...
SENSED HE WAS BOTH EXCITED AND A LITTLE NERVOUS.
D/FW Airport
YOU GOT THIS LEONARD, YOU GOT THIS...

*HAVING A SMOKE

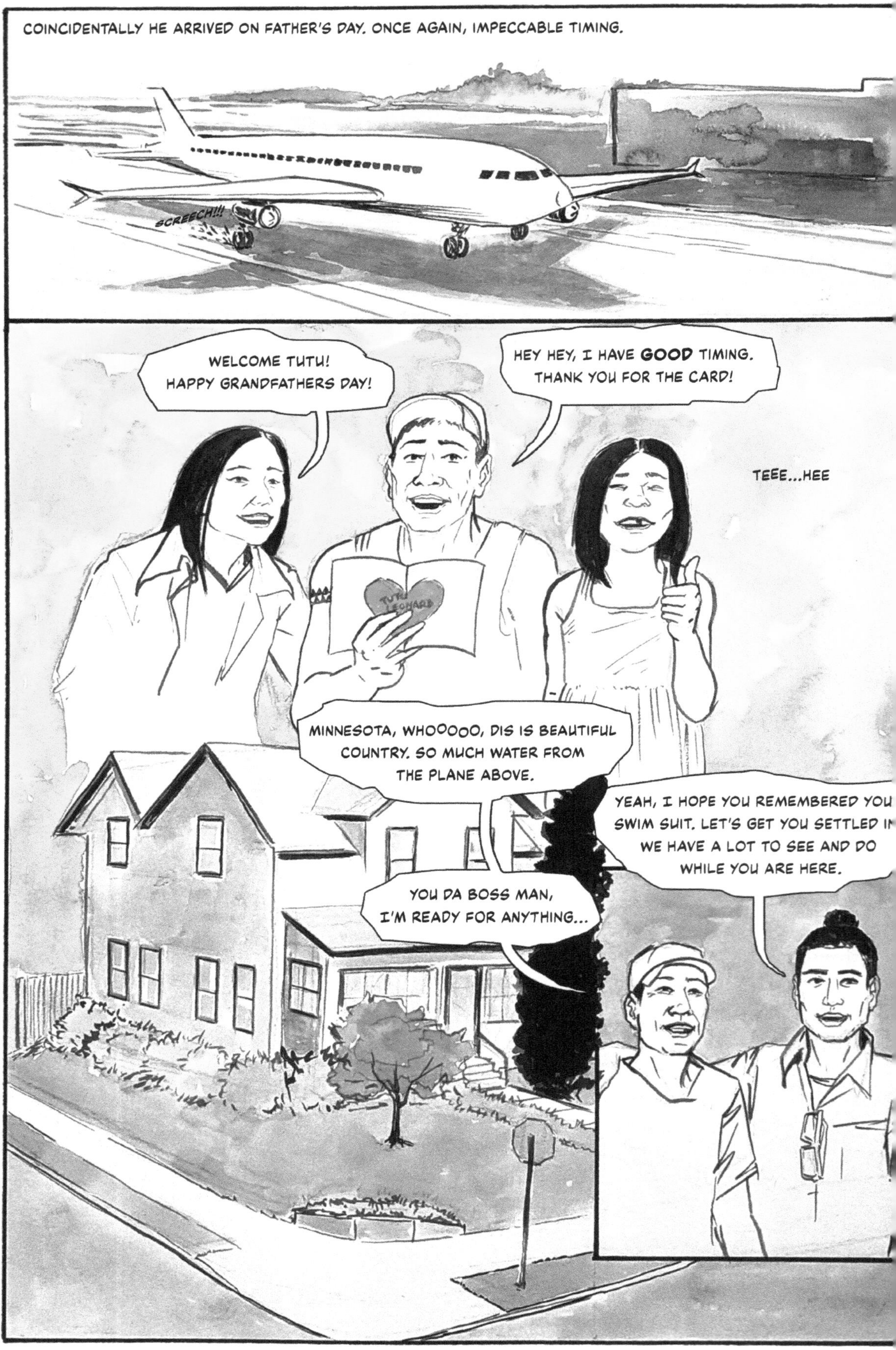
COINCIDENTALLY HE ARRIVED ON FATHER'S DAY. ONCE AGAIN, IMPECCABLE TIMING.
SCREECH!!!
WELCOME TUTU! HAPPY GRANDFATHERS DAY!
HEY HEY, I HAVE **GOOD** TIMING. THANK YOU FOR THE CARD!
TEEE...HEE
MINNESOTA, WHOOOOO, DIS IS BEAUTIFUL COUNTRY. SO MUCH WATER FROM THE PLANE ABOVE.
YEAH, I HOPE YOU REMEMBERED YOU SWIM SUIT. LET'S GET YOU SETTLED I WE HAVE A LOT TO SEE AND DO WHILE YOU ARE HERE.
YOU DA BOSS MAN, I'M READY FOR ANYTHING...

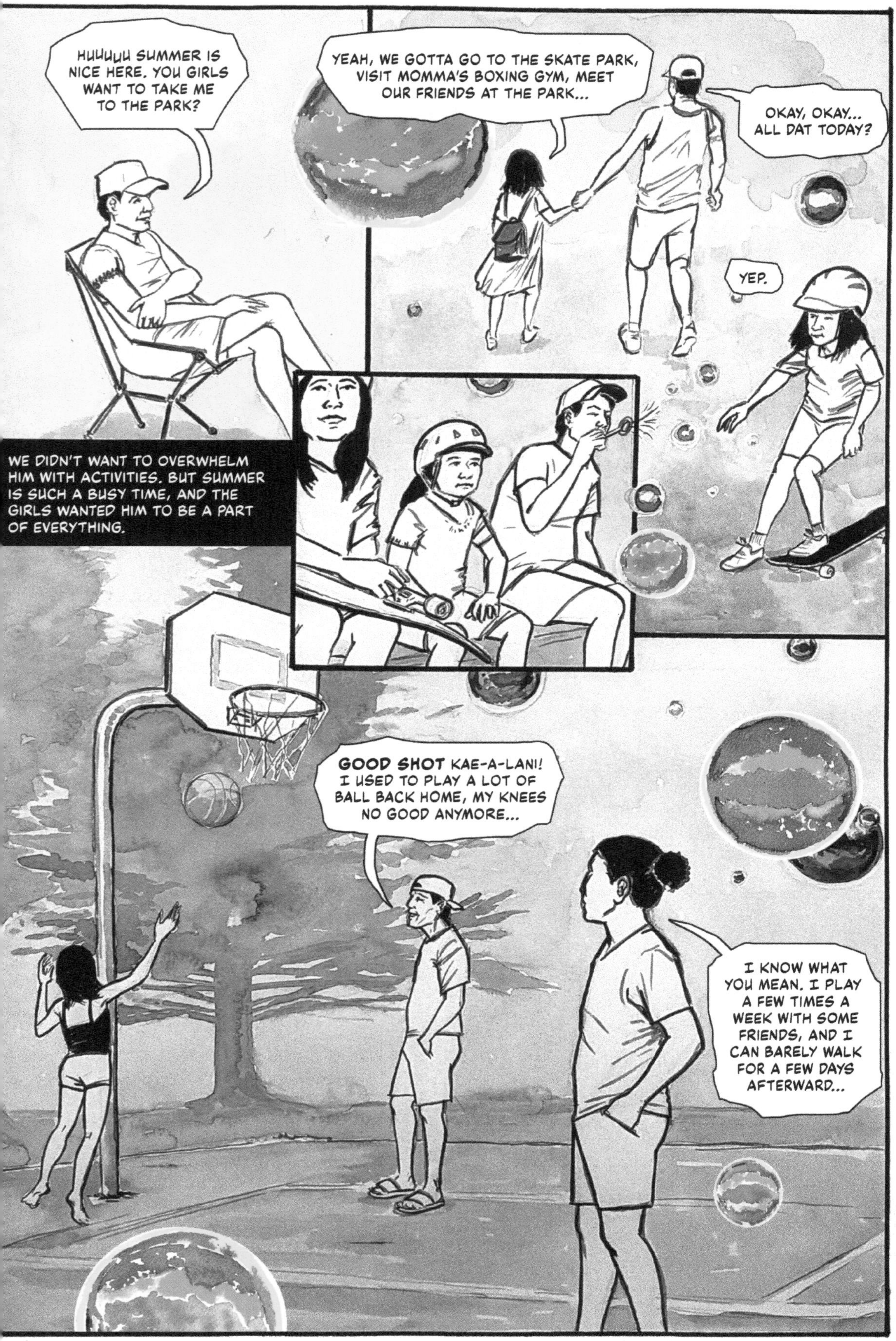
HUUUUU SUMMER IS NICE HERE. YOU GIRLS WANT TO TAKE ME TO THE PARK?
YEAH, WE GOTTA GO TO THE SKATE PARK, VISIT MOMMA'S BOXING GYM, MEET OUR FRIENDS AT THE PARK...
OKAY, OKAY... ALL DAT TODAY?
YEP.
WE DIDN'T WANT TO OVERWHELM HIM WITH ACTIVITIES. BUT SUMMER IS SUCH A BUSY TIME, AND THE GIRLS WANTED HIM TO BE A PART OF EVERYTHING.
GOOD SHOT KAE-A-LANI! I USED TO PLAY A LOT OF BALL BACK HOME, MY KNEES NO GOOD ANYMORE...
I KNOW WHAT YOU MEAN. I PLAY A FEW TIMES A WEEK WITH SOME FRIENDS, AND I CAN BARELY WALK FOR A FEW DAYS AFTERWARD...

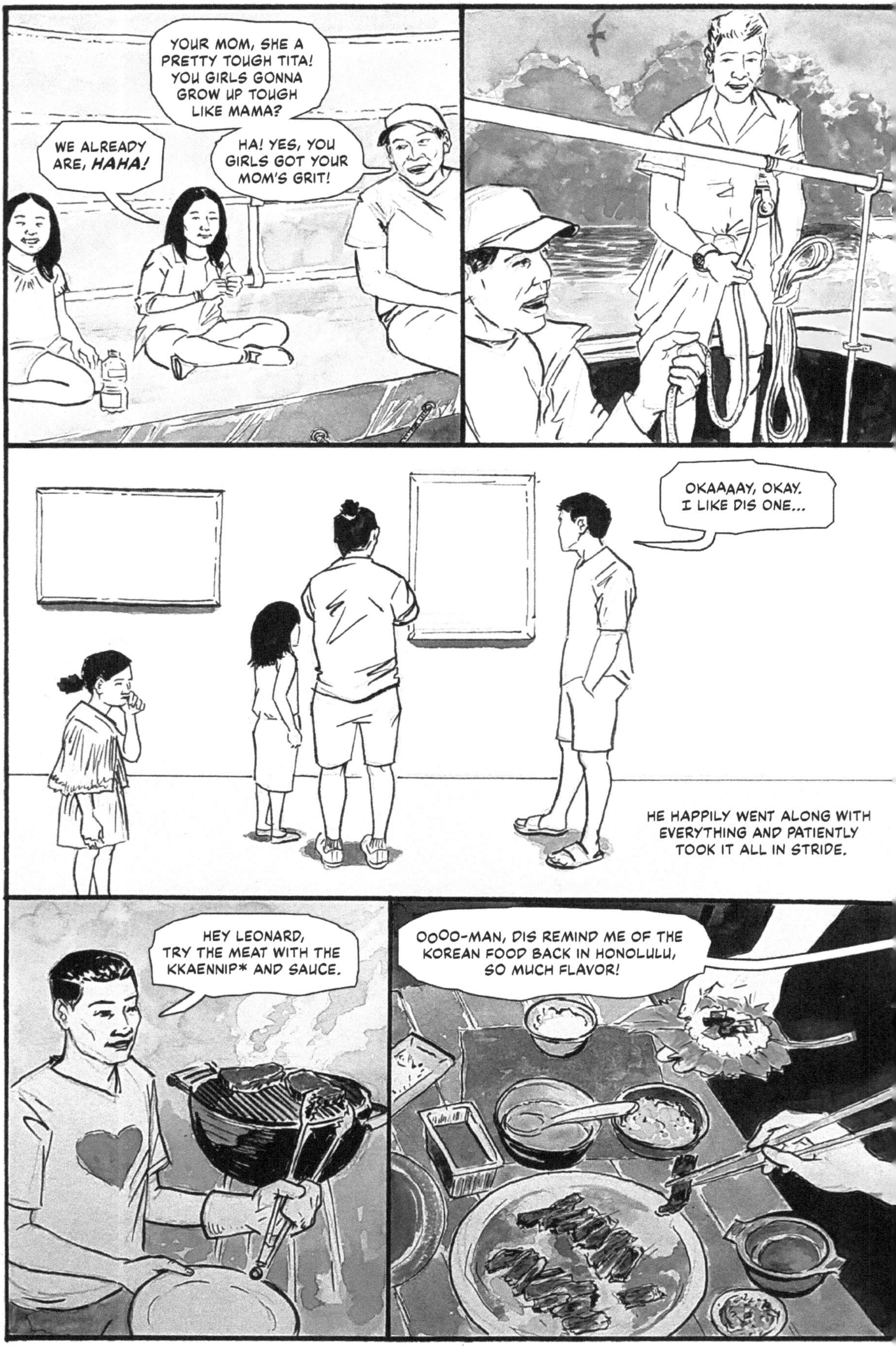
YOUR MOM, SHE A PRETTY TOUGH TITA! YOU GIRLS GONNA GROW UP TOUGH LIKE MAMA?
WE ALREADY ARE, HAHA!
HA! YES, YOU GIRLS GOT YOUR MOM'S GRIT!
OKAAAAY, OKAY. I LIKE DIS ONE...
HE HAPPILY WENT ALONG WITH EVERYTHING AND PATIENTLY TOOK IT ALL IN STRIDE.
HEY LEONARD, TRY THE MEAT WITH THE KKAENNIP* AND SAUCE.
OOOO-MAN, DIS REMIND ME OF THE KOREAN FOOD BACK IN HONOLULU, SO MUCH FLAVOR!

*PERILLA LEAV

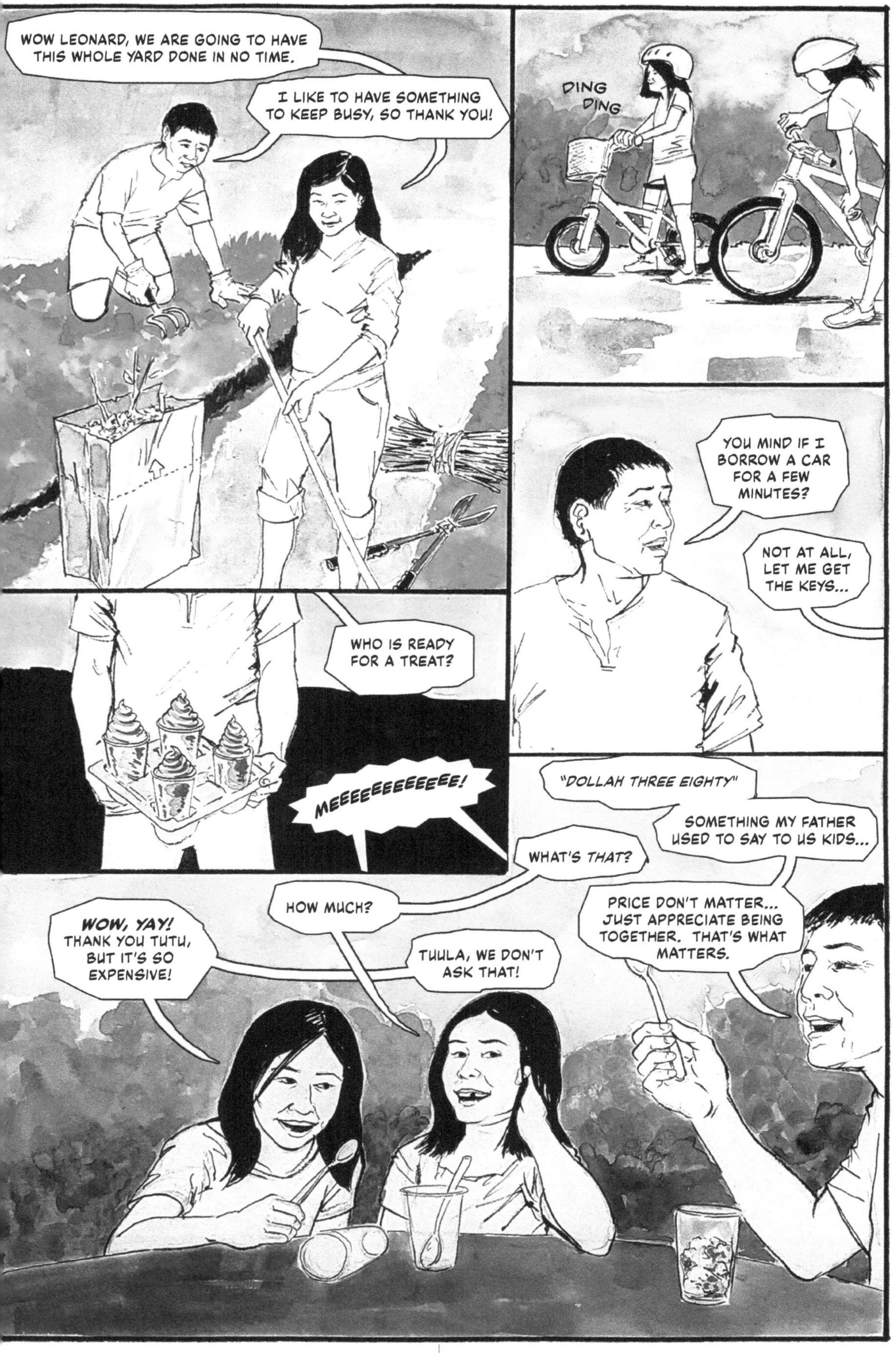
WOW LEONARD, WE ARE GOING TO HAVE THIS WHOLE YARD DONE IN NO TIME.
I LIKE TO HAVE SOMETHING TO KEEP BUSY, SO THANK YOU!
DING DING
YOU MIND IF I BORROW A CAR FOR A FEW MINUTES?
NOT AT ALL, LET ME GET THE KEYS...
WHO IS READY FOR A TREAT?
MEEEEEEEEEEEE!
"DOLLAH THREE EIGHTY"
SOMETHING MY FATHER USED TO SAY TO US KIDS...
WHAT'S *THAT*?
WOW, YAY! THANK YOU TUTU, BUT IT'S SO EXPENSIVE!
HOW MUCH?
TUULA, WE DON'T ASK THAT!
PRICE DON'T MATTER... JUST APPRECIATE BEING TOGETHER. THAT'S WHAT MATTERS.

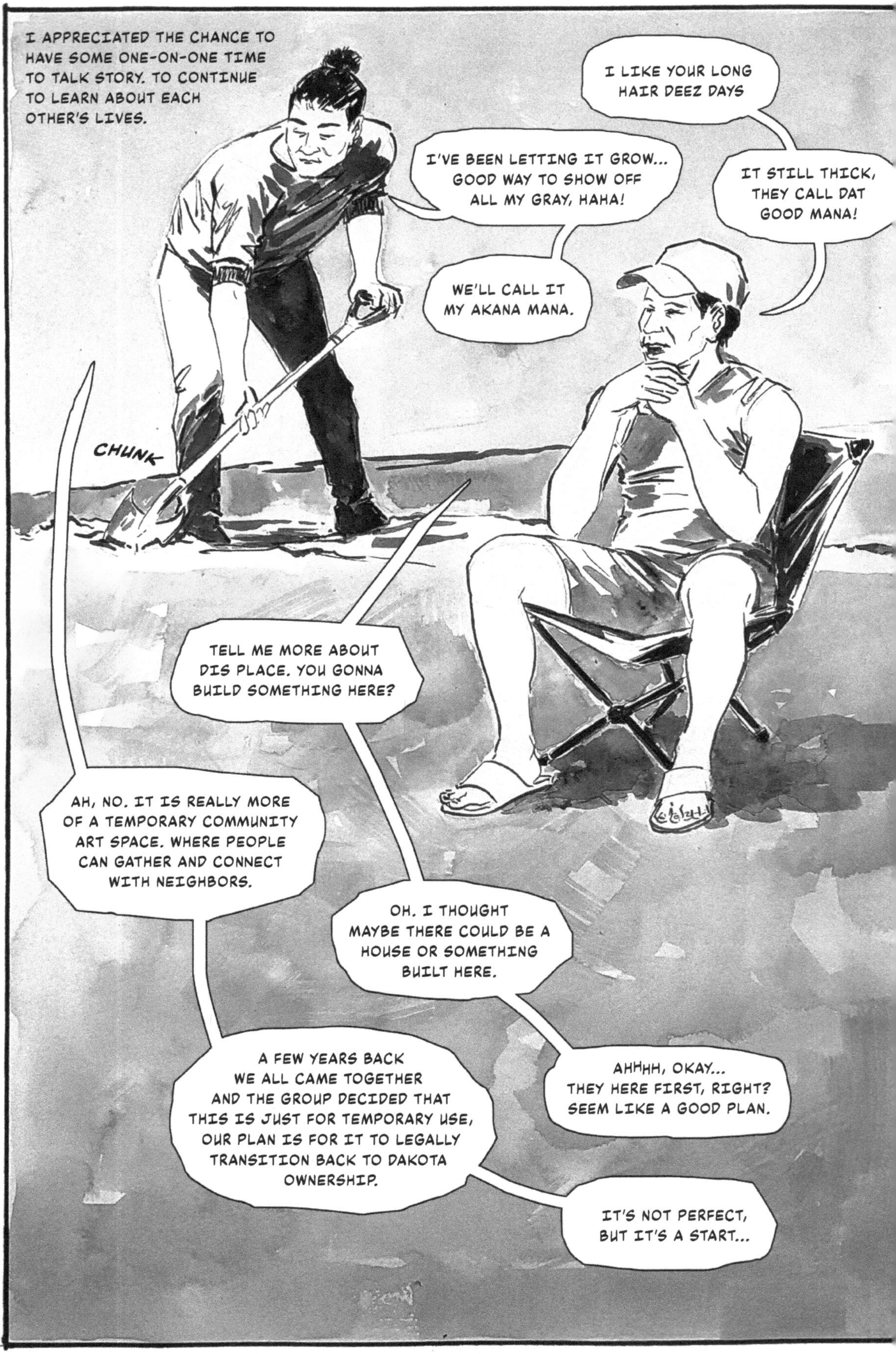
I APPRECIATED THE CHANCE TO HAVE SOME ONE-ON-ONE TIME TO TALK STORY. TO CONTINUE TO LEARN ABOUT EACH OTHER'S LIVES.
I LIKE YOUR LONG HAIR DEEZ DAYS
I'VE BEEN LETTING IT GROW... GOOD WAY TO SHOW OFF ALL MY GRAY, HAHA!
IT STILL THICK, THEY CALL DAT GOOD MANA!
WE'LL CALL IT MY AKANA MANA.
CHUNK
TELL ME MORE ABOUT DIS PLACE. YOU GONNA BUILD SOMETHING HERE?
AH, NO. IT IS REALLY MORE OF A TEMPORARY COMMUNITY ART SPACE. WHERE PEOPLE CAN GATHER AND CONNECT WITH NEIGHBORS.
OH. I THOUGHT MAYBE THERE COULD BE A HOUSE OR SOMETHING BUILT HERE.
A FEW YEARS BACK WE ALL CAME TOGETHER AND THE GROUP DECIDED THAT THIS IS JUST FOR TEMPORARY USE, OUR PLAN IS FOR IT TO LEGALLY TRANSITION BACK TO DAKOTA OWNERSHIP.
AHHHH, OKAY... THEY HERE FIRST, RIGHT? SEEM LIKE A GOOD PLAN.
IT'S NOT PERFECT, BUT IT'S A START...

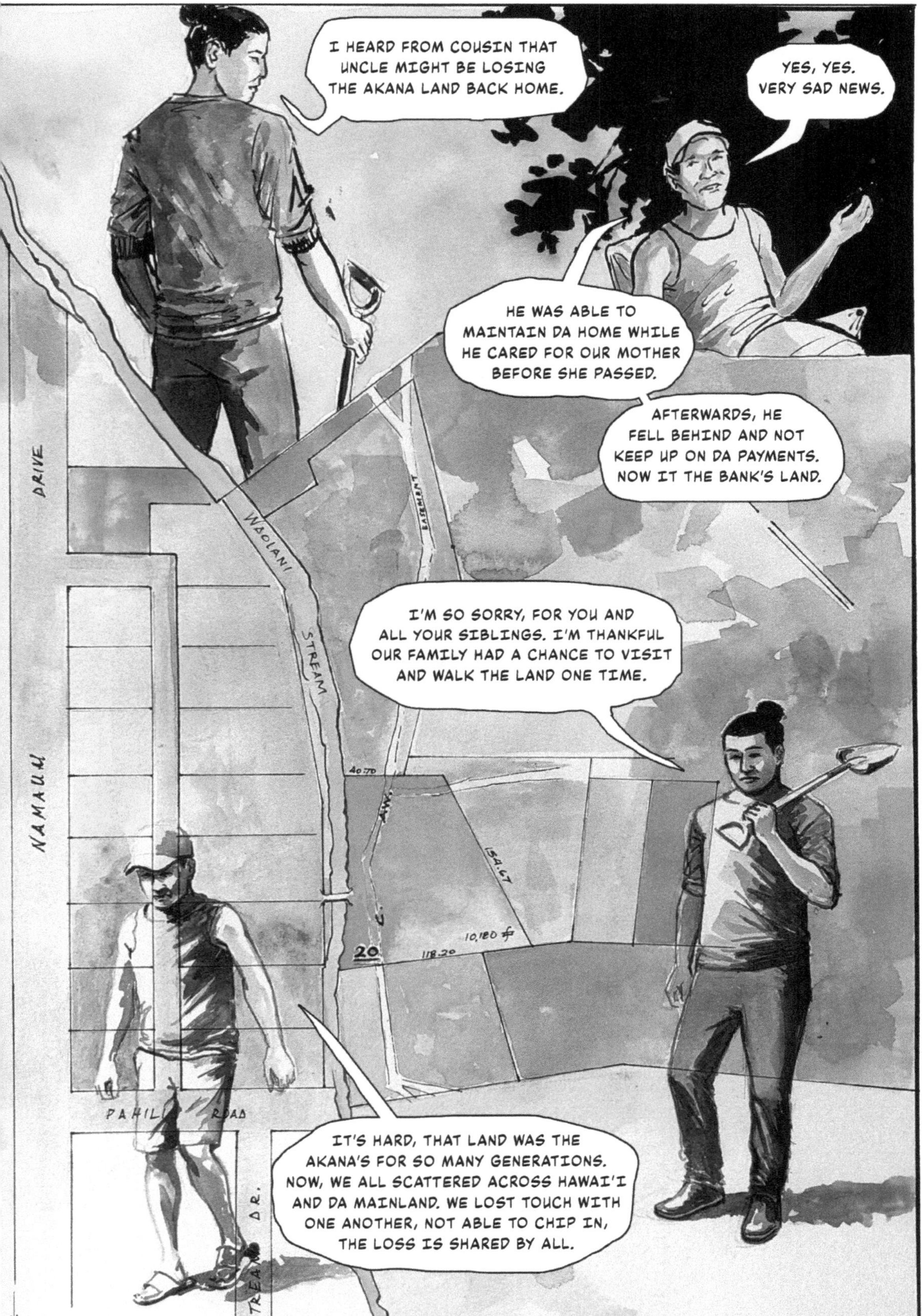
I HEARD FROM COUSIN THAT UNCLE MIGHT BE LOSING THE AKANA LAND BACK HOME.
YES, YES. VERY SAD NEWS.
HE WAS ABLE TO MAINTAIN DA HOME WHILE HE CARED FOR OUR MOTHER BEFORE SHE PASSED.
AFTERWARDS, HE FELL BEHIND AND NOT KEEP UP ON DA PAYMENTS. NOW IT THE BANK'S LAND.
I'M SO SORRY, FOR YOU AND ALL YOUR SIBLINGS. I'M THANKFUL OUR FAMILY HAD A CHANCE TO VISIT AND WALK THE LAND ONE TIME.
IT'S HARD, THAT LAND WAS THE AKANA'S FOR SO MANY GENERATIONS. NOW, WE ALL SCATTERED ACROSS HAWAI'I AND DA MAINLAND. WE LOST TOUCH WITH ONE ANOTHER, NOT ABLE TO CHIP IN, THE LOSS IS SHARED BY ALL.
DRIVE
WOOLANI
STREAM
EASEMENT
40.70
154.67
20
118.20
ROAD
DR.
PUUNUI, HONOLULU, OAHU

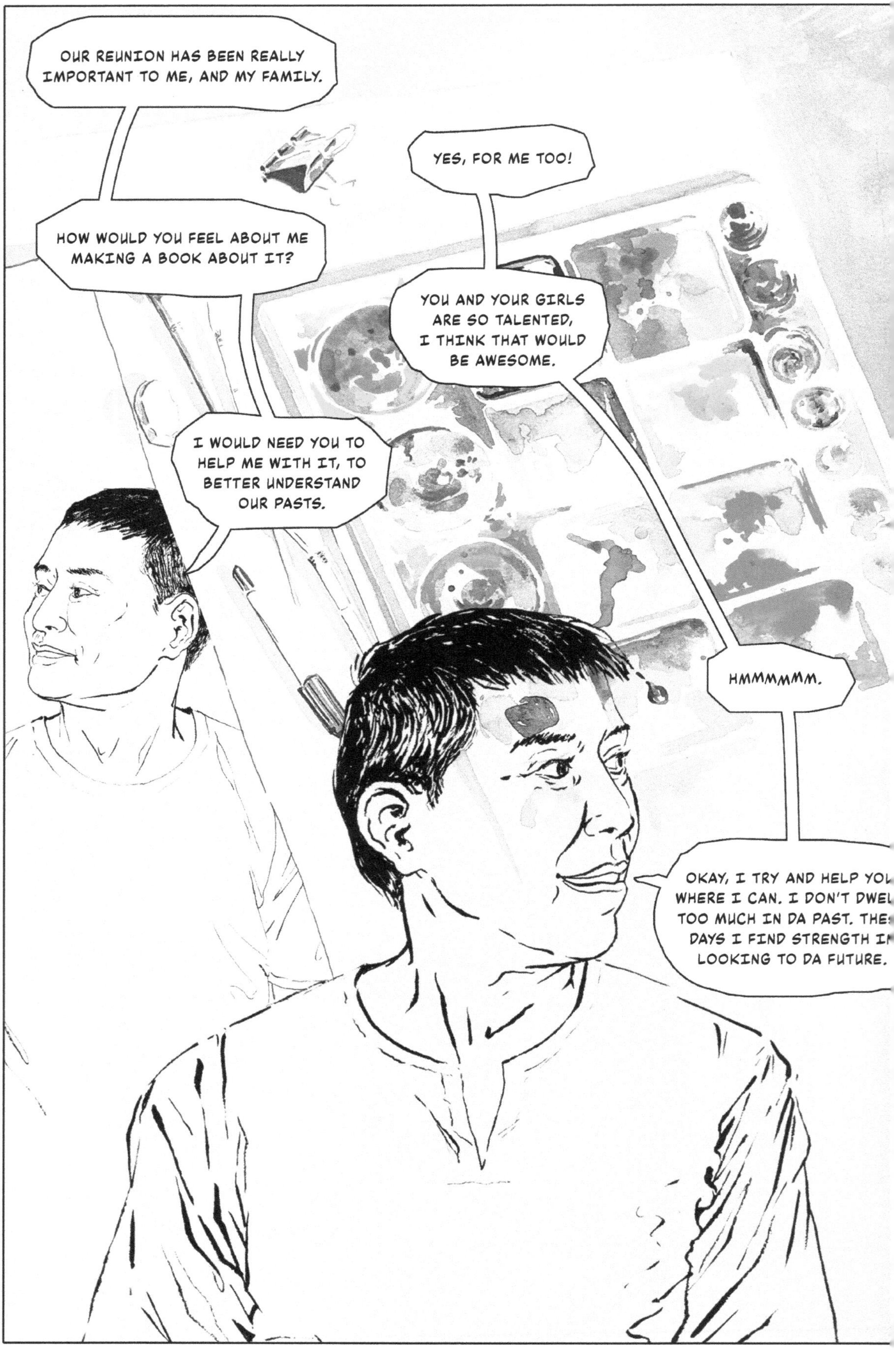
OUR REUNION HAS BEEN REALLY IMPORTANT TO ME, AND MY FAMILY.
HOW WOULD YOU FEEL ABOUT ME MAKING A BOOK ABOUT IT?
I WOULD NEED YOU TO HELP ME WITH IT, TO BETTER UNDERSTAND OUR PASTS.
YES, FOR ME TOO!
YOU AND YOUR GIRLS ARE SO TALENTED, I THINK THAT WOULD BE AWESOME.
HMMMMMM.
OKAY, I TRY AND HELP YO WHERE I CAN. I DON'T DWEL TOO MUCH IN DA PAST. THE DAYS I FIND STRENGTH I LOOKING TO DA FUTURE.

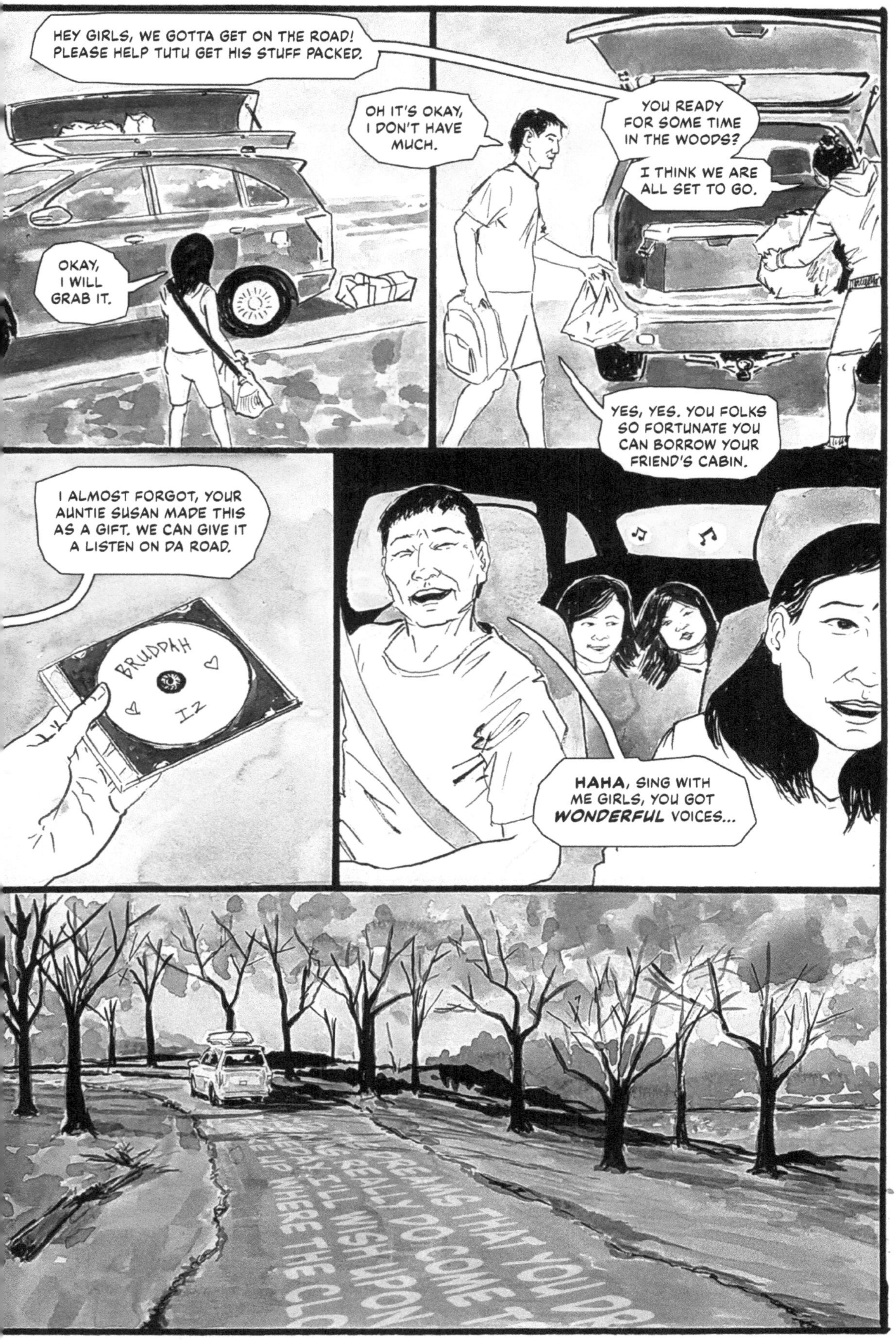
HEY GIRLS, WE GOTTA GET ON THE ROAD! PLEASE HELP TUTU GET HIS STUFF PACKED.
OKAY, I WILL GRAB IT.
OH IT'S OKAY, I DON'T HAVE MUCH.
YOU READY FOR SOME TIME IN THE WOODS?
I THINK WE ARE ALL SET TO GO.
YES, YES. YOU FOLKS SO FORTUNATE YOU CAN BORROW YOUR FRIEND'S CABIN.
I ALMOST FORGOT, YOUR AUNTIE SUSAN MADE THIS AS A GIFT. WE CAN GIVE IT A LISTEN ON DA ROAD.
BRUDDAH IZ
HAHA, SING WITH ME GIRLS, YOU GOT ***WONDERFUL*** VOICES...
THE DREAMS THAT YOU
REALLY DO COME
I'LL WISH UPON
WHERE THE

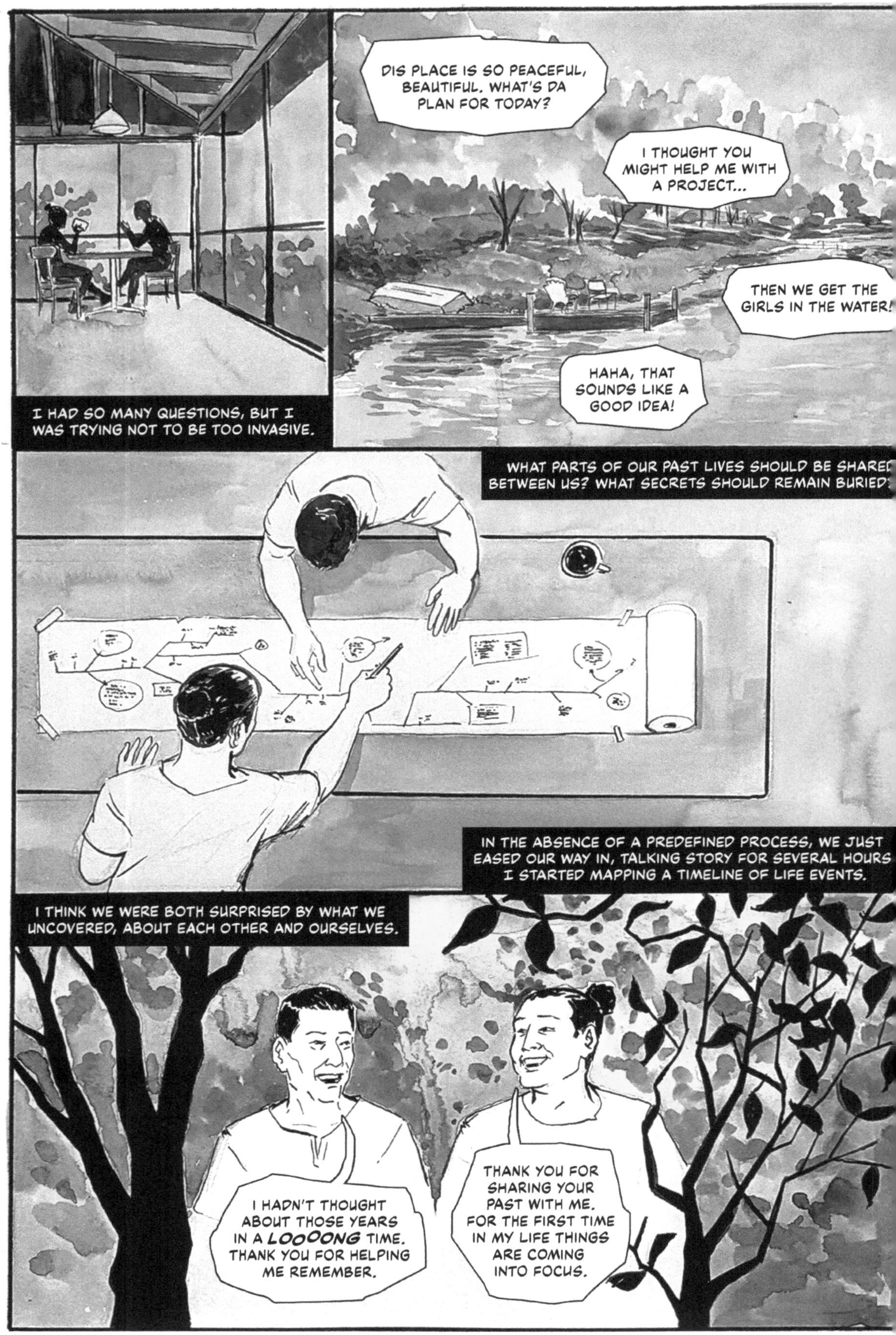
I HAD SO MANY QUESTIONS, BUT I WAS TRYING NOT TO BE TOO INVASIVE.
DIS PLACE IS SO PEACEFUL, BEAUTIFUL. WHAT'S DA PLAN FOR TODAY?
I THOUGHT YOU MIGHT HELP ME WITH A PROJECT...
THEN WE GET THE GIRLS IN THE WATER!
HAHA, THAT SOUNDS LIKE A GOOD IDEA!
WHAT PARTS OF OUR PAST LIVES SHOULD BE SHARED BETWEEN US? WHAT SECRETS SHOULD REMAIN BURIED?
IN THE ABSENCE OF A PREDEFINED PROCESS, WE JUST EASED OUR WAY IN, TALKING STORY FOR SEVERAL HOURS. I STARTED MAPPING A TIMELINE OF LIFE EVENTS.
I THINK WE WERE BOTH SURPRISED BY WHAT WE UNCOVERED, ABOUT EACH OTHER AND OURSELVES.
I HADN'T THOUGHT ABOUT THOSE YEARS IN A LOOOONG TIME. THANK YOU FOR HELPING ME REMEMBER.
THANK YOU FOR SHARING YOUR PAST WITH ME. FOR THE FIRST TIME IN MY LIFE THINGS ARE COMING INTO FOCUS.

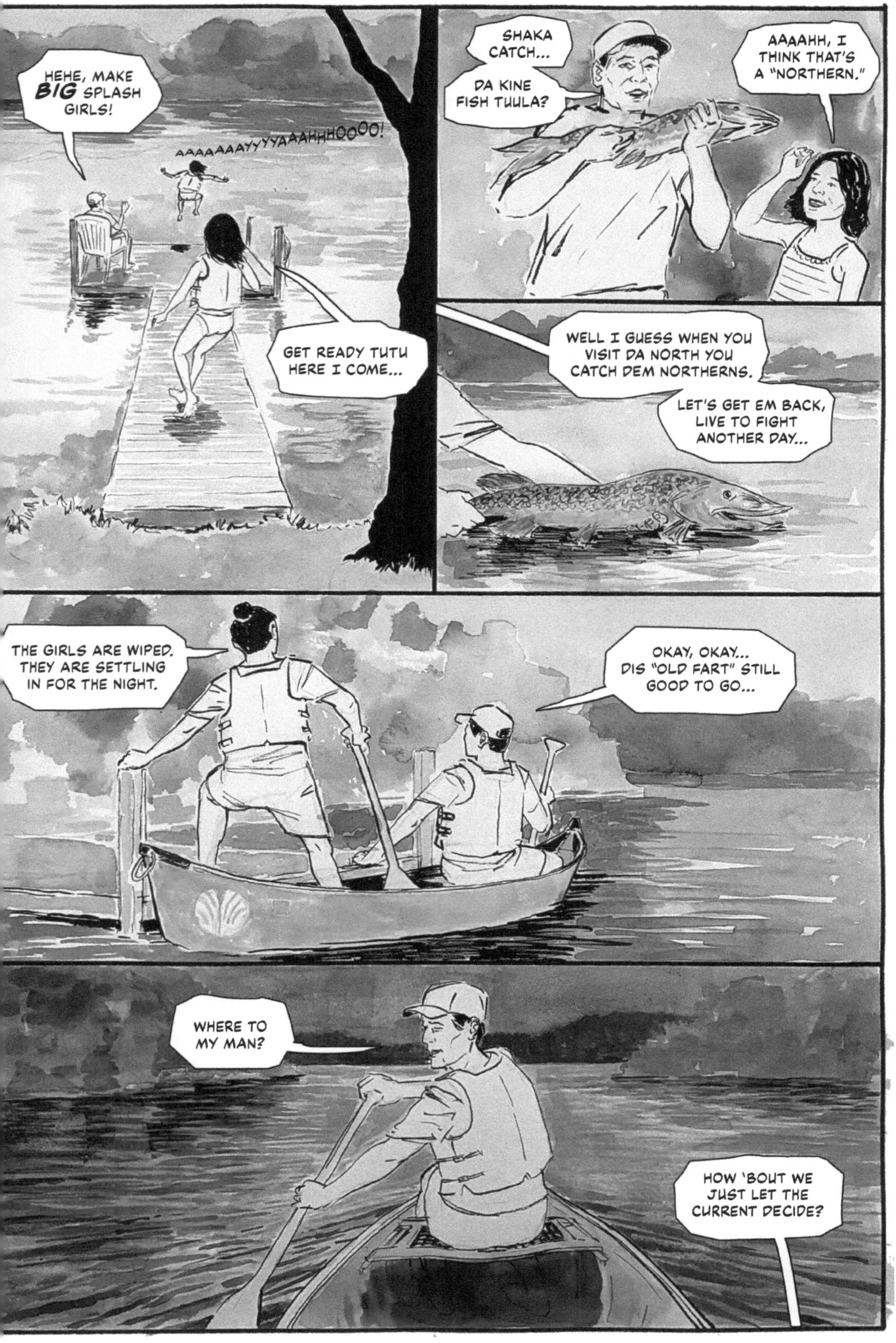
HEHE, MAKE BIG SPLASH GIRLS!
AAAAAAAYYYYAAAHHHOOOO!
GET READY TUTU HERE I COME...
SHAKA CATCH...
DA KINE FISH TUULA?
AAAAHH, I THINK THAT'S A "NORTHERN."
WELL I GUESS WHEN YOU VISIT DA NORTH YOU CATCH DEM NORTHERNS.
LET'S GET EM BACK, LIVE TO FIGHT ANOTHER DAY...
THE GIRLS ARE WIPED. THEY ARE SETTLING IN FOR THE NIGHT.
OKAY, OKAY... DIS "OLD FART" STILL GOOD TO GO...
WHERE TO MY MAN?
HOW 'BOUT WE JUST LET THE CURRENT DECIDE?

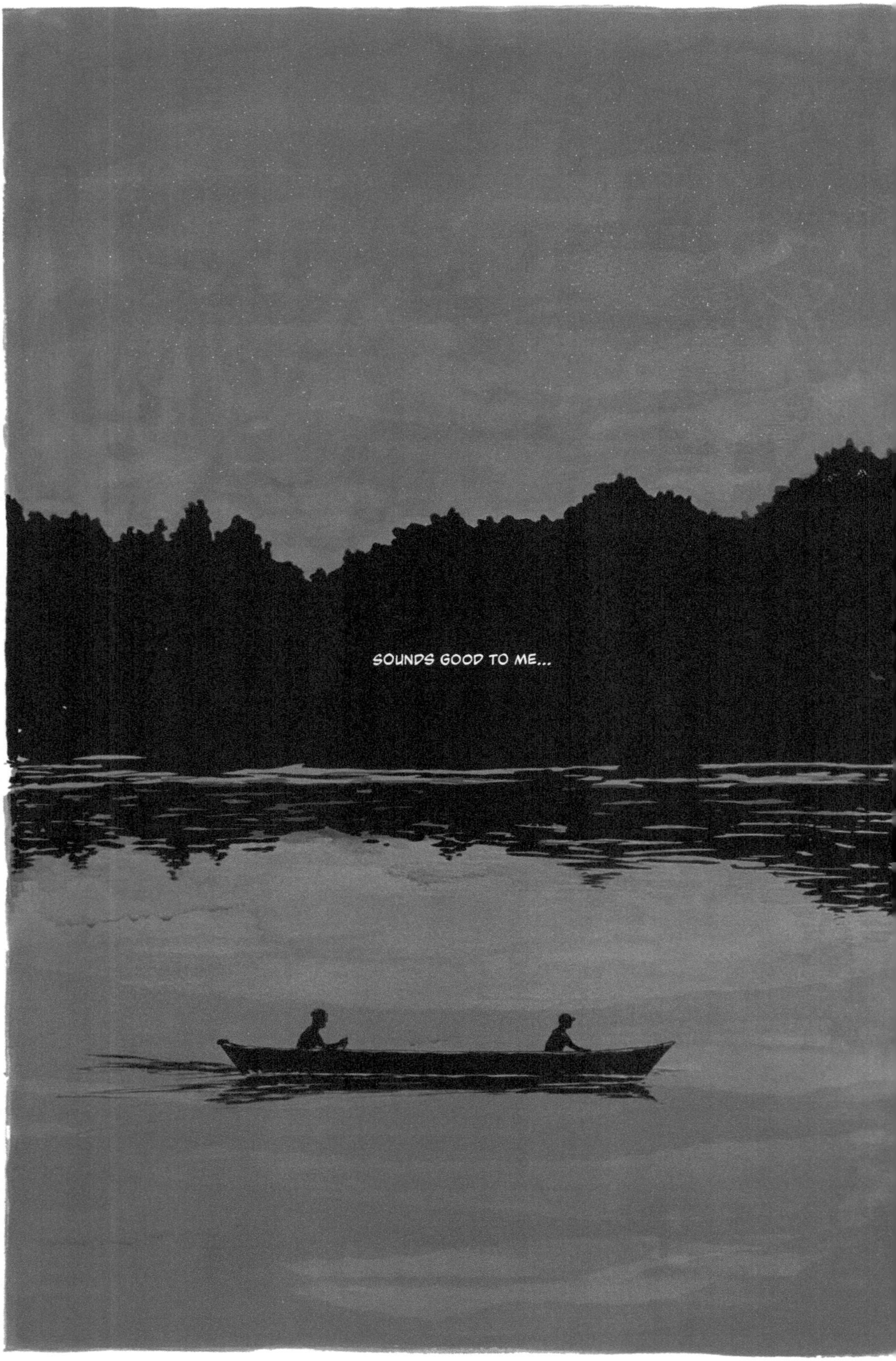
SOUNDS GOOD TO ME...

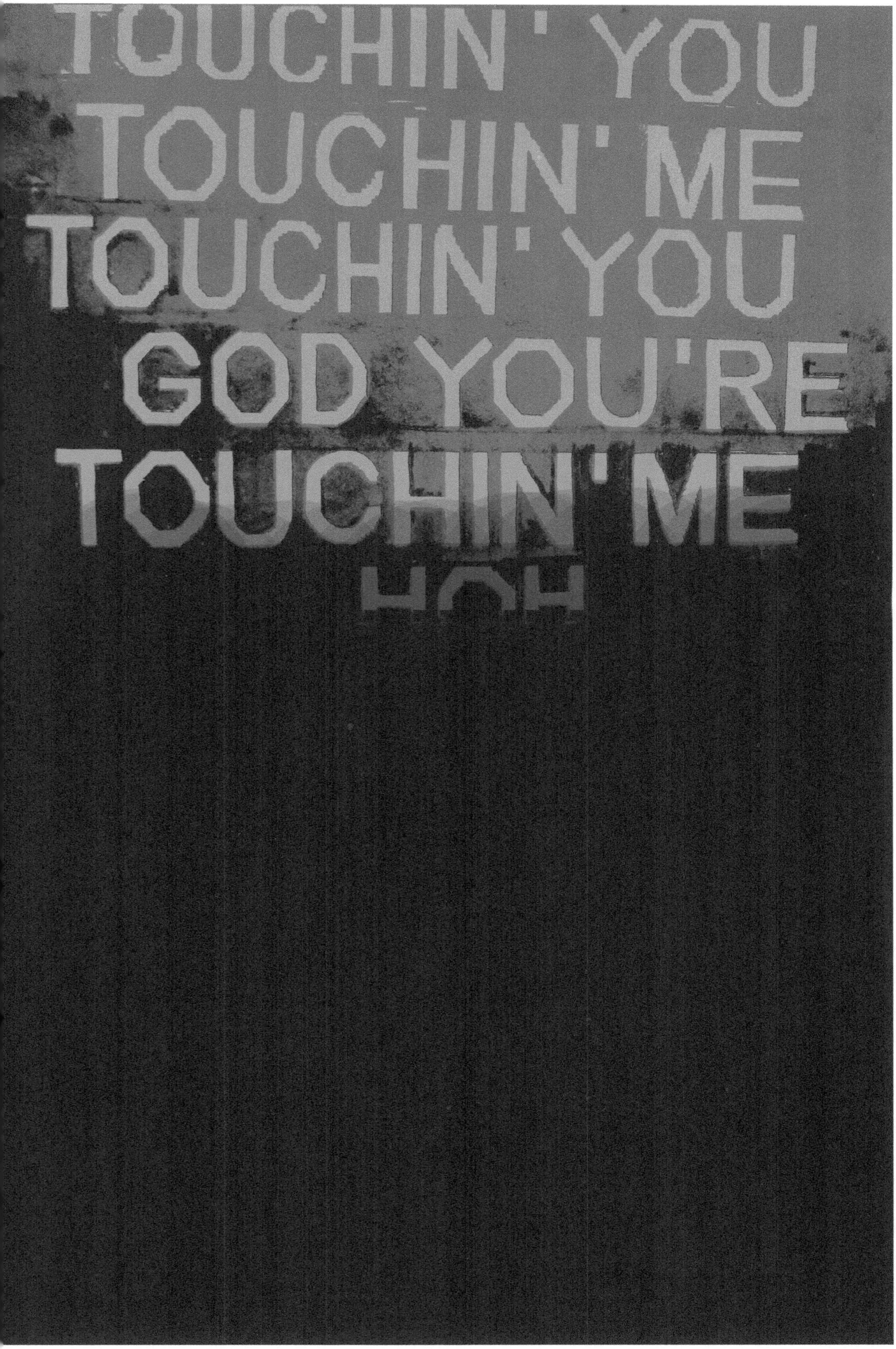
TOUCHIN' YOU
TOUCHIN' ME
TOUCHIN' YOU
GOD YOU'RE
TOUCHIN' ME

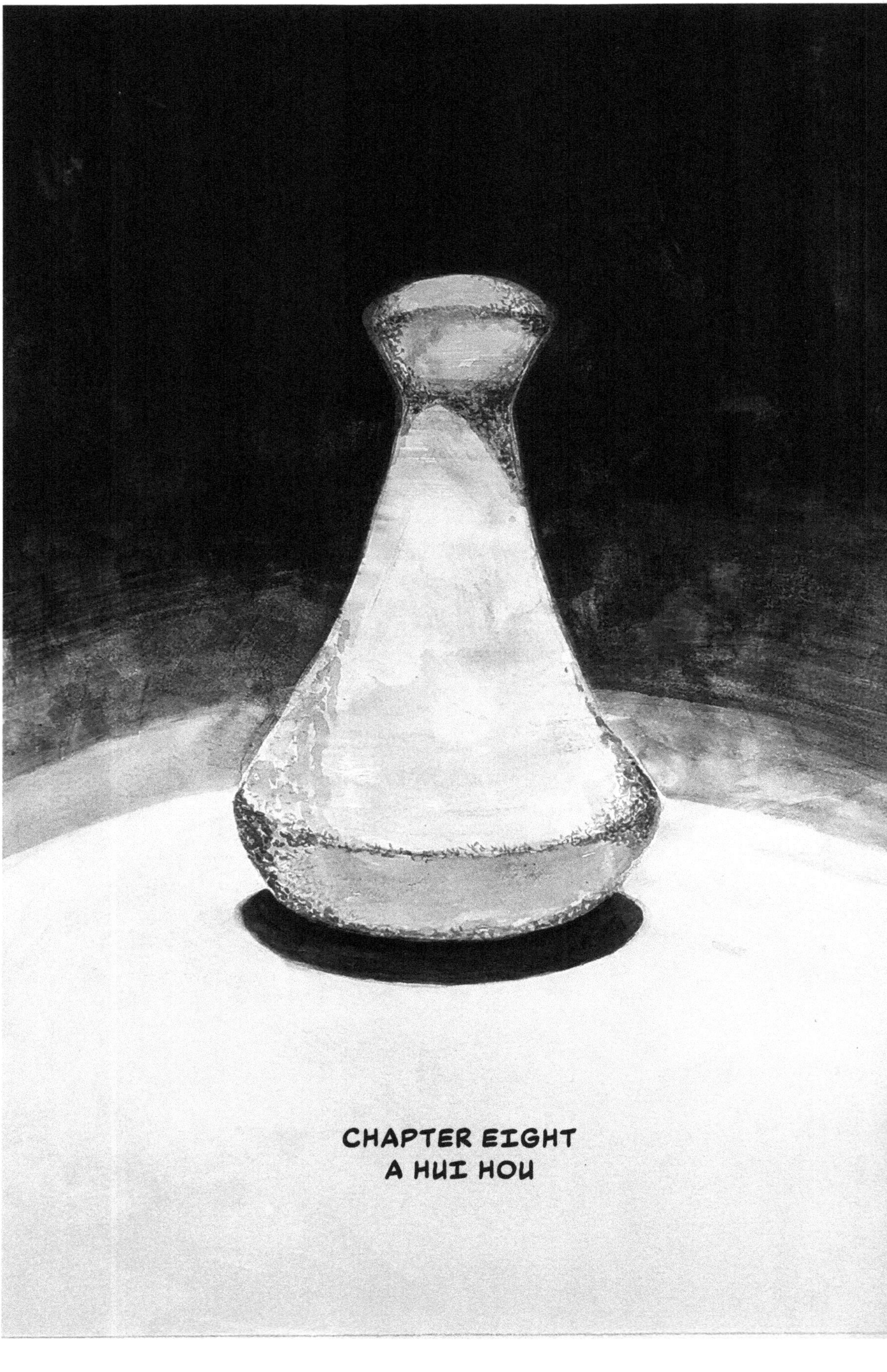

CHAPTER EIGHT
A HUI HOU

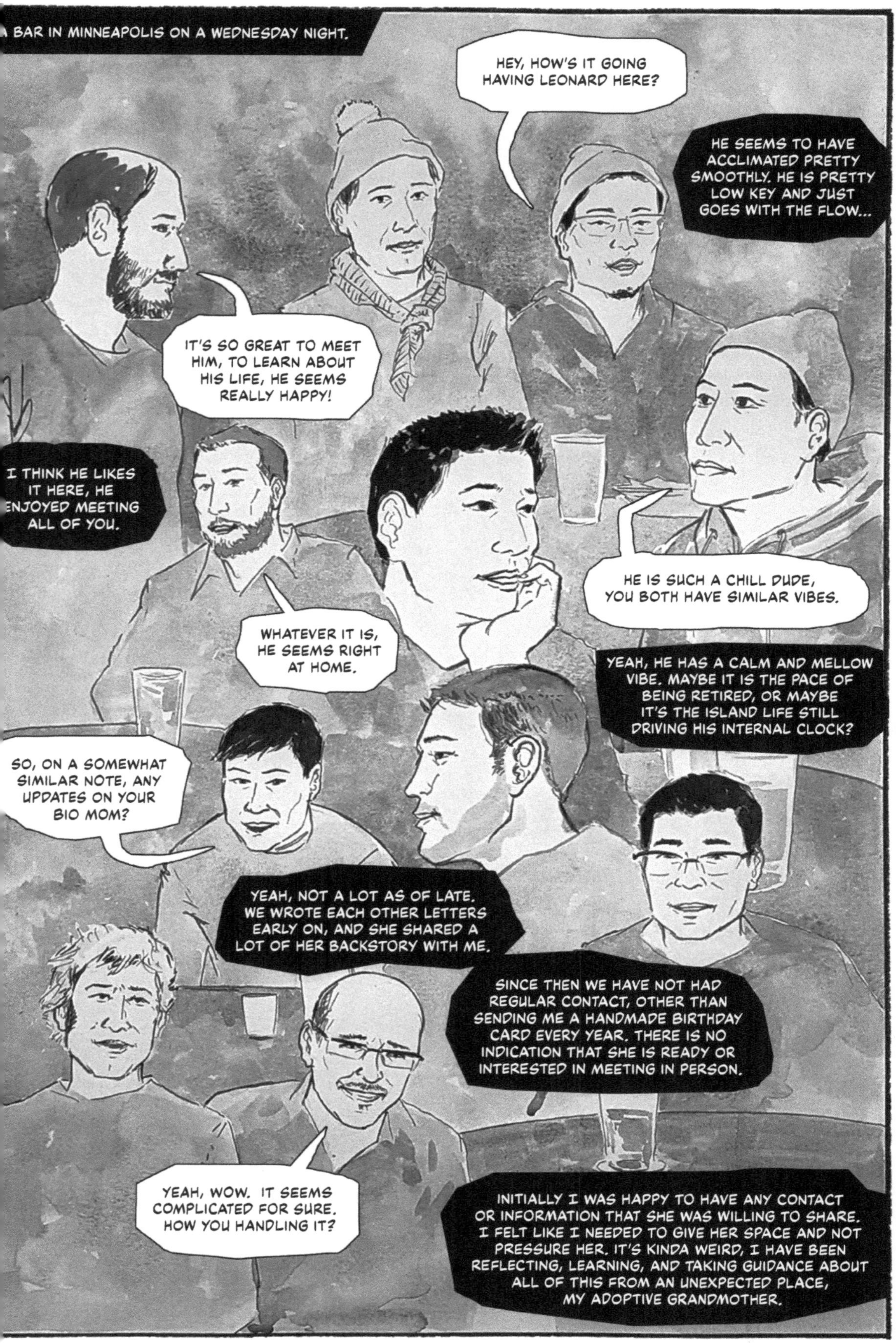
A BAR IN MINNEAPOLIS ON A WEDNESDAY NIGHT.
HEY, HOW'S IT GOING HAVING LEONARD HERE?
HE SEEMS TO HAVE ACCLIMATED PRETTY SMOOTHLY. HE IS PRETTY LOW KEY AND JUST GOES WITH THE FLOW...
IT'S SO GREAT TO MEET HIM, TO LEARN ABOUT HIS LIFE, HE SEEMS REALLY HAPPY!
I THINK HE LIKES IT HERE, HE ENJOYED MEETING ALL OF YOU.
HE IS SUCH A CHILL DUDE, YOU BOTH HAVE SIMILAR VIBES.
WHATEVER IT IS, HE SEEMS RIGHT AT HOME.
YEAH, HE HAS A CALM AND MELLOW VIBE. MAYBE IT IS THE PACE OF BEING RETIRED, OR MAYBE IT'S THE ISLAND LIFE STILL DRIVING HIS INTERNAL CLOCK?
SO, ON A SOMEWHAT SIMILAR NOTE, ANY UPDATES ON YOUR BIO MOM?
YEAH, NOT A LOT AS OF LATE. WE WROTE EACH OTHER LETTERS EARLY ON, AND SHE SHARED A LOT OF HER BACKSTORY WITH ME.
SINCE THEN WE HAVE NOT HAD REGULAR CONTACT, OTHER THAN SENDING ME A HANDMADE BIRTHDAY CARD EVERY YEAR. THERE IS NO INDICATION THAT SHE IS READY OR INTERESTED IN MEETING IN PERSON.
YEAH, WOW. IT SEEMS COMPLICATED FOR SURE. HOW YOU HANDLING IT?
INITIALLY I WAS HAPPY TO HAVE ANY CONTACT OR INFORMATION THAT SHE WAS WILLING TO SHARE. I FELT LIKE I NEEDED TO GIVE HER SPACE AND NOT PRESSURE HER. IT'S KINDA WEIRD, I HAVE BEEN REFLECTING, LEARNING, AND TAKING GUIDANCE ABOUT ALL OF THIS FROM AN UNEXPECTED PLACE, MY ADOPTIVE GRANDMOTHER.

DEAR GRANDMOTHER,

OH GRANDMOTHER, IF YOU WERE STILL WITH US TODAY I IMAGINE YOU WOULD BE SURPRISED TO RECEIVE THIS FROM ME, AS OUR RELATIONSHIP WAS NOT EXPRESSED THROUGH OUTWARD GESTURES OF TENDERNESS. I ADMIT THAT AS YOUR GRANDSON, I NEVER PUT MUCH EFFORT INTO CONNECTING WITH YOU AS I OFTEN FOUND YOU DISTANT AND DETACHED. BUT THINGS HAVE COME TO LIGHT THAT CANNOT BE IGNORED.

I FIND MYSELF TRYING TO LEARN FROM IT ALL, LET IT GUIDE ME, AND POTENTIALLY COMPLICATE MY PERCEPTIONS OF YOU.

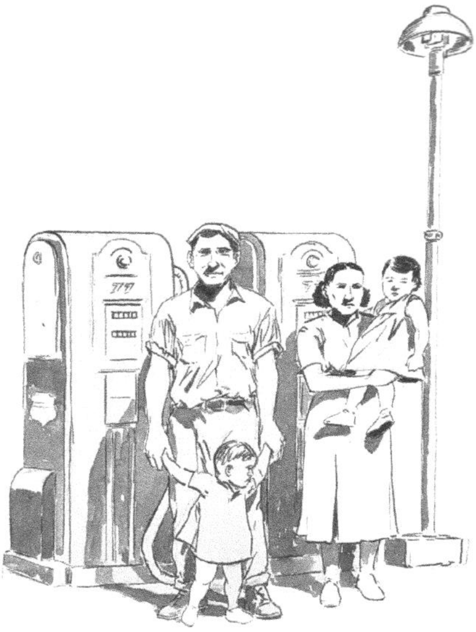

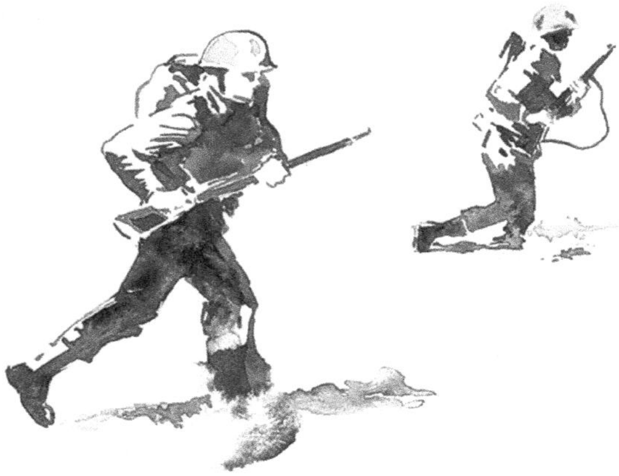

AS A CHILD I UNDERSTOOD YOUR LIFE TO BE ONE OF HARDSHIP AND BITTERNESS. I KNOW NOW THAT WAS A FAIRLY NAIVE OR LIMITED POINT OF VIEW. AND HAD I EXPERIENCED THE LOSSES YOU ENDURED, I PROBABLY WOULD HAVE BEEN CONSUMED WITH BITTERNESS AS WELL.

I CANNOT KNOW THE PAIN OF LOSING A SPOUSE SO EARLY. OF HAVING YOUR DREAMS OF RUNNING A SMALL BUSINESS, OF RAISING A FAMILY TOGETHER IN RURAL MINNESOTA, DASHED ALONG WITH 75 MILLION OTHER FAMILIES WORLDWIDE DURING YOUR GENERATION'S GREAT WAR.

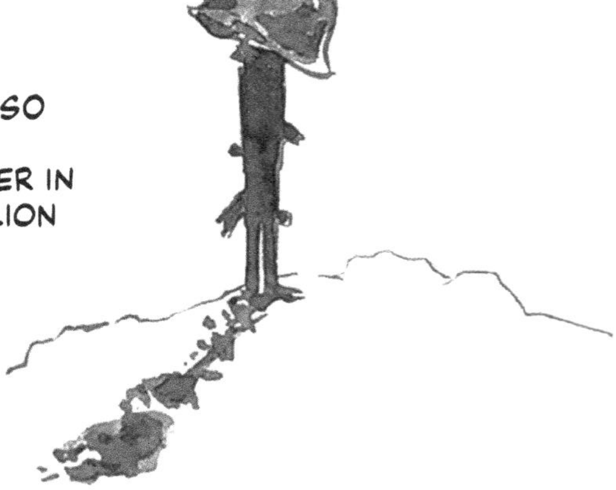

IN A TIMELY PARALLEL CIRCUMSTANCE, ONE OF YOUR GREAT SECRETS HAS NOW COME TO SURFACE. A SECRET YOU NEVER UTTERED TO ANYONE, A DAUGHTER WHO WOULD BE NAMED BY SOMEONE OTHER THAN YOU.

I WILL NEVER KNOW THE WEIGHT OF SOCIETAL SHAME AND CATHOLIC GUILT THAT MADE THIS SECRET SO POTENT. THE IMMENSE BURDEN THAT YOUNG WOMEN EXPERIENCED BEING SENT AWAY TO HAVE A CHILD OUT OF WEDLOCK. I REFLECT DIFFERENTLY NOW, THROUGH CURIOSITY AND A LITTLE MORE COMPASSION.

OH DEAR, GRANDMOTHER, WAS IT EVEN CONSENSUAL?

I WONDER TODAY IF MY SISTER AND I, BOTH BEING ADOPTED BY YOUR YOUNGEST DAUGHTER, WERE A PAINFUL REMINDER OF THE CHILD YOU GAVE UP, AND IF THIS WAS A FACTOR IN OUR STRAINED RELATIONSHIP.

OR WERE WE JUST TOO RAMBUNCTUOUS AND NOISY AND YOU WERE INDIFFERENT? WE WILL NEVER KNOW.

YOUR LIFELONG SECRET GIVES ME NEW INSIGHT AND COMPASSION FOR MY FIRST MOTHER'S EXPERIENCE. SHE CHOSE TO TELL HER HUSBAND AND ADULT CHILDREN ABOUT GIVING BIRTH TO ME AND MY SUBSEQUENT ADOPTION. I'M NOT SAYING THIS WAS WHAT YOU SHOULD HAVE DONE, GRANDMOTHER. SHE MADE A DIFFERENT CHOICE, HER CHOICE. I HOPE THAT BY BREAKING SILENCE WITH HER BELOVED, SHE WILL BE FULLY LIBERATED FROM THE PAIN, GUILT, JUDGEMENT, OR SHAME YOU INTERNALIZED AND SHOULDERED THROUGHOUT YOUR LIFETIME.

I'LL NEVER KNOW HOW DIFFICULT THAT MUST HAVE BEEN FOR YOU. IN RETROSPECT I WONDER WHAT IT WOULD HAVE BEEN LIKE FOR YOU TO BE RELEASED FROM IT. YOUR UNNAMED DAUGHTER AND I LIVE ON SEPARATE LINES OF TIME AND GENEALOGY, YET WE PLAY A SIMILAR ROLE IN ALL OF THIS. ALTHOUGH YOU REMAINED SILENT THROUGHOUT, SILENCE DOES NOT PREVENT SECRETS FROM RETURNING.

-M

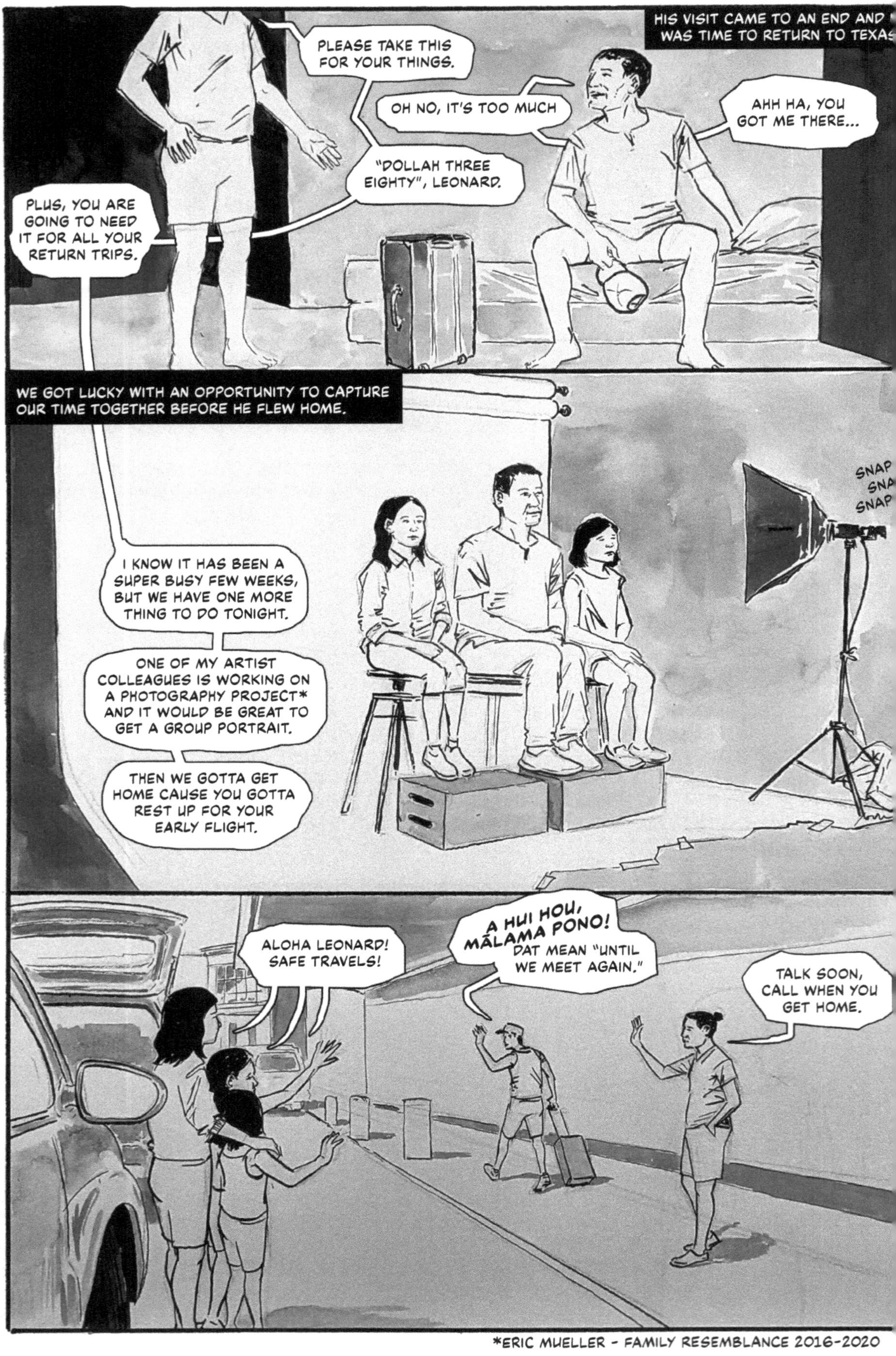
HIS VISIT CAME TO AN END AND IT WAS TIME TO RETURN TO TEXAS
PLEASE TAKE THIS FOR YOUR THINGS.
OH NO, IT'S TOO MUCH
"DOLLAH THREE EIGHTY", LEONARD.
PLUS, YOU ARE GOING TO NEED IT FOR ALL YOUR RETURN TRIPS.
AHH HA, YOU GOT ME THERE...
WE GOT LUCKY WITH AN OPPORTUNITY TO CAPTURE OUR TIME TOGETHER BEFORE HE FLEW HOME.
I KNOW IT HAS BEEN A SUPER BUSY FEW WEEKS, BUT WE HAVE ONE MORE THING TO DO TONIGHT.
ONE OF MY ARTIST COLLEAGUES IS WORKING ON A PHOTOGRAPHY PROJECT* AND IT WOULD BE GREAT TO GET A GROUP PORTRAIT.
THEN WE GOTTA GET HOME CAUSE YOU GOTTA REST UP FOR YOUR EARLY FLIGHT.
SNAP SNAP SNAP
ALOHA LEONARD! SAFE TRAVELS!
A HUI HOU, MĀLAMA PONO! DAT MEAN "UNTIL WE MEET AGAIN."
TALK SOON, CALL WHEN YOU GET HOME.

*ERIC MUELLER - FAMILY RESEMBLANCE 2016-2020

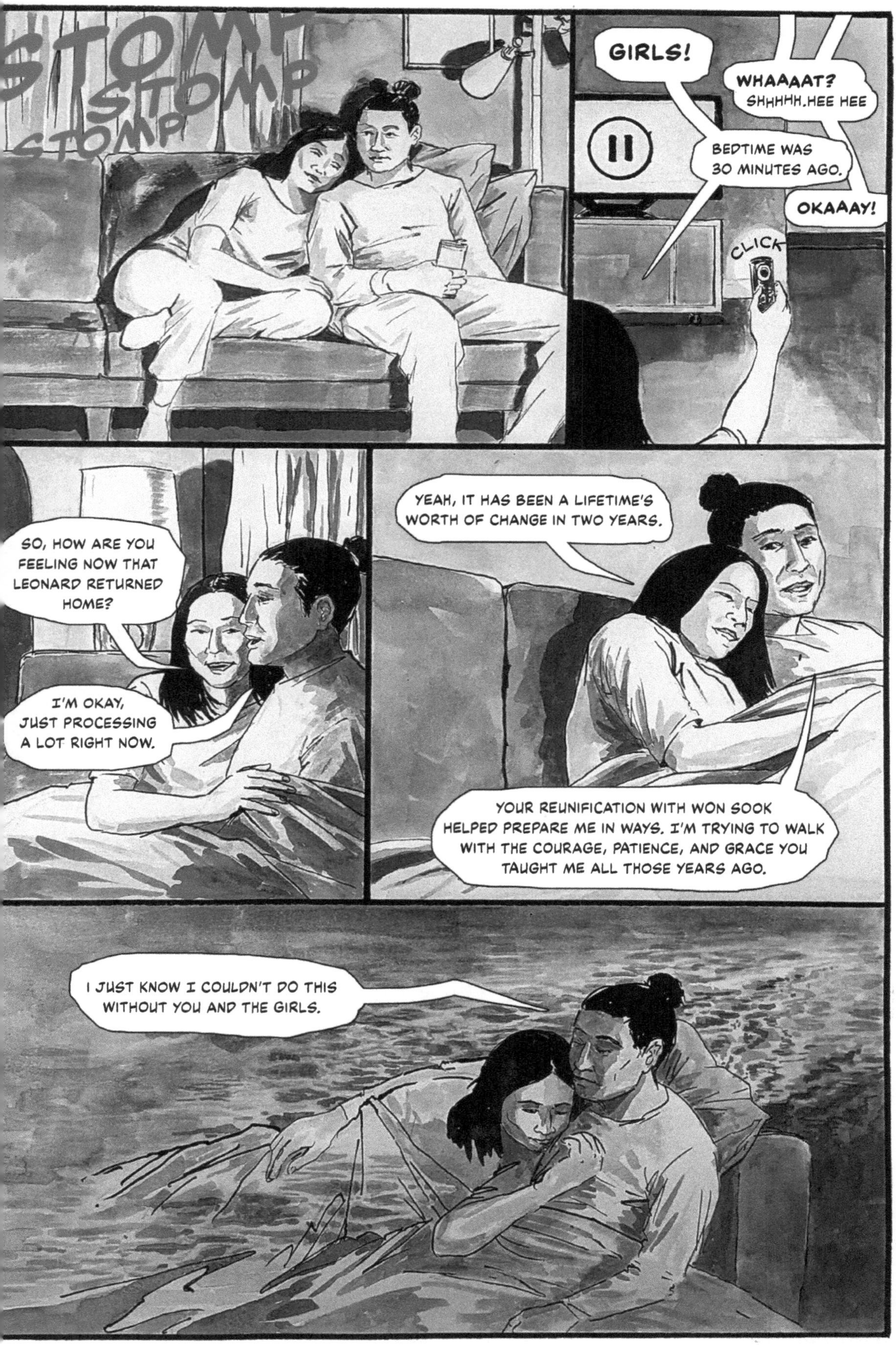
STOMP
STOMP
STOMP
GIRLS!
WHAAAAT?
SHHHHH.HEE HEE
BEDTIME WAS 30 MINUTES AGO.
OKAAAY!
CLICK
SO, HOW ARE YOU FEELING NOW THAT LEONARD RETURNED HOME?
I'M OKAY, JUST PROCESSING A LOT RIGHT NOW.
YEAH, IT HAS BEEN A LIFETIME'S WORTH OF CHANGE IN TWO YEARS.
YOUR REUNIFICATION WITH WON SOOK HELPED PREPARE ME IN WAYS. I'M TRYING TO WALK WITH THE COURAGE, PATIENCE, AND GRACE YOU TAUGHT ME ALL THOSE YEARS AGO.
I JUST KNOW I COULDN'T DO THIS WITHOUT YOU AND THE GIRLS.

DEAR KYONG-HEE (SARAH),

YOU HAVE ALWAYS BEEN A COLLECTOR, A KEEPER OF THINGS THAT CARRY MEANING. AND ALTHOUGH I GIVE YOU A HARD TIME ABOUT LETTING GO OF THINGS (BOXES OF OLD HIPSTER BOOTS, CUPBOARDS OF DUSTY GLASSWARE, RUSTY ILL-FITTING ICE SKATES), I ALSO KNOW EVERY SINGLE WORD I HAVE WRITTEN TO YOU OVER OUR LAST 30 YEARS LIVES IN AN UNMARKED PLASTIC TUB SOMEWHERE IN OUR BASEMENT. LIKE A FERMENTING CAPSULE OF COMMINGLED SENTIMENTALITY, PUNGENT AND JUST A LITTLE SPICY. AND JUST SO YOU KNOW, OF ALL THE RANDOM DUSTY OLD THINGS I WOULD LIKE TO CLEAR FROM OUR CLUTTERED HOME, THIS IS NOT ONE OF THEM.

YOU, MORE THAN ANYONE ON THIS PLANET, KNOWS THE TOTALITY OF ME. THE WAYS IN WHICH I HAVE BROUGHT BOTH LOVE AND HARM INTO THIS WORLD. ALL OF THE THINGS I HAVE ASPIRED TO AND STRETCHED FOR AND HAVE YET TO SUCCEED IN ACHIEVING. YOU HAVE WITNESSED ALL TOO MANY TIMES MY BRASH, SELFISH, AND STUBBORN TAURUS SELF. AND YOU HAVE HELD ME WITH TENDERNESS WHEN I HAVE FALTERED OR SUCCUMBED TO QUIET FEAR OR INSECURITY.

I HAVE GAINED SO MUCH WISDOM IN YOUR PRESENCE AND I HAVE DRAWN ON THE COURAGE AND GRACE YOU HAVE QUIETLY MODELED THROUGHOUT YOUR LIFE. THERE IS NO GREATER EXAMPLE OF THIS THAN WHEN YOU BOLDLY REUNITED WITH YOUR FIRST MOTHER AND FAMILY IN YOUR LATE 20'S. IT FEELS SO UNCANNY HOW OUR LIVES, OUR RETURNINGS, HAVE MIRRORED OVER TIME. I KNOW I WOULD NOT HAVE THE CONFIDENCE TO PRESS FORWARD WITHOUT HAVING WITNESSED YOUR OWN DELICATE STEPS TWO DECADES PRIOR. I SAY THESE WORDS NOW BECAUSE I WANT THEM TO PERMEATE EVERY CELL WITHIN YOU. FOR MY LOVE AND ADMIRATION TO ALIGN WITH THE RHYTHMS OF YOUR HEART, SYNAPSE, YOUR EVER NEXT BREATH.

I KNOW I HAVE BEEN NURTURED WITHIN YOUR LOVE, A FORM OF CARE AND PATIENCE I NEVER KNEW EXISTED OR COULD EVER HAVE IMAGINED NEEDING FROM YOU IN OUR LIVES TOGETHER. I DON'T KNOW IF YOU ALWAYS POSSESSED THESE EMOTIONAL COMPETENCIES OR IF IT IS A BYPRODUCT OF YOUR SPECIFIC EXPERIENCE NAVIGATING (DIS)BELONGING. YOU HAVE WITNESSED ME NOW IN MY MOST RAW MOMENT, A WAVE OF CHILDHOOD EMOTIONS THAT HAVE BEEN DORMANT FOR 40 YEARS, ERUPTING. LIKE THE CHEST-QUAKING BREATHLESSNESS ONE EXPERIENCES WHEN A BODY SEARCHES FOR AIR AFTER A DEEP PENETRATING CRY. YET WITH YOU I KNOW I'M NOT SUFFOCATING OR DROWNING IN THE MOMENT. HUHH HUHH HUHH... BECAUSE YOU ARE MY RESUSCITATION.

MY HOPE IS THAT SOMEHOW THESE WORDS EVENTUALLY FIND THEMSELVES TUCKED AWAY IN THAT BIN IN THE BASEMENT, ADDING TO THE SLURRY OF SCRAWLED EXPRESSIONS, BAD POETRY, AND INK DRAWINGS.

I THINK THESE WORDS WOULD BE GOOD COMPANY WITH THE VERY FIRST THING YOU EVER RECEIVED FROM ME, AN ANONYMOUS POSTCARD MAILED TO YOU WITH THREE SIMPLE WORDS.

-M

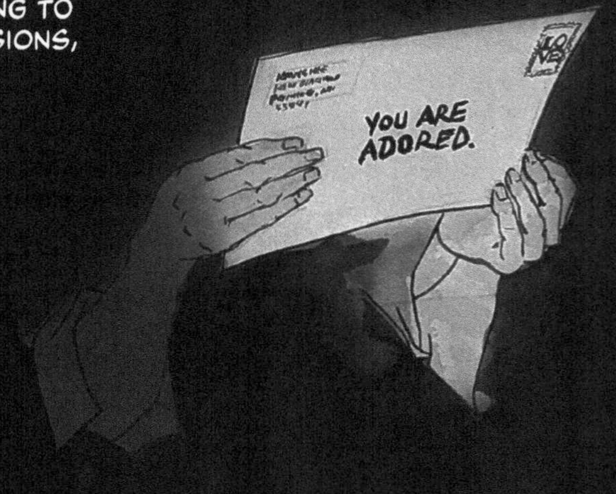
YOU ARE ADORED.

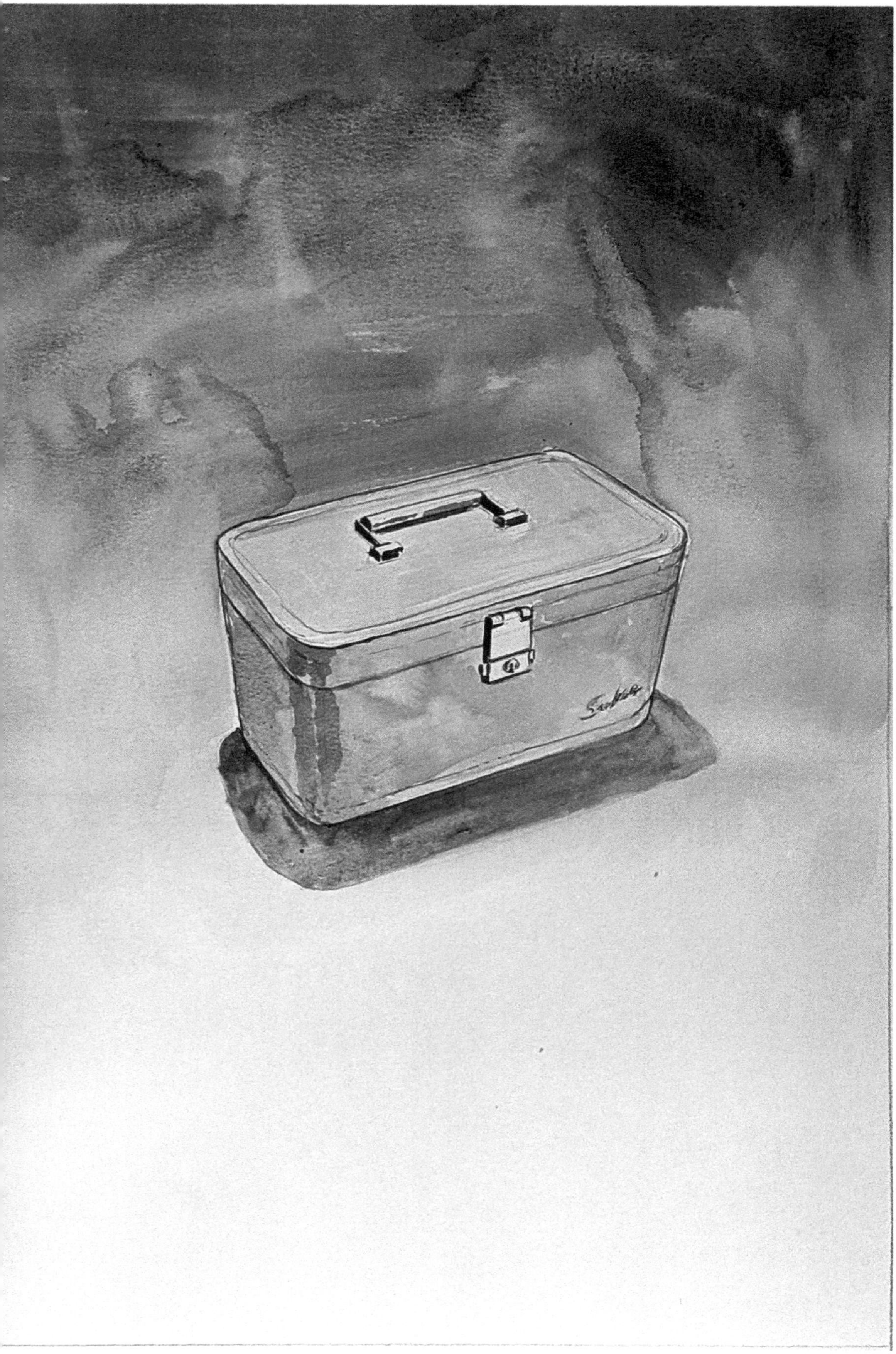

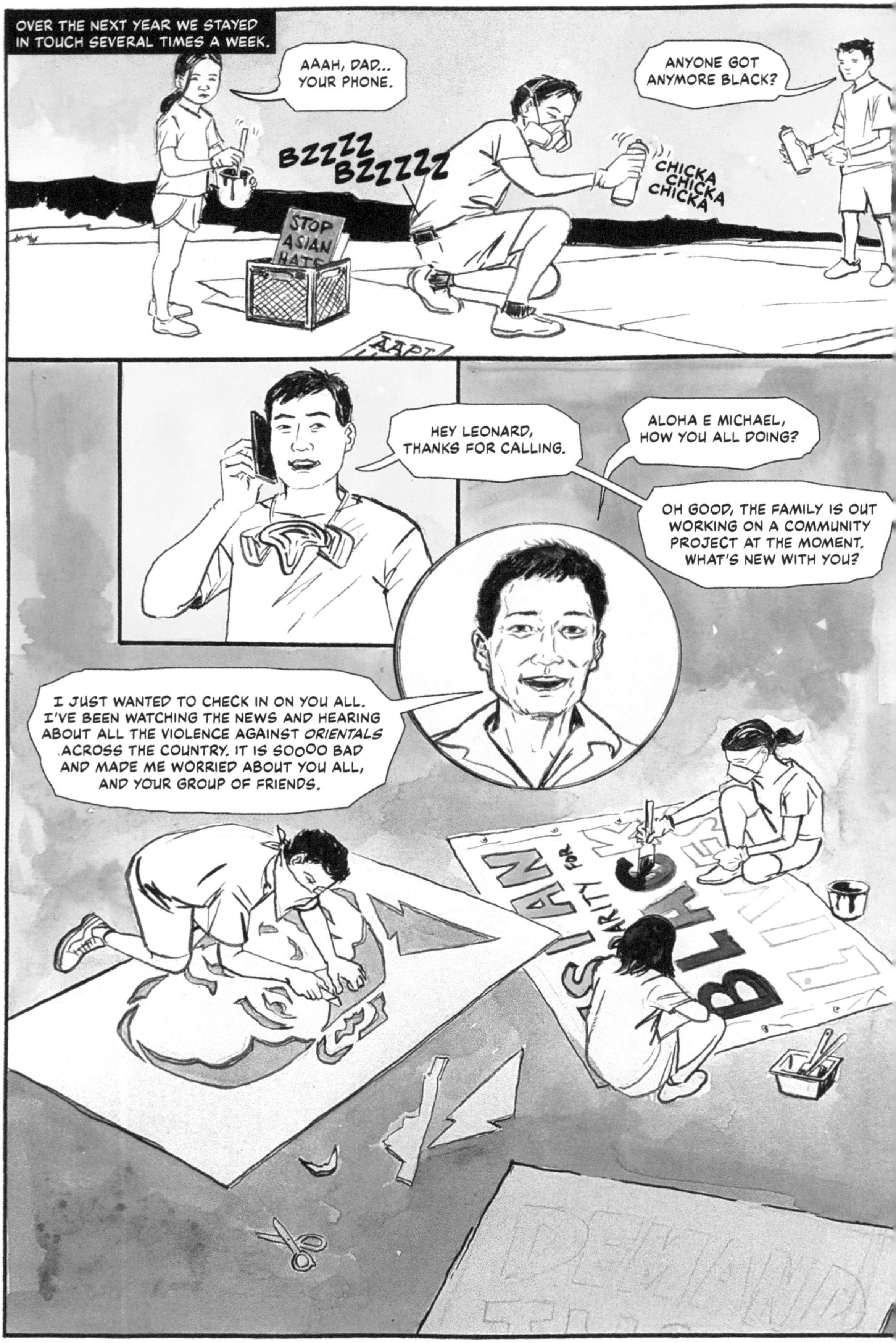
OVER THE NEXT YEAR WE STAYED IN TOUCH SEVERAL TIMES A WEEK.
AAAH, DAD... YOUR PHONE.
BZZZZ BZZZZZ
ANYONE GOT ANYMORE BLACK?
CHICKA CHICKA CHICKA
STOP ASIAN
HEY LEONARD, THANKS FOR CALLING.
ALOHA E MICHAEL, HOW YOU ALL DOING?
OH GOOD, THE FAMILY IS OUT WORKING ON A COMMUNITY PROJECT AT THE MOMENT. WHAT'S NEW WITH YOU?
I JUST WANTED TO CHECK IN ON YOU ALL. I'VE BEEN WATCHING THE NEWS AND HEARING ABOUT ALL THE VIOLENCE AGAINST *ORIENTALS* ACROSS THE COUNTRY. IT IS SOOOO BAD AND MADE ME WORRIED ABOUT YOU ALL, AND YOUR GROUP OF FRIENDS.

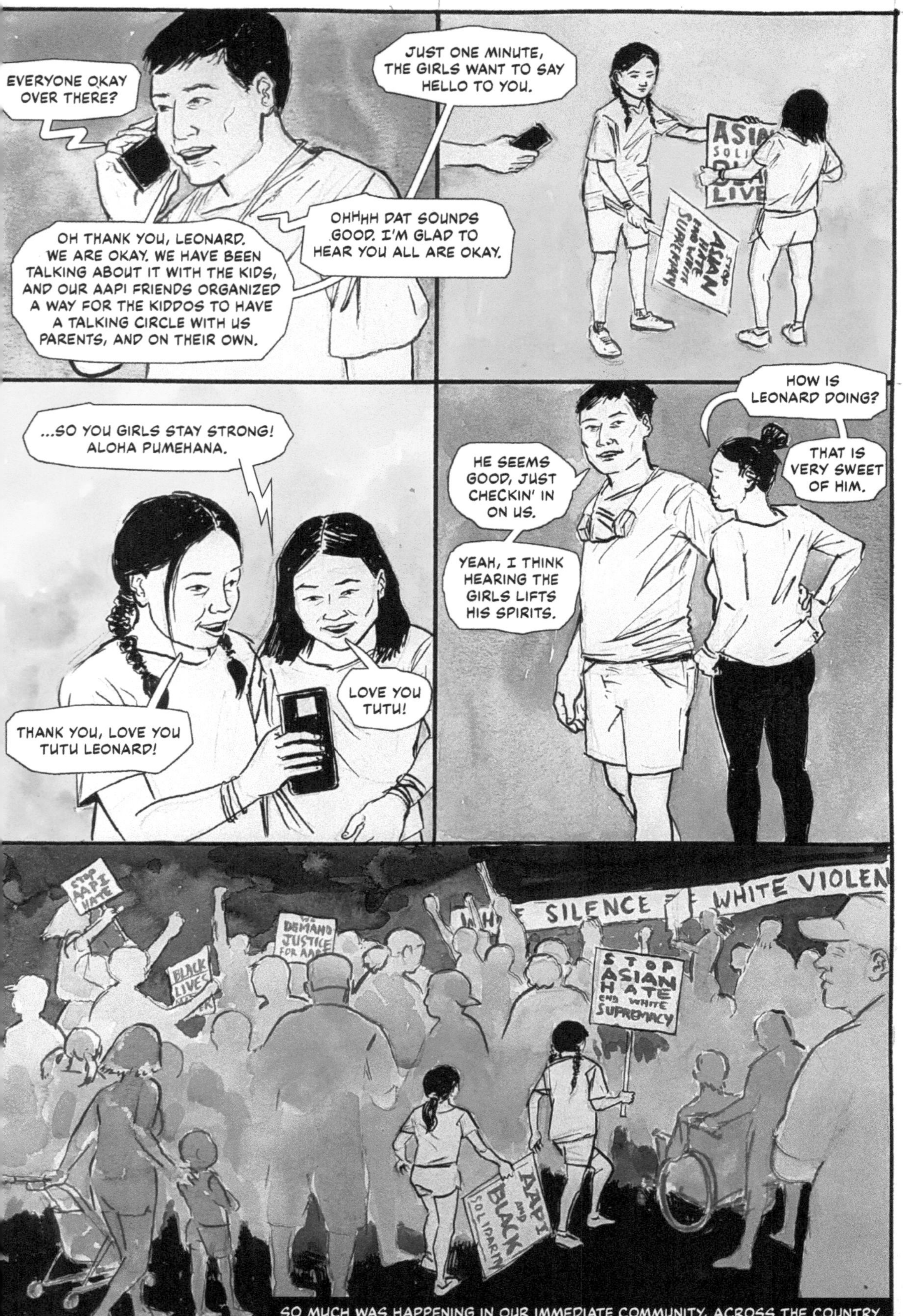
EVERYONE OKAY OVER THERE?
JUST ONE MINUTE, THE GIRLS WANT TO SAY HELLO TO YOU.
OH THANK YOU, LEONARD. WE ARE OKAY. WE HAVE BEEN TALKING ABOUT IT WITH THE KIDS, AND OUR AAPI FRIENDS ORGANIZED A WAY FOR THE KIDDOS TO HAVE A TALKING CIRCLE WITH US PARENTS, AND ON THEIR OWN.
OHHHH DAT SOUNDS GOOD. I'M GLAD TO HEAR YOU ALL ARE OKAY.
ASIAN SOLI... BLA... LIVE...
STOP ASIAN HATE END WHITE SUPREMACY
...SO YOU GIRLS STAY STRONG! ALOHA PUMEHANA.
THANK YOU, LOVE YOU TUTU LEONARD!
LOVE YOU TUTU!
HOW IS LEONARD DOING?
HE SEEMS GOOD, JUST CHECKIN' IN ON US.
THAT IS VERY SWEET OF HIM.
YEAH, I THINK HEARING THE GIRLS LIFTS HIS SPIRITS.
STOP AAPI HATE
DEMAND JUSTICE FOR AAPI
BLACK LIVES
SILENCE WHITE VIOLEN
STOP ASIAN HATE END WHITE SUPREMACY
AAPI AND BLACK SOLIDARITY
SO MUCH WAS HAPPENING IN OUR IMMEDIATE COMMUNITY, ACROSS THE COUNTRY. IT WAS COMFORTING TO KNOW HE WAS LOOKING OUT FOR OUR WELL-BEING.

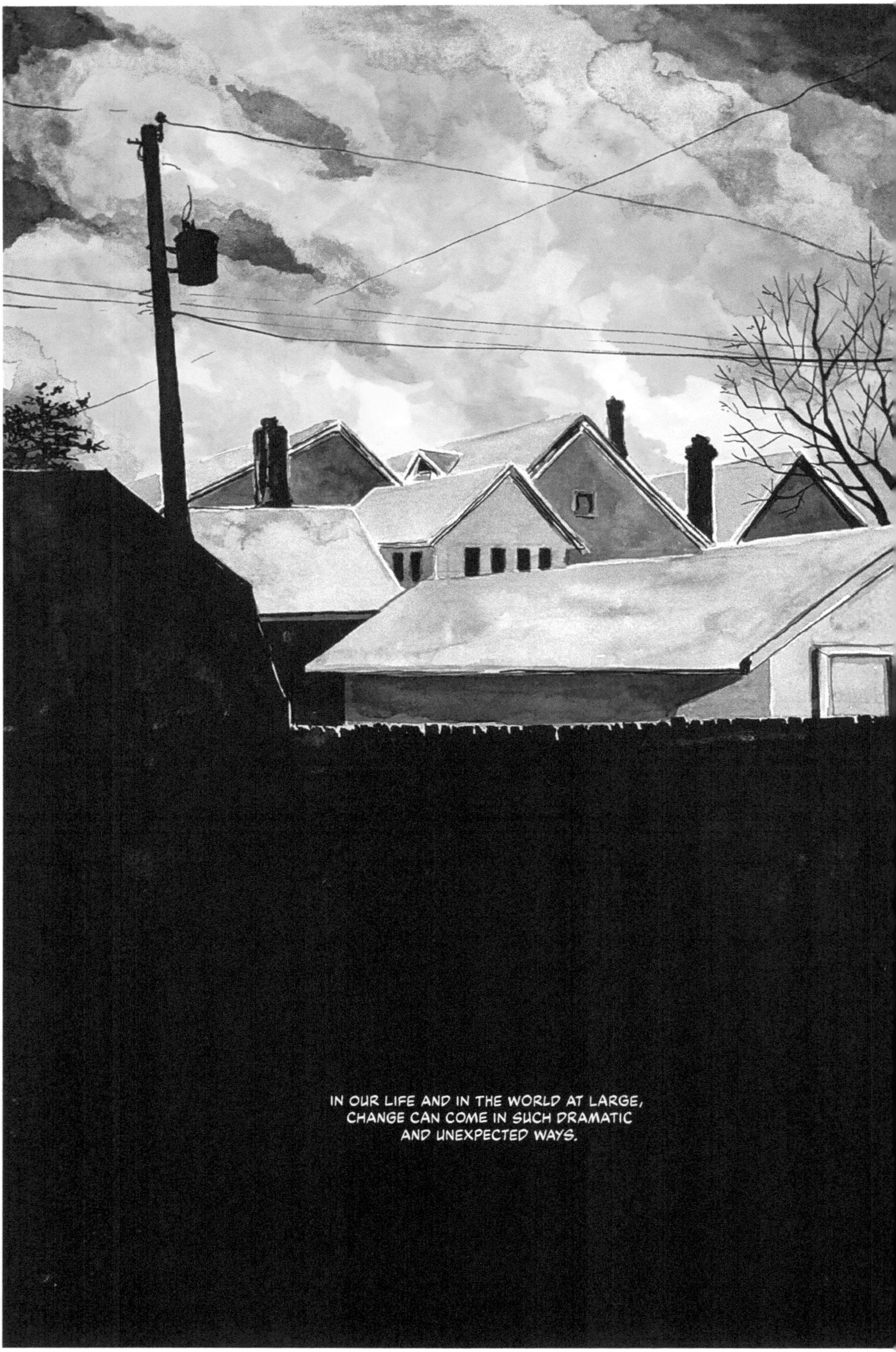
IN OUR LIFE AND IN THE WORLD AT LARGE, CHANGE CAN COME IN SUCH DRAMATIC AND UNEXPECTED WAYS.

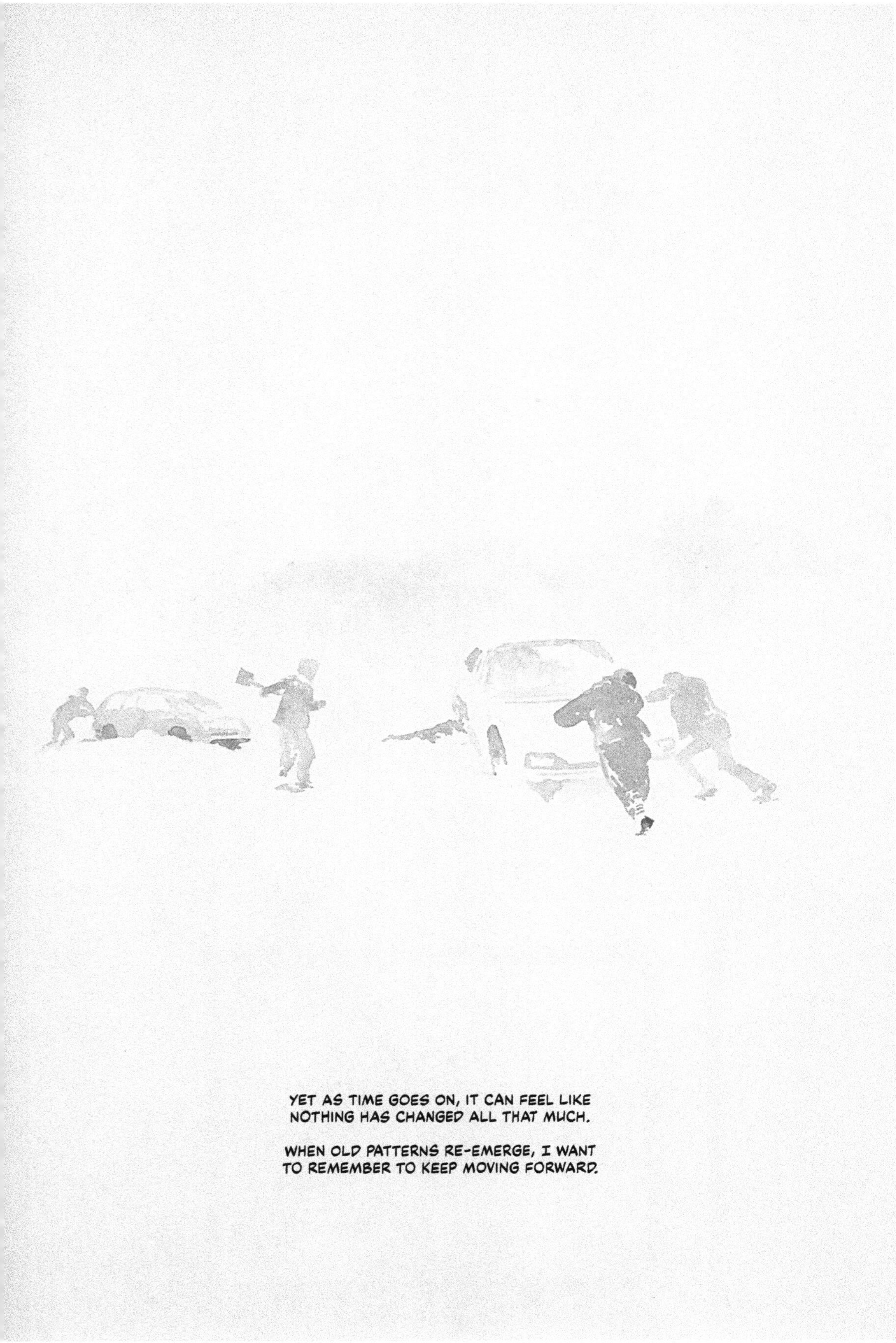
YET AS TIME GOES ON, IT CAN FEEL LIKE NOTHING HAS CHANGED ALL THAT MUCH.
WHEN OLD PATTERNS RE-EMERGE, I WANT TO REMEMBER TO KEEP MOVING FORWARD.

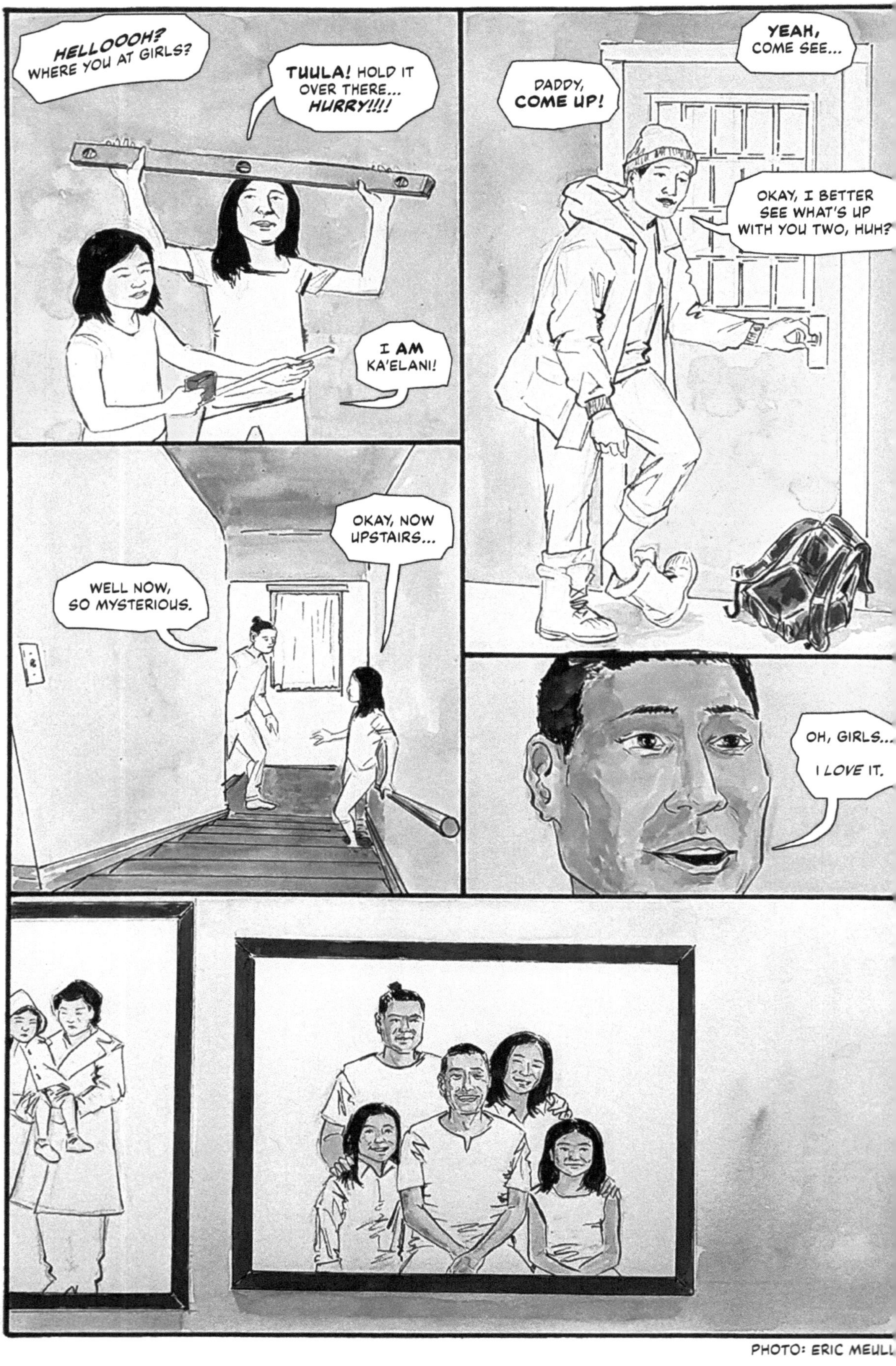
HELLOOOH? WHERE YOU AT GIRLS?
TUULA! HOLD IT OVER THERE... HURRY!!!!
I AM KA'ELANI!
DADDY, COME UP!
YEAH, COME SEE...
OKAY, I BETTER SEE WHAT'S UP WITH YOU TWO, HUH?
WELL NOW, SO MYSTERIOUS.
OKAY, NOW UPSTAIRS...
OH, GIRLS...
I LOVE IT.
PHOTO: ERIC MEULI

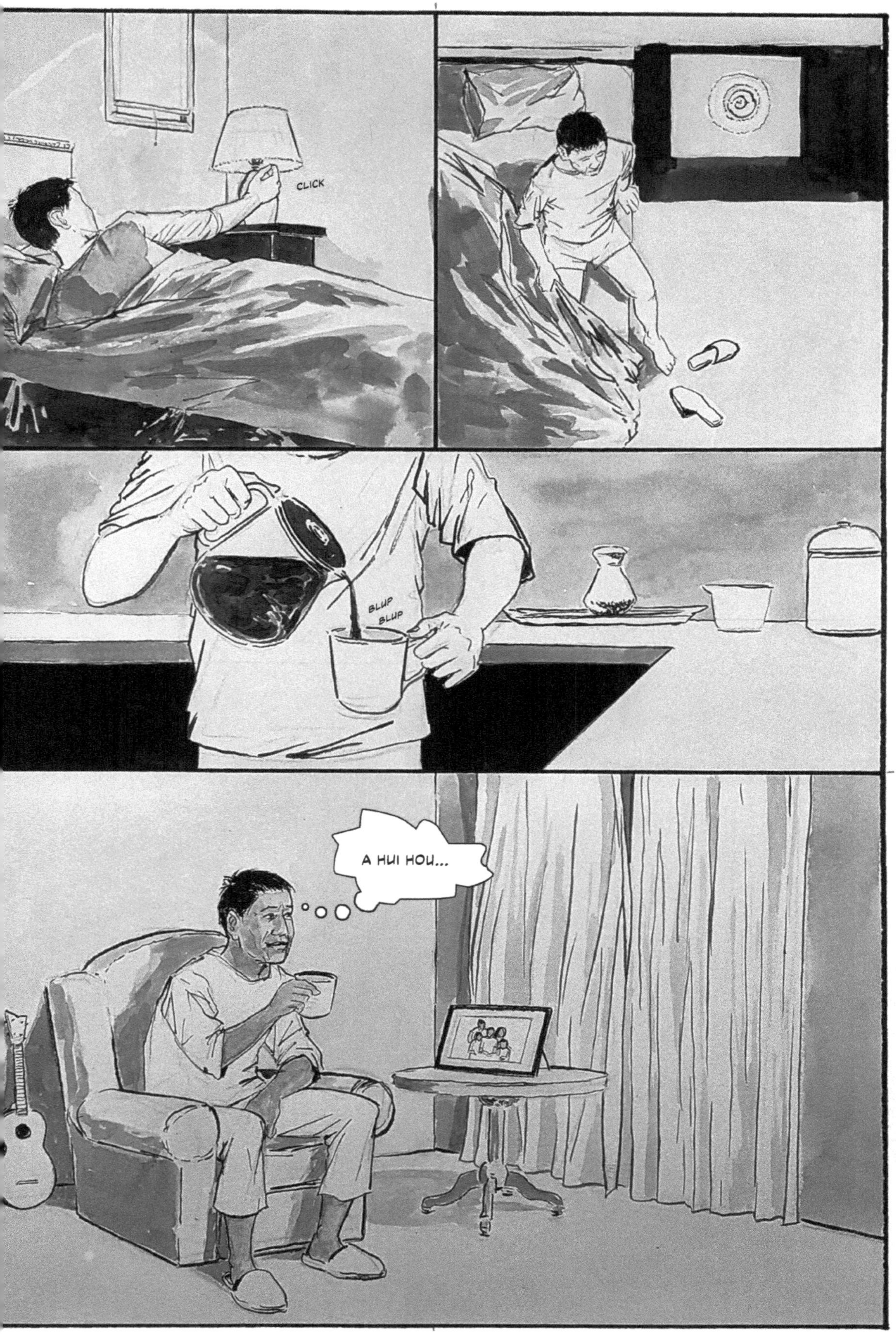
CLICK
BLUP
BLUP
A HUI HOU...

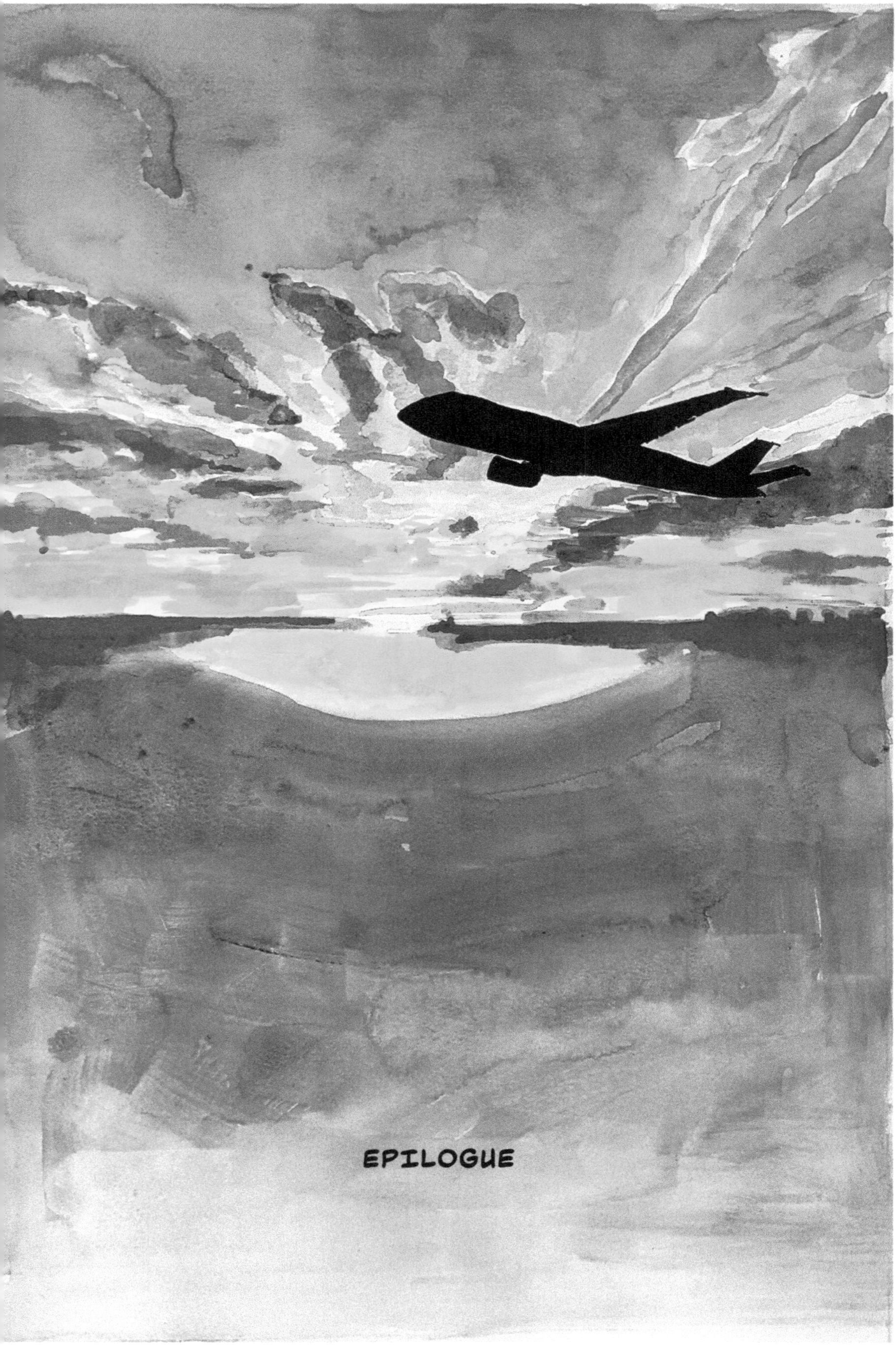
EPILOGUE

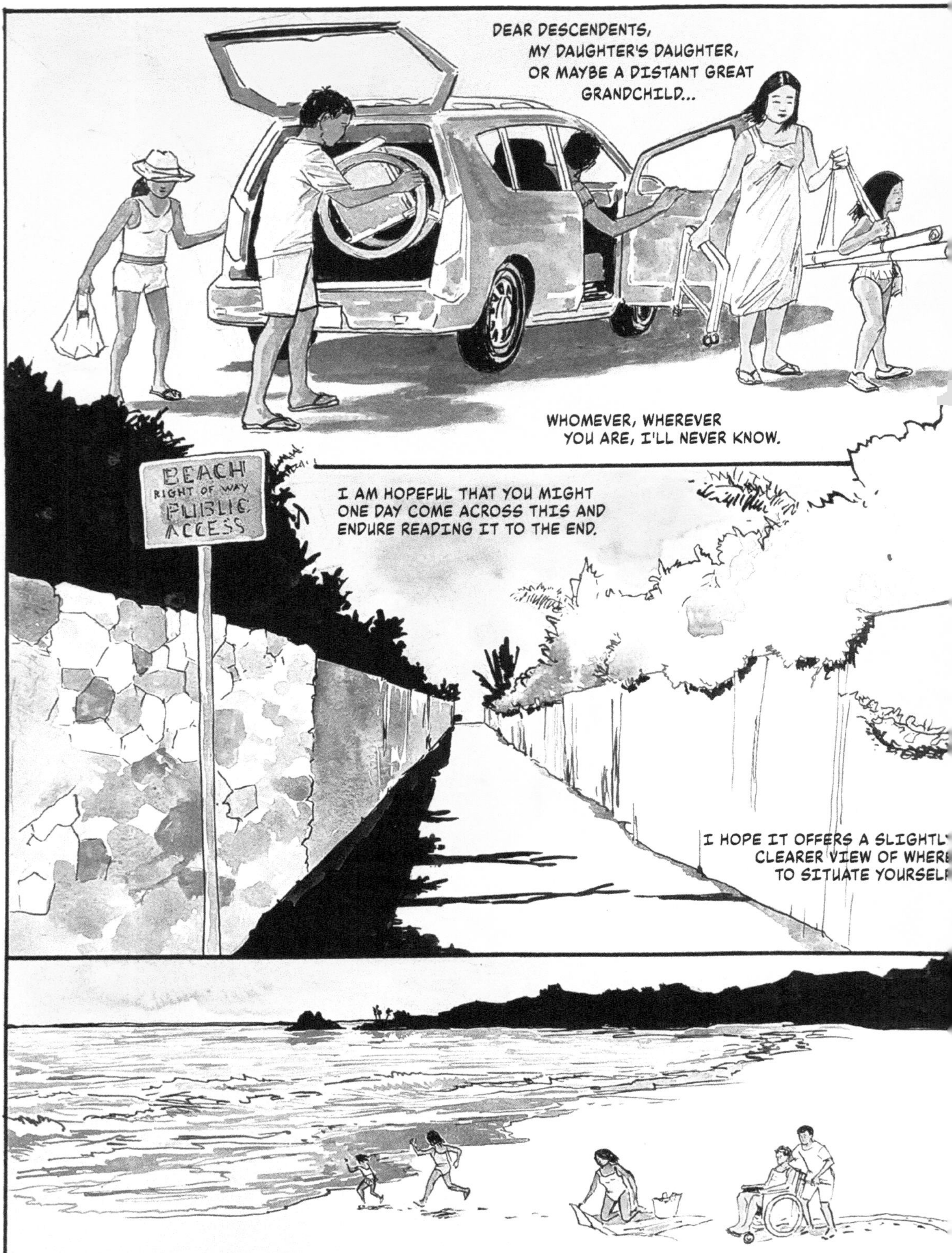
DEAR DESCENDENTS,
MY DAUGHTER'S DAUGHTER,
OR MAYBE A DISTANT GREAT GRANDCHILD...
WHOMEVER, WHEREVER YOU ARE, I'LL NEVER KNOW.
BEACH
RIGHT OF WAY
PUBLIC
ACCESS
I AM HOPEFUL THAT YOU MIGHT ONE DAY COME ACROSS THIS AND ENDURE READING IT TO THE END.
I HOPE IT OFFERS A SLIGHTLY CLEARER VIEW OF WHERE TO SITUATE YOURSELF
IT IS IMPOSSIBLE TO PREDICT IF, AFTER READING THIS, YOU WILL CONSIDER MY STORY COMPLETE. FOR NOW I HAVE GIVEN WHAT I HAVE COME TO KNOW AND UNDERSTAND. THE REST I MUST MAKE MEANING OF BY LIVING IT FORWARD.

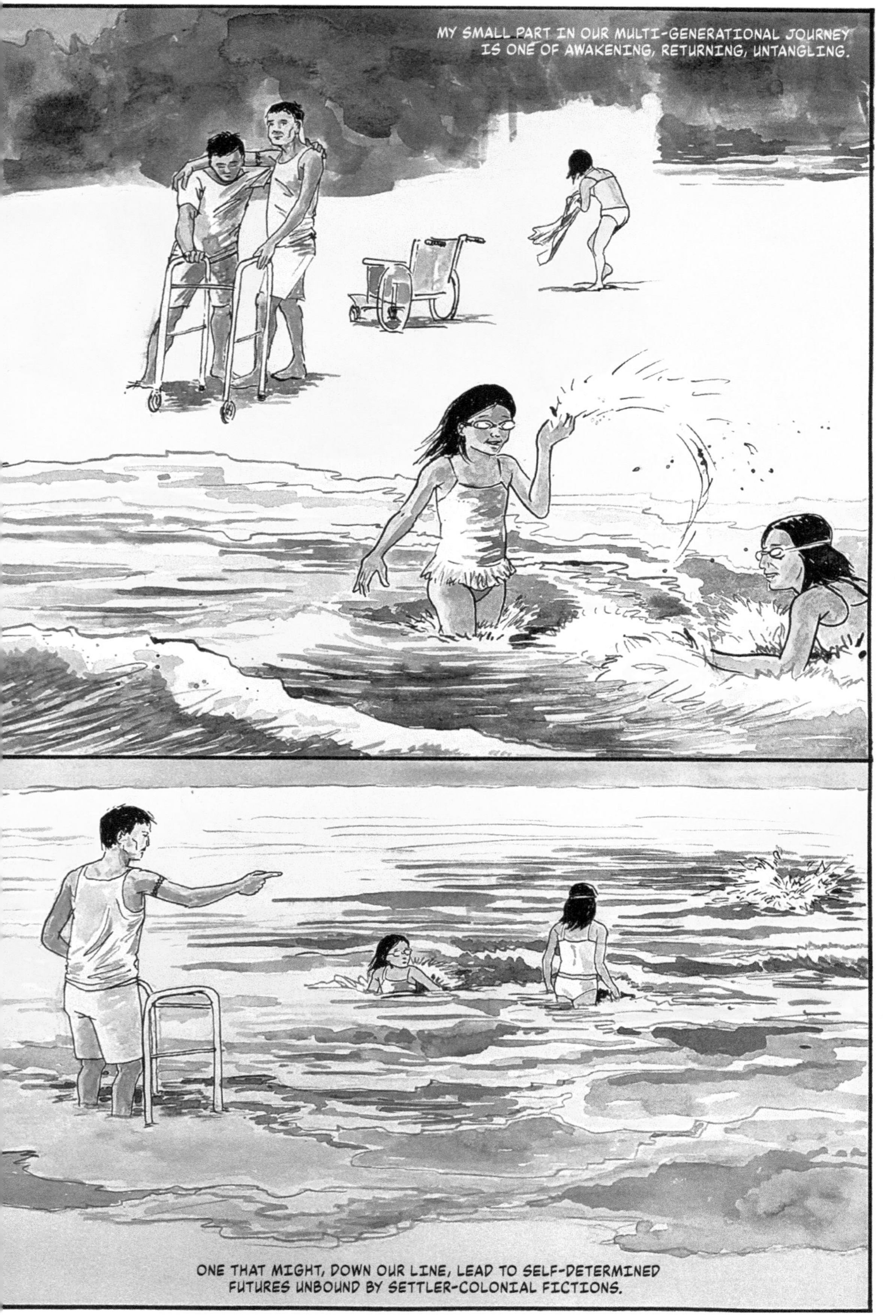
MY SMALL PART IN OUR MULTI-GENERATIONAL JOURNEY IS ONE OF AWAKENING, RETURNING, UNTANGLING.
ONE THAT MIGHT, DOWN OUR LINE, LEAD TO SELF-DETERMINED FUTURES UNBOUND BY SETTLER-COLONIAL FICTIONS.

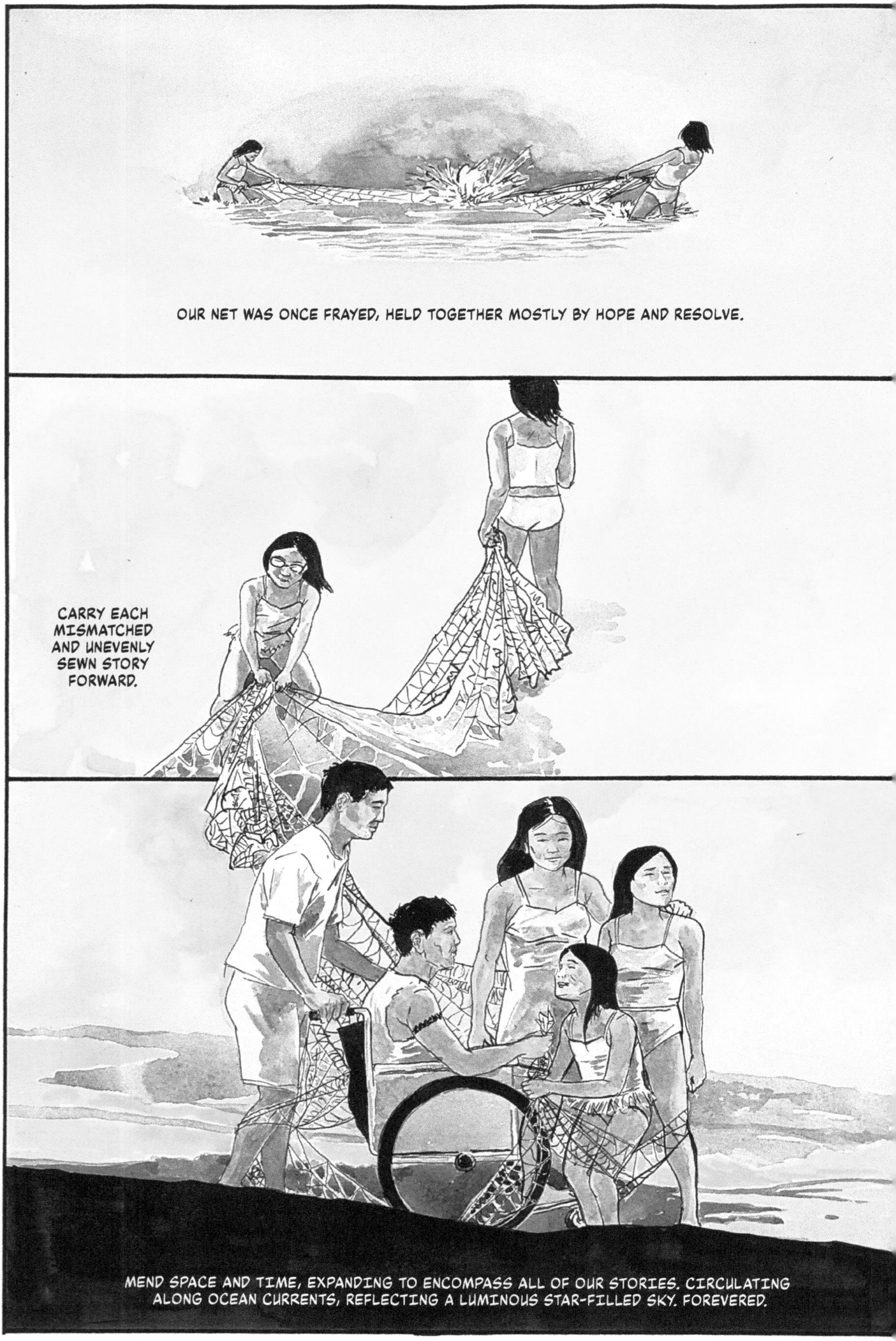
OUR NET WAS ONCE FRAYED, HELD TOGETHER MOSTLY BY HOPE AND RESOLVE.
CARRY EACH MISMATCHED AND UNEVENLY SEWN STORY FORWARD.
MEND SPACE AND TIME, EXPANDING TO ENCOMPASS ALL OF OUR STORIES. CIRCULATING ALONG OCEAN CURRENTS, REFLECTING A LUMINOUS STAR-FILLED SKY. FOREVERED.

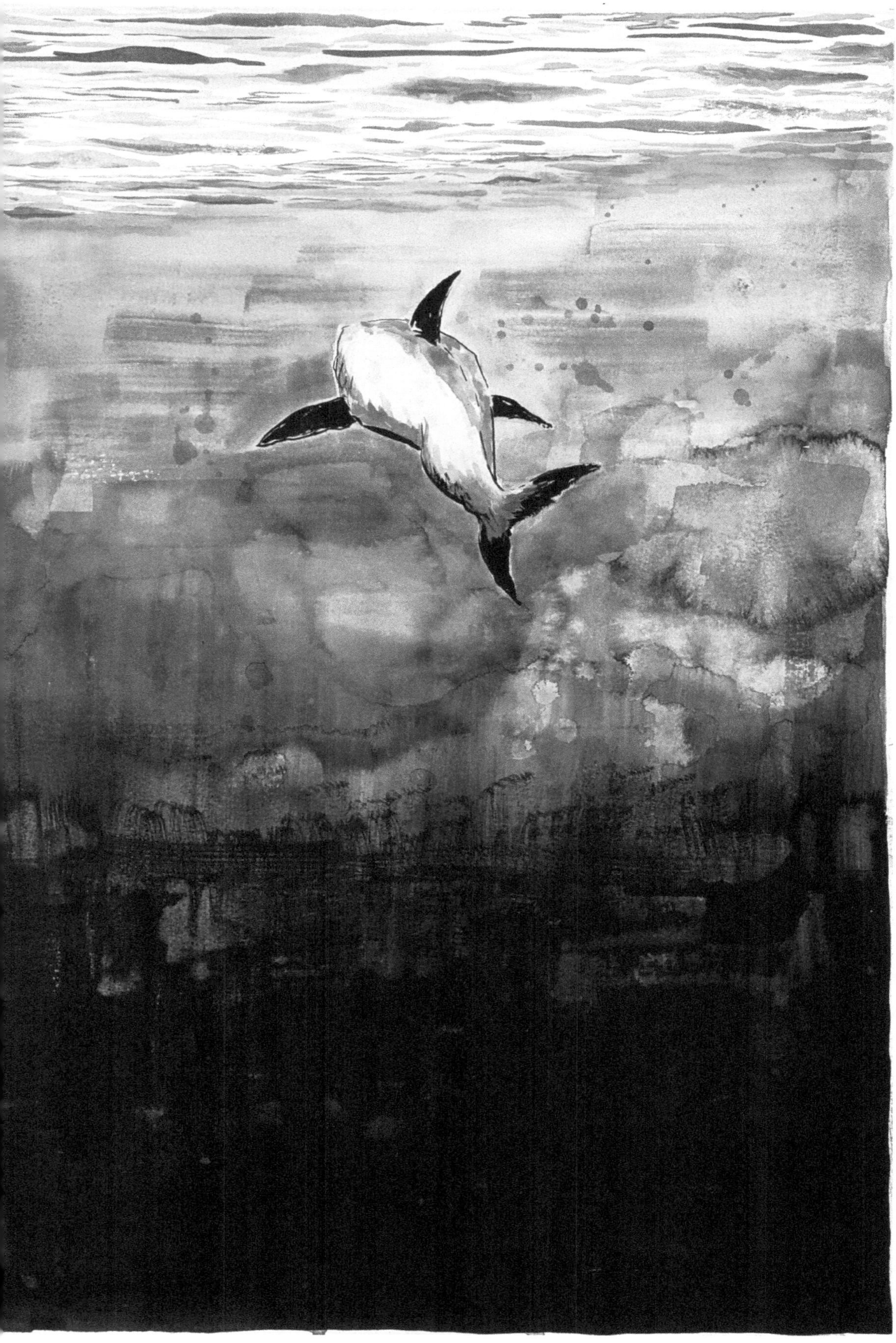

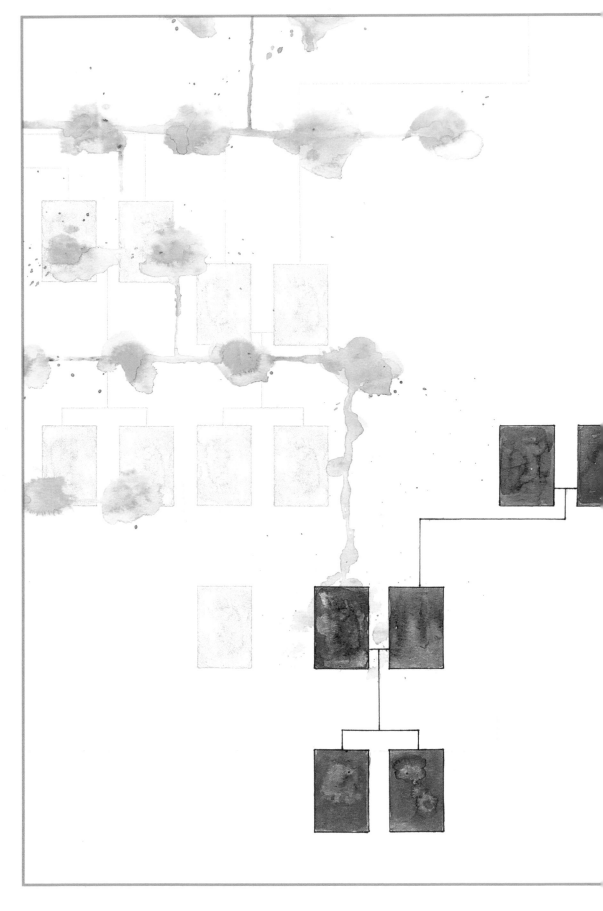

ACKNOWLEDGMENTS

This project was created from a slow and meandering process of personal and cultural reclamation compelled by hope and longing. This is not in any way the product of a single person's wisdom or smarts, quite the contrary. It was made possible through many beautiful and complicated conversations, the immense support of a peer network of care, and an expanding web of Ohana tenderness, vulnerability, and generosity.

This represents one transracial adoption story. It seeks to explore two lives impacted by different forms of colonization, silence, and ambiguous longing. Each seeking to reckon with their complex pasts towards reclamation. It is not intended to, and could never adequately, represent the multitudes of transracial and transnational adoptees diasporic experiences. It respectfully exists as one additional story, alongside the many adoptee voices, seeking answers to lifelong questions while working to make meaning from these experiences.

I am deeply grateful for all of the people willing to sift through rough ideas, review in-progress drafts, provide critical feedback, and offer encouragement to stay the course. My sincere thanks go out to: Ed Bok Lee, Wing Young Huie, Stephanie Rogers, Masanari Kawahara, Kaleo Nadal, Diver Van Avery, Richard M. Lee, Ryan Stopera, Noel Raymond, Kenji Okumura, Witt Siasoco, Stephanie DeArmond, Heewon Lee, Kurt Kwan, and Eric F. Avery. Thank you to Jasmine Tang for coaching me to "read to believe," to David A. Chang for cultural and historical accuracy and support, for Eric Mueller's permission to incorporate his photography, Alex DeArmond's help with formatting, and to Jake Nassif for much-needed copyediting and proofreading. Thank you to my friends and colleagues at the Pillsbury House + Theatre and the Tofte Lake Center.

Love and appreciation go out to my Ohana: Uncle Alan, Auntie Susan, Auntie Molly, and Uncle Anthony for illuminating the past with warmth, humor, and aloha. And a special shout out to Cousin Kimlen for her tender care and for playing a significant role in making this reunification possible.

To my beloved Kyong-Hee (Sarah) Mickelson: I am eternally indebted to you for 30 years of unwavering support and for granting me hundreds of late-night hours squirreled away in a half-heated Airstream studio as we continue to navigate the pandemics. To my dearest daughters Ka'elani and Tuula for taking active roles in this expanding family line and for being my inspiration and light in life.

Finally, thank you to my first father, Leonard Akana. Your enthusiasm, sincerity, laughter, and kindness has been a buoy throughout this time as we heal forward together.